American Christian Missionary Society

Christian Hymnal

a choice collection of hymns and tunes for congregational and social worship

American Christian Missionary Society

Christian Hymnal

a choice collection of hymns and tunes for congregational and social worship

ISBN/EAN: 9783337286286

Printed in Europe, USA, Canada, Australia, Japan

Cover: Foto ©Lupo / pixelio.de

More available books at **www.hansebooks.com**

THE
CHRISTIAN HYMNAL:

A CHOICE COLLECTION OF

Hymns and Tunes

FOR CONGREGATIONAL AND SOCIAL WORSHIP.

Arranged by a Committee of Harmonists and Musical Authors.

UNDER THE DIRECTION OF

THE CHRISTIAN HYMN-BOOK COMMITTEE,

AND

PUBLISHED BY AUTHORITY OF THE TRUSTEES.

CINCINNATI:
CHASE & HALL, PUBLISHERS.
No. 180 ELM STREET.
1875.

Entered according to Act of Congress, in the year 1871, by
R. M. BISHOP, C. H. GOULD, J. B. BOWMAN, O. A. BURGESS, W. H. LAPE, *Trustees*,
In the Office of the Librarian of Congress, at Washington.

ELECTROTYPED AT
THE FRANKLIN TYPE FOUNDRY,
CINCINNATI.

PREFACE.

The Christian Hymnal has been prepared to meet a want that has long been felt in our churches. The same meeting of the American Christian Missionary Society which authorized the publication of our present Hymn Book, unanimously recommended that, as soon as practicable, a Hymn and Tune Book should also be published. Since that time the Trustees of the Christian Hymn Book have had the matter under advisement, but, on account of having to make the plates for the several editions of the Hymn Book, the copyright accruing from the sale of that book has not been sufficient to justify them at an earlier day in going forward with the Hymn and Tune Book; they take pleasure, however, in saying that they hope the thoroughness and completeness of the present work will justify the delay.

In the compilation of the Christian Hymnal, the Trustees beg leave to say that, while they have had an eye to a just economy, they have, at the same time, spared no means to make the book as perfect as possible. To this end, they have not only secured the best copyrighted music now in use, but have also had written expressly for this work a number of new tunes by some of the most talented and popular composers in this country. Such names as Dr. Thomas Hastings, T. J. Cook, John Zundel, T. E. Perkins, Silas J. Vail, Philip Phillips, W. H. Doane, Solon Wilder, A. Squire, etc., need only be mentioned to assure the superior character of the new music introduced. These men have all been in constant correspondence with the Editing Committee in Cincinnati, and have rendered valuable assistance in the preparation of the work. Thanks are especially due to Mr. W. H. Doane, of this city, for suggestions in reference to the general plan and style of the book, as well as for his admirable contributions to it.

The Editing Committee have kept constantly in view the importance of meeting the wants of all classes in our churches; hence they have attempted to bring the Old and New together in such a dress, and in such relations to each other, as that there shall be no incompatibility between them. The old standard tunes that have stood the test of long use will be found always to occupy the first place, while many familiar pieces, that are especially valuable because of endearing associations, have been harmonized expressly for this work by the best harmonists in the United States. These, with all other new arrangements, are marked with a star—thus: ✻—and should not be used in other works without permission. The same caution should be observed in reference to all music marked (New), such pieces having been written expressly for the Christian Hymnal.

The hymns, with a few exceptions, have been selected from the Christian Hymn Book, and embrace every variety of meter in that book. An index has been arranged, in which all the omitted hymns of the Christian Hymn Book are referred to pages in this book where suitable tunes may be found. Hence a complete adaptation to the entire Hymn Book is provided for, and this, of itself, renders the Hymnal invaluable, as it contains a larger variety of metrical music than any other book now published.

PREFACE.

Special attention has been given to the adaptation of music to the hymns. Where hymns and tunes have been long associated, they have not been divorced, except for very obvious reasons. The value of both a hymn and tune is often largely dependent upon their association; hence a separation would tend to render both comparatively useless. In all the adaptations, it has been the aim of the Committee to select such music as would best harmonize with the spirit of the words. In this it is believed they have succeeded—at least, to a reasonable degree. They have, however, placed in the margin of the pages other tunes, and the keys in which they are written, so that singers may take their choice.

It will readily be seen that most of the tunes are suitable for congregational singing—simple carols—easily sung, but very effective when well sung. A few of the more difficult pieces of this kind have been inserted to meet the wants of those who would not be satisfied without them, while special attention has been given to the selection of a fine class of music for social meetings and the home circle. Many of the new pieces are set to the most beautiful hymns in the Hymn Book—hymns that have been, heretofore, almost useless for the want of music adapted to them.

During the preparation of the work, both the Editing Committee and Trustees have been in correspondence with a number of leading brethren known to possess good musical taste, who have kindly furnished contributions and valuable suggestions. It is, however, but just to say that, for the arrangement of the book, selection of tunes, adaptations, proof-reading, etc., etc., grateful acknowledgments should be made to Prof. J. P. Powell and Miss Bettie Wilson, of this city, to whose enthusiasm and interest in the work the public is largely indebted for much that is valuable in it. Mention should also be made of the generous courtesy of a number of authors, who have granted the privilege of using their copyrighted music free of charge: among these, T. E. Perkins, S. J. Vail, Solon Wilder, J. M. Pelton, and T. J. Cook, are gratefully remembered.

In conclusion, the Trustees desire to say that they feel a special pleasure in being able to furnish the book at such low rates. Notwithstanding the heavy outlay—which they had necessarily to make—by a careful economy of space, they have been able, it is believed, to produce a book containing more hymns and tunes than are generally found in larger works of the kind, furnishing a complete adaptation of music to the 1324 hymns of the Christian Hymn Book, of convenient size and shape, published in good style, and at rates at least fifty per cent. cheaper than any other book known to them, containing the same amount of matter. Hence it is hoped that the book will be acceptable to the Brotherhood for whom specially it has been published, and that it will prove to be a great blessing to the churches by exciting a more general and active interest in an important though much neglected part of Christian worship.

R. M. BISHOP,
C. H. GOULD,
J. B. BOWMAN, *Trustees of the Christian Hymn Book.*
O. A. BURGESS,
W. H. LAPE,

CINCINNATI, *February*, 1871.

THE CHRISTIAN HYMNAL.

THE HOLY SCRIPTURES.

UXBRIDGE. L. M.   Dr. L. MASON.

1. The heavens declare thy glory, Lord; In every star thy wis-dom shines;
But when our eyes behold thy word, We read thy name in fair-er lines.

1   *The works and the word of God.*   (1)

2 The rolling sun, the changing light,
And nights and days, thy power confess;
But the blest volume thou hast writ,
Reveals thy justice and thy grace.

3 Sun, moon, and stars, convey thy praise
Round the whole earth, and never stand;
So when thy truth began its race,
It touched and glanced on every land.

4 Nor shall thy spreading gospel rest
Till thro' the world thy truth has run;
Till Christ has al' the nations blest
That see the light or feel the sun.

5 Great Sun of Righteousness! arise;
Bless the dark world with heavenly light:
Thy gospel makes the simple wise.
Thy laws are pure, thy judgments right.

6 Thy noblest wonders here we view,
In souls renewed and sins forgiven;
Lord! cleanse my sins, my soul renew,
And make thy word my guide to heaven.

2   *The Scriptures our light and guide.*   (5)

1 When Israel thro' the desert passed,
A fiery pillar went before,
To guide them thro' the dreary waste,
And lessen the fatigues they bore.

2 Such is thy glorious word, O God;
'T is for our light and guidance given;
It sheds a luster all abroad,
And points the path to bliss and heaven.

3 It fills the soul with sweet delight,
And quickens its inactive powers;
It sets our wandering footsteps right,
Displays thy love and kindles ours.

4 Its promises rejoice our hearts;
Its doctrine is divinely true;
Knowledge and pleasure it imparts;
It comforts and instructs us too.

5 Ye favored lands, who have this word
Ye saints, who feel its saving power
Unite your tongues to praise the Lord.
And his distinguished grace adore.

N. B.—The small figures in brackets at the right-hand corner of hymns indicate their number in the "Christian Hymn Book."

THE HOLY SCRIPTURES.

WARD. L. M.   Arr. by Dr. L. MASON.

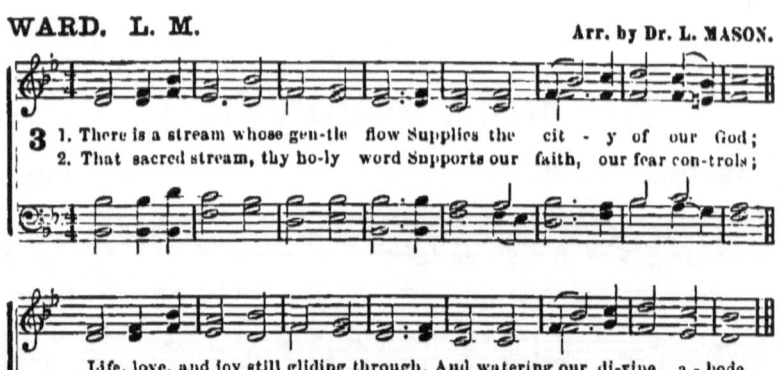

3 1. There is a stream whose gen-tle flow Supplies the cit - y of our God;
   2. That sacred stream, thy ho-ly word Supports our faith, our fear con-trols;

Life, love, and joy still gliding through, And watering our di-vine a - bode.
Sweet peace thy promises af - ford, And give new strength to fainting souls.

4   *Divine love displayed.*   (2)

1 To thee, my heart, Eternal King!
Would now its thankful tribute bring,
To thee its humble homage raise
In songs of ardent, grateful praise.

2 All nature shows thy boundless love,
In worlds below and worlds above;
But in thy blessed word I trace
The richer glories of thy grace.

3 There what delightful truths are given;
There Jesus shows the way to heaven;
His name salutes my listening ear,
Revives my heart and checks my fear.

4 For love like this, oh, may our song
Thro' endless years thy praise prolong;
And distant climes thy name adore,
Till time and nature are no more!

5   *Hold fast the form of sound words.*   (7)

1 God's law demands one living faith,
Not a gaunt crowd of lifeless creeds;
Its warrant is a firm " God saith;"
   Its claim, not words, but living deeds.

2 Yet, Lord, forgive; thy simple law
Grows tarnished in our earthly grasp;
Pure in itself, without a flaw,
   It dims in our too-worldly clasp.

3 We handle it with unwashed hands;
We stain it with unhallowed breath;
We gloss it with device of man's,
And hide thine image underneath.

4 Forgive the sacrilege, and take
From off our souls the unworthy stain;
And show us, for thy Son's dear sake,
Thy pure and perfect law again.

6   *The power of God unto salvation.*   (268)

1 God, in the gospel of his Son,
Makes his eternal counsels known;
'T is here his richest mercy shines;
And truth is drawn in fairest lines.

2 Here sinners of a humble frame
May taste his grace and learn his name;
'T is writ in characters of blood,
Severely just—immensely good.

3 Here Jesus, in ten thousand ways,
His soul-attracting charms displays;
Recounts his poverty and pains,
And tells his love in melting strains.

4 May this blest volume ever lie
Close to my heart, and near my eye—
Till life's last hour my soul engage,
And be my chosen heritage!

THE HOLY SCRIPTURES.

HEBER. C. M.   GEO. KINGSLEY.

1. Fath-er of Mer-cies! in thy word What end-less glo-ry shines! For-ev-er be thy name a-dored For these ce-les-tial lines.

7   *Thy testimonies are my delight.*   (10)

2 Here may the wretched sons of want
   Exhaustless riches find;
Riches above what earth can grant,
   And lasting as the mind.

3 Here the fair tree of knowledge grows,
   And yields a rich repast;
Sublimer sweets than nature knows
   Invite the longing taste.

4 Here springs of consolation rise
   To cheer the fainting mind,
And thirsty souls receive supplies,
   And sweet refreshment find.

5 Here the Redeemer's welcome voice
   Spreads heavenly peace around;
And life and everlasting joys
   Attend the blissful sound.

6 Oh may these heavenly pages be
   My ever dear delight;
And still new beauties may I see,
   And still increasing light.

8   *A light unto my path.*   (11)

1 What glory gilds the sacred page,
   Majestic like the sun!
It gives a light to every age—
   It gives, but borrows none.

2 The hand that gave it, still supplies
   His gracious light and heat;
His truths upon the nations rise—
   They rise, but never set.

3 Let everlasting thanks be thine
   For such a bright display,
As makes the world of darkness shine
   With beams of heavenly day.

4 My soul rejoices to pursue
   The paths of truth and love,
Till glory breaks upon my view
   In brighter worlds above.

9   *Thy word is a lamp.*   (9)

1 How precious is the book divine,
   By inspiration given!
Bright as a lamp its precepts shine,
   To guide our souls to heaven.

2 It sweetly cheers our drooping hearts
   In this dark vale of tears;
Life, light, and joy, it still imparts,
   And quells our rising fears.

3 This lamp through all the tedious night
   Of life, shall guide our way,
Till we behold the clearer light
   Of an eternal day.

THE HOLY SCRIPTURES.

MARLOW. C. M. — English.

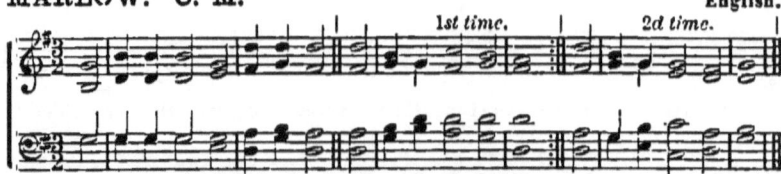

10 *Word of the everlasting God.* (16)

1 Lamp of our feet! whereby we trace
  Our path when wont to stray;
Stream from the fount of heavenly grace!
  Brook by the traveler's way!

2 Bread of our souls, whereon we feed!
  True manna from on high!
Our guide and chart, wherein we read
  Of realms beyond the sky!

3 Pillar of fire through watches dark,
  And radiant cloud by day!
When waves would whelm our tossing bark,
  Our anchor and our stay!

4 Word of the everlasting God!
  Will of his glorious Son!
Without thee, how could earth be trod,
  Or heaven itself be won?

11 *Wherewithal shall a young man, etc.* (15)

1 How shall the young secure their hearts,
  And guard their lives from sin?
Thy word the choicest rule imparts
  To keep the conscience clean.

2 'T is, like the sun, a heavenly light,
  That guides us all the day;
And, through the dangers of the night,
  A lamp to lead our way.

3 Thy precepts make us truly wise;
  We hate the sinner's road;
We hate our own vain thoughts that rise,
  But love thy law, O God!

4 Thy word is everlasting truth:
  How pure is every page!
That holy book shall guide our youth,
  And well support our age.

WILMOT. 7s. — VON WEBER.

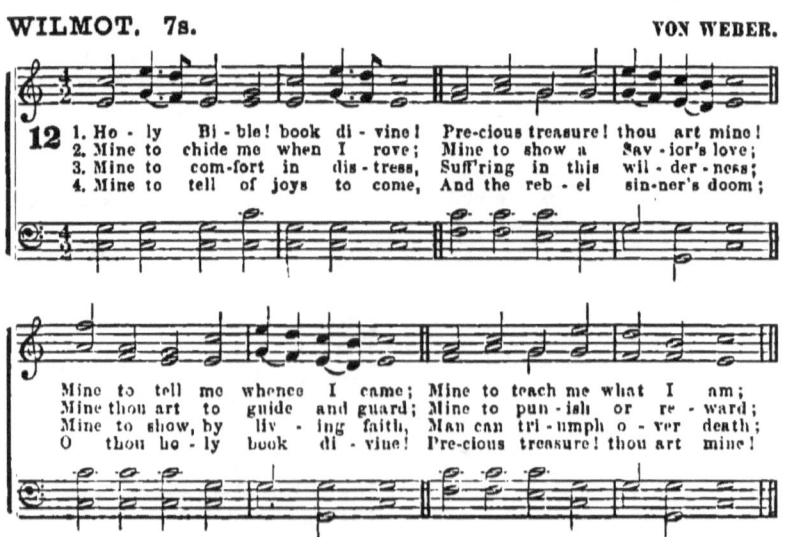

12
1. Holy Bible! book divine! Precious treasure! thou art mine!
2. Mine to chide me when I rove; Mine to show a Savior's love;
3. Mine to comfort in distress, Suff'ring in this wilderness;
4. Mine to tell of joys to come, And the rebel sinner's doom;

Mine to tell me whence I came; Mine to teach me what I am;
Mine thou art to guide and guard; Mine to punish or reward;
Mine to show, by living faith, Man can triumph over death;
O thou holy book divine! Precious treasure! thou art mine!

THE HOLY SCRIPTURES.

HARWELL. 8, 7, 8, 7, 7, 7. Arr. from Dr. L. MASON.

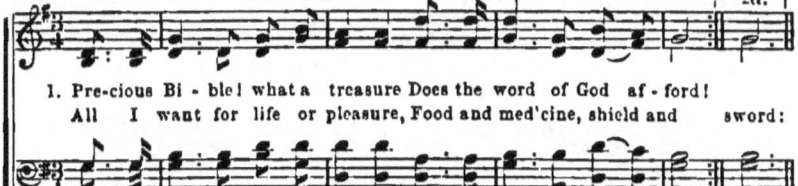

1. Pre-cious Bi-ble! what a treasure Does the word of God af-ford!
All I want for life or pleasure, Food and med'cine, shield and sword:
D. C. Hal-le-lu-jah, hal-le-lu-jah, Hal-le-lu-jah, A-men.

Let the world ac-count me poor, Hav-ing this I need no more.

13 *The word more precious than gold.* (22)

2 Food to which the world's a stranger,
  Here my hungry soul enjoys;
Of excess there is no danger—
  Though it fills, it never cloys:
On a dying Christ I feed;
He is meat and drink indeed!

3 In the hour of dark temptation,
  Satan can not make me yield;
For the word of consolation
  Is to me a mighty shield:
While the Scripture truths are sure,
From his malice I'm secure.

14 *Hark! ten thousand harps.* (663)

1 Hark! ten thousand harps and voices
  Sound the note of praise above;
Jesus reigns, and heaven rejoices—
  Jesus reigns, the God of love.
See: he sits on yonder throne—
Jesus rules the world alone.

2 Jesus, hail! whose glory brightens
  All above, and gives it worth;
Lord of life, thy smile enlightens,
  Cheers, and charms thy saints on earth;
When we think of love like thine,
Lord, we own it love divine.

3 King of glory, reign forever—
  Thine an everlasting crown;
Nothing from thy love shall sever
  Those whom thou hast made thine own;
Happy objects of thy grace,
Destined to behold thy face.

4 Savior, hasten thine appearing;
  Bring, oh bring the glorious day,
When, the awful summons hearing,
  Heaven and earth shall pass away;
Then, with golden harps, we'll sing,
"Glory, glory to our King!"

15 *Invitation.* (1319)

1 Come to Calvary's holy mountain,
  Sinners, ruined by the fall!
Here a pure and healing fountain
  Flows, to cleanse the guilty soul,
In a full, perpetual tide—
Opened when the Savior died.

2 Come in sorrow and contrition,
  Wounded, impotent, and blind;
Here the guilty find remission—
  Here the lost a refuge find:
Health this fountain will restore;
He that drinks shall thirst no more.

3 Come, ye dying, live forever;
  'T is a soul-reviving flood;
God is faithful—he will never
  Break the cov'nant sealed in blood:
Signed when our Redeemer died;
Sealed when he was crucified.

THE HOLY SCRIPTURES.

THE FAMILY BIBLE. 12s & 11s.   T. J. COOK, by permission.*

1. How painfully pleasing the fond re-col-lection Of youthful con-nections and
   When blessed with parental advice and affection,
   in-no-cent joy, Surrounded with mercies—with peace from on high! I still view the
   chairs of my father and mother, The seats of their offspring as ranged on each hand;
   And that richest of books, which excelled every other, The fam-i-ly Bi-ble that
   D. S. The fam-i-ly Bi-ble that
   lay on the stand: The old-fash-ioned Bi-ble, the dear, bles-sed Bi-ble,
   lay on the stand.

16   *The family Bible.*   (23)

2 That Bible, the volume of God's inspiration,
   At morn and at evening could yield us delight;
   And the prayer of our sire was a sweet invocation
   For mercy by day and for safety through night;
   Our hymn of thanksgiving with harmony swelling
   All warm from the heart of the family band,
   Has raised us from earth to that rapturous dwelling,
   Described in the Bible that lay on the stand.

* Written expresely for this work, but the copyright is retained by Mr. Cook.

GOD—HIS BEING AND PERFECTION. 11

BEETHOVEN. L. M.   **HAYDN.**

1 Praise ye the Lord! 'tis good to raise Our hearts and voices in his praise; His na-ture and his works in-vite To make this du-ty our de-light.

17   *Great is the Lord.*   (24)

2 Great is the Lord! and great his might,
And all his glories infinite;
His wisdom vast, and knows no bound—
A deep where all our thoughts are drowned.

3 He loves the meek, rewards the just,
Humbles the wicked in the dust,
Melts and subdues the stubborn soul,
And makes the broken spirit whole.

4 His saints are precious in his sight;
He views his children with delight;
He sees their hope, he knows their fear,
Approves and loves his image there.

18   *Omnipresence of God.*   (27)

1 Father of spirits! nature's God!
Our inmost thoughts are known to thee;
Thou, Lord, canst hear each idle word,
And every private action see.

2 Could we, on morning's swiftest wings,
Pursue our flight thro' trackless air,
Or dive beneath deep ocean's springs,
Thy presence still would meet us there.

3 In vain may guilt attempt to fly,
Concealed beneath the pall of night:
One glance from thy all-piercing eye
Can kindle darkness into light.

4 Search thou our hearts, and there destroy
Each evil thought, each secret sin,
And fit us for those realms of joy
Where naught impure shall enter in.

19   *Eternity of God.*   (25)

1 Ere mountains reared their forms sublime,
Or heaven and earth in order stood—
Before the birth of ancient time,
From everlasting thou art God.

2 A thousand ages, in their flight,
With thee are as a fleeting day;
Past, present, future, to thy sight
At once their various scenes display.

3 But our brief life's a shadowy dream—
A passing thought, that soon is o'er—
That fades with morning's earliest beam,
And fills the musing mind no more.

4 To us, O Lord, the wisdom give
Each passing moment so to spend,
That we at length with thee may live,
Where life and bliss shall never end.

20   *Doxology.*   (728)

Praise God, ye heavenly hosts above!
Praise him all creatures of his love!
Praise him each morning, noon, and night!
Praise him with holy, sweet delight!

Old Hundred, Key A.

GOD.

AVON. C. M. — Scotch.

1 Lord, all I am is known to thee; In vain my soul would try
To shun thy pres-ence, or to flee The no-tice of thine eye.

21 *Lord, thou hast searched me, etc.* (35)

2 Thy all-observing eye surveys
   My rising and my rest,
My public walks, my private ways,
   The secrets of my breast.

3 My thoughts lie open to thee, Lord,
   Before they're formed within;
And ere my lips pronounce the word,
   Thou knowest all I mean.

4 Oh let thine arms surround me still,
   And like a bulwark prove,
To guard my soul from every ill,
   Secured by sovereign love.

22 *He trieth the reins.* (40)

1 Great God! thy penetrating eye
   Pervades my inmost powers;
With awe profound my wondering soul
   Falls prostrate and adores.

2 To be encompassed round with God,
   The Holy and the Just,
Armed with omnipotence to save,
   Or crush me to the dust—

3 Oh how tremendous is the thought!
   Deep may it be impressed;
And may thy Spirit firmly 'grave
   This truth within my breast.

4 Begirt with thee, my fearless soul
   The gloomy vale shall tread;
And thou wilt bind the immortal crown
   Of glory on my head.

23 *God seen in his works.* (52)

1 There's not a tint that paints the rose
   Or decks the lily fair,
Or streaks the humblest flower that blows,
   But God has placed it there.

2 There's not a star whose twinkling light
   Illumes the distant earth,
And cheers the solemn gloom of night,
   But goodness gave it birth.

3 There's not a cloud whose dews distill
   Upon the parching clod,
And clothe with verdure vale and hill,
   That is not sent by God.

4 There's not a place in earth's vast round,
   In ocean deep, or air,
Where skill and wisdom are not found:
   For God is every-where.

5 Around, beneath, below, above,
   Wherever space extends,
There heaven displays its boundless love
   And power with goodness blends.

Balerma, Key D♭. Dundee, Key F.

GOD IN CREATION.

MENDON. L. M. ✳︎   Arr. from the German.

1. The spacious fir-ma-ment on high, With all the blue e-the-real sky,
And spangled heav'ns, a shining frame, Their great O-ri-gi-nal proclaim.

24 *The heavens declare the glory of God.* (43)

2 Th' unwearied sun, from day to day,
Does his Creator's power display,
And publishes to every land
The work of an almighty hand.

3 Soon as the evening shades prevail,
The moon takes up the wondrous tale,
And nightly to the listening earth
Repeats the story of her birth:

4 While all the stars that round her burn,
And all the planets in their turn,
Confirm the tidings as they roll,
And spread the truth from pole to pole.

5 What though in solemn silence all
Move round this dark terrestrial ball—
What though no real voice nor sound
Amid their radiant orbs be found—

6 In reason's ear they all rejoice,
And utter forth a glorious voice;
Forever singing as they shine,
The hand that made us is divine!

25 *The all-seeing God.* (32)

1 Lord, thou hast searched and seen me thro';
Thine eye commands with piercing view
My rising and my resting hours,
My heart and flesh, with all their powers.

2 My thoughts, before they are my own,
Are to my God distinctly known;
He knows the words I mean to speak,
Ere from my opening lips they break.

3 Within thy circling power I stand;
On every side I find thy hand:
Awake, asleep, at home, abroad,
I am surrounded still with God.

4 Amazing knowledge, vast and great!
What large extent! what lofty height!
My soul, with all the powers I boast,
Is in the boundless prospect lost.

26 *He is clothed with majesty.* (44)

1 Jehovah reigns: he dwells in light,
Arrayed with majesty and might;
The world, created by his hands,
Still on its firm foundation stands.

2 But ere this spacious world was made,
Or had its first foundation laid,
His throne eternal ages stood,
Himself the ever-living God.

3 Forever shall his throne endure;
His promise stands forever sure;
And everlasting holiness
Becomes the dwellings of his grace.

Uxbridge, Key E.   Duke Street, Key E♭.

GOD IN CREATION.

CADDO. C. M.   W. B. BRADBURY, by permission.

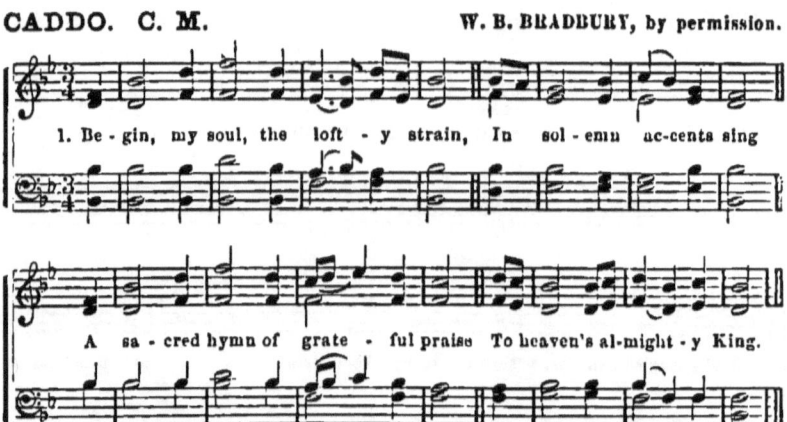

1. Be-gin, my soul, the loft-y strain, In sol-emn ac-cents sing A sa-cred hymn of grate-ful praise To heaven's al-might-y King.

27 *Praise him in the firmament of his power.* (53)

2 Ye curling fountains, as ye roll
  Your silver waves along,
Whisper to all your verdant shores
  The subject of my song.

3 Retain it long, ye echoing rocks,
  The sacred sound retain,
And from your hollow winding caves
  Return it oft again.

4 Bear it, ye winds, on all your wings,
  To distant climes away,
And round the wide-extended world
  The lofty theme convey.

5 Take the glad burden of his name,
  Ye clouds, as you arise,
Whether to deck the golden morn
  Or shade the evening skies.

28   *God of Bethel.*   (73)

1 O God of Bethel, by whose hand
  Thy people still are fed;
Who through this weary pilgrimage
  Hast all our fathers led—

2 Our vows, our prayers, we now present
  Before thy throne of grace;
God of our fathers, be the God
  Of their succeeding race.

3 Through each succeeding path of life,
  Our wandering footsteps guide;
Give us each day our daily bread,
  And raiment fit provide.

4 Oh spread thy covering wings around,
  Till all our wanderings cease,
And at our Father's loved abode
  Our souls arive in peace.

29   *Our dwelling place in all generations.* (75)

1 Our God, our help in ages past,
  Our hope for years to come,
Our shelter from the stormy blast,
  And our eternal home!

2 Under the shadow of thy throne
  Thy saints have dwelt secure;
Sufficient is thine arm alone,
  And our defense is sure.

3 Before the hills in order stood,
  Or earth received her frame,
From everlasting thou art God,
  To endless years the same.

4 A thousand ages in thy sight
  Are like an evening gone;
Short as the watch that ends the night
  Before the rising sun.

5 Time, like an ever-rolling stream,
  Bears all its sons away;
They fly, forgotten, as a dream
  Dies at the opening day.

6 Our God, our help in ages past,
  Our hope for years to come,
Be thou our guard while troubles last,
  And our eternal home.

Arlington, Key G.   Evan, Key A♭.

GOD IN CREATION. 15

DALSTON. S. P. M.   A. WILLIAMS.

1. The Lord Jehovah reigns, And royal state maintains, His head with awful glories crowned; Arrayed in robes of light, Begirt with sovereign might, And rays of majesty around.

30   *Jehovah reigns.*   (57)

1 The Lord Jehovah reigns,
   And royal state maintains,
His head with awful glories crowned;
   Arrayed in robes of light,
   Begirt with sovereign might,
And rays of majesty around.

2 Upheld by thy commands,
   The world securely stands,
And skies and stars obey thy word:
   Thy throne was fixed on high
   Before the starry sky:
Eternal is thy kingdom, Lord!

3 Thy promises are true;
   Thy grace is ever new;
There fixed, thy church shall ne'er remove:
   Thy saints with holy fear,
   Shall in thy courts appear,
And sing thine everlasting love.

31   *I was glad.*   (027)

1 How pleased and blessed was I,
   To hear the people cry—
"Come, let us seek our God to-day!"
   Yes, with a cheerful zeal,
   We haste to Zion's hill,
And there our vows and honors pay.

2 Zion! thrice happy place,
   Adorned with wondrous grace,
And walls of strength embrace thee round;
   In thee our tribes appear,
   To pray, and praise, and hear
The sacred gospel's joyful sound.

3 May peace attend thy gate,
   And joy within thee wait,
To bless the soul of every guest:
   The man who seeks thy peace,
   And wishes thine increase—
A thousand blessings on him rest!

32   *Laban, Key D.*   (56)

1 The Lord Jehovah reigns,
   Let all the nations fear;
Let sinners tremble at his throne,
   And saints be humble there.

2 Jesus, the Savior, reigns;
   Let earth adore its Lord;
Bright cherubs his attendants wait,
   Swift to fulfill his word.

3 In Zion stands his throne;
   His honors are divine;
His church shall make his wonders known,
   For there his glories shine.

4 How holy is his name!
   How fearful is his praise!
Justice, and truth, and judgment join
   In all the works of grace.

Peters, Key C.

ROCKINGHAM. L. M.
Dr. L. MASON.

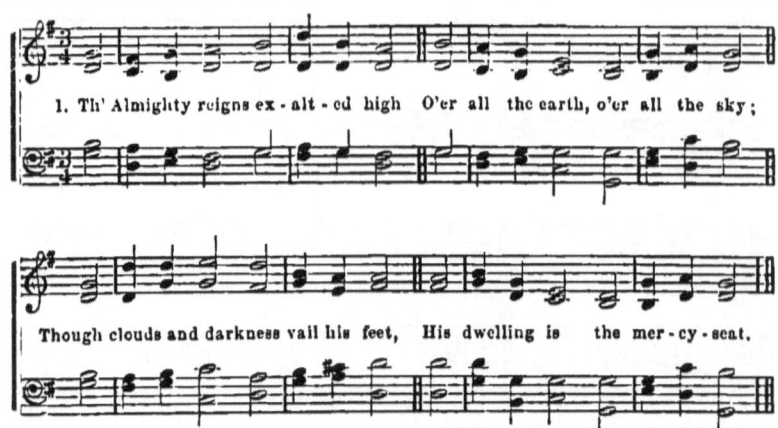

1. Th' Almighty reigns ex-alt-ed high O'er all the earth, o'er all the sky;
Though clouds and darkness vail his feet, His dwelling is the mer-cy-seat.

33 *Grace and glory.* (62)

2 Oh ye that love his holy name,
Hate every work of sin and shame;
He guards the souls of all his friends,
And from the snares of hell defends.

3 Immortal light and joys unknown
Are for the saints in darkness sown:
Those glorious seeds shall spring and rise,
And the bright harvest bless our eyes.

4 Rejoice, ye righteous, and record
The sacred honors of the Lord:
None but the soul that feels his grace
Can triumph in his holiness.

34 *Be thou exalted, O my God.* (64)

1 My God, in whom are all the springs
Of boundless love and grace unknown,
Hide me beneath thy spreading wings,
Till the dark cloud is overblown.

2 Up to the heavens I send my cry,
The Lord will my desires perform;
He sends his angels from the sky,
And saves me from the threatening storm.

3 My heart is fixed: my song shall raise
Immortal honors to thy name;
Awake, my tongue, to sound his praise,
My tongue, the glory of my frame.

4 High o'er earth his mercy reigns,
And reaches to the utmost sky;
His truth to endless years remains,
When lower worlds dissolve and die.

5 Be thou exalted, O my God!
Above the heavens where angels dwell;
Thy power on earth be known abroad,
And land to land thy wonders tell.

35 *God ever near.* (66)

1 O love divine, that stooped to share
Our sharpest pang, our bitterest tear,
On thee is cast each earth-born care,
We smile at pain while thou art near!

2 Though long the weary way we tread,
And sorrow crown each lingering year,
No path we shun, no darkness dread,
Our hearts still whispering, thou art near!

3 When drooping pleasure turns to grief,
And trembling faith is changed to fear
The murmuring wind, the quivering leaf,
Shall softly tell us, thou art near!

4 On thee we fling our burdening woe,
O love divine, for ever dear,
Content to suffer while we know,
Living and dying, thou art near!

Ward, Key B♭. Hamburg, Key F.

GOD IN PROVIDENCE.

HE LEADETH ME. L. M. 6 lines.
W. B. BRADBURY, by per.

1. He lead-eth me! Oh, blessed thought! Oh, words with heavenly comfort fraught!
Whate'er I do, whate'er I be, Still 't is God's hand that lead-eth me!

Refrain.
He lead-eth me! he lead-eth me! By his own hand he lead-eth me!
He lead-eth me! he lead-eth me! By his own hand he lead-eth me!

36   *He leadeth me.*   (768)

2 Sometimes 'midst scenes of deepest gloom,
Sometimes where Eden's bowers bloom;
By waters still, o'er troubled sea—
Still 't is his hand that leadeth me!
  He leadeth me! he leadeth me!
  By his own hand he leadeth me.

3 Lord, I would clasp thy hands in mine,
Nor ever murmur nor repine—
Content, whatever lot I see,
Since 't is my God that leadeth me.
  He leadeth me, etc.

4 And when my task on earth is done,
When, by thy grace, the victory's won,
E'en death's cold wave I will not flee;
Since God through Jordan leadeth me.
  He leadeth me, etc.

37   *Thy will be done.*   (68)

1 He sendeth sun, he sendeth shower;
Alike they're needful for the flower;
And joys and tears alike are sent
To give the soul fit nourishment:
As comes to me or cloud or sun,
Father, thy will, not mine, be done!

2 Can loving children e'er reprove
With murmurs whom they trust and love?
Creator, I would ever be,
A trusting, loving child to thee:
  As comes, etc.

3 Oh ne'er will I at life repine!
Enough that thou hast made it mine;
When fall the shadow cold of death,
I yet will sing, with parting breath—
  As comes, etc.

2

GOD IN PROVIDENCE.

ST. PETERSBURG. L. M. 6 lines. BORTNIANSKY.

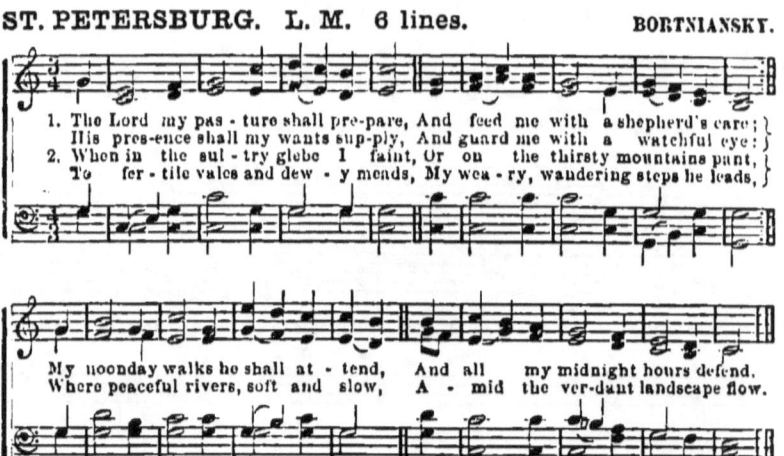

1. The Lord my pas-ture shall pre-pare, And feed me with a shepherd's care;
His pres-ence shall my wants sup-ply, And guard me with a watchful eye:
2. When in the sul-try glebe I faint, Or on the thirsty mountains pant,
To fer-tile vales and dew-y meads, My wea-ry, wandering steps he leads,

My noonday walks he shall at-tend, And all my midnight hours defend.
Where peaceful rivers, soft and slow, A-mid the ver-dant landscape flow.

38 *Psalm 23.* (70)
3 Though in a bare and rugged way,
Through devious, lonely wilds I stray,
His bounty shall my pains beguile;
The barren wilderness shall smile,
With lively greens and herbage crowned,
And streams shall murmur all around.

4 Though in the paths of death I tread,
With gloomy horrors overspread,
My steadfast heart shall fear no ill,
For thou, O Lord! art with me still;
Thy friendly crook shall give me aid,
And guide me through the dismal shade.

39 *Touched with the feeling of, etc.* (999)
1 When gathering clouds around I view,
And days are dark and friends are few;
On him I lean, who, not in vain,
Experienced every human pain.
He sees my wants, allays my fears,
And counts and treasures up my tears.

2 If aught should tempt my soul to stray
From heavenly wisdom's narrow way,
To fly the good I would pursue,
Or do the ill I would not do;
Still he who felt temptation's power,
Will guard me in that dangerous hour.

3 When, sorrowing, o'er some stone I bend,
Which covers all that was a friend;
And from his hand, his voice, his smile,
Divides me for a little while—
My Savior marks the tears I shed,
For "Jesus wept" o'er Lazarus dead.

4 And, oh! when I have safely passed
Through every conflict but the last,
Still, Lord, unchanging, watch beside
My dying bed, for thou hast died;
Then point to realms of cloudless day,
And wipe the latest tear away.

AMOY. 6s & 4s. (323) Dr. L. MASON.

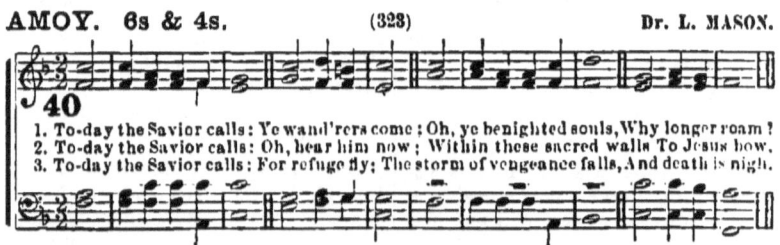

40
1. To-day the Savior calls: Ye wand'rers come; Oh, ye benighted souls, Why longer roam?
2. To-day the Savior calls: Oh, hear him now; Within these sacred walls To Jesus bow.
3. To-day the Savior calls: For refuge fly; The storm of vengeance falls, And death is nigh.

GOD IN PROVIDENCE.

NASHVILLE. L. P. M. Arr. by Dr. L. MASON.

1. I'll praise my Maker while I've breath, And when my voice is lost in death, Praise shall employ my nobler powers: { My days of praise shall ne'er be past, While life, and tho't, and being last, } And D. S. im-mor-tal - i - ty endures.

41 Psalm 146. (72)

2 Happy the man whose hopes rely
On Israel's God: he made the sky,
And earth, and seas, with all their train.
His truth forever stands secure:
He saves the oppressed, he feeds the poor,
And none shall find his promise vain.

3 The Lord pours eyesight on the blind;
The Lord supports the fainting mind,
He sends the laboring conscience peace:
He helps the stranger in distress,
The widow and the fatherless,
And grants the prisoner sweet release.

42 *The entrance of thy word giveth light.* (8)
1 I love the volume of thy word;
What light and joy those leaves afford

To souls benighted and distressed!
Thy precepts guide my doubtful way,
Thy fear forbids my feet to stray,
Thy promise leads my heart to rest.

2 Thy threatenings wake my slumbering eyes,
And warn me where my danger lies;
But 'tis thy blessed gospel, Lord,
That makes my guilty conscience clean,
Converts my soul, subdues my sin,
And gives a free but large reward.

3 Who knows the errors of his thoughts?
My God, forgive my secret faults,
And from presumptuous sins restrain;
Accept my poor attempts of praise,
That I have read thy book of grace,
And book of nature, not in vain.

WELLS. L. M. (71) HOLDROYD.

43
1. With Israel's God who can compare? Or who, like Israel, hap-py are?
2. Up-held by ev - er - last-ing arms, We are se-cure from foes and harms!

Oh, peo-ple sav-ed by the Lord, He is our shield and great re-ward:
In vain their plots, and false their boasts—Our refuge is the Lord of hosts!

GOD IN PROVIDENCE.

GENEVA. C. M. — COLE.

1. When all thy mer-cies, O my God, My ris-ing soul sur-veys,
2. Un-num-bered comforts on my soul Thy ten-der care be-stowed,

Transport-ed with the view I'm lost In won-der, love, and praise.
Be-fore my in-fant heart con-ceived From whom those com-forts flowed.

---

44   *Gratitude.*   (78)

3 When in the slippery paths of youth
   With heedless steps I ran,
Thine arm, unseen, conveyed me safe,
   And led me up to man.

4 Ten thousand thousand precious gifts
   My daily thanks employ,
Nor is the least a cheerful heart,
   That tastes those gifts with joy.

5 Through every period of my life
   Thy goodness I'll pursue;
And after death, in distant worlds,
   The glorious theme renew.

6 Through all eternity, to thee
   A joyful song I'll raise;
But oh! eternity's too short
   To utter all thy praise!

45   *The God of my life.*   (81)

1 Father of mercies! God of love!
   My Father and my God!
I'll sing the honors of thy name,
   And spread thy praise abroad.

2 In every period of my life
   Thy thoughts of love appear;
Thy mercies gild each transient scene,
   And crown each passing year.

3 In all thy mercies, may my soul
   A Father's bounty see;
Nor let the gifts thy grace bestows
   Estrange my heart from thee.

4 Teach me, in times of deep distress,
   To own thy hand, O God!
And in submissive silence learn
   The lessons of thy rod.

5 Then may I close my eyes in death,
   Redeemed from anxious fear:
For death itself, my God, is life,
   If thou be with me there.

46   *Majesty of God.*   (90)

1 The Lord descended from above
   And bowed the heavens most high,
And underneath his feet he cast
   The darkness of the sky.

2 On cherubim and seraphim
   Full royally he rode;
And on the wings of mighty winds,
   Came flying all abroad.

3 He sat serene upon the floods,
   Their fury to restrain;
And he, as sovereign Lord and King,
   For evermore shall reign.

Zanesville, Key G.   Heber, Key C.

GOD IN PROVIDENCE.

DUNDEE. C. M.   Scotch.

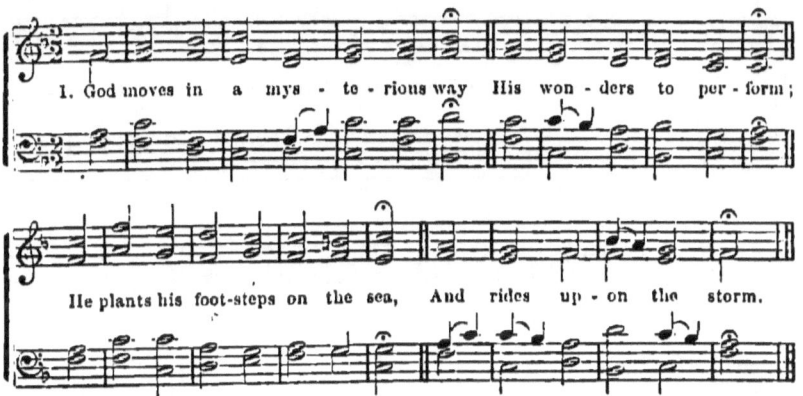

1. God moves in a mys-te-rious way His won-ders to per-form;
He plants his foot-steps on the sea, And rides up-on the storm.

47 *The judgments are a great deep.* (79)
2 Deep in unfathomable mines
Of never-failing skill,
He treasures up his bright designs,
And works his gracious will.

3 You fearful saints, fresh courage take;
The clouds you so much dread
Are big with mercy, and shall break
In blessings on your head.

4 Judge not the Lord by feeble sense,
But trust him for his grace;
Behind a frowning providence
He hides a smiling face.

5 His purposes will ripen fast,
Unfolding every hour;
The bud may have a bitter taste,
But sweet will be the flower.

6 Blind unbelief is sure to err,
And scan his work in vain:
God is his own interpreter,
And he will make it plain.

48 *Thou hast taught me from my youth* (87)
1 Almighty Father of mankind!
On thee my hopes remain;
And when the day of trouble comes,
I shall not trust in vain.

2 In early years, thou wast my guide,
And of my youth the friend;
And, as my days began with thee,
With thee my days shall end.

3 I know the power in whom I trust,
The arm on which I lean;
He will my Savior ever be,
Who has my Savior been.

4 Thou wilt not cast me off, when age
And evil days descend;
Thou wilt not leave me in despair,
To mourn my latter end.

49 *His tender mercies.* (83)
1 Thy goodness, Lord, our souls confess;
Thy goodness we adore;
A spring whose blessings never fail;
A sea without a shore.

2 Sun, moon, and stars thy love attest
In every golden ray;
Love draws the curtains of the night,
And love brings back the day.

3 Thy bounty every season crowns
With all the bliss it yields,
With joyful clusters loads the vines,
With strengthening grain the fields

4 But chiefly thy compassion, Lord,
Is in the gospel seen;
There, like a sun, thy mercy shines,
Without a cloud between.

5 There, pardon, peace, and holy joy
Through Jesus' name are given;
He on the cross was lifted high,
That we might reign in heaven.

Balerma, Key B♭.   Mear, Key F.

GOD IN PROVIDENCE.

GERAR. S. M.   Dr. L. MASON.

1. God is the foun-tain whence Ten thousand bless-ings flow; To him my life, my health, and friends, And ev-ery good, I owe.

50   *The fountain.*   (96)

2 The comforts he affords
  Are neither few nor small;
He is the source of fresh delights,
  My portion and my all.

3 He fills my heart with joy,
  My lips attunes for praise;
And to his glory I'll devote
  The remnant of my days.

51   *Psalm 23.*   (94)

1 The Lord my shepherd is;
  I shall be well supplied;
Since he is mine, and I am his,
  What can I want beside?

2 He leads me to the place
  Where heavenly pasture grows,
Where living waters gently pass,
  And full salvation flows.

3 If e'er I go astray,
  He doth my soul reclaim,
And guides me in his own right way,
  For his most holy name.

4 While he affords his aid,
  I can not yield to fear;
Though I should walk through death's dark shade,
  My shepherd's with me there.

52   *His mercy endureth forever.*   (95)

1 My soul, repeat his praise
  Whose mercies are so great;
Whose anger is so slow to rise,
  So ready to abate.

2 High as the heavens are raised
  Above the ground we tread,
So far the riches of his grace
  Our highest thoughts exceed.

3 His power subdues our sins,
  And his forgiving love,
Far as the east is from the west,
  Doth all our guilt remove.

4 The pity of the Lord,
  To those that fear his name,
Is such as tender parents feel:
  He knows our feeble frame.

5 Our days are as the grass,
  Or like the morning flower:
If one sharp blast sweeps o'er the field,
  It withers in an hour.

6 But thy compassions, Lord,
  To endless years endure;
And children's children ever find
  Thy words of promise sure.

Laban, Key C.   Boylston, Key C.

GOD IN PROVIDENCE.

DORRNANCE. 8s & 7s. I. B. WOODBURY.

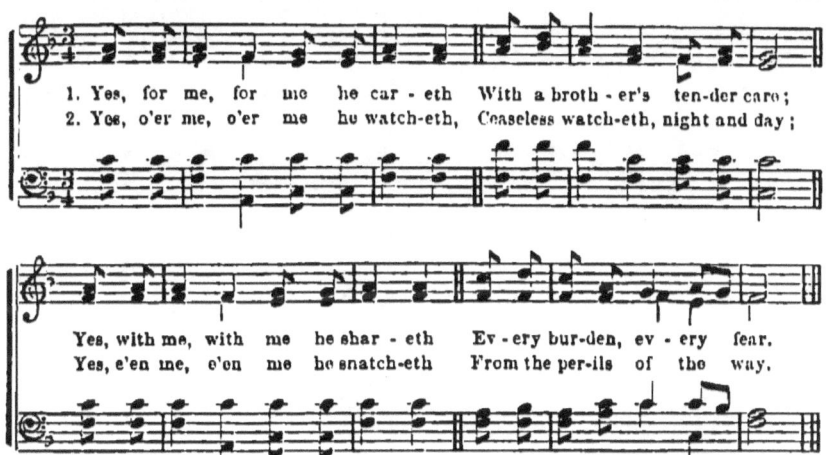

1. Yes, for me, for me he car-eth With a broth-er's ten-der care;
   Yes, with me, with me he shar-eth Ev-ery bur-den, ev-ery fear.
2. Yes, o'er me, o'er me he watch-eth, Ceaseless watch-eth, night and day;
   Yes, e'en me, e'en me he snatch-eth From the per-ils of the way.

53 *The elder brother.* (99)

3 Yes, for me he standeth pleading
  At the mercy-seat above;
Ever for me interceding;
  Constant in untiring love.

4 Yes, in me abroad he sheddeth
  Joys unearthly, love and light;
And to cover me he spreadeth
  His paternal wing of might.

5 Yes, in me, in me he dwelleth;
  I in him, and he in me;
And my empty soul he filleth,
  Here and through eternity.

6 Thus I wait for his returning,
  Singing all the way to heaven;
Such the joyful song of morning,
  Such the tranquil song of even.

54 *Arise and depart, etc.* (1142)

1 This is not my place of resting,
  Mine, a city yet to come;
Onward to it I am hasting—
  On to my eternal home.

2 In it, all is light and glory,
  O'er it shines a nightless day:
Every trace of sin's sad story,
  All the curse has passed away.

3 There the Lamb, our Shepherd, leads us,
  By the streams of life along;
On the freshest pastures feeds us,
  Turns our sighing into song.

4 Soon we pass this desert dreary,
  Soon we bid farewell to pain;
Never more be sad or weary,
  Never, never sin again.

55 *God is light and love.* (116)

1 God is love; his mercy brightens
  All the path in which we move!
Bliss he grants, and woe he lightens;
  God is light, and God is love.

2 Chance and change are busy ever;
  Worlds decay and ages move;
But his mercy waneth never;
  God is light, and God is love.

3 E'en the hour that darkest seemeth,
  His unchanging goodness proves;
From the cloud his brightness streameth;
  God is light, and God is love.

4 He our earthly cares entwineth
  With his comforts from above:
Every-where his glory shineth;
  God is light, and God is love.

Stockwell, Key B♭.

GOD IN PROVIDENCE.

LYONS. 10 & 11s. HAYDN.

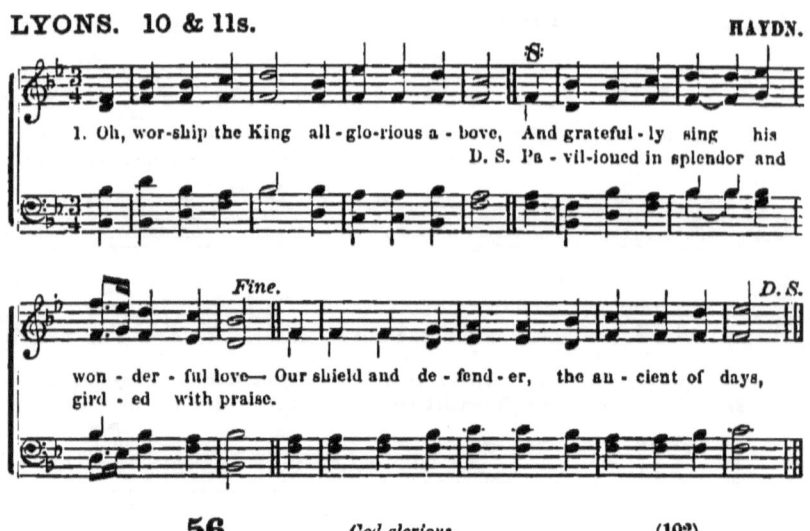

1. Oh, wor-ship the King all-glo-rious a-bove, And grateful-ly sing his
D. S. Pa-vil-ioned in splendor and
won-der-ful love— Our shield and de-fend-er, the an-cient of days,
gird-ed with praise.

56 *God glorious.* (102)

2 Oh tell of his might and sing of his grace,
Whose robe is the light, whose canopy space;
His chariots of wrath the deep thunder-clouds form,
And dark is his path on the wings of the storm.

3 Thy bountiful care, what tongue can recite?
It breathes in the air, it shines in the light,
It streams from the hills, it descends to the plain,
And sweetly distills in the dew and the rain.

4 Frail children of dust, and feeble as frail,
In thee do we trust, nor find thee to fail;
Thy mercies, how tender! how firm to the end,
Our Maker, Defender, Preserver, and Friend.

5 O Father Almighty, how faithful thy love!
While angels delight to hymn thee above,
The humbler creation, though feeble their lays,
With true adoration shall lisp to thy praise.

57 *"Preach the word."* (474)

1 You servants of God, your Master proclaim,
And publish abroad his wonderful name:
The name all victorious of Jesus extol:
His kingdom is glorious, and rules over all.

2 Christ ruleth on high, almighty to save:
And still he is nigh—his presence we have:
The great congregation his triumph shall sing,
Ascribing salvation to Jesus our King.

GOD IN PROVIDENCE.

COMFORT. 10, 10, 11, 11. From Social H. & T. Book.

1. Tho' troubles assail, and dangers affright,
Tho' friends should all fail, and foes all unite,
Yet one thing secures us, whatever betide,
The scripture assures us, The Lord will provide.

2. The birds without barn or storehouse are fed;
From them let us learn to trust for our bread,
His saints what is fitting ne'er be denied,
So long as 'tis written, The Lord will provide.

3. We may, like the ships, by tempests be tossed
On perilous deeps, but can not be lost;
Tho' Satan enrages the wind and the tide,
The promise engages, The Lord will provide.

58 *Jehovah-jireh.* (100)

4 His call we obey, like Abrah'm of old,
Not knowing our way, but faith makes us bold:
For though we are strangers, we have a good guide,
And trust, in all dangers, the Lord will provide.

59 *Oh tell me no more.* (841)

1 Oh tell me no more of this world's vain store:
The time for such trifles with me now is o'er;
A country I've found where true joys abound,
To dwell I'm determined on that happy ground.

2 The souls that believe, in glory shall live,
And me in that number will Jesus receive;
My soul, do n't delay, he calls thee away,
Rise, follow the Savior, and bless the glad day.

3 No mortal doth know what he can bestow,
What light, strength, and comfort—go after him, go;
Lo, onward I move to a city above,
None guesses how wondrous my journey will prove.

4 Great spoils I shall win from death, hell, and sin,
'Midst outward afflictions I feel Christ within;
And when I'm to die, receive me, I'll cry,
For Jesus has loved me—I can not tell why.

GOD IN REDEMPTION.

DUKE STREET. L. M.   HATTON.

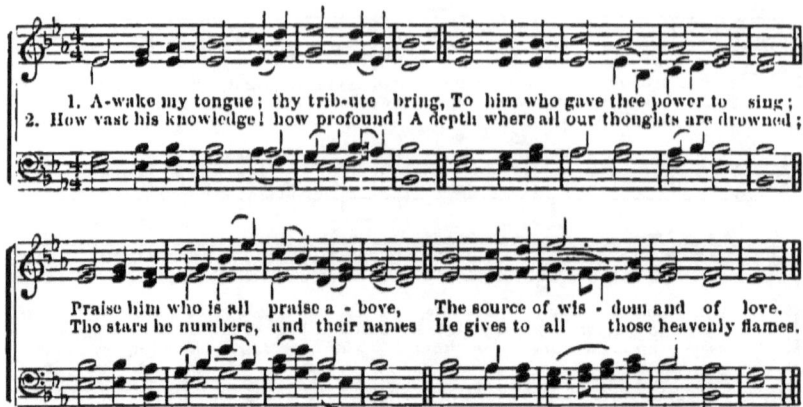

1. A-wake my tongue; thy trib-ute bring, To him who gave thee power to sing;
Praise him who is all praise a-bove, The source of wis-dom and of love.

2. How vast his knowledge! how profound! A depth where all our thoughts are drowned;
The stars he numbers, and their names He gives to all those heavenly flames.

60   *God only wise.*   (105)
3 Through each bright world above, behold
Ten thousand thousand charms unfold;
Earth, air, and mighty seas combine
To speak his wisdom all divine.

4 But in redemption, oh what grace!
Its wonders, oh, what thought can trace!
Here, wisdom shines for ever bright;
Praise him, my soul, with sweet delight.

61   *What is man?*   (109)
1 Lord, what is man? Extremes how wide
In this mysterious nature join!
The flesh to worms and dust allied,
The soul immortal and divine.

2 Divine at first, a holy flame
Kindled by heaven's inspiring breath;
Till sin, with power prevailing, came,
Then followed darkness, shame and death.

3 But Jesus, oh amazing grace!
Assumed our nature as his own,
Obeyed and suffered in our place,
Then took it with him to his throne.

4 Now, what is man, when grace reveals
The virtue of a Savior's blood?
Again a life divine he feels,
Despises earth and walks with God.

5 And what, in yonder realms above,
Is ransomed man ordained to be?
With honor, holiness, and love,
No seraph more adorned than he.

6 Nearest the throne, and first in song,
Man shall his hallelujahs raise;
While wondering angels round him throng
And swell the chorus of his praise.

62   *The reconciliation.*   (108)
1 Oh love beyond conception great,
That formed the vast, stupendous plan,
Where all divine perfections meet
To reconcile rebellious man:

2 There wisdom shines in fullest blaze,
And justice all her right maintains—
Astonished angels stoop to gaze,
While mercy o'er the guilty reigns.

3 Yes, mercy reigns, and justice too;
In Christ they both harmonious meet;
He paid to justice all her due,
And now he fills the mercy-seat.

63   *Love—that passeth knowledge.*   (110)
1 O love of God, how strong and true!
Eternal and yet ever new:
Above all price, and still unbought;
Beyond all knowledge and all thought.

2 O wide embracing, wondrous love,
We read thee in the sky above;
We read thee in the earth below,
In seas that swell and streams that flow.

3 We read thee best in him who came
To bear for us the Cross of shame;
Sent by the Father from on high,
Our life to live, our death to die.

Uxbridge, Key E.   Rockingham, Key G.

GOD IN REDEMPTION.

PERON. 8s, 7s & 4.

1. Guide me, O thou great Jehovah,
   Pilgrim thro' this barren land:
   I am weak, but thou art mighty,
   Hold me with thy powerful hand;
   Bread of heaven, Bread of heaven,
   Feed me till I want no more.

64 *Jehovah my strength.* (115)

2 Open thou the crystal fountain
   Whence the healing waters flow;
   Let the fiery, cloudy pillar,
   Lead me all my journey through;
   Strong Deliverer,
   Be thou still my strength and shield.

3 When I tread the verge of Jordan,
   Bid the swelling stream divide;
   Death of death, and hell's destruction,
   Land me safe on Canaan's side!
   Songs of praises
   I will ever give to thee.

65 *Praise the King of heaven.* (101)

1 Praise, my soul, the King of heaven;
   To his feet thy tribute bring;
   Ransomed, healed, restored, forgiven,
   Who like me his praise should sing?
   Praise him! praise him!
   Praise the everlasting King!

2 Praise him for his grace and favor
   To our fathers in distress;
   Praise him, still the same forever:
   Slow to chide, and swift to bless;
   Praise him! praise him!
   Glorious in his faithfulness!

3 Father-like he tends and spares us;
   Well our feeble frame he knows;
   In his hands he gently bears us—
   Rescues us from all our foes;
   Praise him! praise him!
   Widely as his mercy flows!

66 *It is finished.* (178)

1 Hark! the voice of love and mercy
   Sounds aloud from Calvary;
   See! it rends the rocks asunder,
   Shakes the earth and vails the sky!
   It is finished!
   Hear the dying Savior cry.

2 It is finished! Oh what pleasure
   Do these precious words afford!
   Heavenly blessings without measure
   Flow to us from Christ the Lord;
   It is finished!
   Saints, the dying words record.

3 Finished all the types and shadows
   Of the ceremonial law!
   Finished all that God had promised;
   Death and hell no more shall awe:
   It is finished!
   Saints, from this your comfort draw

Oliphant, Key D.   Osgood, Key E♭.

CHRIST—HIS NATIVITY.

PARK STREET. L. M. VENUA.

1. When Jordan hushed his waters still, And silence slept on Zion's hill; When Bethlehem's shepherds thro' the night, Watched o'er their flocks by starry light, Watched o'er their flocks by starry light—

67 *Luke 2: 11.* (117)

2 Hark! from the midnight hills around,
A voice of more than mortal sound,
In distant hallelujahs stole,
Wild murmuring o'er the raptured soul.

3 On wheels of light, on wings of flame,
The glorious hosts of Zion came;
High heaven with songs of triumph rung,
While thus they struck their harps and sang:

4 "O Zion, lift thy raptured eye;
The long-expected hour is nigh;
The joys of nature rise again;
The Prince of Salem comes to reign.

5 "See, Mercy, from her golden urn,
Pours a rich stream to them that mourn;
Behold, she binds with tender care,
The bleeding bosom of despair.

6 "He comes to cheer the trembling heart:
Bids Satan and his hosts depart;
Again the day-star gilds the gloom,
Again the bowers of Eden bloom."

68 *Genesis 3: 15.* (118)

1 Behold the woman's promised seed !
Behold the great Messiah come!
Behold the prophets all agreed
To give him the superior room!

2 Abrah'm, the saint, rejoiced of old,
When visions of the Lord'he saw;
Moses, the man of God, foretold
This great fulfiller of his law.

3 The types bore witness to his name,
Obtained their chief design, and ceased—
The incense and the bleeding lamb,
The ark, the altar, and the priest.

4 Predictions in abundance join
To pour their witness on his head:
Jesus, we bow before thy throne,
And own thee as the promised seed.

69 *He hath the keys of hell and of death* (218)

1 Hail to the Prince of Life and Peace,
Who holds the keys of death and hell;
The spacious world unseen is his,
The sovereign power becomes him well.

2 In shame and anguish once he died;
But now he lives for evermore;
Bow down, you saints, around his seat,
And all you angel bands adore;

3 Live, live forever, glorious Lord,
To crush thy foes and guard thy friends,
While all thy chosen tribes rejoice
That thy dominion never ends.

4 Worthy thy hand to hold the keys,
Guided by wisdom and by love;
Worthy to rule our mortal lives,
O'er worlds below and worlds above.

5 Forever reign, victorious King!
Wide through the earth thy name be known,
And call our longing souls to sing
Sublimer anthems near thy throne.

Sessions, Key C.   Duke Street, Key E♭.

BOONTON. C. H. M.
W. B. BRADBURY, by permission.

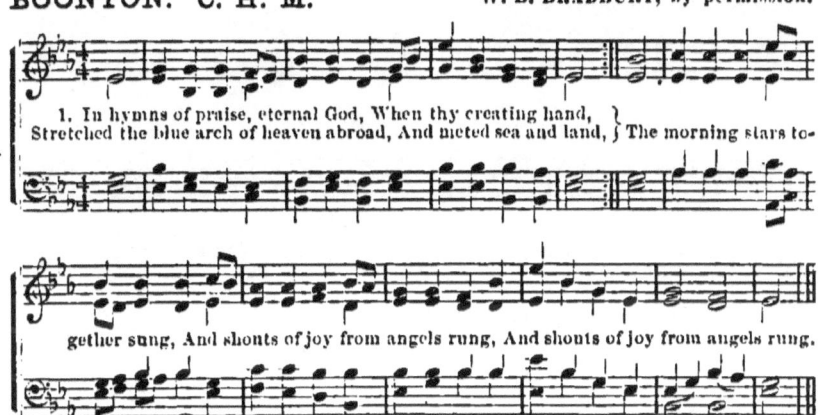

1. In hymns of praise, eternal God, When thy creating hand,
Stretched the blue arch of heaven abroad, And meted sea and land,
The morning stars together sung, And shouts of joy from angels rung, And shouts of joy from angels rung.

70 *Glory to God—good will to men.* (119)

2 Than earth's prime hour, more joyous far,
 Was the eventful morn,
When the bright beam of Bethlehem's star
 Announced a Savior born!
Then sweeter strains from heaven began,
 "Glory to God—good will to man."

3 Babe of the manger! can it be?
 Art thou the Son of God?
Shall subject nations bow the knee,
 And kings obey thy nod?
Shall thrones and monarchs prostrate fall
Before the tenant of a stall?

4 'T is he! the hymning seraphs cry,
 While hovering drawn to earth;
'T is he! the shepherds' songs reply;
 Hail! hail! Immanuel's birth;
The rod of peace those hands shall bear,
That brow a crown of glory wear.

71 *The ineffable glory of God.* (55)

1 Since o'er thy footstool here below
 Such radiant gems are strewn,
Oh what magnificence must glow,
 Great God, about thy throne!
So brilliant here these drops of light—
There the full ocean rolls, how bright!

2 If night's blue curtain of the sky—
 With thousand stars inwrought,
Hung like a royal canopy
 With glittering diamonds fraught—
Be, Lord, thy temple's outer vail,
What splendor at the shrine must dwell!

3 The dazzling sun at noonday hour—
 Forth from his flaming vase
Flinging o'er earth the golden shower
 Till vale and mountain blaze—
But shows, O Lord, one beam of thine;
What, then, the day where thou dost shine!

4 Oh how shall these dim eyes endure
 That noon of living rays!
Or how our spirits so impure,
 Upon thy glory gaze!
Anoint, O Lord, anoint our sight,
And fit us for that world of light.

72 *Job 1: 21.* (777)

1 When I can trust my all with God,
 In trial's fearful hour—
Bow all resigned beneath his rod,
 And bless his sparing power;
A joy springs up amid distress,
A fountain in the wilderness.

2 Oh! to be brought to Jesus' feet,
 Though trials fix me there,
Is still a privilege most sweet;
 For he will hear my prayer;
Though sighs and tears its language be,
The Lord is nigh to answer me.

3 Then, blessed be the hand that gave,
 Still blessed when it takes;
Blessed be he who smites to save,
 Who heals the heart he breaks;
Perfect and true are all his ways,
Whom heaven adores and death obeys.

CHRIST—HIS NATIVITY.

WAYNE. C. M. Double.   Dr. L. MASON.

1. It came up-on the mid-night clear, That glorious song of old,
From an-gels bend-ing near the earth, To touch their harps of gold;
"Peace to the earth, good will to men, From heaven's all-gracious King;"
The world in sol-emn still-ness lay To hear the an-gels sing.

2. Still thro' the clo-ven skies they come, With peaceful wings un-furled;
And still their heavenly mu-sic floats O'er all the wear-y world;
A-bove its sad and low-ly plains, They bend on heavenly wing,
And ev-er o'er its Ba-bel sounds, The bles-sed an-gels sing.

73   *Song of the angels.*   (120)

3 Yet with the woes of sin and strife
The world has suffered long;
Beneath the angel-strain have rolled
Two thousand years of wrong;
And men, at war with men, hear not
The love-song which they bring:
Oh! hush the noise, ye men of strife,
And hear the angels sing!

4 And ye, beneath life's crushing load,
Whose forms are bending low,
Who toil along the climbing way
With painful steps and slow;
Look now! for glad and golden hours
Come swiftly on the wing:
Oh! rest beside the weary road,
And hear the angels sing!

5 For lo! the days are hast'ning on,
By prophet-bards foretold,
When with the ever-circling years
Comes round the age of gold;

When peace shall over all the earth
Its ancient splendor fling,
And the whole world send back the song
Which now the angels sing.

74   *The Advent.*   (124)

1 Hark, the glad sound! the Savior comes!
The Savior promised long!
Let every heart prepare a throne,
And every voice a song.
He comes, the prisoner to release
In Satan's bondage held;
The gates of brass before him burst,
The iron fetters yield.

2 He comes, from thickest films of vice
To clear the mental ray,
And on the eyeballs of the blind
To pour celestial day.
He comes, the broken heart to bind,
The bleeding soul to cure.
And with the treasures of his grace
To enrich the humble poor.

Drake, Key F.   Fleming, Key G.

CHRIST—HIS NATIVITY.

ANTIOCH. C. M. Arranged from Handel by Dr. L. MASON.

1. Joy to the world, the Lord is come! Let earth re-ceive her King: Let ev-ery heart prepare him room, And heaven and nature sing, And heaven and na-ture sing, And heaven, And heaven and na-ture sing.

75 *Joy to the World.* (125)
2 Joy to the earth, the Savior reigns!
Let men their songs employ;
While fields and floods, rocks, hills, and plains,
Repeat the sounding joy.

3 No more let sins and sorrows grow,
Nor thorns infest the ground;
He comes to make his blessings flow
Far as the curse is found.

4 He rules the world with truth and grace,
And makes the nations prove
The glories of his righteousness,
And wonders of his love.

76 *God is gone up with a shout.* (199)
1 Arise, ye people, and adore,
Exulting strike the chord;
Let all the earth, from shore to shore,
Confess the almighty Lord.

2 Glad shouts aloud—wide echoing round,
The ascending Lord proclaim;
The angelic choir respond the sound,
And shake creation's frame.

3 They sing of death and hell o'erthrown
In that triumphant hour;
And God exalts his conquering Son
To his right hand of power.

77 *Mortals, awake.* (121)
1 Mortals! awake, with angels join,
And chant the solemn lay;
Love, joy, and gratitude combine
To hail the auspicious day.

2 In heaven the rapturous song began,
And sweet seraphic fire
Through all the shining legions ran,
And swept the sounding lyre.

3 The theme, the song, the joy was new
To each angelic tongue;
Swift through the realms of light it flew,
And loud the echo rung.

4 Down through the portals of the sky
The pealing anthem ran,
And angels flew with eager joy
To bear the news to man.

Zerah, Key C.

CHRIST—HIS NATIVITY.

ZERAH. C. M.   Dr. L. MASON.

1. To us a child of hope is born, To us a Son is given;
Him shall the tribes of earth o-bey, Him, all the hosts of heaven;
Him shall the tribes of earth o-bey, Him, all the hosts of heaven.

78   *Isaiah 9: 6.*   (122)

2 His name shall be the Prince of Peace,
   For evermore adored,
The Wonderful, the Counselor,
   The great and mighty Lord.

3 His power, increasing, still shall spread;
   His reign no end shall know;
Justice shall guard his throne above,
   And peace abound below.

79   *He shall save his people.*   (254)

1 Salvation! oh the joyful sound;
   'Tis pleasure to our ears;
A sovereign balm for every wound,
   A cordial for our fears.

2 Buried in sorrow and in sin,
   At hell's dark door we lay;
But we arise by grace divine,
   To see a heavenly day.

3 Salvation! let the echo fly
   The spacious earth around;
While all the armies of the sky
   Conspire to raise the sound.

80   *Children's Hymn.*   (234)

1 Hosanna! raise the pealing hymn
   To David's Son and Lord;
With cherubim and seraphim
   Exalt the incarnate Word.

2 Hosanna! Lord, our feeble tongue
   No lofty strains can raise:
But thou wilt not despise the young
   Who meekly chant thy praise.

3 Hosanna! Sovereign, Prophet, Priest,
   How vast thy gifts, how free!
Thy Blood, our life; thy Word, our feast;
   Thy Name, our only plea.

4 Hosanna! Master, lo! we bring
   Our offerings to thy throne;
Not gold, nor myrrh, nor mortal thing,
   But hearts to be thine own.

5 O Savior, if, redeemed by thee
   Thy temple we behold,
Hosannas through eternity
   We'll sing to harps of gold.

Antioch, Key E.   Brown, Key C.

CHRIST—HIS NATIVITY. 33

WATCHMAN. 7s, Double.   Dr. L. MASON.

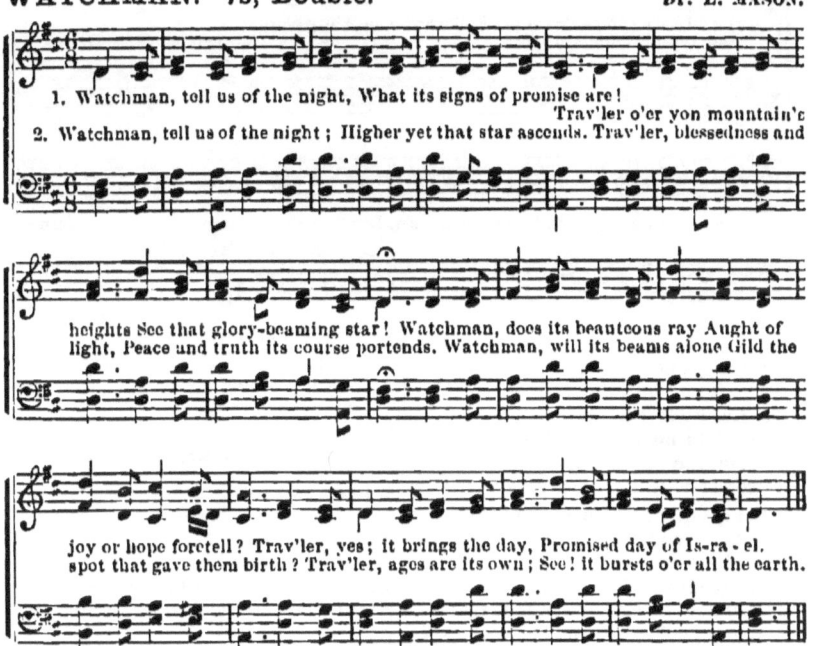

1. Watchman, tell us of the night, What its signs of promise are! Trav'ler o'er yon mountain's heights See that glory-beaming star! Watchman, does its beauteous ray Aught of joy or hope foretell? Trav'ler, yes; it brings the day, Promised day of Is-ra-el.

2. Watchman, tell us of the night; Higher yet that star ascends. Trav'ler, blessedness and light, Peace and truth its course portends. Watchman, will its beams alone Gild the spot that gave them birth? Trav'ler, ages are its own; See! it bursts o'er all the earth.

81   *Watchman, what of the night!*   (128)
3 Watchman, tell us of the night,
For the morning seems to dawn.
Trav'ler, darkness takes its flight,
Doubt and terror are withdrawn.
Watchman, let thy wandering cease;
Hie thee to thy quiet home.
Trav'ler, lo! the Prince of Peace,
Lo! the Son of God is come!

82   *Christ is born in Bethlehem.*   (126)
1 Hark! the herald angels sing,
"Glory to the new-born King!
Peace on earth, and mercy mild;
God and sinners reconciled."
Joyful, all ye nations, rise;
Join the triumphs of the skies;
With th' angelic host proclaim,
"Christ is born in Bethlehem."

2 See, he lays his glory by;
Born that man no more may die;
Born to raise the sons of earth;
Born to give them second birth.

Vailed in flesh the Godhead see!
Hail, th' incarnate Deity!
Pleased as man with man to dwell,
Jesus, our Immanuel!

3 Hail, the heaven-born Prince of Peace!
Hail, the Son of Righteousness!
Light and life to all he brings,
Risen with healing in his wings.
Let us then with angels sing,
"Glory to the new-born King!
Peace on earth, and mercy mild
God and sinners reconciled!"

83   *Col. 1: 11, 12.*   (747)
1 Glorious in thy saints appear;
Plant thy heavenly kingdom here;
Light and life to all impart;
Shine on each believing heart;
And, in every grace complete,
Make us, Lord, for glory meet;
Till we stand before thy sight,
Partners with the saints in light.

Eltham, Key G.

HADDAM. H. M.   English.

1. Hark! hark! the notes of joy Roll o'er the heav'nly plains,
And seraphs find em-ploy — — — — — For their sublimest strains;
Some new de-light in heaven is known, Loud sound the harps around the throne.

84   *Good tidings of great joy.*   (132)
2 Hark! hark! the sound draws nigh—
  The joyful host descends;
The Lord forsakes the sky,
  To earth his footsteps bends:
He comes to bless our fallen race;
He comes with messages of grace.

3 Bear, bear the tidings round!
  Let every mortal know
What love in God is found,
  What pity he can show:
Ye winds that blow, ye waves that roll,
Bear the glad news from pole to pole.

4 Strike, strike the harps again,
  To great Immanuel's name!
Arise, ye sons of men,
  And all his grace proclaim:
Angels and men, wake every string,
'Tis God the Savior's praise we sing!

85   *A birthday hymn.*   (1174)
1 God of my life, to thee
  My cheerful soul I raise,
Thy goodness bade me be,
  And still prolongs my days:
I see my natal hour return,
And bless the day that I was born.

2 Though but a child of earth,
  I glorify thy name,
From whom alone my birth,
  And all my blessing came;
Creating and preserving grace
Let all that is within me praise.

3 My soul and all its powers,
  Thine, wholly thine, shall be;
All, all my happy hours
  I consecrate to thee;
Whate'er I have, whate'er I am,
Shall magnify my Maker's name.

4 Long as I live beneath,
  To thee oh let me live,
To thee my ev'ry breath
  In thanks and blessings give;
Me to thine image, Lord, restore,
And I shall praise thee evermore.

86   *Believing, we rejoice.*   (545)
1 Ye saints, your music bring,
  Attuned to sweetest sound,
Strike every trembling string,
  Till earth and heaven resound;
The triumphs of the cross we sing;
Awake, ye saints, each joyful string.

2 The cross, the cross alone,
  Subdued the powers of hell;
Like light'ning from his throne
  The prince of darkness fell.
The triumphs of the cross we sing,
Awake, ye saints, each joyful string.

3 The cross hath power to save
  From all the foes that rise;
The cross hath made the grave
  A passage to the skies;
The triumphs of the cross we sing;
Awake, ye saints, each joyful string.

Lenox, Key B♭.   Zebulon, Key F.   Lischer, Key G.

CHRIST—HIS NATIVITY.

87 *Chorus of the angels.* (134)

2 See all darkness disappearing
　As the star begins to rise!
Sin and death stand trembling, fearing,
　As the light falls on their eyes:
Now, again, the earth rejoices,
　Satan's powerful kingdom shakes,
As, from all the heavenly voices,
　Louder still the chorus breaks!

3 Rise and shine, Star of Salvation!
　Spread thy beams o'er all the earth,
Till each distant land and nation
　Owns and speaks thy matchless worth!
Till all tongues, thy praises singing,
　Shall thy mighty wonders tell!
Till all heaven with joy is ringing,
　As our hearts the chorus swell!

4 When our days on earth are ended,
　And we rise to worlds above,
Then our songs shall all be blended
　In one song of pardoning love!
Then we'll tell the wondrous story,
　And our blessed Lord adore;
In our home of bliss and glory
　We shall sing for evermore!

88 *Shepherds, hail the wondrous, etc.* (133)

Shepherds, hail the wondrous stranger!
　Now to Bethlehem speed your way;
Lo! in yonder humble manger,
　Christ the Lord is born to-day.
Bright the star of your salvation,
　Pointing to his rude abode;
Rapturous news for every nation·
　Now, behold the Son of God!

CHRIST—HIS NATIVITY.

MANOR. 8s & 7s, Double. ✷ Arr. fr. the Oriola, by J. P. POWELL.

1. Hark! what mean those holy voices, Sweetly sounding thro' the skies? Lo! th' angel-ic host re-joices, ——— Heavenly hal-le-lujahs rise. Hear them tell the wondrous story, Hear them chant in hymns of joy— "Glo-ry to the highest, glo-ry; Glo-ry be to God most high!"

89 *Hark! what mean those holy voices?* (135)

2 "Peace on earth, good-will from heaven,
  Reaching far as man is found;
Souls redeemed and sins forgiven!"
  Loud our golden harps shall sound.
"Christ is born, the great anointed;
  Heaven and earth his praises sing;
Oh receive whom God appointed,
  For your Prophet, Priest, and King!

90 *Christ, the Savior, born.* (136)

1 Hail, thou long-expected Jesus!
  Born to set thy people free;
From our sins and fears release us,
  Let us find our rest in thee.
Israel's strength and consolation,
  Hope of all the saints, thou art;
Long-desired of every nation,
  Joy of every waiting heart.

2 Born, thy people to deliver—
  Born a child, yet Christ, our king—
Born to reign in us forever—
  Now thy gracious kingdom bring.
By thine own eternal Spirit,
  Rule in all our hearts alone;
By thine all-sufficient merit,
  Raise us to thy glorious throne.

91 *Onward!* (1275)

1 Onward, onward, men of heaven!
  Bear the gospel banner high;
Rest not till its light is given—
  Star of every pagan sky;
Send it where the pilgrim stranger
  Faints beneath the torrid ray;
Bid the hearty forest ranger
  Hail it ere he fades away.

2 Where the Arctic ocean thunders,
  Where the tropics fiercely glow,
Broadly spread its page of wonders,
  Brightly bid its radiance flow;
India marks its luster stealing;
  Shivering Greenland loves its rays;
Afric, 'mid her deserts kneeling,
  Lifts the untaught strain of praise.

CHRIST—HIS NATIVITY.

STAR IN THE EAST. 11s & 10s. ※   Arr. by J. ZUNDEL.

1. Hail the blest morn! when the great Mediator Down from the regions of glory descends!
Shepherds, go worship the babe in the manger; Lo! for your guide the bright angel attends!
D. C. Star of the East, the horizon adorning, Guide where our infant Redeemer is laid.

VOCAL OR INSTRUMENTAL BASE.

*Sing small notes in repeat.

Chorus.

Brightest and best of the sons of the morning, Dawn on our darkness, and lend us thy aid;

92   *Hail the blest morn.*   (138)

2 Cold on his cradle the dew-drops are shining,
Low lies his head with the beasts of the stall:
Angels adore him in slumbers reclining,
Maker, and Monarch, and Savior of all!

3 Say, shall we yield him, in costly devotion,
Oders of Eden, and offerings divine;
Gems from the mountain, and pearls from the ocean,
Myrrh from the forest, and gold from the mine?

SILENT NIGHT. 6, 6, 9, 9, 6.   Tyrolese Melody.

1. Silent night! hallowed night! Land and deep si-lent sleep; { Softly glitters bright
Beck'ning Is-ra el's
Bethlehem's star,
eye from a-far, } Where the Savior is born, Where the Sav-ior is born.

93   *Silent night.*   (131)

2 Silent night! hallowed night!
On the plain wakes the strain,
Sung by heavenly harbingers bright,
Fraught with tidings of boundless delight:
Christ the Savior has come.

3 Silent night! hallowed night!
Earth awake, silence break,
High your anthems of melody raise,
Heaven and earth in full chorous of praise:
Peace forever shall reign.

CHRIST—HIS NATIVITY.

SCOTLAND. 12s.   Dr. CLARKE.

94   *Hallelujah to the Lamb.*   (139)
2 Glad tidings I bring unto you and each nation!
Glad tidings of joy—now behold your salvation;
Then suddenly multitudes raise their glad voices,
And shout hallelujahs, while heaven rejoices!

3 Now glory to God in the highest be given,
All glory to God is re-echoed from heaven;
Around the whole earth let us tell the glad story,
And sing of his love, his salvation, and glory.

95   *The voice of free grace.*   (332)
1 The voice of free grace cries, "Escape to the mountain!"
For Adam's lost race Christ hath opened a fountain;
For sin and uncleanness, and every transgression,
His blood flows most freely in streams of salvation.

2 Ye souls that are wounded! O! flee to the Savior;
He calls you in mercy—'t is infinite favor;
Your sins are increasing—escape to the mountain—
His blood can remove them, it flows from the fountain.

GRATITUDE. L. M.
BOST.

1. How sweetly flowed the gospel sound
From lips of gentleness and grace,
When list'ning thousands gathered round,
And joy and gladness filled the place.

96 *His teaching.* (141)

2 From heaven he came, of heaven he spoke,
To heaven he led his followers' way;
Dark clouds of gloomy night he broke,
Unvailing an immortal day.

3 "Come, wanderers, to my Father's home;
Come, all ye weary ones, and rest!"
Yes, sacred teacher, we will come,
Obey thee, love thee, and be blest.

97 *Meekness and gentleness of Christ.* (144)

1 How bounteous were the marks divine,
That in thy meekness used to shine;
That lit thy lonely pathway, trod
In wondrous love, O Son of God!

2 Oh, who like thee—so calm, so bright,
So pure, so made to live in light?
Oh, who like thee did ever go
So patient through a world of woe?

3 Oh, who like thee so humbly bore
The scorn, the scoffs of men, before?
So meek, forgiving, godlike, high,
So glorious in humility?

4 Oh, in thy light be mine to go,
Illuming all my way of woe;
And give me ever on the road
To trace thy footsteps, Son of God!

98 *His example.* (146)

1 My dear Redeemer and my Lord,
I read my duty in thy word;
But in thy life the law appears
Drawn out in living characters.

2 Such was thy truth, and such thy zeal,
Such deference to thy Father's will,
Such love, and meekness so divine,
I would transcribe and make them mine.

4 Be thou my pattern; make me bear
More of thy gracious image here;
Then God the judge shall own my name
Among the followers of the Lamb.

99 *His holy life.* (143)

1 And is the gospel peace and love?
Such let our conversation be;
The serpent blended with the dove—
Wisdom and meek simplicity.

2 Whene'er the angry passions rise,
And tempt our thoughts or tongues to strife,
On Jesus let us fix our eyes,
Bright pattern of the Christian life.

3 Oh how benevolent and kind!
How mild! how ready to forgive!
Be his the temper of our mind,
And his the rules by which we live.

4 To do his heavenly Father's will
Was his employment and delight;
Humility, and love, and zeal,
Shone through his life divinely bright.

5 Dispensing good where'er he came,
The labors of his life were love—
Oh! if we love the Savior's name,
Let his divine example move.

Zephyr, Key C.   Ward, Key Eb.   Amboy, Key G.

EDMESTON. C. M.

1. A pilgrim thro' this lonely world The blessed Savior passed;
A mourner all his life was he, A dying Lamb at last.

100 *The man of sorrows.* (150)

2 That tender heart which felt for all,
For us its life-blood gave;
It found on earth no resting-place,
Save only in the grave!

3 Such was our Lord: and shall we fear
The cross with all its scorn?
Or love a faithless, evil world,
That wreathed his brow with thorn?

4 No; facing all its frowns or smiles,
Like him, obedient still,
We homeward press, through storm or calm,
To Zion's blessed hill.

101 *He went about doing good.* (149)

1 Behold, where, in a mortal form,
Appears each grace divine;
The virtues, all in Jesus met,
With mildest radiance shine.

2 To spread the rays of heavenly light,
To give the mourner joy,
To preach glad tidings to the poor,
Was his divine employ.

3 'Midst keen reproach, and cruel scorn,
Patient and meek he stood;
His foes, ungrateful, sought his life:
He labored for their good.

4 In the last hour of deep distress,
Before his Father's throne,
With soul resigned, he bowed, and said,
"Thy will, not mine, be done!"

5 Be Christ our pattern and our guide;
His image may we bear;
Oh, may we tread his holy steps,
His joy and glory share!

102 *The bitter cup.* (160)

1 Dark was the night and cold the ground
On which the Lord was laid:
His sweat like drops of blood ran down;
In agony he prayed:

2 "Father, remove this bitter cup,
If such thy sacred will;
If not, content to drink it up,
Thy pleasure I fulfill."

3 Go to the garden, sinner: see
Those precious drops that flow,
The heavy load he bore for thee:
For thee he lies so low.

4 Then learn of him the cross to bear,
Thy Father's will obey;
And when temptations press thee near,
Awake to watch and pray.

Naomi, Key D.   Siloam, Key D.   Evan, Key A♭.

CHRIST—LIFE AND MINISTRY.

ARIEL. C. P. M.   Dr. L. MASON.

1. Oh, could I speak the matchless worth, Oh, could I sound the glories forth Which in my Sav-ior shine! I'd soar and touch the heavenly strings, And vie with Gabriel while he sings, In notes al-most di-vine, In notes al-most di-vine.

103   *His unsearchable riches.*   (152)

2 I'd sing the precious blood he spilt,
My ransom from the dreadful guilt
    Of sin, and wrath divine;
I'd sing his glorious righteousness,
In which all-perfect, heavenly dress,
    My soul shall ever shine.

3 I'd sing the characters he bears,
And all the forms of love he wears,
    Exalted on his throne;
In loftiest songs of sweetest praise,
I would to everlasting days
    Make all his glories known.

4 Well, the delightful day will come,
When my dear Lord will bring me home,
    And I shall see his face;
Then, with my Savior, Brother, Friend,
A blest eternity I'll spend,
    Triumphant in his grace.

104   *The only foundation.*   (257)

1 Had I ten thousand gifts beside,
I'd cleave to Jesus crucified,
    And build on him alone;
For no foundation is there given
On which to place my hopes of heaven,
    But Christ the corner-stone.

2 Possessing Christ, I all possess,
Wisdom, and strength, and righteousness,
    And holiness complete;
Bold in his name, I dare draw nigh
Before the Ruler of the sky,
    And all his justice meet.

3 There is no path to heavenly bliss,
To solid joy or lasting peace,
    But Christ, th' appointed road;
Oh may we tread the sacred way,
By faith rejoice, and praise, and pray.
    Till we sit down with God!

CHRIST—LIFE AND MINISTRY.

JESUS WEPT. 8, 7, 8, 7, 7, 7. ✷   JAMES CHALLEN.

1. Je-sus wept! those tears are o-ver, But his heart is still the same;
   Kinsman, Friend, and El-der Brother, Is his ev-er-last-ing name.
   Sav-ior, who can love like thee? Gra-cious one of Beth-a-ny!

2. When the pangs of tri-al seize us, When the waves of sor-row roll,
   I will lay my head on Je-sus— Pil-low of the trou-bled soul.
   Tru-ly, none can feel like thee, Weep-ing one of Beth-a-ny!

105   *Jesus wept.*   (156)

3 Jesus wept, and still in glory
  He can mark each mourner's tear—
Living to retrace the story
  Of the hearts he solaced here.
Lord, when I am called to die,
Let me think of Bethany!

4 Jesus wept! that tear of sorrow
    Is a legacy of love;
Yesterday, to-day, to-morrow,
    He the same shall ever prove.
Thou art all in all to me,
Living one of Bethany!

106   *Sweet it is to trust in thee.*   (1206)

1 Through the day thy love hath spared us,
    Wearied we lie down to rest;
Through the silent watches guards us,
    Let no foe our peace molest.
Father! thou our guardian be;
Sweet it is to trust in thee.

2 Wandering in the land of strangers,
    Dwelling in the midst of foes,
Us and ours preserve from dangers:
    In thy love we all repose.
Father! thou our guardian be;
Sweet it is to trust in thee.

107 *What is your life? Even a vapor.* (1078)

1 What is life? 'T is but a vapor;
    Soon it vanishes away.
Life is but a dying taper—
    O my soul, why wish to stay?
Why not spread thy wings and fly
Straight to yonder world of joy!

2 See that glory, how resplendent!
    Brighter far than fancy paints;
There, in majesty transcendent,
    Jesus reigns, the King of saints:
Why not spread thy wings and fly
Straight to yonder world of joy!

3 Joyful crowds, his throne surrounding
    Sing with rapture of his love;
Through the heavens his praise resounding
    Filling all the courts above:
Why not spread thy wings and fly
Straight to yonder world of joy!

CHRIST—LIFE AND MINISTRY.

OLIVES' BROW. L. M.   W. B. BRADBURY, by permission.

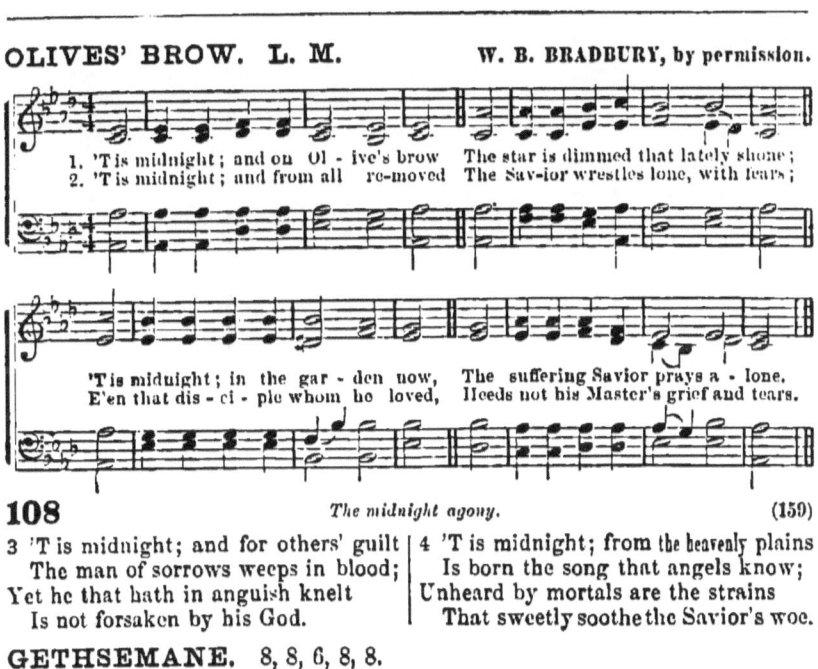

108   *The midnight agony.*   (159)

3 'T is midnight; and for others' guilt
The man of sorrows weeps in blood;
Yet he that hath in anguish knelt
Is not forsaken by his God.

4 'T is midnight; from the heavenly plains
Is born the song that angels know;
Unheard by mortals are the strains
That sweetly soothe the Savior's woe.

GETHSEMANE.   8, 8, 6, 8, 8.

109   *Gethsemane.*   (164)

2 He bows beneath the sins of men;
He cries to God, and cries again,
  In sad Gethsemane:
He lifts his mournful eyes above—
"My Father, can this cup remove?"

3 With gentle resignation still,
He yielded to his Father's will
  In sad Gethsemane:
"Behold me here, thine only Son;
And, Father, let thy will be done."

4 The Father heard; and angels there
Sustained the Son of God in prayer,
  In sad Gethsemane:
He drank the dreadful cup of pain—
Then rose to life and joy again.

5 When storms of sorrow round us sweep,
And scenes of anguish make us weep,
  To sad Gethsemane
We'll look and see the Savior there,
And humbly bow, like him, in prayer

CHRIST—LIFE AND MINISTRY.

CALM. C. L. M. Dr. HASTINGS.

1. How calm and beau-ti-ful the morn
That gilds the sa-cred tomb,
Where once the Cru-ci-fied was borne,
And veiled in mid-night gloom!
Oh, weep no more the Sav-ior slain;
The Lord is risen, he lives a-gain.

110 *The Lord is risen.* (186)

2 Ye mourning saints! dry every tear
For your departed Lord;
"Behold the place—he is not here;"
The tomb is all unbarred:
The gates of death were closed in vain;
The Lord is risen—he lives again.

3 Now cheerful to the house of prayer
Your early footsteps bend,
The Savior will himself be there,
Your advocate and friend:
Once by the law your hopes were slain,
But now in Christ ye live again.

4 How tranquil now the rising day!
'T is Jesus still appears,
A risen Lord to chase away
Your unbelieving fears;
Oh weep no more your comforts slain;
The Lord is risen—he lives again.

5 And when the shades of evening fall,
When life's last hour draws nigh—
If Jesus shine upon the soul,
How blissful then to die:
Since he has risen who once was slain,
Ye die in Christ to live again.

111 *Agony in the garden.* (165)

1 He knelt; the Savior knelt and prayed
When but his Father's eye
Looked, through the lonely garden shade,
On that dread agony:
The Lord of high and heavenly birth
Was bowed with sorrow unto death.

2 The sun went down in fearful hour;
The heavens might well grow dim,
When this mortality had power
Thus to o'ershadow him;
That he who came to save might know
The very depths of human woe.

3 He knew them all—the doubt, the strife,
The faint, perplexing dread:
The mists that hang o'er parting life
All darkened round his head;
And the deliverer knelt to pray:
Yet passed it not, that cup, away.

4 It passed not, though the stormy wave
Had sunk beneath his tread;
It passed not, though to him the grave
Had yielded up its dead;
But there was sent him, from on high,
A gift of strength, for man to die.

CHRIST'S SUFFERINGS. 45

CHRIST—THE BETRAYAL.

THE BETRAYAL. S. H. M. ✻   Harmonized by S. J. VAIL.

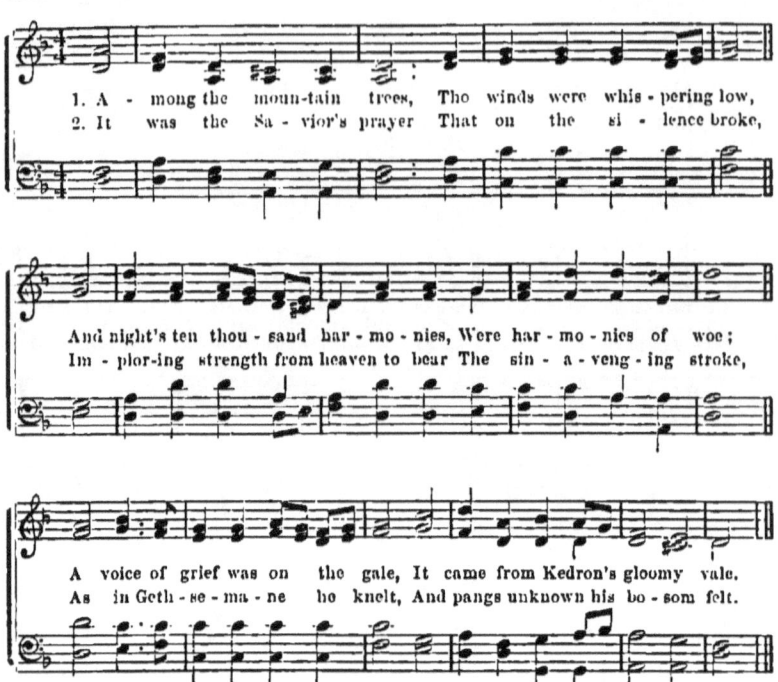

1. A-mong the moun-tain trees, Tho winds were whis-pering low,
2. It was the Sa-vior's prayer That on the si-lence broke,

And night's ten thou-sand har-mo-nies, Were har-mo-nies of woe;
Im-plor-ing strength from heaven to bear The sin-a-veng-ing stroke,

A voice of grief was on the gale, It came from Kedron's gloomy vale.
As in Geth-se-ma-ne he knelt, And pangs unknown his bo-som felt.

113   *The Betrayal.*   (166)

3 The fitful starlight shone,
  In dim and misty gleams;
Deep was his agonizing groan,
  And large the vital streams
That trickled to the dewy sod,
While Jesus raised his voice to God.

4 The chosen three that staid,
  Their nightly watch to keep,
Left him through sorrows deep to wade,
  And gave themselves to sleep;
Meekly and sad he prayed alone;
Strangely forgotten by his own.

5 Along the streamlet's banks
  The reckless traitor came,
And heavy on his bosom sank
  The load of guilt and shame;
Yet unto them that waited nigh
He gave the Lamb of God to die.

114   *Friend after friend departs.*   (1090)

1 Friend after friend departs—
  Who hath not lost a friend?
There is no union here of hearts
  That finds not here an end.
Were this frail world our only rest,
Living or dying, none were blest.

2 There is a world above
  Where parting is unknown—
A whole eternity of love,
  Formed for the good alone;
And faith beholds the dying here
Translated to that happier sphere.

3 Thus star by star declines,
  Till all are passed away,
As morning high and higher shines
  To pure and perfect day;
Nor sink those stars in empty night—
They hide themselves in heaven's own light.

CHRIST'S SUFFERINGS. 47

SACRED TEARS. 10s & 11s, Peculiar. (New.) SILAS J. VAIL.

1. Draw near, ye wea-ry, bowed, and broken-heart-ed, Ye on-ward trav-'lers
Ye from whose path the light hath all de-part-ed; Ye . . . .
to a peaceful bourne; who are left in sol-itude to mourn; Tho' o'er your spirits
hath the storm-cloud swept, Sacred are sor-row's tears, since "Je-sus wept."

115 *Sacred tears.* (154)

3 But with the friends he loved, whose
   hope had perished,
The Savior stood, while through his
   bosom rushed
A tide of sympathy for those he cherished,
And from his eyes the burning tear-
   drops gushed;
And bending o'er the tomb where Laz-
   arus slept,
In agony of spirit, "Jesus wept."

4 Lo! Jesus' power, the sleep of death
   hath broken,
And wiped the tear from sorrow's
   drooping eye!
Look up, ye mourners, hear what he hath spoken:
"He that believes on me shall never die,"
Through faith and love your spirits shall
   be kept;
Hope brighter grew on earth when "Je-
   sus wept."

116 *Dennis, Key F.* (92)

1 How gentle God's commands!
   How kind his precepts are!
Come, cast your burdens on the Lord,
   And trust his constant care.

2 His bounty will provide,
   His saints securely dwell;
That hand which bears creation up,
   Shall guard his children well.

3 Why should this anxious load
   Press down your weary mind?
Oh, seek your heavenly Father's throne,
   And peace and comfort find.

4 His goodness stands approved,
   Unchanged from day to day;
I'll drop my burden at his feet,
   And bear a song away.

CHRIST'S SUFFERINGS.

SWEET KEDRON. ✻   Harmonized by T. J. COOK.

117   *Thou sweet gliding Kedron.*   (167)

2 How damp were the vapors that fell on his head,
How hard was his pillow, how humble his bed;
The angels beholding, amazed at the sight,
Attended their Master with solemn delight.

3 Oh garden of Olives! thou dear honored spot,
The fame of thy wonders shall ne'er be forgot:
The theme most transporting to seraphs above,
The triumph of sorrow, the triumph of love!

CHRIST'S CRUCIFIXION. 49

SALEM. L. M. (New.) Dr. THOMAS HASTINGS.

1. He dies, the friend of sin-ners dies! Lo! Salem's daughters weep around! A sol-emn darkness vails the skies, A sudden trembling shakes the ground.

118 *Darkness and light.* (172)

2 Here's love and grief beyond degree!
The Lord of glory dies for men!
But, lo! what sudden joys we see—
Jesus the dead revives again!

3 The rising Lord forsakes the tomb!
(The tomb in vain forbids his rise!)
Cherubic legions guard him home,
And shout him welcome to the skies.

4 Break off your tears, you saints, and tell
How high our great Deliverer reigns;
Sing how he spoiled the hosts of hell,
And led the monster Death in chains.

5 Say, "Live forever, wondrous King!
Born to redeem, and strong to save!"
Then ask the monster, "Where's thy sting?
And where's thy victory, boasting grave?"

119 *The last scenes.* (517)

1 'T was on that night, when doomed to know
The eager rage of every foe,
That night in which he was betrayed,
The Savior of the world took bread;

2 And, after thanks and glory given
To him that rules in earth and heaven,
That symbol of his flesh he broke,
And thus to all his followers spoke:

3 My broken body thus I give
To you, my friends; take, eat, and live;
And oft the sacred feast renew,
That brings my wondrous love to view.

4 Then in his hands the cup he raised,
And God anew he thanked and praised;
While kindness in his bosom glowed,
And from his lips salvation flowed.

5 My blood I thus pour forth, he cries,
To cleanse the soul in sin that lies;
In this the covenant is sealed,
And heaven's eternal grace revealed.

6 This cup is fraught with love to men;
Let all partake who love my name;
Through latest ages let it pour
In memory of my dying hour.

120 *Looking to the cross.* (169)

1 O Lord! when faith with fixed eyes
Beholds thy wondrous sacrifice,
Love rises to an ardent flame,
And we all other hope disclaim.

2 With cold affections who can see
The thorns, the scourge, the nails, the tree,
The flowing tears, and crimson sweat,
The bleeding hands, and head, and feet?

3 Jesus, what millions of our race
Have seen the triumphs of thy grace!
And millions more to thee shall fly,
And on thy sacrifice rely.

4 The sorrow, shame, and death were thine
And all the stores of wrath divine!
Ours are the pardon, life, and bliss;
What love can be compared to this!

Ward, Key B♭.   Olive's Brow, Key A♭.   Hamburg, Key F.

CHRIST'S CRUCIFIXION.

BRADBURY. C. M. SOLON WILDER, by permission.

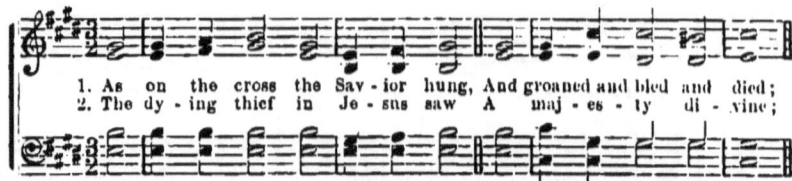

1. As on the cross the Sav-ior hung, And groaned and bled and died;
2. The dy-ing thief in Je-sus saw A maj-es-ty di-vine;

He looked with pit-y on a wretch That languished by his side.
While scoffing Jews a-round him stood, And asked him for a sign.

121 *The dying penitent.* (176)
3 The kingdom, Lord, is thine, he said;
 'Tis thine o'er men to reign:
Thy wondrous works thy Lordship prove,
 These pains thy love proclaim:

4 Honors divine await thee soon
 A scepter and a crown:
With shame thy foes shall yet behold
 Thee seated on a throne.

5 Then gracious Lord, remember me!
 Is not forgiveness thine?
My crimes have brought me to thy side—
 Thy love brought thee to mine.

6 His prayer the dying Jesus hears,
 And instantly replies,
To-day your parting soul shall be
 With me in paradise.

122 *His condescension.* (173)
1 And did the holy and the just,
 The Sovereign of the skies,
Stoop down to wretchedness and dust,
 That guilty man might rise?

2 Yes, the Redeemer left his throne,
 His radiant throne on high;
Surpassing mercy! love unknown!
 To suffer, bleed, and die.

3 He took the dying rebel's place,
 And suffered in our stead;
For sinful man, oh wondrous grace!
 For sinful man he bled!

123 *They nailed him to the cross.* (175)
1 Behold the Savior of mankind
 Nailed to the shameful tree!
How vast the love that him inclined
 To bleed and die for me!

2 Hark! how he groans, while nature shakes,
 And earth's strong pillars bend!
The temple's vail asunder breaks,
 The solid marbles rend.

3 'Tis finished! now the ransom's paid,
 "Receive my soul!" he cries:
See—how he bows his sacred head!
 He bows his head and dies!

4 But soon from death he'll rise again,
 And in full glory shine;
O Lamb of God! was ever pain—
 Was ever love like thine?

124 *He conquered when he fell.* (174)
1 We sing the Savior's wondrous death—
 He conquered when he fell:
'Tis finished, said his dying breath,
 And shook the gates of hell.

2 'Tis finished, our Immanuel cries,
 The dreadful work is done;
Hence shall his sovereign throne arise,
 His kingdom is begun.

3 His cross a sure foundation laid
 For glory and renown,
When through the regions of the dead
 He passed to reach the crown.

Chimes, Key C. Edmeston, Key C.

CHRIST ON THE CROSS.

MONTAGUE. 7s & 6s, Double.   J. P. HOLBROOK.

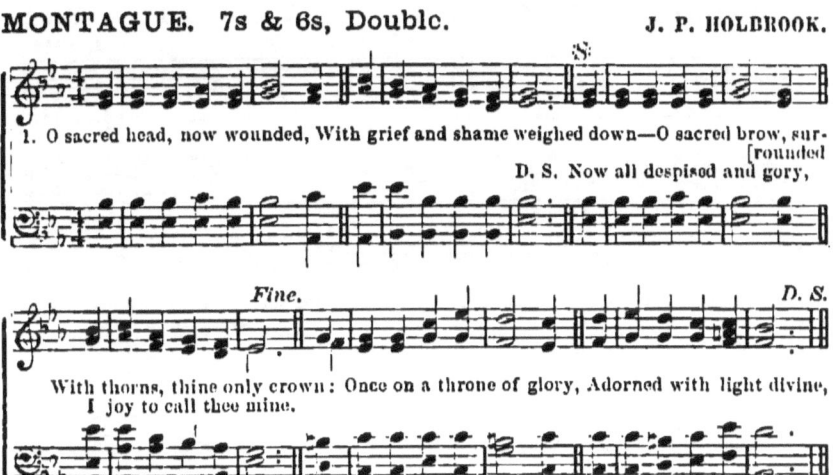

1. O sacred head, now wounded, With grief and shame weighed down—O sacred brow, sur-[rounded
D. S. Now all despised and gory,

With thorns, thine only crown: Once on a throne of glory, Adorned with light divine,
I joy to call thee mine.

125 *"Surely he hath borne our griefs."* (177)

2 On me, as thou art dying,
  Oh turn thy pitying eye!
To thee for mercy crying,
  Before thy cross I lie.
Thine, thine the bitter passion;
  Thy pain is all for me;
Mine, mine the deep transgression;
  My sins are all on thee.

3 What language can I borrow
  To praise thee, heav'nly Friend,
For all this dying sorow,
  Of all my woes the end?
Oh, can I leave thee ever?
  Then do not thou leave me;
Lord, let me never, never
  Outlive my love to thee.

4 Be near when I am dying;
  Then close beside me stand;
Let me, while faint and sighing,
  Lean calmly on thy hand:
These eyes, new faith receiving,
  From thee shall never move,
For he who dies believing,
  Dies safely—in thy love.

126 *The cross—"the power of God."* (543)

1 I saw the cross of Jesus
  When burdened with my sin;
I sought the cross of Jesus
  To give me peace within:
I brought my soul to Jesus;
  He cleans'd it in his blood;
And in the cross of Jesus
  I found my peace with God.

2 I love the cross of Jesus—
  It tells me what I am;
A vile and guilty creature,
  Saved only through the Lamb.
No righteousness, no merit,
  No beauty can I plead;
Yet in the cross I glory,
  My title there I read.

3 I clasp the cross of Jesus
  In every trying hour,
My sure and certain refuge,
  My never-failing tower.
In every fear and conflict,
  I more than conqueror am;
Living I'm safe, or dying,
  Through Christ the risen Lamb.

4 Sweet is the cross of Jesus!
  There let my weary heart
Still rest in peace and safety
  Till life itself depart.
And then in strains of glory
  I'll sing thy wondrous power,
Where sin can never enter,
  And death is known no more.

Webb, Key B♭.   Western, Key G.

CHRIST ON THE CROSS.

BEHOLD THE LAMB OF GOD. 8s & 6s, Peculiar. (New.)

S. J. VAIL.

1. The Son of Man they did betray;
He was condemned, and led away;
Look on Mount Calvary; Behold him, lamb-like, led along
Surrounded by a wicked throng,
Accus'd by ev'ry lying tongue, And thus the Lamb of God they hung Upon the shameful tree.
Think, O my soul, on that dread day,

127 *Behold the Lamb of God.* (179)

2 Now, hung between the earth and skies,
Behold! in agony he dies;
O sinners, hear his mournful cries—
Come, see his torturing pain!
The morning sun withdrew his light,
Blushed, and refused to view the sight,
The azure clothed in robes of night,
All nature mourned, and stood affright,
When Christ the Lord was slain.

3 All glory be to God on high,
Who reigns enthroned above the sky;
Who sent his Son to bleed and die;
Glory to him be given:
While heaven above his praise resounds,
O Zion, sing—his grace abounds;
I hope to shout eternal rounds,
In flaming love that knows no bounds,
When glorified in heaven.

CORONAL. 8s, 7s & 4. (207)

128
1. Look, ye saints, the sight is glo-ri-ous, See the Man of Sor-rows now;
From the fight returned vic-to-rious, Ev-ery knee to him shall bow.
2. Crown the Sav-ior, an-gels, crown him; Rich the tro-phies Je-sus brings;
In the seat of power enthrone him, While the heaven-ly con-cert rings.

Crown him, crown him, Crowns become the victor's brow, Crowns become the Victor's brow.
Crown him, crown him, Crown the Savior King of kings, Crown the Savior King of kings.

CHRIST—BURIAL AND RESURRECTION.

ARLINGTON. C. M. — Dr. ARNE.

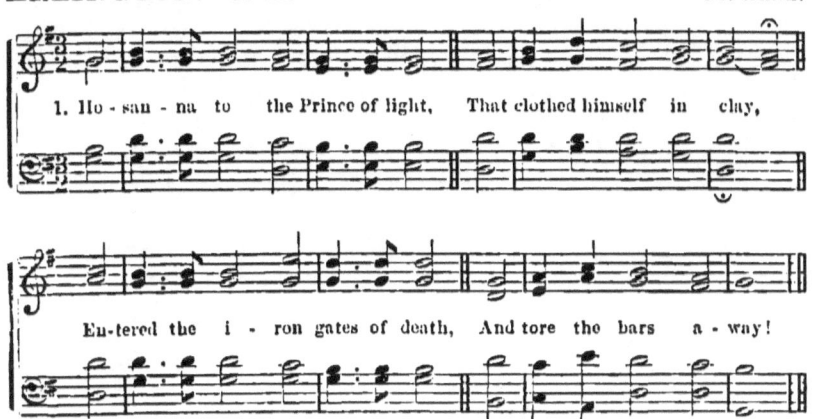

1. Ho-san-na to the Prince of light, That clothed himself in clay, Entered the i-ron gates of death, And tore the bars a-way!

129 *The Resurrection, and the Life.* (185)
2 Death is no more the king of dread,
  Since our Immanuel rose;
He took the tyrant's sting away,
  And spoiled our hellish foes.

3 Raise your devotion, mortal tongues,
  To reach his blest abode;
Sweet be the accents of your songs
  To our incarnate God.

4 Bright angels, strike your loudest strings,
  Your sweetest voices raise;
Let heaven, and all created things,
  Sound our Immanuel's praise.

130 *Now is Christ risen from the dead.* (183)
1 Blest morning! whose young dawning rays
  Beheld our rising Lord;
That saw him triumph o'er the dust,
  And leave his dark abode.

2 In the cold prison of a tomb
  The great Redeemer lay,
Till the revolving skies had brought
  The third, the appointed day.

3 Hell and the grave unite their force
  To hold our Lord, in vain;
The sleeping Conqueror arose,
  And burst their feeble chain.

4 To thy great name, Almighty Lord,
  These sacred hours we pay;
And loud hosannas shall proclaim
  The triumph of the day.

5 Salvation and immortal praise
  To our victorious King!
Let heaven, and earth, and rocks, and seas,
  With glad hosannas ring.

131 *The day-spring from on high.* (123)
1 Calm, on the listening ear of night,
  Come heaven's melodious strains,
Where wild Judea stretches far
  Her silver-mantled plains.

2 Celestial choirs, from courts above,
  Shed sacred glories there,
And angels, with their sparkling lyres,
  Make music on the air.

3 The answering hills of Palestine
  Send back the glad reply,
And greet, from all their holy heights,
  The day-spring from on high.

4 O'er the blue depths of Galilee
  There comes a holier calm;
And Sharon waves, in solemn praise,
  Her silent groves of palm.

5 "Glory to God!" the sounding skies
  Loud with their anthems ring—
"Peace to the earth, good will to men,
  From heaven's eternal King."

6 Light on thy hills, Jerusalem!
  The Savior now is born!
And bright on Bethlehem's joyous plains
  Breaks the first Advent morn.

Caddo, Key B♭.   Zerah, Key C.

54 CHRIST—BURIAL AND RESURRECTION.

ZEBULON. H. M.
Dr. L. MASON.

1. Yes, the Redeem-er rose: The Sav-ior left the dead,
And o'er his hell-ish foes High raised his conquering head:
In wild dis-may, the guards a-round Fall to the ground, and sink a-way.

132 *Thou reigning Son of God.* (188)

1 Yes, the Redeemer rose:
  The Savior left the dead,
And o'er his hellish foes
  High raised his conquering head:
In wild dismay, the guards around
Fall to the ground, and sink away.

2 Lo! the angelic bands
  In full assembly meet,
To wait his high commands,
  And worship at his feet:
Joyful they come, and wing their way
From realms of day to Jesus' tomb.

3 Then back to heaven they fly,
  The joyful news to bear;
Hark! as they soar on high,
  What music fills the air:
Their anthems say, Jesus who bled
Has left the dead—he rose to day!

4 You mortals, catch the sound,
  Redeemed by him from hell,
And send the echo round
  The globe on which you dwell:
Transported cry, Jesus who bled
Has left the dead, no more to die!

5 All hail! triumphant Lord,
  Who saved us by thy blood:
Wide be thy name adored,
  Thou reigning Son of God!
With thee we rise, with thee we reign,
And kingdoms gain beyond the skies.

133 *Declare among the people his doings.* (670)

1 Come, every pious heart
  That loves the Savior's name.
Your noblest powers exert
  To celebrate his fame:
Tell all above and all below
The debt of love to him you owe.

2 Such was his zeal for God,
  And such his love for you,
He nobly undertook
  What angels could not do:
His every deed of love and grace
All words exceed, all thoughts surpass.

3 He left his starry crown,
  And laid his robes aside;
On wings of love came down,
  And wept, and bled, and died:
What he endured, oh who can tell,
To save our souls from death and hell!

4 From the dark grave he rose,
  The mansion of the dead;
And thence his mighty foes
  In glorious triumph led:
Up through the sky the Conqueror rode,
And reigns on high, the Son of God.

5 From thence he'll quickly come—
  His chariot will not stay—
And bear our spirits home
  To realms of endless day:
There shall we see his lovely face,
And ever be in his embrace.

Lischer, Key G.   Lenox, Key B♭.

CHRIST—BURIAL AND RESURRECTION.

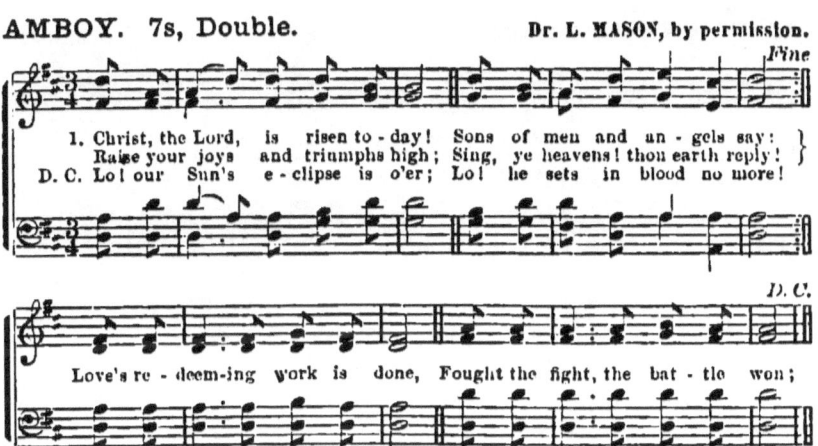

AMBOY. 7s, Double.   Dr. L. MASON, by permission.

1. Christ, the Lord, is risen to-day! Sons of men and angels say:
Raise your joys and triumphs high; Sing, ye heavens! thou earth reply!
D. C. Lo! our Sun's e-clipse is o'er; Lo! he sets in blood no more!

Love's re-deem-ing work is done, Fought the fight, the bat-tle won;

134   *Christ the first fruits.*   (190)

2 Vain the stone, the watch, the seal—
Christ hath burst the gates of hell;
Death in vain forbids his rise,
Christ hath opened paradise.
Lives again our glorious King!
Where, O Death, is now thy sting?
Once he died, our souls to save:
Where's thy victory, boasting grave?

3 Soar we now where Christ hath led,
Following our exalted Head:
Made like him, like him we rise,
Ours the cross, the grave, the skies!
King of glory, Fount of bliss,
Everlasting life is this:
Thee to know, thy power to prove,
Thus to sing, and thus to love.

135   *The stone rolled away.*   (189)

1 Angels! roll the rock away;
Death! yield up thy mighty prey;
See! the Savior leaves the tomb,
Glowing with immortal bloom.
Hark! the wondering angels raise
Louder notes of joyful praise;
Let the earth's remotest bound
Echo with the blissful sound.

2 Now, ye saints! lift up your eyes,
See him high in glory rise!
Ranks of angels, on the road,
Hail him—the incarnate God.

Heaven unfolds its portals wide,
See the Conqueror through them ride!
King of glory! mount thy throne—
Boundless empire is thine own.

136   *The Resurrection.*   (191)

1 Morning breaks upon the tomb,
Jesus scatters all its gloom;
Day of triumph through the skies—
See the glorious Savior rise!
Ye who are of death afraid,
Triumph in the scattered shade;
Drive your anxious cares away;
See the place where Jesus lay!

137   *I, the Lord, will hasten it.*   (599)

1 Hasten, Lord! the glorious time,
When, beneath Messiah's sway,
Every nation, every clime,
Shall the gospel call obey.
Mightiest Kings his power shall own,
Heathen tribes his name adore;
Satan and his host, o'erthrown,
Bound in chains, shall hurt no more.

2 Then shall wars and tumults cease,
Then be banished grief and pain;
Righteousness, and joy, and peace,
Undisturbed shall ever reign.
Bless we, then, our gracious Lord!
Ever praise his glorious name;
All his mighty acts record,
All his wondrous love proclaim.

Hendon, Key G.   Nuremberg, Key A♭.

CHRIST—BURIAL AND RESURRECTION.

MARTYN. 7s, Double. MARSH.

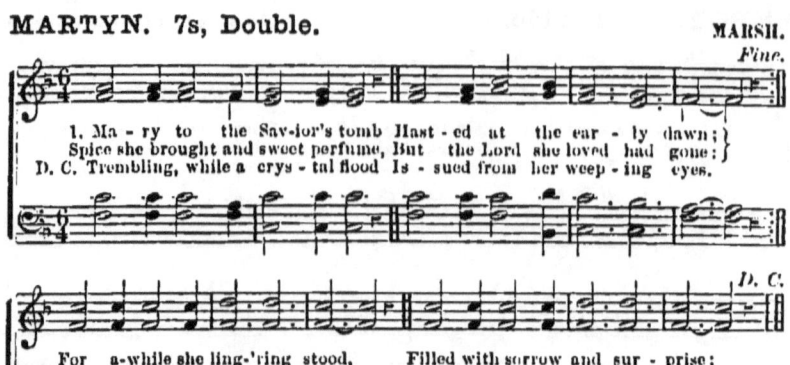

1. Mary to the Savior's tomb Hasted at the early dawn;
Spice she brought and sweet perfume, But the Lord she loved had gone;
D. C. Trembling, while a crystal flood Is sued from her weeping eyes.
For a-while she ling-'ring stood, Filled with sorrow and sur-prise;

138 *Mary at the tomb.* (192)

2 Jesus who is always near,
Though too often unperceived,
Came her drooping heart to cheer,
Kindly asking why she grieved:
Though at first she knew him not,
When he called her by her name,
She her heavy griefs forgot,
For she found him still the same.

3 And her sorrows quickly fled,
When she heard his welcome voice;
Christ had risen from the dead,
Now he bids her heart rejoice:
What a change his word can make—
Turning darkness into day;
You who weep for Jesus' sake,
He will wipe your tears away.

139 *What could have been done, etc.* (305)

1 What could your Redeemer do
More than he has done for you?
To procure your peace with God,
Could he more than shed his blood?
After all this flow of love,
All his drawings from above,
Why will you your Lord deny?
Why will you resolve to die?

2 Turn, he cries, O sinner, turn!
By his life your God hath sworn
He would have you turn and live,
He would all the world receive:

If your death were his delight,
Would he thus to life invite?
Would he ask, beseech, and cry,
Why will you resolve to die?

3 Sinners, turn, while God is near!
He has left you naught to fear:
Now, e'en now, your Savior stands;
All day long he spreads his hands:
Cries—"You will not happy be,
No, you will not come to me:
Me who life to none deny—
Why will you resolve to die?"

4 Can you doubt that God is love,
Who thus calls you from above?
Will you not his word receive?
Will you not his oath believe?
See, the suffering Lord appears;
Jesus weeps—believe his tears!
Mingled with his blood, they cry,
"Why will you resolve to die?"

140 *Doxology.* (749)

Father! glory be to thee,
Source of all the good we see!
Glory for the blessed Light
Rising on the ancient night!
Glory for the hopes that come
Streaming through the silent tomb!
Glory for thy Spirit given,
Guiding us in peace to heaven!

Eltham, Key G.   Essex, Key B♭.

CLARINGTON. ✱

Harmony by J. ZUNDEL.

1. The angels that watched round the tomb Where low the Redeem-er was laid,
D. C. Have witnessed his ris-ing and swept The chords with the triumphs of joy.
When deep in mor-tal-i-ty's gloom He hid for a sea-son his head;
That veiled their fair face while he slept, And ceased their sweet harps to employ,

141 "*He hath abolished death.*" *(193)

2 You saints, who once languished below,
  But long since have entered your rest,
I pant to be glorified, too—
  To lean on Immanuel's breast.
The grave in which Jesus was laid
  Has buried my guilt and my fears;
And while I contemplate its shade,
  The light of his presence appears.

3 Oh sweet is the season of rest,
  When life's weary journey is done!
The blush that spreads over its west,
  The last lingering ray of its sun!
Though dreary the empire of night,
  I soon shall emerge from its gloom,
And see immortality's light
  Arise on the shades of the tomb.

4 Then welcome the last rending sighs,
  When these aching heart-strings shall break,
When death shall extinguish these eyes,
  And moisten with dew the pale cheek.
No terror the prospect begets—
  I am not mortality's slave—
The sunbeam of life, as it sets,
  Paints a rainbow of peace on the grave.

142 "*The darkness is passed.*" (194)

1 Behold! the bright morning appears,
  And Jesus revives from the grave;
His rising removes all our fears,
  And shows him almighty to save.
How strong were his tears and his cries!
  The worth of his blood, how divine!
How perfect was his sacrifice,
  Who rose, though he suffered for sin!

2 The man that was crowned with thorns,
  The man that on Calvary died,
The man that bore scourging and scorns,
  Whom sinners agreed to deride—
Now blessed forever is made,
  And life has rewarded his pain;
Now glory has crowned his head;
  Heaven sings of the Lamb that was slain.

143 "*The first and the last.*" (658)

This Lord is the Lord we adore,
  Our faithful, unchangeable friend,
Whose love is as large as his power,
  And neither knows measure nor end.
'T is Jesus, the First and the Last,
  Whose Spirit shall guide us safe home;
We'll praise him for all that is past,
  And trust him for all that's to come.

CHRIST—THE ASCENSION.

LUTON. L. M.   BURDER.

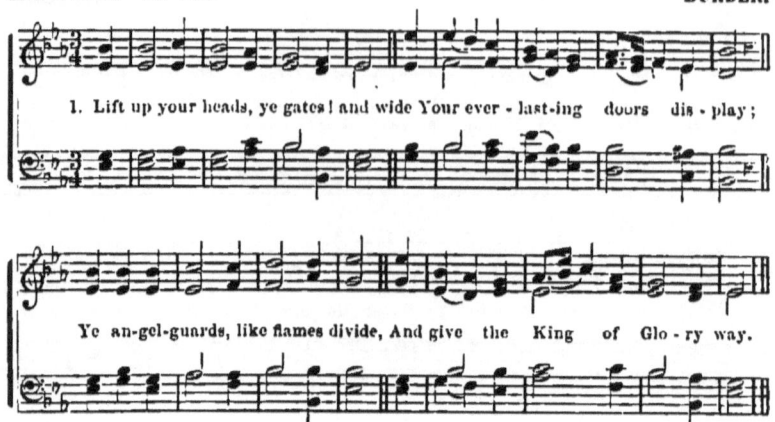

1. Lift up your heads, ye gates! and wide Your ever-last-ing doors dis-play; Ye an-gel-guards, like flames divide, And give the King of Glo-ry way.

144   *The King of Glory.*   (196)

2 Who is the King of glory? He,
The Lord omnipotent to save,
Whose own right arm, in victory,
Led captive death, and spoiled the grave.

3 Lift up your heads, ye gates! and high
Your everlasting portals heave;
Welcome the King of glory nigh:
Him must the heaven of heavens receive.

4 Who is the King of glory—who?
The Lord of hosts; behold his name!
The Kingdom, power, and honor due,
Yield him, ye saints, with glad acclaim.

145   *Lift up your heads, ye gates.*   (195)

1 Our Lord is risen from the dead,
Our Jesus is gone up on high;
The powers of hell are captive led,
Dragged to the portals of the sky.

2 There his triumphal chariot waits,
And angels chant the solemn lay:
Lift up your heads, you heavenly gates!
You everlasting doors, give way!

3 Loose all your bars of massy light,
And wide unfold the radiant scene!
He claims those mansions as his right—
Receive the King of glory in!

4 Who is the King of glory—who?
The Lord, who all his foes o'ercame;
The world, sin, death, and hell o'erthrew,
And Jesus is the Conqueror's name.

5 Lo! his triumphal chariot waits,
And angels chant the solemn lay:
Lift up your heads, you heavenly gates!
You everlasting doors, give way!

6 Who is the King of glory—who?
The Lord, of boundless might possessed,
The King of saints and angels, too—
Lord over all, forever blest.

146   *The fullness of God.*   (979)

1 My God, my heart with love inflame,
That I may, in thy holy name,
Aloud in songs of praise rejoice,
While I have breath to raise my voice.

2 No more let my ungrateful heart
One moment from thy praise depart;
But live and sing, in sweet accord,
The glories of my sovereign Lord.

3 Jesus, thou hope of glory! come.
And make my heart thy constant home
Through all the remnant of my days.
Oh let me speak and live thy praise!

Duke Street, Key Eb.   Sessions. Key C.

CHRIST—THE ASCENSION. 59

ALLEN. C. M., with Chorus. (197)

147
1. Lift up your state-ly heads, yo doors, With has-ty rev-erence rise,
2. Swift from your golden hing-es leap, Your bar-riers roll a-way,

Ye ev-er-last-ing doors that guard The pass-age to the skies.
And throw your blaz-ing por-tals wide, And burst the gates of day.

Chorus.

For see, for see, the King of Glo-ry comes, The King of Glo-ry comes a-
long the e-ter-nal road, For see, the King, the King of Glo-ry comes,

For see, he comes

---

148 *Received up into glory.* (198)

1 Triumphant Christ ascends on high,
  The glorious work complete;
  Sin, death, and hell, now vanquished lie
  Beneath his awful feet.

2 There with eternal glory crowned,
  The Lord, the Conqueror, reigns;
  His praise the heavenly choirs resound,
  In their immortal strains.

3 Amid the splendors of his throne,
  Unchanging love appears;
  The names he purchased for his own,
  Still on his heart he bears.

4 Oh, the rich depths of love divine!
  Of bliss a boundless store:
  Dear Savior, let me call thee mine;
  I can not wish for more.

---

149 *Laban, Key C.* (93)

1 Oh bless the Lord, my soul!
  Let all within me join,
  And aid my tongue to bless his name
  Whose favors are divine.

2 Oh bless the Lord, my soul!
  Nor let his mercies lie
  Forgotten in unthankfulness,
  And without praises die.

3 'T is he forgives thy sins;
  'T is he relieves thy pain;
  'T is he that heals thy sicknesses,
  And gives thee strength again.

4 He crowns thy life with love,
  When rescued from the grave;
  He that redeemed our souls from death,
  Hath boundless power to save.

5 He fills the poor with good;
  He gives the sufferers rest:
  The Lord hath justice for the proud,
  And mercy for the oppressed.

6 His wondrous works and ways
  He made by Moses known;
  But sent the world his truth and grace
  By his beloved Son.

(Reigns †Upon :Throne for Hymn 148.)

CHRIST—THE ASCENSION.

BE WITH US THROUGH THE STRIFE. 6s & 10s. (New.)
SILAS J. VAIL.

150 *He became obedient unto death.* (200)

2 It was no path of flowers,
 Through this dark world of ours,
Beloved of the Father! thou didst tread;
 And shall we in dismay
 Shrink from the narrow way,
When clouds and darkness are around it spread?
3 Oh thou who art our Life,
 Be with us through the strife;
Thy own meek head with rudest storms was bowed!

Raise thou our eyes above
 To see a Father's love
Beam, like the bow of promise, through the cloud.
4 E'en through the awful gloom
 Which hovers o'er the tomb,
That light of love our guiding star shall be;
 Our spirits shall not dread
 The shadowy way to tread,
Friend, Guardian, Savior! which doth lead to thee.

MERDIN. 7s, 6s & 7s.
Dr. L. MASON, by permission.

151 *Psalm 45.* (202)

2 Floods of everlasting light
 Freely flash before him;
Myriads, with supreme delight,
 Instantly adore him;
Trumpets loud resound his fame;
Lutes of lucid gold proclaim
All the music of his name;
 Heaven resounding with the theme.

3 Hark! the thrilling symphonies
 Seem, methinks, to seize us;
Join we too the holy lays—
 Jesus, Jesus, Jesus!
Sweetest sound in seraph's song,
Sweetest note on mortal tongue,
Sweetest carol ever sung—
 Jesus, Jesus, flow along.

CHRIST—THE CORONATION.

CORONATION. C. M.   O. HOLDEN.

1. All hail the power of Jesus' name! Let angels prostrate fall; Bring forth the royal diadem, And crown him Lord of all; Bring forth the royal diadem, And crown him Lord of all.

152   *The Coronation.*   (203)

2 Crown him, you martyrs of our God,
Who from his altar call;
Extol the stem of Jesse's rod,
And crown him Lord of all.

3 You chosen seed of Israel's race,
A remnant weak and small,
Hail him who saves you by his grace,
And crown him Lord of all.

4 You gentile sinners ne'er forget
The wormwood and the gall;
Go, spread your trophies at his feet,
And crown him Lord of all.

5 Babes, men, and sires, who know his love,
Who feel your sin and thrall,
Now join with all the hosts above
And crown him Lord of all.

6 Let every kindred, every tribe,
On this terrestrial ball,
To him all majesty ascribe,
And crown him Lord of all.

153   *Worthy the Lamb.*   (206)

1 Come, let us join our cheerful songs
With angels round the throne;
Ten thousand thousand are their tongues,
But all their joys are one.

2 Worthy the Lamb that died, they cry,
To be exalted thus!
Worthy the Lamb, our lips reply,
For he was slain for us!

3 Jesus is worthy to receive
Honor and power divine;
And blessings more than we can give,
Be, Lord, forever thine.

4 Let all who dwell above the sky,
On earth, in air, and seas,
Conspire to lift thy glories high,
And speak thy endless praise.

5 The whole creation join in one,
To bless the sacred name
Of him that sits upon the throne,
And to adore the Lamb.

154   *His kingdom is everlasting.*   (451)

1 Oh where are kings and empires now,
Of old that went and came?
But Holy Church is praying yet,
A thousand years the same.

2 Mark ye her holy battlements,
And her foundations strong:
And hear within, the solemn voice,
And her unending song.

3 For not like kingdoms of the world,
The Holy Church of God!
Though earthquake shocks are rocking her,
And tempests are abroad;

4 Unshaken as eternal hills,
Unmovable she stands—
A mountain that shall fill the earth,
A fane unbuilt by hands.

Zanesville, Key G.   Arlington, Key G.   Peterboro, Key G.

CHRIST—MEDIATORIAL REIGN.

SESSIONS. L. M. L. O. EMERSON.

1. King Jesus reign for-ev-er-more, Un-ri-valed in thy courts above,
While we, with all thy saints, adore The wonders of re-deem-ing love.

* 2 Beats.

155 *Everlasting Kingdom.* (208)
2 No other Lord but thee we'll know,
No other power but thine confess;
We'll spread thine honors while below,
And heaven shall hear us shout thy grace.

3 We'll sing along the heavenly road
That leads us to thy blest abode:
Till with the vast unnumbered throng
We join in heaven's triumphant song—

4 Till with pure hands and voices sweet,
We cast our crowns at Jesus' feet,
And sing of everlasting love
In everlasting strains above.

156 *All nations shall serve him.* (209)
1 Jesus shall reign where'er the sun
Does his successive journeys run;
His kingdom stretch from shore to shore,
Till moons shall wax and wane no more.

2 For him shall endless prayer be made
And praises throng to crown his head;
His name like sweet perfume shall rise
With every morning sacrifice.

3 People and realms of every tongue
Dwell on his love with sweetest song;
And infant voices shall proclaim
Their early blessings on his name.

4 Blessings abound where'er he reigns;
The prisoner leaps to loose his chains,
The weary find eternal rest,
And all the sons of want are blest.

5 Where he displays his healing power,
Death and the curse are known no more;
In him the tribes of Adam boast
More blessings than their father lost.

6 Let every creature rise, and bring
Peculiar honors to our King;
Angels descend with songs again,
And earth repeat the long Amen.

157 1 Cor. 15: 4. (180)
1 When we the sacred grave survey
In which the Savior deigned to lie,
We see fulfilled what prophets say,
And all the power of death defy.

2 This empty tomb shall now proclaim
How weak the bands of conquered death;
Sure pledge that all who trust his name
Shall rise and draw immortal breath.

3 Our surety freed declares us free,
For whose offenses he was seized:
In his release our own we see,
And joy to see Jehovah pleased.

4 Jesus, once numbered with the dead,
Unseals his eyes to sleep no more;
And ever lives their cause to plead,
For whom the pains of death he bore.

5 Then, though in dust we lay our head,
Yet, gracious God, thou wilt not leave
Our flesh forever with the dead,
Nor lose thy children in the grave!

Rockingham, Key G.   Ward, Key B♭.

CHRIST—MEDIATORIAL REIGN.

158 *My heart is inditing a good matter.* (211)

1 Now be my heart inspired to sing
The glories of my Savior King;
He comes with blessings from above,
And wins the nations to his love.

2 Thy throne, O Lord, forever stands;
Grace is the scepter in thy hands;
Thy laws and works are just and right,
But truth and mercy thy delight.

3 Let endless honors crown thy head;
Let every age thy praises spread;
Let all the nations know thy word,
And every tongue confess thee Lord.

159 *Let the earth be filled with his glory.* (213)

1 Great God! whose universal sway
The known and unknown worlds obey,
Now give the kingdom to thy Son;
Extend his power, exalt his throne.

2 Thy scepter well becomes his hands;
All heaven submits to his commands;
His justice shall avenge the poor,
And pride and rage prevail no more.

3 The heathen lands, that lie beneath
The shades of overspreading death,
Revive at his first dawning light;
And deserts blossom at the sight.

4 The saints shall flourish in his days,
Dressed in the robes of joy and praise;
Peace, like a river, from his throne
Shall flow to nations yet unknown.

160 *My Redeemer liveth.* (219)

1 I know that my Redeemer lives;
What comfort this sweet sentence gives!
He lives, he lives who once was dead,
He lives, my ever-living Head!

2 He lives to bless me with his love,
He lives to plead for me above,
He lives my hungry soul to feed,
He lives to bless in time of need.

3 He lives to grant me rich supply,
He lives to guide me with his eye,
He lives to comfort me when faint,
He lives to hear my soul's complaint.

4 He lives, my kind, wise, heavenly friend;
He lives, and loves me to the end;
He lives, and while he lives I'll sing,
He lives, my Prophet, Priest, and King!

5 He lives, all glory to his name!
He lives, my Jesus, still the same!
Oh the sweet joy this sentence gives
I know that my Redeemer lives!

161 *No other name.* (220)

1 Jesus, the spring of joys divine,
Whence all our hopes and comforts flow;
Jesus, no other name but thine
Can save us from eternal woe.

2 In vain would boasting reason find
Thy way to happiness and God;
Her weak directions leave the mind
Bewildered in a dubious road.

3 No other name will heaven approve;
Thou art the true, the living way,
Ordained by everlasting love,
To the bright realms of endless day.

4 Here let our constant feet abide,
Nor from the heavenly path depart;
Oh let thy Spirit, gracious Guide!
Direct our steps, and cheer our heart.

162 *He is precious.* (227)

1 Jesus! the very thought is sweet;
In that dear name all heart-joys meet;
But sweeter than the honey far
The glimpses of his presence are.

2 No word is sung more sweet than this;
No name is heard more full of bliss;
No thought brings sweeter comfort nigh,
Than Jesus, Son of God most high.

3 Jesus, the hope of souls forlorn!
How good to them for sin that mourn;
To them that seek thee, oh how kind!
But what art thou to them that find?

4 No tongue of mortal can express,
No letters write its blessedness;
Alone, who hath thee in his heart,
Knows, love of Jesus, what thou art.

Duke Street, Key E♭.   Uxbridge, Key E.   Duane Street, Key A.

CHIMES. C. M.
Dr. L. MASON, by permission.

1. With joy we med-i-tate the grace Of our High Priest a-bove:
His heart is full of ten-der-ness, His bo-som glows with love.

163 *Christ a merciful High Priest.* (228)

2 Touched with a sympathy within,
 He knows our feeble frame;
 He knows what sore temptations mean,
 For he has felt the same.

3 He in the days of feeble flesh,
 Poured out his cries and tears;
 And in his measure feels afresh
 What every member bears.

4 Then let our humble faith address
 His mercy and his power;
 We shall obtain delivering grace
 In each distressing hour.

164 *The bright and morning star.* (229)

1 Bright was the guiding star that led,
 With mild, benignant ray,
 The Gentiles to the lowly shed
 Where the Redeemer lay.

2 But, lo! a brighter, clearer light
 Now points to his abode;
 It shines through sin and sorrow's night
 To guide us to our God.

3 Oh haste to follow where it leads;
 The gracious call obey,
 Be rugged wilds or flowery meads
 The Christian's destined way.

4 Oh gladly tread the narrow path
 While light and grace are given:
 Who meekly follow Christ on earth,
 Shall reign with him in heaven.

165 *He suffered, the Just for the unjust.* (240)

1 Alas! and did my Savior bleed?
 And did my Sovereign die?
 Would he devote that sacred head
 For such a worm as I?

2 Was it for crimes that I had done
 He groaned upon the tree?
 Amazing pity! grace unknown!
 And love beyond degree!

3 Well might the sun in darkness hide,
 And shut his glories in,
 When God's own Son was crucified
 For man the creature's sin.

4 Thus might I hide my blushing face
 While his dear cross appears,
 Dissolve my heart in thankfulness,
 And melt mine eyes to tears.

5 But drops of grief can ne'er repay
 The debt of love I owe;
 Here, Lord, I give myself away;
 'T is all that I can do.

166 *He is Lord of all.* (243)

1 Hosanna to our conquering King!
 All hail, incarnate Love!
 Ten thousand songs and glories wait
 To crown thy head above.

2 Thy victories and thy deathless fame
 Through all the world shall run
 And everlasting ages sing
 The triumphs thou hast won.

Marlow, Key G.   Zerah, Key C.   Fountain, Key E♭.

CHRIST—HIS MEDIATORIAL REIGN.

167 *He died for our sins.* (238)

1 Jesus, in thy transporting name,
   What blissful glories rise!
Jesus, the angels' sweetest theme—
   The wonder of the skies!

2 Well might the skies with wonder view
   A love so strange as thine!
No thought of angels ever knew
   Compassion so divine!

3 Jesus, and didst thou leave the sky
   To bear our sins and woes?
And didst thou bleed, and groan, and die,
   For vile, rebellious foes?

4 Victorious love! can language tell
   The wonders of thy power,
Which conquered all the force of hell
   In that tremendous hour!

5 What glad return can I impart
   For favors so divine?
Oh take this heart, this worthless heart,
   And make it only thine!

168 *The Name above every name.* (239)

1 The Savior! Oh what endless charms
   Dwell in the blissful sound!
Its influence every fear disarms,
   And spreads sweet peace around.

2 Here pardon, life, and joys divine,
   In rich profusion flow;
For guilty rebels, lost in sin,
   And doomed to endless woe.

3 The almighty Former of the skies
   Stooped to our vile abode;
While angels viewed with wondering eyes,
   And hailed the incarnate God.

4 Oh the rich depths of love divine!
   Of bliss, a boundless store!
Blest Savior, let me call thee mine;
   I can not wish for more.

5 On thee, alone, my hope relies;
   Beneath thy cross I fall;
My Lord, my life, my sacrifice,
   My Savior, and my all.

169 *Consider—the High Priest, etc.* (235)

1 Now let our cheerful eyes survey
   Our great High Priest above,
And celebrate his constant care
   And sympathetic love.

2 Though raised to heaven's exalted throne,
   Where angels bow around,
And high o'er all the hosts of light,
   With matchless honors crowned—

3 The names of all his saints he bears
   Deep graven on his heart;
Nor shall the weakest Christian say
   That he has lost his part.

4 Those characters shall fair abide,
   Our everlasting trust,
When gems, and monuments, and crowns,
   Have moldered down to dust.

170 *An unchangeable priesthood.* (242)

1 Jesus, in thee our eyes behold
   A thousand glories more
Than the rich gems and polished gold
   The sons of Aaron wore.

2 They first their own burnt-offerings brought,
   To purge themselves from sin:
Thy life was pure, without a spot,
   And all thy nature clean.

3 Fresh blood, as constant as the day,
   Was on their altar spilt;
But thy one offering takes away
   Forever all our guilt.

4 Their priesthood ran through several hands,
   For mortal was their race:
Thy never-changing office stands
   Eternal as thy days.

5 Once, in the circuit of a year,
   With blood, but not his own,
Aaron with the vail appeared,
   Before the golden throne;

6 But Christ, with his own precious blood,
   Ascends above the skies,
And, in the presence of our God,
   Shows his own sacrifice.

Ortonville, Key B♭. Devizes, Key G. Howard, Key C. Balerma, Key B♭.

CHRIST—HIS MEDIATORIAL REIGN.

ORTONVILLE. C. M.   Dr. T. HASTINGS.

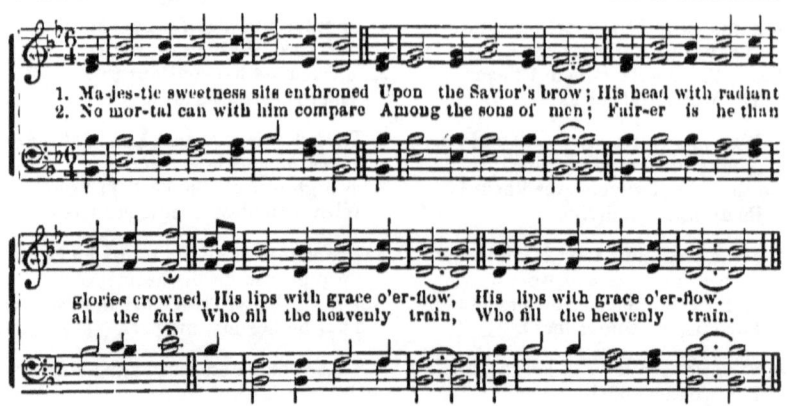

1. Ma-jes-tic sweetness sits enthroned Upon the Savior's brow; His head with radiant
2. No mor-tal can with him compare Among the sons of men; Fair-er is he than

glories crowned, His lips with grace o'er-flow, His lips with grace o'er-flow.
all the fair Who fill the heavenly train, Who fill the heavenly train.

171   *Chief among ten thousand.*   (250)
3 He saw me plunged in deep distress
    And flew to my relief;
For me he bore the shameful cross,
    And carried all my grief.

4 To him I owe my life and breath,
    And all the joys I have!
He makes me triumph over death,
    And saves me from the grave.

5 To heaven, the place of his abode,
    He brings my weary feet;
Shows me the glories of my God,
    And makes my joys complete.

6 Since from thy bounty I receive
    Such proofs of love divine,
Had I a thousand hearts to give,
    Lord, they should all be thine.

172   *Ye are complete in him.*   (217)
1 How sweet the name of Jesus sounds
    In a believer's ear;
It soothes his sorrows, heals his wounds,
    And drives away his fear!

2 It makes the wounded spirit whole,
    And calms the troubled breast;
'Tis manna to the hungry soul,
    And to the weary rest.

3 By thee my prayers acceptance gain,
    Although with sin defiled;
Satan accuses me in vain,
    And I am owned a child.

4 Jesus, my Shepherd, Guardian, Friend,
    My Prophet, Priest, and King,
My Lord, my Life, my Way, my End,
    Accept the praise I bring.

5 Weak is the effort of my heart,
    And cold my warmest thought,
But when I see thee as thou art,
    I'll praise thee as I ought.

6 Till then I would thy love proclaim
    With every fleeting breath;
And may the music of thy name
    Refresh my soul in death!

173   *Blessed are all they, etc.*   (249)
1 My Savior! my almighty Friend!
    When I begin thy praise,
Where will the growing numbers end—
    The numbers of thy grace?

2 Thou art my everlasting trust;
    Thy goodness I adore;
And since I knew thy graces first,
    I speak thy glories more.

3 My feet shall travel all the length
    Of the celestial road;
And march with courage in thy strength
    To see my Father God.

4 How will my lips rejoice to tell
    The victories of my King!
My soul, redeemed from sin and hell,
    Shall thy salvation sing.

Heber, Key C.   Brown, Key C.   Caddo Key B♭.

CHRIST—HIS MEDIATORIAL REIGN. 67

174 *Worthy is the Lamb that was slain.* (236)

1 Behold the glories of the Lamb
 Amidst his Father's throne;
Prepare new honors for his name,
 And songs before unknown.

2 Let elders worship at his feet,
 The church adore around,
With vials full of odors sweet,
 And harps of sweeter sound.

3 Now to the Lamb that once was slain
 Be endless blessings paid;
Salvation, glory, joy remain
 Forever on thy head!

4 Thou hast redeemed our souls with blood,
 Hast set the prisoners free,
Hast made us kings and priests to God,
 And we shall reign with thee.

175 *Come to the Ark.* (292)

1 Come to the ark, come to the ark;
 To Jesus come away:
The pestilence walks forth by night,
 The arrow flies by day.

2 Come to the ark; the waters rise,
 The seas their billows rear;
While darkness gathers o'er the skies,
 Behold a refuge near!

3 Come to the ark, all, all that weep
 Beneath the sense of sin:
Without, deep calleth unto deep,
 But all is peace within.

4 Come to the ark, ere yet the flood
 Your lingering steps oppose;
Come, for the door, which open stood,
 Is now about to close.

176 *Let him that is athirst come.* (290)

1 Oh what amazing words of grace
 Are in the gospel found,
Suited to every sinner's case
 Who hears the joyful sound!

2 Come, then, with all your wants and wounds,
 Your every burden bring;
Here love, unchanging love, abounds—
 A deep celestial spring.

3 This spring with living water flows,
 And heavenly joy imparts;
Come, thirsty souls! your wants disclose,
 And drink with thankful hearts.

4 Millions of sinners, vile as you,
 Have here found life and peace;
Come, then, and prove its virtues, too,
 And drink, adore, and bless.

177 *The true and living Way.* (248)

1 Thou art the Way—to thee alone
 From sin and death we flee;
And he who would the Father seek,
 Must seek him, Lord, by thee.

2 Thou art the Truth—thy word alone
 True wisdom can impart;
Thou, only, canst inform the mind,
 And purify the heart.

3 Thou art the Life—the rending tomb
 Proclaims thy conquering arm;
And those who put their trust in thee,
 Nor death nor hell shall harm.

4 Thou art the Way, the Truth, the Life;
 Grant us that way to know,
That truth to keep, that life to win,
 Whose joys eternal flow.

178 *Altogether lovely.* (251)

1 Jesus, I love thy charming name;
 'Tis music to my ear;
Fain would I sound it out so loud
 That all the earth might hear.

2 Yes, thou art precious to my soul,
 My transport and my trust;
Jewels to thee are gaudy toys,
 And gold is sordid dust.

3 All that my ardent soul can wish,
 In thee doth richly meet;
Nor to my eyes is light so dear,
 Nor friendship half so sweet.

4 Thy grace shall dwell upon my heart,
 And shed its fragrance there—
The noblest balm of all its wounds,
 The cordial of its care.

Balerma, Key B♭. Ohio, Key B♭. Azmon, Key A. Arlington, Key G.

CHRIST—THE MEDIATORIAL REIGN.

FOUNTAIN. C. M. Dr. L. MASON.

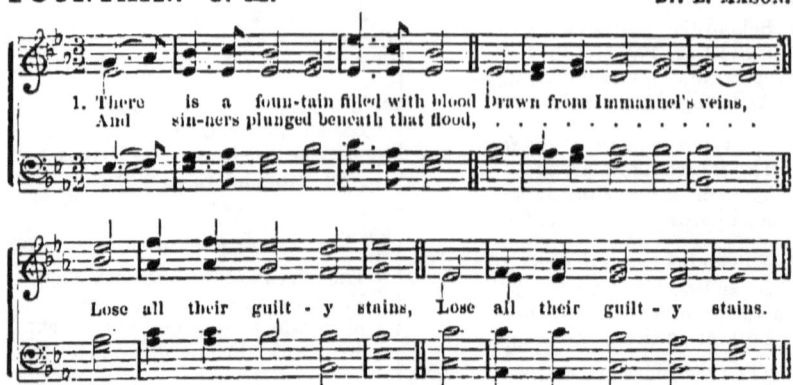

1. There is a fountain filled with blood
Drawn from Immanuel's veins,
And sinners plunged beneath that flood,
Lose all their guilty stains,
Lose all their guilty stains.

179 *A fountain for sin.* (253)

2 The dying thief rejoiced to see
That fountain in his day;
And there have I, as vile as he,
Washed all my sins away.

3 O Lamb of God, thy precious blood
Shall never lose its power,
Till all the ransomed Church of God
Be saved to sin no more.

4 E'er since by faith I saw the stream
Thy flowing wounds supply,
Redeeming love has been my theme,
And shall be till I die.

5 And when this lisping, stammering tongue
Lies silent in the grave,
Then, in a nobler, sweeter song,
I'll sing thy power to save.

180 *I looked, and there was none to help.* (252)

1 Plunged in a gulf of dark despair,
We wretched sinners lay,
Without one cheerful beam of hope,
Or spark of glimmering day.

2 With pitying eyes the Prince of grace
Beheld our helpless grief;
He saw, and—O! amazing love!
He ran to our relief.

3 Down from the shining seats above,
With joyful haste he fled,
Entered the grave in mortal flesh,
And dwelt among the dead.

4 Oh! for this love let rocks and hills
Their lasting silence break;
And all harmonious human tongues
The Savior's praises speak.

5 Angels! assist our mighty joys;
Strike all your harps of gold;
But, when you raise your highest notes
His love can ne'er be told.

181 *The reign of Christ.* (255)

1 Let earth, with every isle and sea,
Rejoice; the Savior reigns:
His word, like fire, prepares his way,
And mountains melt to plains.

2 His presence sinks the proudest hills
And makes the valleys rise;
The humble soul enjoys his smiles,
The haughty sinner dies.

3 Adoring angels, at his birth,
Made our Redeemer known;
Thus shall he come to judge the earth,
And angels guard his throne.

4 His foes shall tremble at his sight,
And hills and seas retire;
His children take their upward flight,
And leave the world on fire.

5 The seeds of joy and glory sown
For saints in darkness here,
Shall rise and spring in worlds unknown,
And a rich harvest bear.

Woodstock, Key G.   Arlington, Key G.

CHRIST—HIS MEDIATORIAL REIGN. 69

YOAKLEY. L. M. 6 lines. YOAKLEY.

1. Jesus, thou source of calm re-pose,
All fullness dwells in thee divine;
Our strength, to quell the proudest foes;
Our light, in deepest gloom to shine;
Thou art our fortress, strength, and tower,
Our trust and por-tion ev-er-more.

182 *Christ all and in all.* (225)

2 Jesus, our Comforter, thou art
 Our rest in toil, our ease in pain;
The balm to heal each broken heart:
 In storms our peace, in loss our gain;
Our joy, beneath the worldling's frown;
 In shame, our glory and our crown:

3 In want, our plentiful supply;
 In weakness our almighty power;
In bonds, our perfect liberty;
 Our refuge in temptation's hour;
Our comfort 'midst all grief and thrall;
 Our life in death; our all in all.

183 *Prophet, Priest, and King.* (226)

1 My Prophet thou, my heavenly Guide,
 Thy sweet instructions I will hear;
The words that from my lips proceed,
 Oh how divinely sweet they are!
Thee, my great Prophet, I would love,
And imitate the blest above.

2 My great High Priest, whose precious blood
 Did once atone upon the cross,
Who now dost intercede with God,
 And plead the friendless sinner's cause;
In thee I trust, thee would I love,
And imitate the blest above.

3 My King supreme, to thee I bow,
 A willing subject at thy feet;

All other lords I disavow,
 And to thy government submit;
My Savior King, this heart would love,
And imitate the blest above.

184 *God is my light and my salvation.* (764)

1 Fountain of light, and living breath,
 Whose mercies never fail nor fade,
Fill me with life that hath no death,
 Fill me with light that hath no shade;
Appoint the remnant of my days
To see thy power, and sing thy praise.

2 O Lord, our God, before whose throne
 Stand storms and fire, oh what shall we
Return to heaven, that is our own,
 When all the world belongs to thee?
We have no offering to impart,
But praises, and a broken heart.

3 Oh thou who sittest in heaven, and seest
 My deeds without, my thoughts within,
Be thou my prince, be thou my priest—
 Command my soul, and cure my sin:
How bitter my afflictions be,
I care not, so I rise to thee.

4 What I possess, or what I crave,
 Brings no content, great God, to me,
If what I would, or what I have,
 Be not possessed and blest in thee:
What I enjoy, oh, make it mine,
In making me—that have it—**thine.**

Belleville, Key D.

70 CHRIST—HIS MEDIATORIAL REIGN.

ROCK OF AGES. 7s. 6 lines.
Dr. HASTINGS.

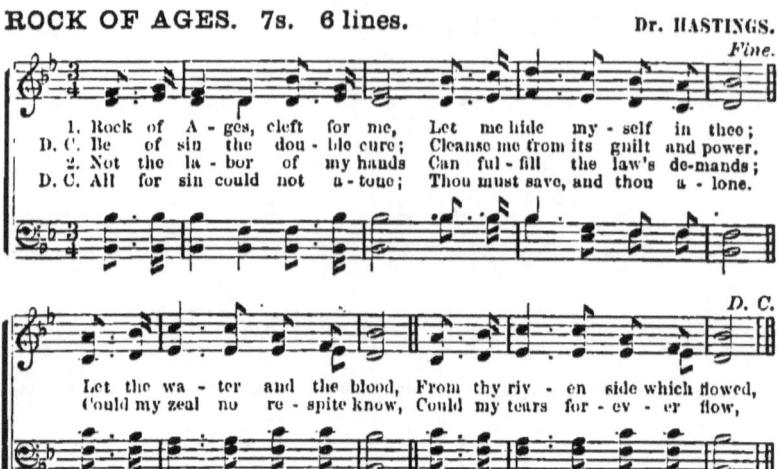

1. Rock of A-ges, cleft for me, Let me hide my-self in thee;
D. C. Be of sin the dou-ble cure; Cleanse me from its guilt and power.
2. Not the la-bor of my hands Can ful-fill the law's de-mands;
D. C. All for sin could not a-tone; Thou must save, and thou a-lone.

Let the wa-ter and the blood, From thy riv-en side which flowed,
Could my zeal no re-spite know, Could my tears for-ev-er flow,

185 *And that rock was Christ.* (261)

3 Nothing in my hand I bring,
Simply to thy cross I cling;
Naked, come to thee for dress;
Helpless, look to thee for grace;
Foul, I to the fountain fly;
Wash me, Savior, or I die.

4 While I draw this fleeting breath,
When my heart-strings break in death,
When I soar to worlds unknown,
See thee on thy judgment throne,
Rock of ages, cleft for me,
Let me hide myself in thee.

THE LORD IS GREAT.

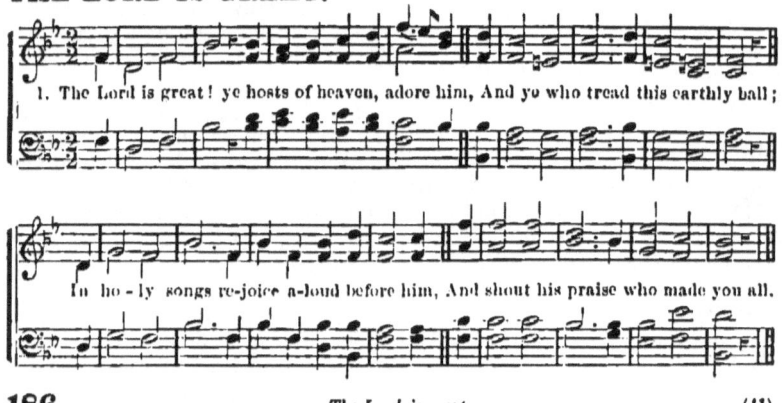

1. The Lord is great! ye hosts of heaven, adore him, And ye who tread this earthly ball;

In ho-ly songs re-joice a-loud before him, And shout his praise who made you all.

186 *The Lord is great.* (41)

2 The Lord is great! his majesty how glorious!
Resound his praise from shore to shore;
O'er sin, and death, and hell, now made victorious,
He rules and reigns for evermore.

3 The Lord is great; his mercy how abounding!
Ye angels, strike your golden chords,
Oh praise our God, with voice and harp resounding;
The King of kings, and Lord of lords.

CHRIST—MEDIATORIAL REIGN. 71

WILSON. 7s, Double. (New.)   W. T. MOORE.

187   *A covert from the storm.*   (262)

2 Other refuge have I none,
  Hangs my helpless soul on thee!
Leave, oh leave me not alone,
  Still support and comfort me:
All my trust on thee is stayed,
  All my help from thee I bring,
Cover my defenseless head
  With the shadow of thy wing.

3 Thou, O Christ, art all I want,
  Boundless love in thee I find;
Raise the fallen, cheer the faint,
  Heal the sick, and lead the blind.
Just and holy is thy name,
  Prince of Peace and Righteousness;
Most unworthy, Lord, I am,
  Thou art full of love and grace.

4 Plenteous grace with thee is found,
  Grace to pardon all my sins;
Let the healing streams abound,
  Make and keep me pure within.
Thou of life the fountain art,
  Freely let me take of thee;
Spring thou up within my heart,
  Rise to all eternity.

188   *Hail the day that saw him rise.*   (628)

1 Hail the day that saw him rise,
  Ravished from his people's eyes;
Christ, awhile to mortals given,
  Re-ascends his native heaven.
There the glorious triumph waits—
  "Lift your heads, you heavenly gates!
Wide unfold the radiant scene;
  Take the King of glory in."

2 He, whom highest heaven receives,
  Ever loves the friends he leaves;
Though returning to his throne,
  Still he calls his saints his own;
Still for us he intercedes,
  Prevalent his death he pleads;
Near himself prepares a place,
  Harbinger of human race.

3 Taken from our eyes to-day,
  Master, hear us when we pray;
See thy needy servants, see,
  Ever gazing up to thee:
Grant, though parted from our sight,
  Far above yon azure height,
Grant our hearts may thither rise,
  Follow thee beyond the skies.

Eltham, Key G.   Amboy, Key D.   Martyn, Key F.

THE ROCK. 11s & 12s.

1. In sea-sons of grief to my God I'll re-pair, When my heart is o'er-whelmed with sorrow and care; From the ends of the earth unto thee will I cry, Lead me to the Rock that is high-er than I, High-er than I, High-er than I, Lead me to the Rock that is high-er than I.

189   *The Rock that is higher than I.*   (264)

2 When Satan the tempter comes in like a flood,
To drive my poor soul from the fountain of good,
I'll pray to the Lord, who for sinners did die—
Lead me to the Rock that is higher than I!
   Higher than I, higher than I,
   Lead me to the Rock that is higher than I!

3 And when I have finished my pilgrimage here,
Complete in Christ's righteousness I shall appear;
In the swellings of Jordan, all dangers defy,
And look to the Rock that is higher than I!
   Higher than I, higher than I,
   And look to the Rock that is higher than I!

4 And when the last trumpet shall sound thro' the skies,
And the dead from the dust of the earth shall arise,
Transported I'll join with the ransomed on high,
To praise the great Rock that is higher than I!
   Higher than I, higher than I,
   To praise the great Rock that is higher than I!

DUANE STREET. L. M.
G. COLES.

1. The Christian banner! dread no loss Where that broad ensign floats unrolled;
But let the fair and sacred cross Blaze out from ev'ry radiant fold:
D. S. But though the strife be fierce and long, That cross shall wave in vic-to-ry.
Stern foes a-rise, a countless throng, Loud as the storms of Kara's sea,

190 *The Christian banner.* (266)

2 Sound the shrill trumpet, sound, and call
  The people of the mighty King,
And bid them keep that standard all
  In martial thousands gathering:
Let them come forth from every clime
  That lies beneath the circling sun,
Various, as flowers in that sweet clime
  Where flowers are, in heart, but one.

3 Soldiers of heaven! take sword and shield,
  Look up to him who rules on high,
And forward to the glorious field
  Where noble martyrs bleed and die;
Press onward, scorning flight or fear,
  As deep waves burst on Norway's coast,
And let the startled nations hear
  The war-shout of the Christian host.

4 Lift up the banner: rest no more,
  Nor let this righteous warfare cease,
Till man's last tribe shall bow before
  The Lord of lords—the Prince of Peace.
Go, bear it forth, ye strong and brave;
  Let not those bright folds once be furled
Till that high sun shall see them wave
  Above a blest but conquered world.

191 *Christ the Way, Truth, and Life.* (223)

1 Thou art the Way; and he who sighs,
  Amid this starless waste of woe,
To find a pathway to the skies,
  A light from heaven's eternal glow.
By thee must come, thou gate of love,
  Through which the saints undoubting trod,
Till faith discovers, like the dove,
  An ark, a resting-place in God.

2 Thou art the truth, whose steady day
  Shines on thro' earthly blight and bloom;
The pure, the everlasting Ray,
  The lamp that shines e'en in the tomb;
The Light that out of darkness springs,
  And guideth them that blindly go;
The Word whose precious radiance flings
  Its luster upon all below.

3 Thou art the Life, the blessed Well,
  With living waters gushing o'er,
Which those that drink shall ever dwell
  Where sin and thirst are known no more;
Thou art the mystic Pillar given,
  Our Lamp by night, our Light by day;
Thou art the sacred bread from heaven;
  Thou art the Life, the Truth, the Way.

THE GOSPEL PROCLAMATION.

WARE. L. M. — **KINGSLEY.**

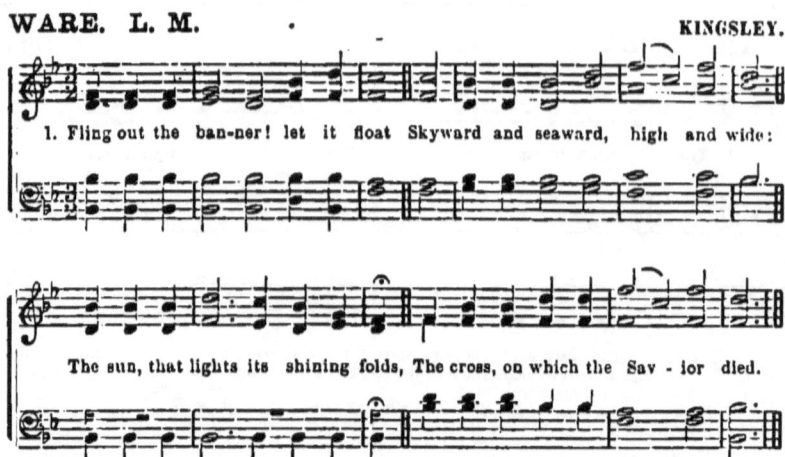

1. Fling out the ban-ner! let it float Skyward and seaward, high and wide: The sun, that lights its shining folds, The cross, on which the Sav-ior died.

192   *The Spirit of the Lord, etc.*   (267)

2 Fling out the banner! angels bend,
In anxious silence, o'er the sign;
And vainly seek to comprehend
The wonder of the love divine.

3 Fling out the banner! heathen lands
Shall see, from far, the glorious sight,
And nations, crowding to be born,
Baptize their spirits in its light.

4 Fling out the banner! sin-sick souls,
That sink and perish in the strife,
Shall touch in faith its radiant hem,
And spring immortal into life.

5 Fling out the banner! let it float
Skyward and seaward, high and wide;
Our glory, only in the cross;
Our only hope, the Crucified.

6 Fling out the banner! wide and high,
Seaward and skyward, let it shine:
Nor skill, nor might, nor merit, ours;
We conquer only in that sign.

193   *Pentecost.*   (269)

1 Great was the day, the joy was great,
When the beloved disciples met;
And on their heads the Spirit came,
And sat like tongues of cloven flame.

2 What gifts, what miracles he gave—
The power to kill, the power to save;
Furnished their tongues with wondrous words
Instead of shields, and spears, and swords.

3 Thus armed, he sent the champions forth;
From east to west, from south to north;
Go, and assert your Savior's cause—
Go, spread the mystery of the cross!

4 These weapons of the holy war,
Of what almighty force they are
To make our stubborn passions bow,
And lay the proudest rebel low!

5 The Greeks, and Jews, the learned and rude,
Are by these heavenly arms subdued;
While Satan rages at his loss,
And hates the doctrine of the cross.

194   *Give unto him thanks.*   (727)

1 To God, the great, the ever-blest,
Let songs of honor be addressed!
His mercy firm forever stands;
Give him the thanks his love demands!

2 Who knows the wonder of his ways?
Who can make known his boundless praise?
Blest are the souls that fear him still,
And learn submission to his will.

Anvern, Key F.   Rockingham, Key G.

GOSPEL PROCLAMATION. 75

SILVER STREET. S. M.
I. SMITH.

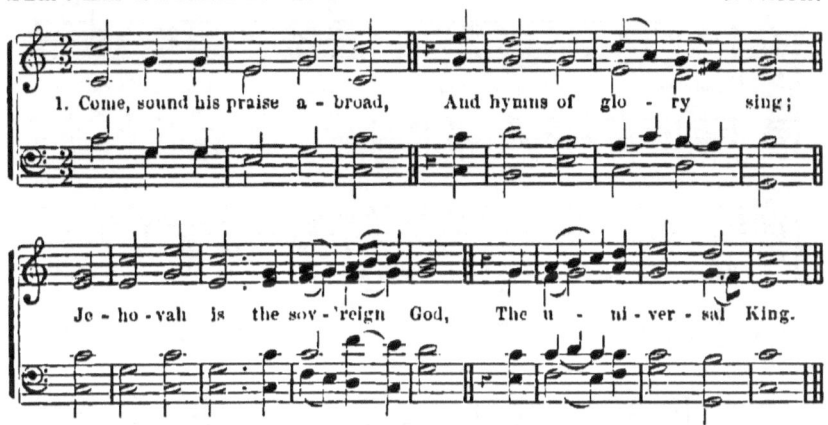

195 *Come, sound his praise abroad.* (702)

1. Come, sound his praise abroad,
And hymns of glory sing;
Jehovah is the sov'reign God,
The universal King.

2 He formed the deeps unknown;
He gave the seas their bound;
The watery worlds are all his own,
And all the solid ground.

3 Come, worship at his throne;
Come, bow before the Lord;
We are his work, and not our own;
He formed us by his word.

4 To-day attend his voice,
Nor dare provoke his rod;
Come, like the people of his choice,
And own your gracious God.

196 *Seen of angels.* (259)

1 Beyond the starry skies,
Far as the eternal hills,
Yon heaven of heavens, with living light,
Our great Redeemer fills.

2 Around him angels fair,
In countless armies, shine;
And ever, in exalted lays,
They offer songs divine.

3 "Hail, Prince of life!" they cry,
"Whose unexampled love
Moved thee to quit those glorious realms
And royalties above."

4 And when he stooped to earth,
And suffered rude disdain,
They cast their honors at his feet,
And waited in his train.

5 They saw him on the cross,
While darkness veiled the skies;
And when he burst the gates of death,
They saw the Conqueror rise.

6 They thronged his chariot wheels,
And bore him to his throne;
Then swept their golden harps and sung,
"The glorious work is done."*

197 *How beautiful are the feet, etc.* (270)

1 How beauteous are their feet
Who stand on Zion's hill!
Who bring salvation on their tongues,
And words of peace reveal!

2 How charming is their voice!
How sweet the tidings are!
"Zion, behold thy Savior King!
He reigns and triumphs here."

3 How happy are our ears
That hear this joyful sound,
Which kings and prophets waited for,
And sought, but never found!

4 How blessed are our eyes
That see this heavenly light!
Prophets and kings desired it long,
But died without the sight.

5 The watchmen join their voice,
And tuneful notes employ;
Jerusalem breaks forth in songs,
And deserts learn the joy.

Browne, Key D. Laban, Key C. Luther, Key F.

THE GOSPEL PROCLAMATION.

LENOX. H. M.

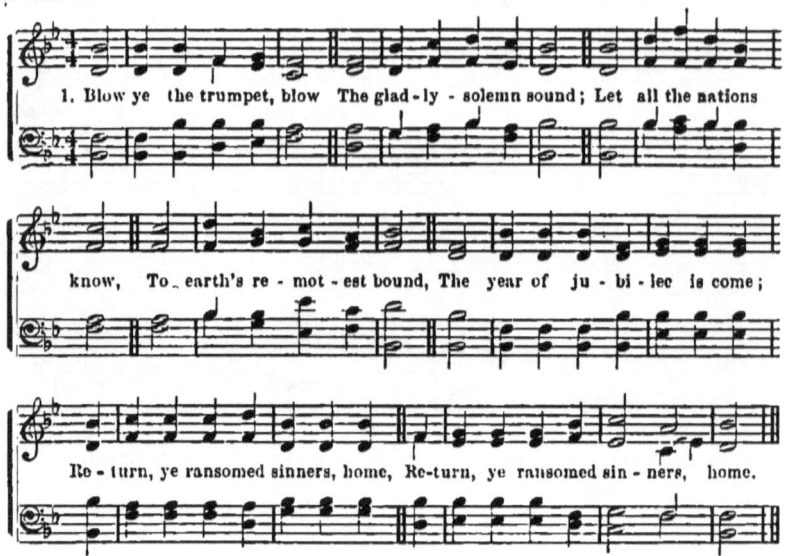

1. Blow ye the trumpet, blow The glad-ly-solemn sound; Let all the nations know, To earth's re-mot-est bound, The year of ju-bi-lee is come; Re-turn, ye ransomed sinners, home, Re-turn, ye ransomed sin-ners, home.

198 *The year of Jubilee.* (273)

2 Exalt the Lamb of God,
   The sin-atoning Lamb;
Redemption by his blood,
   Through all the lands proclaim:
The year of jubilee is come;
Return, ye ransomed sinners, home.

3 Ye slaves of sin and hell,
   Your liberty receive,
And safe in Jesus dwell,
   And blest in Jesus live:
The year of jubilee is come;
Return, ye ransomed sinners, home.

4 The gospel trumpet hear,
   The news of pardoning grace:
Ye happy souls, draw near;
   Behold your Savior's face:
The year of jubilee is come;
Return, ye ransomed sinners, home.

5 Jesus, our great High Priest,
   Has full atonement made:
Ye weary spirits, rest;
   Ye mourning souls, be glad:
The year of jubilee is come;
Return, ye ransomed sinners, home.

199 *The year of Jubilee.* (326)

1 Fair shines the morning star,
   The silver trumpets sound—
Their notes re-echoing far—
   While dawns the day around:
Joy to the slave—the slave is free—
It is the year of jubilee.

2 Prisoners of hope, in gloom
   And silence left to die,
With Christ's unfolding tomb,
   Your portals open fly:
Rise with your Lord; he sets you free;
It is the year of jubilee.

3 Ye who yourselves have sold
   For debts to justice due,
Ransomed, but not with gold,
   He gave himself for you!
The blood of Christ hath made you free;
It is the year of jubilee.

4 Captives of sin and shame,
   O'er earth and ocean, bear
An angel's voice proclaim
   The Lord's accepted year:
Let Jacob rise—be Israel free;
It is the year of jubilee.

Lischer, Key G.   Zebulon, Key F.

THE GOSPEL PROCLAMATION. 77

URMUND. 8, 8, 8, 8, 8, 4.   Dr. L. MASON, by permission.

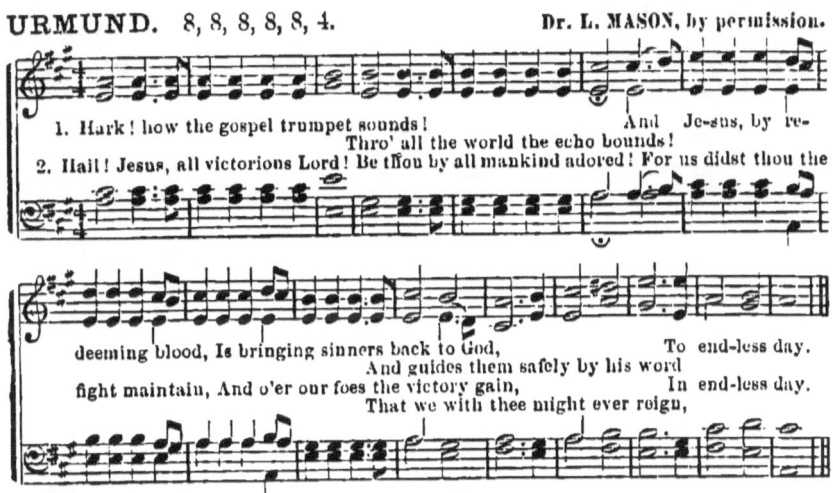

1. Hark! how the gospel trumpet sounds! And Jesus, by redeeming blood, Is bringing sinners back to God, Thro' all the world the echo bounds! To end-less day.
2. Hail! Jesus, all victorious Lord! Be thou by all mankind adored! For us didst thou the fight maintain, And o'er our foes the victory gain, And guides them safely by his word That we with thee might ever reign, In end-less day.

200   *The gospel trumpet.*   (272)

3 Fight on, ye conquering souls, fight on,
And when the conquest you have won,
Then palms of victory you shall bear,
And in his kingdom have a share,
And crowns of glory ever wear,
   In endless day.

4 There we shall in full chorus join,
With saints and angels all combine
To sing of his redeeming love,
When rolling years shall cease to move,
And this shall be our theme above,
   In endless day.

THE ROYAL PROCLAMATION.   From Chapel Melodies.
Very Spirited.   *Chorus.*

1. Hear the royal proclamation, The glad tidings of salvation, Publishing to every creature, To the ruined sons of nature; Jesus reigns, Jesus reigns.
Jesus reigns, { Jesus reigns, he reigns victorious, } [reigns.
{ Over heaven and earth most glorious, } Jesus reigns, Jesus reigns, Jesus

201   *The royal proclamation.*   (274)

2 See the royal banners flying,
Hear the heralds loudly crying,
" Rebel sinners, royal favor
Now is offered by the Savior."

3 " Here is wine, and milk, and honey,
Come and purchase without money;
Mercy like a flowing fountain,
Streaming from the holy mountain."

4 Shout, you tongues of every nation,
To the bound of the creation:
Shout the praise of Judah's Lion,
The Almighty King of Zion.

5 Shout, O saints, make joyful mention,
Christ hath purchased our redemption;
Angels, shout the joyful story,
Through the brighter worlds of glory.

THE GOSPEL PROCLAMATION.

DORT. 6s & 4s.

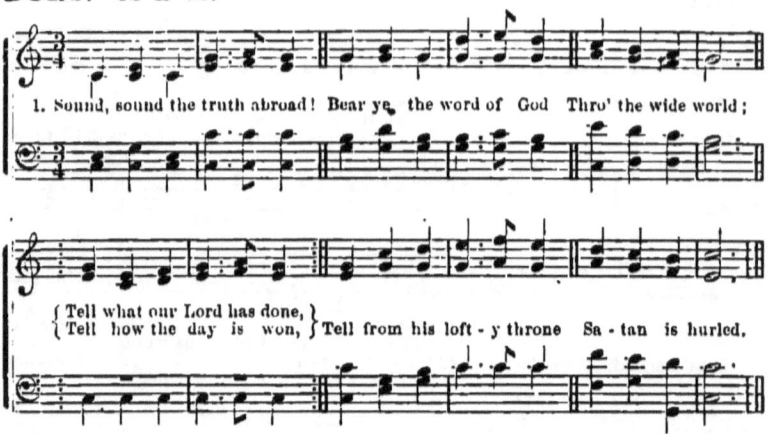

1. Sound, sound the truth abroad! Bear ye the word of God Thro' the wide world; Tell what our Lord has done, Tell how the day is won, Tell from his lofty throne Sa-tan is hurled.

202 *Holding forth the word of life.* (275)

1 Sound, sound the truth abroad!
Bear ye the word of God
　Through the wide world;
Tell what our Lord has done,
Tell how the day is won,
Tell from his lofty throne
　Satan is hurled.

2 Far over sea and land,
Go, at your Lord's command;
　Bear ye his name;
Bear it to every shore,
Regions unknown explore,
Enter at every door;
　Silence is shame.

3 Speed on the wings of love;
Jesus, who reigns above,
　Bids us to fly;
They who his message bear
Should neither doubt nor fear;
He will their friend appear,
　He will be nigh.

4 When on the mighty deep,
He will their spirits keep,
　Stayed on his word;
When in a foreign land,
No other friend at hand,
Jesus will by them stand—
　Jesus, their Lord.

203 *Rule in the midst of thine enemies.* (201)

1 Rise, glorious Conqueror, rise
Into thy native skies—
　Assume thy right;
And where, in many a fold,
The clouds are backward rolled,
Pass through those gates of gold,
　And reign in light!

2 Victor o'er death and hell!
Cherubic legions swell
　The radiant train;
Praises all heaven inspire,
Each angel sweeps his lyre,
And waves his wings of fire,
　Thou Lamb once slain!

3 Enter, incarnate God!
No feet but thine have trod
　The serpent down:
Blow the full trumpets—blow!
Wider yon portals throw!
Savior, triumphant go
　And take thy crown!

4 Lion of Judah, hail!
And let thy name prevail
　From age to age:
Lord of the rolling years,
Claim for thine own the spheres,
For thou hast bought with tears
　Thy heritage.

Olivet, Key E♭   America, Key G.

THE GOSPEL INVITATIONS.

HASTE, TRAVELER, HASTE. 8, 8, 8, 8, 4.* NAGELI.

1. Haste, trav'ler, haste! the night comes on, And many a shining hour is gone;
The storm is gath'ring in the west, And thou art far from home and rest.
Haste, trav'ler, haste!

* Or L. M., without the repeat.

204 *Haste thee; escape thither.* (276)

2 Awake, awake! pursue thy way
With steady course, while yet 't is day;
While thou art sleeping on the ground,
Danger and darkness gather round;
Haste, traveler, haste!

3 The rising tempest sweeps the sky;
The rains descend, the winds are high;
The waters swell, and death and fear
Beset thy path—no refuge near—
Haste, traveler, haste!

4 Haste while a shelter you may gain—
A covert from the wind and rain;
A hiding-place, a rest, a home—
A refuge from the wrath to come—
Haste, traveler, haste!

5 Then linger not in all the plain;
Flee for thy life—the mountain gain;
Look not behind, make no delay;
Oh speed thee, speed thee on thy way!
Haste, traveler, haste!

205 *An evening expostulation.* (280)

1 Oh do not let the word depart,
And close thine eye against the light;
Poor sinner, harden not thy heart—
Thou wouldst be saved: why not to-night?
Why not to-night?

2 To-morrow's sun may never rise
To bless thy long deluded sight:
This is the time; Oh then be wise!
Thou wouldst be saved: why not to-night?

3 Our God in pity lingers still;
And wilt thou thus his love requite?
Renounce at length thy stubborn will—
Thou wouldst be saved: why not to-night?

4 Our blessed Lord refuses none
Who would to him their souls unite;
Then be the work of grace begun—
Thou wouldst be saved: why not to-night?

206 *Come unto me.* (278)

1 With tearful eyes I look around;
Life seems a dark and stormy sea;
Yet 'midst the gloom I hear a sound—
A heavenly whisper—Come to me!

2 It tells me of a place of rest;
It tells me where my soul may flee:
Oh, to the weary, faint, opprest,
How sweet the bidding, Come to me!

3 Come, for all else must fail and die;
Earth is no resting-place for thee;
To heaven direct thy weeping eye—
I am thy portion; Come to me!

4 O voice of mercy, voice of love!
In conflict, grief, and agony,
Support me, cheer me from above,
And gently whisper, Come to me!

Pilesgrove, Key G. Germany, Key B♭.

THE GOSPEL INVITATIONS.

FOREST. L. M.   Arr. by S. J. VAIL.

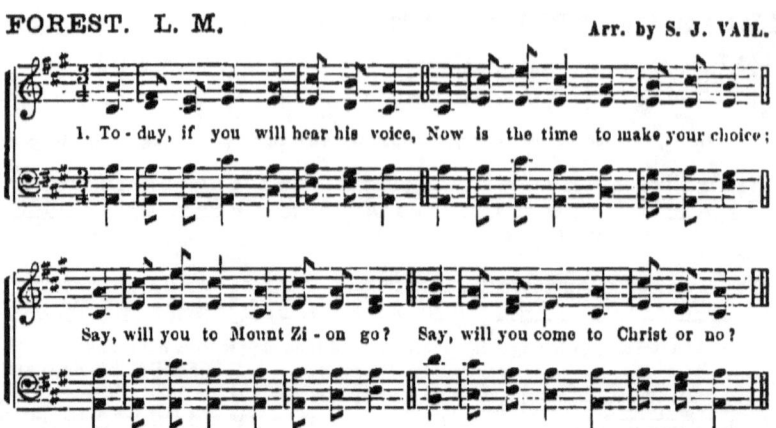

1. To-day, if you will hear his voice, Now is the time to make your choice;
Say, will you to Mount Zi-on go? Say, will you come to Christ or no?

207 *To-day, if you will hear his voice.* (279)

2 Say, will you be forever blest,
And with this glorious Jesus rest?
Will you be saved from guilt and pain?
Will you with Christ forever reign?

3 Make now your choice, and halt no more;
He now is waiting for the poor;
Say, now, poor souls, what will you do?
Say, will you come to Christ or no?

4 Fathers and sons, for ruin bound,
Amidst the gospel's joyful sound,
Come, go with us, and seek to prove
The joys of Christ's redeeming love.

5 Matrons and maids, we look to you,
Are you resolved to perish, too?
To rush in carnal pleasures on,
And sink in flaming ruin down?

6 Once more we ask you, in his name,
(We know his love remains the same,)
Say, will you to Mount Zion go?
Say, will you come to Christ or no?

208   *Ecclesiastes* 9: 10.   (284)

1 Life is the time to serve the Lord,
The time t' insure the great reward;
And while the lamp holds out to burn,
Oh hasten, sinner, to return!

2 Life is the hour that God has given
To 'scape from hell! and fly to heaven,
The day of grace, when mortals may
Secure the blessings of the day.

3 The living know that they must die,
Beneath the clods their dust must lie;
Then have no share in all that's done
Beneath the circle of the sun.

4 Then what my thoughts design to do,
My hands, with all your might pursue:
Since no device nor work is found,
Nor faith, nor hope, beneath the ground.

5 There are no acts of pardon passed
In the cold grave to which we haste;
Oh may we all receive thy grace,
And see with joy thy smiling face.

209   *The broad and the narrow way.* (283)

1 Broad is the road that leads to death;
And thousands walk together there;
But wisdom shows a narrow path,
With here and there a traveler.

2 "Deny thyself, and take thy cross,"
Is the Redeemer's great command;
Nature must count her gold but dross
If she would gain this heavenly land.

3 The fearful soul that tires and faints,
And walks the ways of God no more,
Is but esteemed almost a saint,
And makes his own destruction sure.

4 Lord, let my hopes be not in vain,
Create my heart entirely new;
This, hypocrites could ne'er attain;
This, false apostates never knew.

Hebron, Key B♭.   Devotion, Key C.   Windham, Key F.

THE GOSPEL INVITATIONS. 81

THE GOSPEL FEAST. L. M., with Chorus. ✽

Harmonized by T. E. PERKINS.

1. Come, sin-ners, to the gos-pel feast; Oh, do no lon-ger stay!
You need not one be left be-hind; Oh, do no lon-ger stay!

*Cho. Oh, do no lon-ger stay a-way, For now your Sa-vior calls,

Let ev-ery soul be Je-sus' guest, Oh, do no lon-ger stay a-way!
For God has bid-den all man-kind, Oh, do no lon-ger stay a-way!

The gos-pel sounds the ju-bi-lee, Oh, do no lon-ger stay a-way.

210 *Come, for all things are now ready.* (285)

2 Hark! 'tis the gracious Savior's call:
Oh no longer stay!
The invitation is to all:
Oh do no longer stay away!
Come, all the world—come, sinner, thou—
Oh do no longer stay!
All things in Christ are ready now:
Oh do no longer stay away!—Cho.

3 Come, all you souls by sin oppressed:
Oh do no longer stay!
You weary wanderers after rest,
Oh do no longer stay away!
You poor and maimed, and halt and blind,
Oh do no longer stay!
In Christ a hearty welcome find:
Oh do no longer stay away!—Cho.

4 The message, as from God, receive:
Oh do no longer stay!
You all may come to Christ and live:
Oh do no longer stay away!
Oh let his love your hearts constrain:
Oh do no longer stay!
Nor suffer him to call in vain:
Oh do no longer stay away!—Cho.

5 This is the time—no more delay,
Oh do no longer stay!
The Savior calls you all to-day,
Oh do no longer stay away!

Oh may his call effectual prove,
Oh do no longer stay!
Accept the offers of his love,
Oh do no longer stay away!—Cho.

211 *Inviting.* (281)

1 Come, weary souls with sin distressed
Oh do no longer stay!
Come and accept the promised rest:
Oh do no longer stay away!
The Savior's gracious call obey—
Oh do no longer stay!
And cast your gloomy fears away—
Oh do no longer stay away!—Cho.

2 Oppressed with guilt, a heavy load,
Oh do no longer stay!
Oh come and bow before your God:
Oh do no longer stay away!
Divine compassion, mighty love—
Oh do no longer stay!
Will all the painful load remove:
Oh do no longer stay away!—Cho.

3 Here mercy's boundless ocean flows—
Oh do no longer stay!—
To cleanse your guilt and heal your woes:
Oh do no longer stay away!
Pardon, and life, and endless peace—
Oh do no longer stay!—
How rich the gift, how free the grace!—
Oh do no longer stay away!—Cho.

✽ *Chorus may be omitted.*

IMPORTUNITY. C. M.

1. Let ev-ery mor-tal ear at-tend, And every heart re-joice, And ev-ery heart rejoice; The trumpet of the gos-pel sounds, With an in-vit-ing voice, With an inviting voice, With an in-vit-ing voice.

212 *Hear, and your soul shall live.* (286)

2 Ho! all you hungry, starving souls,
Who feed upon the wind,
And vainly strive with earthly toys
To fill an empty mind;

3 Eternal wisdom has prepared
A soul-reviving feast,
And bids your longing appetites
The rich provision taste.

4 Ho! you that pant for living streams,
And pine away and die,
Here may you quench your raging thirst
With springs that never dry.

5 Rivers of love and mercy here
In a rich ocean join;
Salvation in abundance flows,
Like floods of milk and wine.

6 Great God! the treasures of thy love
Are everlasting mines,
Deep as our helpless miseries are,
And boundless as our sins.

7 The happy gates of gospel grace
Stand open night and day;
Lord, we are come to seek supplies,
And drive our wants away.

213 *For there is no difference.* (287)

1 How free and boundless is the grace
Of our redeeming God!
Extending to the Greek and Jew,
And men of every blood.

2 Come, all you wretched sinners, come,
He'll form your souls anew;
His gospel and his heart have room
For rebels such as you.

3 His doctrine is almighty love;
There's virtue in his name
To turn a raven to a dove,
A lion to a lamb.

4 Come, then, accept the offered grace
And make no more delay;
His love will all your guilt efface,
And soothe your fears away.

Coronation, Key G. Rindge, Key G. Resolution, Key G.

GOSPEL INVITATIONS. 83

RETURN. C. M.   Dr. HASTINGS, by permission.

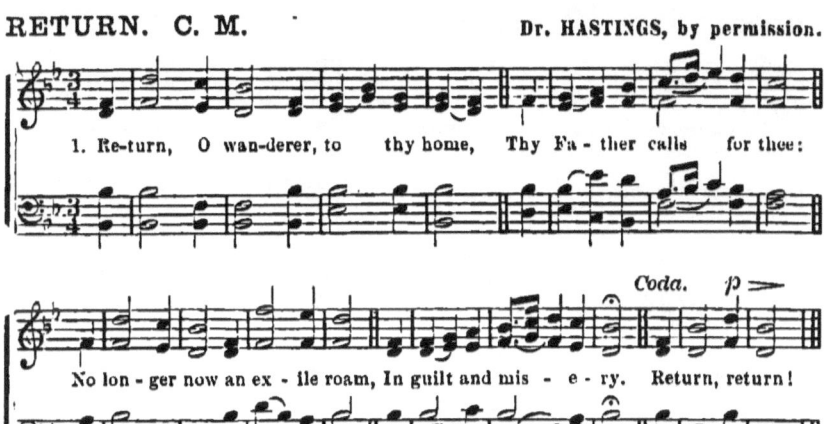

1. Re-turn, O wan-derer, to thy home, Thy Fa-ther calls for thee: No lon-ger now an ex-ile roam, In guilt and mis-e-ry. Return, return!

214 *Draw nigh to God, etc.* (206)

2 Return, O wanderer, to thy home,
  'T is Jesus calls for thee;
The Spirit and the Bride say—come;
Oh! now for refuge flee;
  Return, return!

3 Return, O wanderer, to thy home,
  'T is madness to delay;
There are no pardons in the tomb,
And brief is mercy's day:
  Return, return!

215 *Let him return unto the Lord.* (288)

1 Return, O wanderer, now return,
And seek thy Father's face;
Those new desires which in thee burn
Were kindled by his grace.

2 Return, O wanderer, now return!
He hears thy humble sigh!
He sees thy softened spirit mourn,
When no one else is nigh.

3 Return, O wanderer, now return!
Thy Savior bids thee live;
Go to his feet, and grateful learn
How freely he'll forgive.

4 Return, O wanderer, now return!
And wipe the falling tear;
Thy Father calls—no longer mourn,
'T is love invites thee near.

216 *Remember me.* (241)

1 Jesus, thou art the sinner's friend;
  As such I look to thee;
Now, in the fullness of thy love,
  O Lord, remember me!

2 Remember thy pure word of grace,
  Remember Calvary;
Remember all thy promises,
  And then remember me.

3 Thou mighty Advocate with God!
  I yield myself to thee;
While thou art sitting on thy throne,
  O Lord, remember me!

4 I own I'm guilty—own I'm vile;
  Yet thy salvation's free;
Then in thy all-abounding grace,
  O Lord, remember me!

5 Howe'er forsaken or distressed,
  Howe'er oppressed I be,
Howe'er afflicted here on earth,
  Do thou remember me!

6 And when I close my eyes in death,
  And creature helps all flee,
Then, O my great Redeemer, Lord,
  I pray, remember me!

Prayer, Key C.   Chelmsford, Key A.

THE GOSPEL INVITATIONS.

RESOLUTION. C. M., Double. (Old.)

1. Come, humble sinner, in whose breast, A thousand thoughts revolve;
Come with your guilt and fear oppressed, And make this last resolve:
I'll go to Jesus, tho' my sin Has like a mountain rose;
His kingdom now I'll enter in, What-ever may oppose.

217 *Whoso believeth might not perish.* (291)

2 Humbly I'll bow at his command,
  And there my guilt confess;
I'll own I am a wretch undone,
  Without his sovereign grace.
Surely he will accept my plea,
  For he has bid me come;
Forthwith I'll rise, and to him flee,
  For yet, he says, there's room.

218 *He that cometh shall never hunger.* (293)

1 Ye wretched, hungry, starving poor,
  Behold a royal feast,
Where mercy spreads her bounteous store
  For every humble guest.
See, Jesus stands with open arms;
  He calls, he bids you come;
Guilt holds you back, and fear alarms,
  But see, there yet is room.

2 Room in the Savior's bleeding heart;
  There love and pity meet;
Nor will he bid the soul depart
  That trembles at his feet.
Oh come, and with his children taste
  The blessings of his love,
While hope attends the sweet repast
  Of nobler joys above.

219 *In this mountain shall the Lord.* (294)

1 The King of heaven his table spreads,
  And dainties crown the board;
Not paradise, with all its joys,
  Could such delights afford.
Pardon and peace to dying men,
  And endless life are given,
Through the rich blood that Jesus shed,
  To raise our souls to heaven.

2 You hungry poor, that long have strayed
  In sin's dark mazes, come;
Come from your most obscure retreat,
  And grace shall find you room.
Millions of souls in glory now
  Were fed and feasted here;
And millions more still on the way
  Around the board appear.

3 Yet are his heart and house so large
  That millions more may come;
Nor could the whole assembled world
  O'erfill the spacious room.
All things are ready: come away,
  Nor weak excuses frame;
Crowd to your places at the feast
  And bless the Founder's name.

THE GOSPEL INVITATIONS. 85

KENTUCKY. S. M.

1. Now is th' accepted time— Now is the day of grace;
Now, sinners, come, without delay, And seek the Savior's face.

220   *Now is the accepted time.*   (207)

1 Now is the accepted time,
   Now is the day of grace;
Now, sinners, come, without delay,
   And seek the Savior's face.

2 Now is the accepted time,
   The Savior calls to-day;
To-morrow it may be too late—
   Then why should you delay?

3 Now is the accepted time,
   The gospel bids you come;
And every promise in his word
   Declares there yet is room.

221   *The Gospel call.*   (301)

1 Ye trembling captives! hear;
   The gospel-trumpet sounds;
No music more can charm the ear,
   Or heal your heart-felt wounds.

2 'T is not the trump of war,
   Nor Sinai's awful roar;
Salvation's news it spreads afar,
   And vengeance is no more.

3 Forgiveness, love, and peace,
   Glad heaven aloud proclaims;
And earth, the jubilee's release,
   With eager rapture claims.

4 Far, far to distant lands
   The saving news shall spread;
And Jesus all his willing bands
   In glorious triumph lead.

222   *Give me thy heart.*   (299)

1 Give to the Lord thine heart;
   In him all pleasures meet:
Oh, come and choose the better part,
   Low at the Savior's feet.

2 Hear, and your soul shall live;
   His peace shall be your stay—
Peace, which the world can never give,
   Can never take away.

223   *Boast not thyself of to-morrow.*   (302)

1 To-morrow, Lord! is thine,
   Lodged in thy sovereign hand;
And if its sun arise and shine,
   It shines by thy command.

2 The present moment flies,
   And bears our life away;
Oh, make thy servants truly wise,
   That they may live to-day.

3 Since on this fleeting hour
   Eternity is hung,
Awake, by thine almighty power,
   The aged and the young.

4 One thing demands our care;
   Oh, be it still pursued!
Lest, slighted once, the season fair
   Should never be renewed.

5 To Jesus may we fly,
   Swift as the morning light,
Lest life's young, golden beams should die
   In sudden, endless night.

Gerar, Key F.   Laban, Key C.   Boylston, Key C.

THE GOSPEL INVITATION.

ROSEFIELD. 7s, 6 lines.   Dr. MALAN.

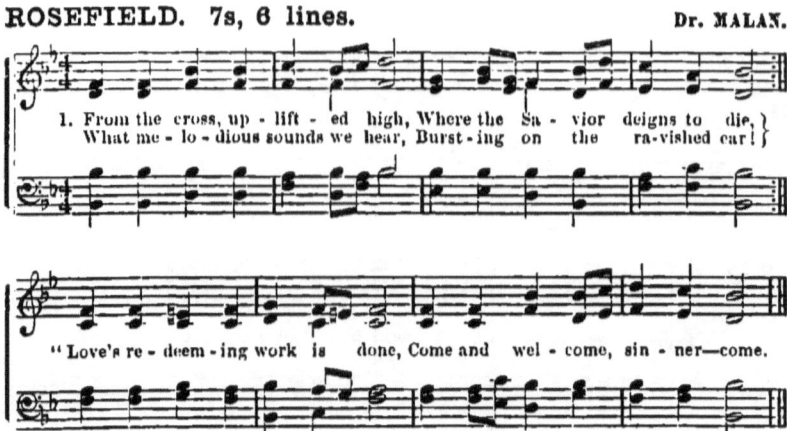

1. From the cross, up-lift-ed high, Where the Sa-vior deigns to die,
What me-lo-dious sounds we hear, Burst-ing on the ra-vished ear!
"Love's re-deem-ing work is done, Come and wel-come, sin-ner—come.

224   *Come and welcome.*   (303)

2 "Sprinkled now with blood the throne,
Why beneath thy burdens groan?
On my pierced body laid,
Justice owns the ransom paid;
Bow the knee, embrace the Son;
Come and welcome, sinner—come.

3 "Spread for thee the festal board:
See, with richest dainties stored;
To thy Father's bosom pressed,
Yet again a child confessed,
Never from his house to roam;
Come and welcome, sinner—come.

4 "Soon the days of life shall end;
Lo! I come, your Savior, Friend,
Safe your spirits to convey
To the realms of endless day,
Up to my eternal home;
Come and welcome, sinner—come."

225   *His example in suffering.*   (162)

1 Go to dark Gethsemane,
Ye that feel the tempter's power;
Your Redeemer's conflict see;
Watch with him one bitter hour:
Turn not from his griefs away;
Learn of Jesus Christ to pray.

2 Follow to the judgment hall;
View the Lord of life arraigned:
Oh the wormwood and the gall!
Oh the pangs his soul sustained!
Shun not suffering, shame, or loss;
Learn of him to bear the cross.

3 Calvary's mournful mountain climb;
There, admiring at his feet,
Mark that miracle of time,
God's own sacrifice complete:
"It is finished," hear him cry;
Learn of Jesus Christ to die.

226   *God is love.*   (61)

1 Earth, with her ten thousand flowers,
Air, with all its beams and showers,
Ocean's infinite expanse,
Heaven's resplendent countenance;
All around, and all above,
Hath this record—God is love.

2 Sounds among the vales and hills,
In the woods, and by the rills,
Of the breeze, and of the bird,
By the gentle murmur stirred:
All these songs, beneath, above,
Have one burden—God is love.

3 All the hopes and fears that start
From the fountain of the heart,
All the quiet bliss that lies
In our human sympathies:
These are voices from above,
Sweetly whispering, God is love.

Ives, Key E♭.   Rock of Ages, Key B♭.   Eltham, Key G.

THE GOSPEL INVITATIONS.

COOKHAM. 7s. Harmonized by T. E. PERKINS.

1. Sin-ners, turn—why will you die? God, your Ma-ker, asks you why; God, who did your be-ing give, Made you with himself to live.

227 *Turn ye; for why will ye die?* (304)

2 Sinners, turn—why will you die?
Christ, your Savior, asks you why;
He, who did your souls retrieve,
He, who died that you might live.

3 Will you let him die in vain?
Crucify your Lord again?
Why, you ransomed sinners, why
Will you slight his grace and die?

4 Will you not his grace receive?
Will you still refuse to live?
Oh! you dying sinners, why—
Why will you forever die?

228 *Earnest entreaty.* (306)

1 Haste, O sinner, to be wise,
Stay not for the morrow's sun;
Wisdom warns thee from the skies
All the paths of death to shun.

2 Haste, and mercy now implore;
Stay not for the morrow's sun;
Thy probation may be o'er
Ere this evening's work is done.

3 Haste, O sinner, now return;
Stay not for the morrow's sun;
Lest thy lamp should cease to burn
Ere salvation's work is done.

4 Haste, while yet thou canst be blest;
Stay not for the morrow's sun,
Death may thy poor soul arrest
Ere the morrow is begun.

229 *Fullness of Christ.* (307)

1 Bleeding hearts, defiled by sin,
Jesus Christ can make you clean;
Contrite souls, with guilt oppressed,
Jesus Christ can give you rest.

2 You that mourn o'er follies past,
Precious hours and years laid waste;
Turn to God, oh turn and live,
Jesus Christ can still forgive.

3 You that oft have wandered far
From the light of Bethlehem's star,
Trembling, now your steps retrace,
Jesus Christ is full of grace.

4 Souls benighted and forlorn,
Grieved, afflicted, tempest-worn,
Now in Israel's rock confide,
Jesus Christ for man has died.

5 Fainting souls, in peril's hour,
Yield not to the tempter's power;
On the risen Lord rely,
Jesus Christ now reigns on high.

230 *The pearl of great price.* (782)

1 'Tis religion that can give
Sweetest pleasure while we live,
'Tis religion must supply
Solid comfort when we die.

2 After death, its joys will be
Lasting as eternity!
Be the living God my friend,
Then my bliss shall never end.

Hendon, Key G. Wilson, Key G. Horton, Key B♭.

THE GOSPEL INVITATIONS.

INVITATION. 8s, 7s & 4.

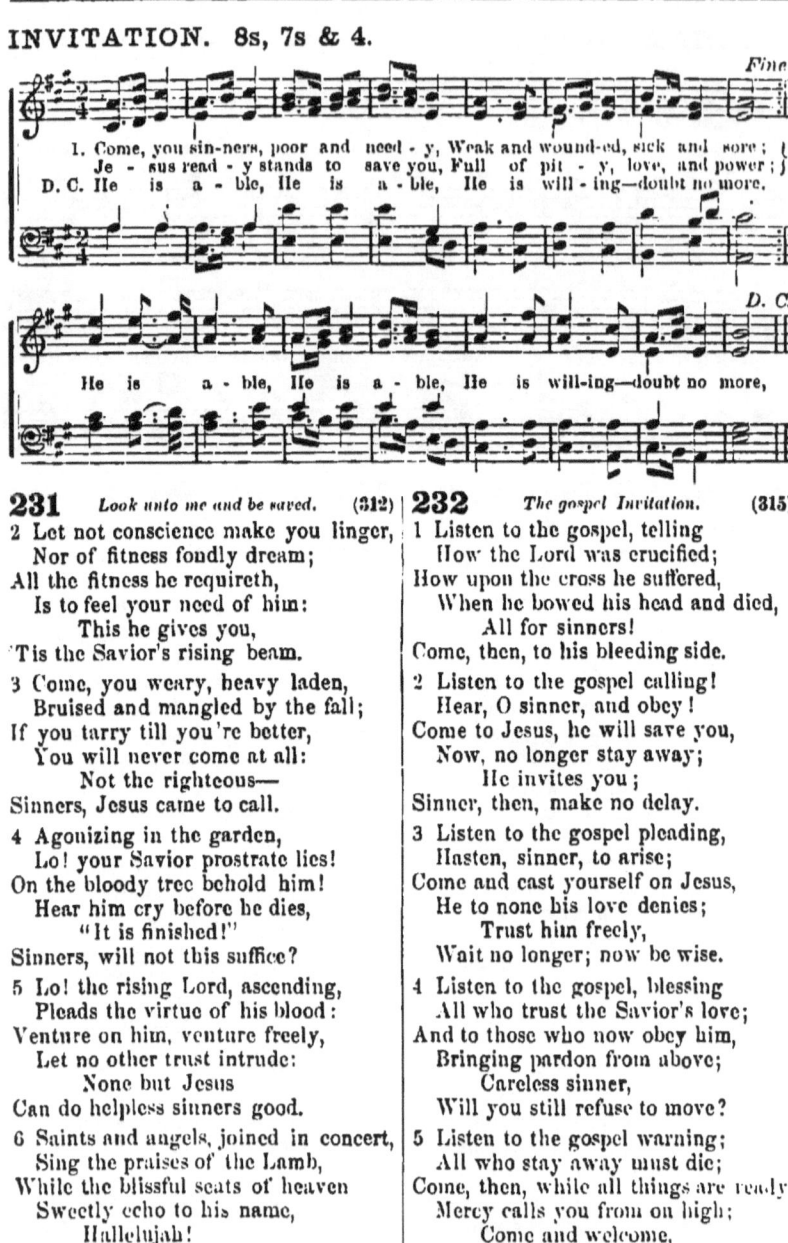

1. Come, you sinners, poor and needy, Weak and wounded, sick and sore;
Jesus ready stands to save you, Full of pity, love, and power;
D. C. He is able, He is able, He is willing—doubt no more.

231 *Look unto me and be saved.* (312)

2 Let not conscience make you linger,
Nor of fitness fondly dream;
All the fitness he requireth,
Is to feel your need of him:
This he gives you,
'Tis the Savior's rising beam.

3 Come, you weary, heavy laden,
Bruised and mangled by the fall;
If you tarry till you're better,
You will never come at all:
Not the righteous—
Sinners, Jesus came to call.

4 Agonizing in the garden,
Lo! your Savior prostrate lies!
On the bloody tree behold him!
Hear him cry before he dies,
"It is finished!"
Sinners, will not this suffice?

5 Lo! the rising Lord, ascending,
Pleads the virtue of his blood:
Venture on him, venture freely,
Let no other trust intrude:
None but Jesus
Can do helpless sinners good.

6 Saints and angels, joined in concert,
Sing the praises of the Lamb,
While the blissful seats of heaven
Sweetly echo to his name,
Hallelujah!
Sinners now his love proclaim.

232 *The gospel Invitation.* (315)

1 Listen to the gospel, telling
How the Lord was crucified;
How upon the cross he suffered,
When he bowed his head and died,
All for sinners!
Come, then, to his bleeding side.

2 Listen to the gospel calling!
Hear, O sinner, and obey!
Come to Jesus, he will save you,
Now, no longer stay away;
He invites you;
Sinner, then, make no delay.

3 Listen to the gospel pleading,
Hasten, sinner, to arise;
Come and cast yourself on Jesus,
He to none his love denies;
Trust him freely,
Wait no longer; now be wise.

4 Listen to the gospel, blessing
All who trust the Savior's love;
And to those who now obey him,
Bringing pardon from above;
Careless sinner,
Will you still refuse to move?

5 Listen to the gospel warning;
All who stay away must die;
Come, then, while all things are ready
Mercy calls you from on high;
Come and welcome,
Hear, oh hear the Savior cry!

Molucca, Key D.   Nettleton, Key E♭.   Osgood, Key E♭.

THE GOSPEL INVITATIONS.

MOLUCCA. 8s, 7s & 4.

1. Sin-ners, will you scorn the message, Sent in mer-cy from a-bove?
Ev'-ry sentence, oh, how ten-der, Ev'-ry line is full of love;
Lis-ten to it, Lis-ten to it, Ev'-ry line is full of love.

233 *He that hath ears, let him hear.* (314)

2 Hear the heralds of the gospel
News from Zion's King proclaim:
"Pardon to each rebel sinner;
Free forgiveness in his name:"
Oh how gracious!
"Free forgiveness in his name."

3 Will you not receive the message—
Listen to the joyful word—
And embrace the news of pardon
Offered to you by the Lord?
Can you slight it—
Offered to you by the Lord?

4 O ye angels, hovering round us,
Waiting spirits, speed your way—
Haste ye to the court of heaven;
Tidings bear without delay;
Rebel sinners
Glad the message will obey.

234 *Friend of Sinners.* (263)

1 One there is above all others,
Well deserves the name of Friend;
His is love beyond a brother's,
Costly, free, and knows no end;
Hallelujah!
Costly, free, and knows no end.

2 Which of all our friends, to save us,
Could or would have shed his blood?
But this Savior died to have us
Reconciled in him to God;
Hallelujah!
Reconciled in him to God.

3 When he lived on earth abased,
Friend of sinners was his name;
Now above all glory raised,
He rejoices in the same;
Hallelujah!
He rejoices in the same.

235 *Love of God, all love excelling.* (1274)

1 Love of God, all love excelling!
How can I its wonders tell!
Now, my troubled spirit quelling,
Now, it breaks the powers of hell:
Oh what mercies
Start beneath its magic spell!

2 Love of God, all love embracing
In its wide-extended arms;
All our doubts and fears displacing,
Saves our souls from death's alarms:
Oh what sweetness
Dwells within its blissful charms!

3 Love of God, all love possessing!
Filling all our souls with joy;
Pouring on each heart a blessing
Which no time can e'er destroy:
Now may praises
All our hearts and tongues employ.

4 Love of God, all love extending
Far o'er sea and ocean strands;
Thou art on the breezes sending
Joyful news to distant lands:
May thy triumphs
Bind the world within thy bands.

8

THE GOLDEN SHORE. 8s & 7s, with Chorus.

WM. B. BRADBURY, by permission.

1. We are on the o-cean sail-ing, Homeward bound we sweetly glide;
We are on the o-cean sail-ing, To a home be-yond the tide.

Chorus.
All the storms will soon be o-ver, Then we'll an-chor in the har-bor;
We are out on the o-cean sail-ing, To a home be-yond the tide;
We are out on the o-cean sail-ing, To a home be-yond the tide.

236   *We are on the ocean sailing.*   (313)

2 Millions now are safely landed
 Over on the golden shore;
Millions more are on their journey,
 Yet there's room for millions more.

3 Come on board; oh ship for glory!
 Be in haste—make up your mind;
For our vessel's weighing anchor;
 You will soon be left behind.

4 You have kindred over yonder,
 On that bright and happy shore;
By and by we'll swell the number,
 When the toils of life are o'er.

5 Spread your sails, while heavenly breezes
 Gently waft our vessel on;
All on board are sweetly singing—
 Free salvation is the song.

6 When we all are safely landed
 Over on the shining shore,
We will walk about the city,
 And we'll sing for evermore.
 CHORUS.
All the storms of life are over,
 Landed in the port of glory:
Now no more on the ocean sailing—
 Safe at home beyond the tide.

THE GOSPEL INVITATIONS.

AMSTERDAM. 7s & 6s, Peculiar. German.

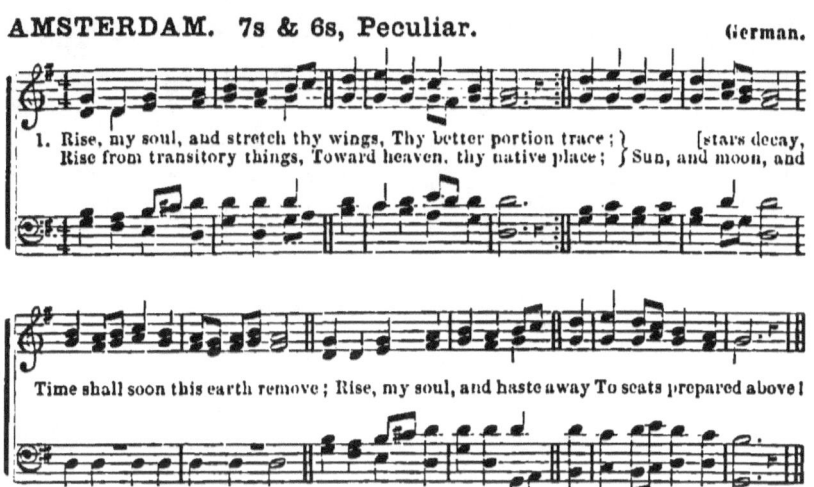

1. Rise, my soul, and stretch thy wings, Thy better portion trace; Rise from transitory things, Toward heaven, thy native place; [stars decay, Sun, and moon, and Time shall soon this earth remove; Rise, my soul, and haste away To seats prepared above!

237 *Aspiration.* (832)

2 Rivers to the ocean run,
Nor stay in all their course;
Fire ascending seeks the sun;
Both speed them to their source:
So a soul that's born of God
Pants to view his glorious face,
Upward tends to his abode,
To rest in his embrace.

3 Cease, ye pilgrims, cease to mourn;
Press onward to the prize;
Soon your Savior will return
Triumphant in the skies:
Yet a season, and you know
Happy entrance will be given—
All your sorrows left below,
And earth exchanged for heaven.

238 *My peace I give unto you.* (537)

1 Lamb of God! whose bleeding love
We now recall to mind,
Send thy blessing from above,
And let us mercy find;
Think on us, who think on thee;
Every burdened soul release;
Oh, remember Calvary,
And bid us go in peace!

2 By thine agonizing pain,
And bloody sweat, we pray—
By thy dying love to man,
Take all our sins away:

By thy passion on the tree,
Let our griefs and troubles cease:
Oh, remember Calvary,
And bid us go in peace!

239 *The alarm.* (317)

1 Stop, poor sinner, stop and think,
Before you further go:
Will you sport upon the brink
Of everlasting woe?
On the verge of ruin stop—
Now the friendly warning take—
Stay your footsteps—ere you drop
Into the burning lake.

2 Say, have you an arm like God,
That you his will oppose?
Fear ye not that iron rod
With which he breaks his foes?
Can you stand in that dread day
Which his justice shall proclaim—
When the earth shall melt away
Like wax before the flame?

3 Ghastly death will quickly come,
And drag you to his bar:
Then, to hear your awful doom,
Will fill you with despair!
All your sins will round you crowd—
You shall mark their crimson dye—
Each for vengeance crying loud;
And what can you reply?

THE GOSPEL INVITATIONS.

WOODWORTH. L. M. WM. B. BRADBURY, by permission.

1. Just as I am, with-out one plea, But that thy blood was shed for me, And that thou bid'st me come to thee, O Lamb of God, I come, I come!

240 *Just as I am.* (343)

2 Just as I am, and waiting not
To rid my soul of one dark blot—
To thee, whose blood can cleanse each spot,
  O Lamb of God, I come.

3 Just as I am, though tossed about
With many a conflict, many a doubt,
With fears within, and foes without—
  O Lamb of God, I come.

4 Just as I am, poor, wretched, blind,
Sight, riches, healing of the mind,
Yea, all I need, in thee to find,
  O Lamb of God, I come.

5 Just as I am, thou wilt receive,
Wilt welcome, pardon, cleanse, relieve,
Because thy promise I believe—
  O Lamb of God, I come.

6 Just as I am—thy love unknown,
Has broken every barrier down;
Now to be thine, yea, thine alone,
  O Lamb of God, I come.

241 *If any man thirst, etc.* (318)

1 Burdened with guilt, wouldst thou be blest?
Trust not the world; it gives no rest:
I bring relief to hearts oppressed:
  O weary sinner, come!

2 Come, leave thy burden at the cross;
Count all thy gains but empty dross:
My grace repays all earthly loss:
  O needy sinner, come!

3 Come, hither bring thy boding fears,
Thine aching heart, thy bursting tears;
'T is mercy's voice salutes thine ears:
  O trembling sinner, come!

4 "The Spirit and the Bride say, Come;"
Rejoicing saints re-echo, Come!
Who faints, who thirsts, who will, may come;
  Thy Savior bids thee come.

242 *God calling yet.* (339)

1 God calling yet! shall I not hear?
Earth's pleasures shall I still hold dear?
Shall life's swift passing years all fly,
And still my soul in slumbers lie?

2 God calling yet! shall I not rise?
Can I his loving voice despise,
And basely his kind care repay?
He calls me still; can I delay?

3 God calling yet! and shall he knock,
And I my heart the closer lock?
He still is waiting to receive,
And shall I dare his Spirit grieve?

4 God calling yet! and shall I give
No heed, but still in bondage live?
I wait, but he does not forsake;
He calls me still! my heart, awake!

5 God calling yet! I can not stay;
My heart I yield without delay;
Vain world, farewell! from thee I part;
The voice of God hath reached my heart.

Sessions, Key C.   Ward, Key B♭.   Devotion, Key C.

THE GOSPEL INVITATIONS. 93

WILL YOU GO? 8s & 3s.

1. We're trav'ling home to heaven a-bove, Will you go? Will you go? Will you go?
   To sing the Sa-vior's dy-ing love, Will you go? Will you go? Will you go?
D. C. And mil-lions more are on the road, Will you go? Will you go? Will you go?

Mil-lions have reached that blest abode, An-oint-ed kings and priests to God,

243 *Will you go?* (320)

2 We're going to see the bleeding Lamb,
   Will you go?
In rapturous strains to praise his name,
   Will you go?
The crown of life we there shall wear,
The conqueror's palms our hands shall bear,
And all the joys of heaven we'll share,
   Will you go?
3 We're going to join the heavenly choir,
   Will you go?
To raise our voice and tune the lyre,
   Will you go?

There saints and angels gladly sing
Hosanna to their God and King,
And make the heavenly arches ring,
   Will you go?
4 Oh could I hear some sinner say,
   I will go,
I'll start this moment—clear the way—
   Let me go!
My old companions, fare you well,
I will not go with you to hell,
With Jesus Christ I mean to dwell—
   Let me go—fare you well!

COME. 6s. (New.)   J. P. POWELL.

1. Sin-ner! come, 'mid thy gloom, All thy guilt con-fess-ing,
2. Sin-ner! come, while there's room, While the feast is wait-ing,

Trembling now, con-trite bow, Take the of-fered bless-ing.
While the Lord, by his word, Kind-ly is in-vit-ing.

244 *Sinner, come.* (319)

3 Sinner! come, ere thy doom
   Shall be sealed forever!
Now return, grieve and mourn,
   Flee to Christ the Savior.

4 Sinner! come to thy home,
   High in heaven gleaming!
To the sky lift thine eye,
   With true sorrow streaming.

FOUNTAIN OF LIFE. 9, 9, 9, 8. *

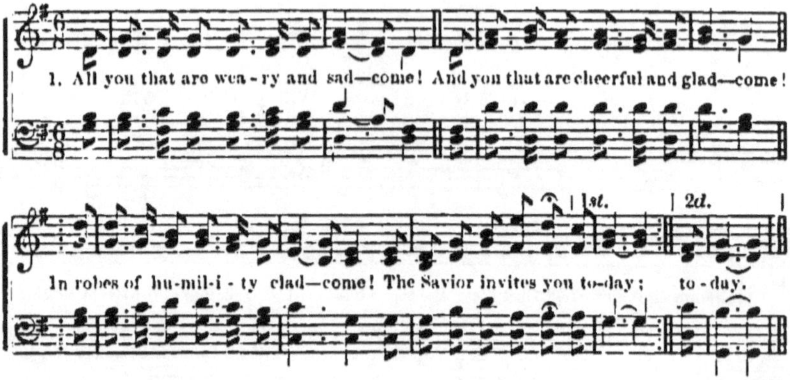
1. All you that are wea - ry and sad—come! And you that are cheerful and glad—come!
In robes of hu-mil-i - ty clad—come! The Savior invites you to-day; to - day.
1st.
2d.

245 *" The Spirit and the Bride say come."* (321)

2 Let youth in its freshness and bloom—come!
Let man in the pride of his noon—come!
Let age on the verge of the tomb—come!
Let none in his pride stay away.

3 Let the halt, and the maimed, and the blind—come!
Let all who are freely inclined—come!
With an humble and peaceable mind—come!
Away from the waters of strife.

4 The Spirit and Bride freely say—come!
And let him that heareth it, say—come!
And let him that thirsteth to-day—come!
And drink of the fountain of life.

CHILD OF SIN AND SORROW. 6s & 4s. Dr. T. HASTINGS.

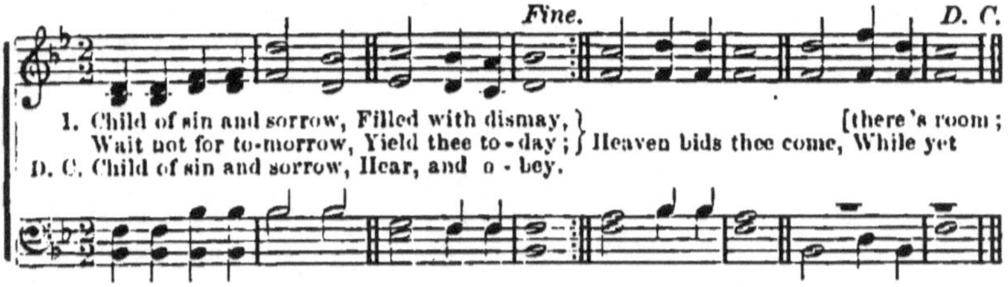
Fine.
D. C.
1. Child of sin and sorrow, Filled with dismay,
Wait not for to-morrow, Yield thee to - day;
Heaven bids thee come, While yet there's room;
D. C. Child of sin and sorrow, Hear, and o - bey.

246 *" The garment of praise."* (322)

2 Child of sin and sorrow,
Why wilt thou die?
Come while thou canst borrow
Help from on high:
Grieve not that love,
Which from above—
Child of sin and sorrow—
Would bring thee nigh.

3 Child of sin and sorrow,
Where wilt thou flee!
Through that long to-morrow,
Eternity!
Exiled from home,
Darkly to roam—
Child of sin and sorrow,
Where wilt thou flee?

4 Child of sin and sorrow,
Lift up thine eye!
Heirship thou canst borrow
In worlds on high!
In that high home,
Graven thy name:
Child of sin and sorrow,
Swift homeward fly!

THE LAND OF PROMISE. 6s & 7s.

Scotch.

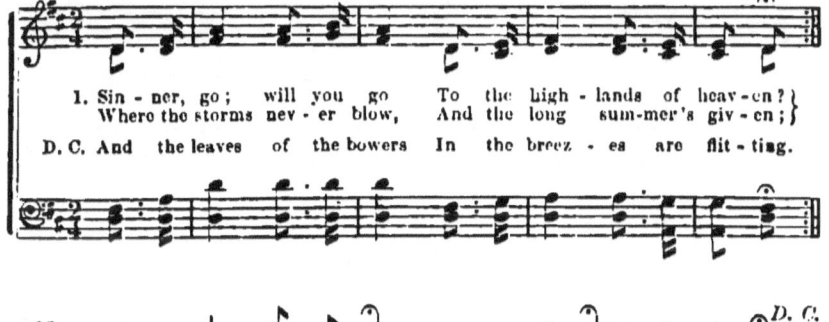

247 *The land of promise.* (327)

1. Sin-ner, go; will you go
To the high-lands of heav-en?
Where the storms nev-er blow,
And the long sum-mer's giv-en;

D. C. And the leaves of the bowers
In the breez-es are flit-ting.

Where the bright, bloom-ing flowers
Are their o-dors e-mit-ting;

2 Where the rich golden fruit
  Is in bright clusters pending,
And the deep laden boughs
  Of life's fair tree are bending;
And where life's crystal stream
  Is unceasingly flowing,
And the verdure is green,
  And eternally growing.

3 Where the saints, robed in white—
  Cleansed in life's flowing fountain—
Shining beauteous and bright,
  They inhabit the mountain;
Where no sin, nor dismay,
  Neither trouble nor sorrow,
Will be felt for a day,
  Nor be feared for the morrow.

4 He's prepared thee a home—
  Sinner, canst thou believe it?
And invites thee to come—
  Sinner, wilt thou receive it?
Oh come, sinner, come,
  For the tide is receding,
And the Savior will soon,
  And forever, cease pleading.

248 *The region above.* (1147)

1 There's a region above,
  Free from sin and temptation,
And a mansion of love,
  For each heir of salvation.
Then dismiss all thy fears,
  Weary pilgrim of sorrow;
Though thy sun set in tears,
  'T will rise brighter to-morrow.

2 There our toils will be done,
  And free grace be our story,
God himself be our Sun,
  And our unsetting glory.
In that world of delight
  Spring shall never be ended,
Nor shall shadows nor night
  With its brightness be blended.

3 There shall friends no more part,
  Nor shall farewells be spoken;
There 'll be balm for the heart
  That with anguish was broken.
From affliction set free,
  And from God ne'er to sever,
We his glory shall see,
  And enjoy him forever.

EXPOSTULATION. 11s.

1. Oh, turn you! oh, turn you, for why will you die, { When God in his mer-cy is com-ing so nigh? } { Now Jesus in-vites you, the Spir-it says, Come, } The brethren are waiting to welcome you home.

249 *Repent and turn.* (329)

2 How vain the delusion, that while you delay
Your hearts may grow better by staying away!
Come wretched, come starving, come just as you be,
Here streams of salvation are flowing most free.

3 Here Jesus is ready your souls to receive;
Oh how can you question, since now you believe?
Since sin is your burden, why will you not come?
He now bids you welcome—he now says there's room.

4 In riches, in pleasure, what can you obtain,
To soothe your affliction, or banish your pain;
To bear up your spirit, when summoned to die,
Or waft you to mansions of glory on high?

250 *Delay not.* (330)

1 Delay not, delay not, O sinner! draw near,
   The waters of life are now flowing for thee;
No price is demanded, the Savior is here,
   Redemption is purchased—salvation is free.

2 Delay not, delay not! why longer abuse
   The love and compassion of Jesus our Lord?
A fountain is opened—how canst thou refuse
   To wash and be cleansed in his pardoning blood?

3 Delay not, delay not, O sinner, to come!
   For mercy still lingers, and calls thee to-day;
Her voice is not heard in the vale of the tomb;
   Her message, unheeded, will soon pass away.

4 Delay not, delay not! the Spirit of grace,
   Long grieved and resisted, entreats thee to come;
Beware, lest in darkness thou finish thy race,
   And sink to the vale of eternity's gloom.

THE GOSPEL INVITATIONS.

THE EDEN ABOVE. P. M. (New.)   T. J. COOK.

1. We are bound for the land of the pure and the ho-ly, The home of the hap-py, the kingdom of love; Ye wanderers from God, in the broad road of fol-ly, Oh, say, will you go to the E-den a-bove? Will you go? Will you go? Oh, say, will you go to the E-den above?

2. In that bless-ed land neither sigh-ing nor an-guish Can breathe in the fields where the glo-ri-fied move. Ye heart-burdened ones, who in mis-e-ry languish, Oh, say, will you go to the E-den a-bove? Will you go? Will you go?

251   *The Eden above.*   (331)

3 Nor fraud, nor deceit, nor the hand of oppression,
  Can injure the dwellers in that holy grove;
No wickedness there, not a shade of transgression—
  O say, will you go to the Eden above?

4 Each saint has a mansion. prepared and all furnished,
  Ere from this clay house he is summoned to move;
Its gates and its towers with glory are burnished—
  O say, will you go to the Eden above?

5 March on, happy pilgrims, that land is before you,
  And soon its ten thousand delights we shall prove;
Yes, soon we shall walk o'er the hills of bright glory,
  And drink the pure joys of the Eden above.
    We will go, etc.

6 And yet, guilty sinner, we would not forsake thee;
  We halt yet a moment as onward we move;
Oh come to thy Lord, in his arms he will take thee,
  And bear thee along to the Eden above.

THE GOSPEL INVITATIONS.

WARNING. 12s & 11s.   W. B. BRADBURY, by permission.

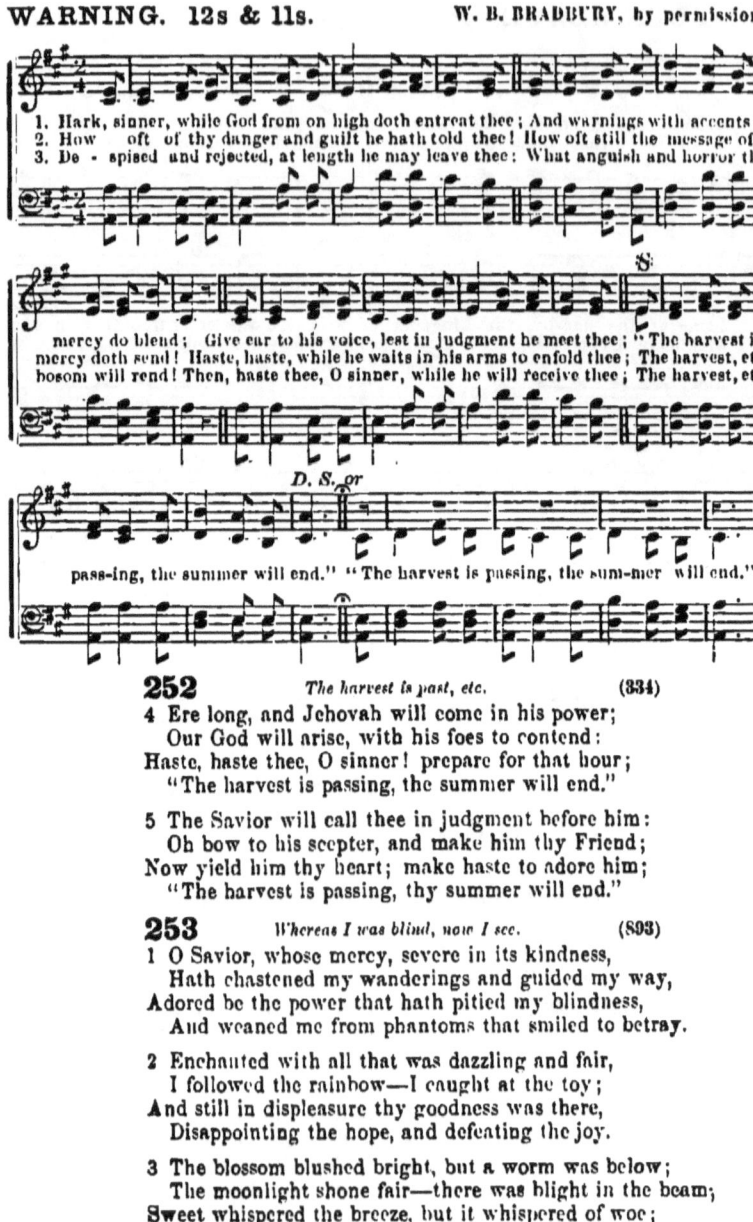

1. Hark, sinner, while God from on high doth entreat thee; And warnings with accents of
2. How oft of thy danger and guilt he hath told thee! How oft still the message of
3. De - spised and rejected, at length he may leave thee: What anguish and horror thy

mercy do blend; Give ear to his voice, lest in judgment he meet thee; "The harvest is
mercy doth send! Haste, haste, while he waits in his arms to enfold thee; The harvest, etc.
bosom will rend! Then, haste thee, O sinner, while he will receive thee; The harvest, etc.

pass-ing, the summer will end." "The harvest is passing, the sum-mer will end."

252   *The harvest is past, etc.*   (334)

4 Ere long, and Jehovah will come in his power;
   Our God will arise, with his foes to contend:
Haste, haste thee, O sinner! prepare for that hour;
   "The harvest is passing, the summer will end."

5 The Savior will call thee in judgment before him:
   Oh bow to his scepter, and make him thy Friend;
Now yield him thy heart; make haste to adore him;
   "The harvest is passing, thy summer will end."

253   *Whereas I was blind, now I see.*   (893)

1 O Savior, whose mercy, severe in its kindness,
   Hath chastened my wanderings and guided my way,
Adored be the power that hath pitied my blindness,
   And weaned me from phantoms that smiled to betray.

2 Enchanted with all that was dazzling and fair,
   I followed the rainbow—I caught at the toy;
And still in displeasure thy goodness was there,
   Disappointing the hope, and defeating the joy.

3 The blossom blushed bright, but a worm was below;
   The moonlight shone fair—there was blight in the beam;
Sweet whispered the breeze, but it whispered of woe;
   And bitterness flowed in the soft flowing stream.

THE GOSPEL INVITATIONS. 99

BILLOW. 8s, 7s & 4s. Dr. L. MASON, by permission.

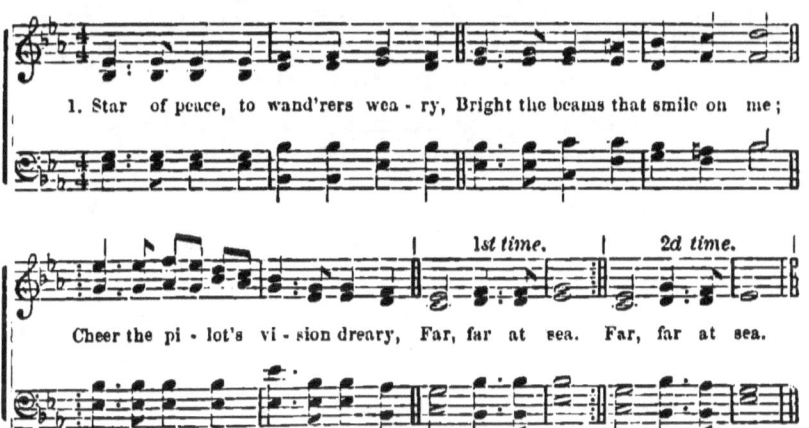

1. Star of peace, to wand'rers wea-ry, Bright the beams that smile on me; Cheer the pi-lot's vi-sion dreary, Far, far at sea. Far, far at sea.

254   *Far, far at sea.*   (1294)

2 Star of Hope, gleam on the billow,
Bless the soul that sighs for thee;
Bless the sailor's lonely pillow,
    Far, far at sea.

3 Star of faith, when winds are mocking
All his toil, he flies to thee;
Save him, on the billows rocking,
    Far, far at sea.

255   *Entreaty.*   (335)

1 Sinners, come, no longer wander;
Turn you from your evil way;
Precious time no longer squander:
    Come, come away.

2 Christ for you his life has offered,
What can you excusing say,
If you slight the pardon proffered?
    Come, come away.

3 Hold not back in hesitation,
There is danger in delay,
Haste, secure your soul's salvation,
    Come, come away.

256   *Book of grace.*   (21)

1 Book of grace, and book of glory!
Gift of God to age and youth;
Wondrous in thy sacred story,
    Bright, bright with truth.

2 Book of love! in accents tender,
Speaking unto such as we;
May it lead us, Lord, to render
    All, all to thee.

3 Book of hope! the spirit, sighing,
Consolation finds in thee;
As it hears the Savior crying—
    "Come, come to me."

4 Book of life! when we, reposing,
Bid farewell to friends we love,
Give us for the life then closing,
    Life, life above.

257   *Praise the Lord.*   (673)

1 Praise the Lord, ye saints, adore him,
All unite with one accord;
Bring your offerings, come before him—
    Oh praise the Lord.

2 Praise the Lord, who every blessing
On our heads hath richly poured;
Sing aloud, his love confessing—
    Oh praise the Lord.

3 Praise the Lord! who would not praise him?
He hath us to grace restored:
To the highest honors raise him—
    Oh praise the Lord.

4 Praise the Lord! your songs excelling
Worldly music's richest chord;
Sing—your Savior's glory telling;
    Oh praise the Lord.

GOSPEL—FAITH AND REPENTANCE.

DEVOTION. L. M. *

1. Show pi-ty, Lord! O Lord, for-give; Let a re-pent-ant re-bel live; Are not thy mer-cies large and free? May not a sin-ner trust in thee?

258 *The contrite heart.* (346)

2 My crimes, though great, can not surpass
The power and glory of thy grace;
Great God, thy nature hath no bound;
So let thy pardoning love be found.

3 Oh, wash my soul from every sin,
And make my guilty conscience clean;
Here, on my heart, the burden lies,
And past offenses pain my eyes.

4 My lips with shame my sins confess,
Against thy law, against thy grace;
Lord, should thy judgment grow severe,
I am condemned, but thou art clear.

5 Should sudden vengeance seize my breath,
I must pronounce thee just in death;
And if my soul were sent to hell,
Thy righteous law approves it well.

6 Yet save a trembling sinner, Lord,
Whose hope, still hovering round thy word,
Would light on some sweet promise there,
Some sure support against despair.

259 *His miracles.* (145)

1 Behold the blind their sight receive!
Behold the dead awake and live!
The damb speak wonders, and the lame
Leap like the hart, and bless his name!

2 Thus doth the Holy Spirit own
And seal the mission of the Son;
The Father vindicates his cause,
While he hangs bleeding on the cross.

260 *The wise choice.* (336)

1 Though all the world my choice deride,
Yet Jesus shall my portion be;
For I am pleased with none beside;
The fairest of the fair is he.

2 Sweet is the vision of thy face,
And kindness o'er thy lips is shed,
Lovely art thou, and full of grace,
And glory beams around thy head.

3 Thy sufferings I embrace with thee,
Thy poverty and shameful cross;
The pleasure of the world I flee,
And deem its treasures only dross.

4 Be daily dearer to my heart,
And ever let me feel thee near;
Then willingly with all I'd part,
Nor count it worthy of a tear.

261 *Restore unto me salvation.* (347)

1 A broken heart, my God, my King,
Is all the sacrifice I bring;
The God of grace will ne'er despise
A broken heart for sacrifice.

2 My soul lies humbled in the dust,
And owns thy dreadful sentence just;
Look down, O Lord, with pitying eye,
And save the soul condemned to die.

3 Then will I teach the world thy ways;
Sinners shall learn thy sovereign grace;
I'll lead them to my Savior's blood,
And they shall praise a pardoning God.

Woodworth, Key E♭.   Gratitude, Key E♭.   Windham, Key F.

GOSPEL—FAITH AND REPENTANCE. 101

PEACE, TROUBLED SOUL. L. M., 6 lines. MAZZINGHI.

262 *Come unto me, all ye that labor.* (350)

1 Peace, troubled soul, whose plaintive moan
  Hath taught each scene the notes of woe;
Cease thy complaint, suppress thy groan,
  And let thy tears forget to flow:
Behold the precious balm is found
To lull thy pain, to heal thy wound.

2 Come, freely come, by sin oppressed;
  On Jesus cast thy weighty load;
In him thy refuge find, thy rest,
  Safe in the mercy of thy God:
Thy God's thy Savior—glorious word!
Oh, hear, believe, and bless the Lord!

263 *Thy footsteps are not known.* (902)

1 Oh let my trembling soul be still,
  While darkness vails this mortal eye,
And wait thy wise, thy holy will,
  Wrapped yet in fears and mystery;
I can not, Lord, thy purpose see;
Yet all is well, since ruled by thee.

2 So trusting in thy love, I tread
  The narrow path of duty on:
What though some cherished joys are fled?
  What though some flattering dreams are gone?
Yet purer, nobler joys remain,
And peace is won through conquered pain.

He leadeth me, Key D. Amber. Key F.

102 GOSPEL—FAITH AND REPENTANCE.

IDUMEA. S. M. ✤

1. Did Christ o'er sin-ners weep, And shall our cheeks be dry? Let tears of pen-i-ten-tial grief Flow forth from ev-ery eye.

264 *He beheld the city and wept over it.* (161)

2 The Son of God in tears,
The wondering angels see:
Be thou astonished, O my soul!
He shed those tears for thee.

3 He wept, that we might weep—
Each sin demands a tear;
In heaven alone no sin is found,
And there's no weeping there.

265 *God's mercy to the penitent.* (366)

1 Sweet is the friendly voice
Which speaks of life and peace;
Which bids the penitent rejoice,
And sin and sorrow cease.

2 No balm on earth like this
Can cheer the contrite heart;
No flattering dreams of earthly bliss
Such pure delight impart.

3 Still merciful and kind,
Thy mercy, Lord, reveal;
The broken heart thy love can bind,
The wounded spirit heal.

266 *Yielding.* (365)

1 And can I yet delay
My little all to give—
To tear my soul from earth away
For Jesus to receive?

2 Nay, but I yield, I yield;
I can hold out no more;
I sink, by dying love compelled,
And own thee Conqueror.

3 Though late, I all forsake;
My friends, my all, resign:
Gracious Redeemer! take, oh take,
And seal me ever thine!

4 Come, and possess me whole,
Nor hence again remove;
Settle and fix my wavering soul
With all thy weight of love.

5 My one desire be this:
Thy only love to know;
To seek and taste no other bliss,
No other good below.

267 *You shall find rest for your souls.* (364)

1 Ah! what avails my strife,
My wandering to and fro?
Thou hast the words of endless life;
Ah! whither should I go?

2 Thy condescending grace
To me did freely move;
It calls me still to seek thy face,
And stoops to ask my love.

3 Lord, at thy feet I fall;
I long to be set free;
I fain would now obey the call,
And give up all for thee.

Golden Hill, Key F. Dennis, Key F. Kentucky, Key A♭.

GOSPEL—FAITH AND REPENTANCE. 103

ALETTA. 7s, 6 Lines. WM. B. BRADBURY, by permission.

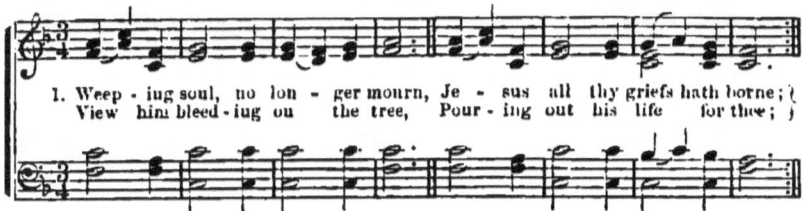

1. Weep-ing soul, no lon-ger mourn, Je-sus all thy griefs hath borne;
View him bleed-ing on the tree, Pour-ing out his life for thee;

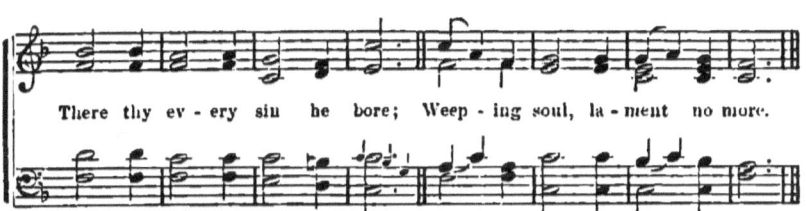

There thy ev-ery sin he bore; Weep-ing soul, la-ment no more.

268 *He hath borne our griefs.* (946)

2 Cast thy guilty soul on him,
Find him mighty to redeem;
At his feet thy burden lay,
Look thy doubts and fears away;
Now by faith the Son embrace,
Plead his promise, trust his grace.

269 *Jesus, Savior, pity me.* (947)

1 Pity, Lord! this child of clay,
Who can only weep and pray—
Only on thy love depend:
Thou who art the sinner's Friend;
Thou the sinner's only plea—
Jesus, Savior, pity me!

2 From thy flock, a straying Lamb,
Tender Shepherd, though I am;
Now, upon the mountain cold,
Lost, I long to gain the fold,
And within thine arms to be:
Jesus, Savior, pity me!

3 Oh where stillest streams are poured,
In green pastures lead me, Lord!
Bring me back where angels sound
Joy to the poor wanderer found;
Evermore my Shepherd be:
Jesus, Savior, pity me!

270 *Heavenly places.* (571)

1 If 't is sweet to mingle where
Christians meet for social prayer;
If 't is sweet with them to raise
Songs of holy joy and praise—
Passing sweet that state must be
Where they meet eternally.

2 Savior, may these meetings prove
Antepasts to that above;
While we worship in this place,
May we go from grace to grace,
Till we each, in his degree,
Fit for endless glory be.

271 *My peace I give unto you.* (300)

1 Ye who in his courts are found
Listening to the joyful sound,
Lost and hopeless as ye are,
Sons of sorrow, sin, and care,
Glorify the King of kings;
Take the peace the gospel brings.

2 Turn to Christ your longing eyes;
View his bleeding sacrifice;
See in him your sins forgiven,
Pardon, holiness, and heaven;
Glorify the King of kings;
Take the peace the gospel brings.

Rosefield, Key B♭.   Horton, Key B♭.   Rock of Ages, Key B♭.

104 GOSPEL—FAITH AND REPENTANCE.

HORTON. 7s.   WARTENSEE.

1. Love for all! and can it be? Can I hope it is for me? I, who strayed so long a-go, Strayed so far, and fell so low!

272 *Father, I have sinned.* (367)
2 I, the disobedient child,
Wayward, passionate, and wild;
I, who left my Father's home
In forbidden ways to roam!
3 I, who spurned his loving hold,
I, who would not be controlled;
I, who would not hear his call,
I, the willful prodigal!
4 I, who wasted and misspent
Every talent he had lent;
I, who sinned again, again,
Giving every passion rein!
5 To my Father can I go?
At his feet myself I'll throw,
In his house there yet may be
Place—a servant's place—for me.
6 See: my Father waiting stands;
See: he reaches out his hands;
God is love! I know, I see,
Love for me—yes, even me.

273 *The night is passed.* (310)
1 Weeping sinners, dry your tears;
Jesus on the throne appears;
Mercy comes with balmy wing,
Bids you his salvation sing.
2 Peace he brings you by his death,
Peace he speaks with every breath:
Can you slight such heavenly charms?
Flee, oh flee to Jesus' arms.

274 *Bond of peace.* (499)
1 Jesus, Lord, we look to thee;
Let us in thy name agree;
Show thyself the Prince of Peace;
Bid our jars forever cease.
2 By thy reconciling love,
Every stumbling-block remove;
Each to each unite, endear;
Come, and spread thy banner here.
3 Make of us one heart and mind—
Courteous, pitiful, and kind:
Lowly, meek, in thought and word—
Altogether like our Lord.
4 Let us for each other care;
Each the other's burden bear:
To thy church the pattern give;
Show how true believers live.
5 Free from anger and from pride,
Let us thus in God abide;
All the depths of love express—
All the heights of holiness.

275 *Lead me, O Lord.* (575)
1 Shepherd of thy little flock,
Lead me to the shadowing rock,
Where the richest pasture grows;
Where the living water flows;
2 By that pure and silent stream.
Sheltered from the scorching beam;
Shepherd, Savior, Guardian, Guide,
Keep me ever near thy side.

Rosefield, Key B♭. Wilson, Key G. Pleyel, Key G.

THE GOSPEL—BAPTISM. 105

STONEFIELD. L. M.   **STANLEY.**

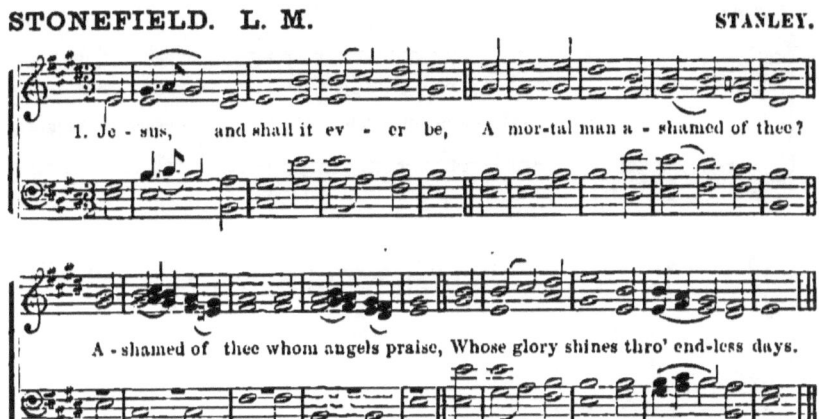

1. Jesus, and shall it ever be, A mortal man ashamed of thee? Ashamed of thee whom angels praise, Whose glory shines thro' endless days.

276   *Ashamed of Jesus.*   (373)

2 Ashamed of Jesus! Sooner far
Let evening blush to own a star!
He sheds the beams of light divine
O'er this benighted soul of mine.

3 Ashamed of Jesus! Just as soon
Let morning be ashamed of noon!
'T is midnight with my soul till he,
Bright Morning Star, bid darkness flee.

4 Ashamed of Jesus—that dear friend
On whom my hopes of heaven depend!
No! when I blush, be this my shame,
That I no more revere his name.

5 Ashamed of Jesus! Yes, I may,
When I 've no guilt to wash away,
No tear to wipe, no good to crave,
No fears to quell, no soul to save.

6 Till then—nor is my boasting vain—
Till then I 'll boast a Savior slain!
And oh! may this my glory be,
That Christ is not ashamed of me!

7 His institutions would I prize,
Take up my cross, the shame despise—
Dare to defend his noble cause,
And yield obedience to his laws.

277   *Christ's example.*   (376)

1 Our Savior bowed beneath the wave,
And meekly sought a watery grave:
Come, see the sacred path he trod—
A path well-pleasing to our God.

2 His voice we hear, his footsteps trace,
And hither come to seek his face,
To do his will, to feel his love,
And join our songs with songs above.

3 Hosanna to the Lamb divine!
Let endless glories round him shine!
High o'er the heavens forever reign.
O Lamb of God! for sinners slain.

278   *The spirit of obedience.*   (374)

1 We love thy name, we love thy laws,
And joyfully embrace thy cause;
We love thy cross, the shame, the pain
O Lamb of God! for sinners slain.

2 We sink beneath the mystic flood:
Oh bathe us in thy cleansing blood!
We die to sin, and seek a grave
With thee beneath the yielding wave.

3 And as we rise, with thee to live,
Oh let the Holy Spirit give
The sealing unction from above,
The breath of life, the fire of love!

279   *A baptismal hymn.*   (378)

1 The great Redeemer we adore,
Who came the lost to seek and save,
Went humbly down from Jordan's shore
To find a tomb beneath its wave!

2 With thee, into thy watery tomb,
Lord, 't is our glory to descend;
'T is wondrous grace that gives us room
To share the grave of such a friend!

Hebron, Key B♭.   Sessions, Key C.   Woodworth, Key E♭.

THE GOSPEL—BAPTISM.

AZMON. C. M. From GLASER.

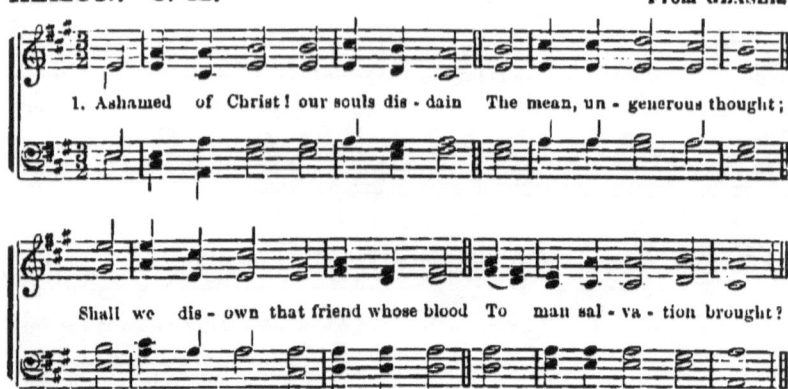

1. Ashamed of Christ! our souls disdain
The mean, ungenerous thought;
Shall we disown that friend whose blood
To man salvation brought?

280 *He that is ashamed of me, etc.* (381)

2 With the glad news of love and peace,
From heaven to earth he came;
For us endured the painful cross,
For us despised the shame.

3 To his command let us submit
Ourselves without delay;
Our lives—yea, thousand lives of ours—
His love can ne'er repay.

4 Each faithful follower Jesus views
With infinite delight;
Their lives to him are dear—their death
Is precious in his sight.

5 To bear his name—his cross to bear—
Our highest honor this!
Who nobly suffers for him now,
Shall reign with him in bliss.

281 *Hinder me not.* (380)

1 In all my Lord's appointed ways,
My journey I'll pursue;
Hinder me not, you much-loved saints,
For I must go with you.

2 Through floods and flames, if Jesus lead,
I'll follow where he goes;
Hinder me not, shall be my cry,
Though earth and hell oppose.

3 Through trials and through sufferings, too,
I'll go at his command;
Hinder me not, for I am bound
To my Immanuel's land.

4 And when my Savior calls me home,
Still this my cry shall be:
Hinder me not—come, welcome death,
I'll gladly go with thee.

282 *Glorying in the cross.* (355)

1 Didst thou, Lord Jesus, suffer shame,
And bear the cross for me?
And shall I fear to own thy name,
Or thy disciple be?

2 Forbid it, Lord, that I should dread
To suffer shame or loss:
Oh let me in thy footsteps tread,
And glory in thy cross.

283 *Call to repentance.* (356)

1 Repent! the voice celestial cries,
No longer dare delay:
The soul that scorns the mandate dies,
And meets a fiery day.

2 No more the sovereign eye of God
O'erlooks the crimes of men;
His heralds now are sent abroad
To warn the world of sin.

3 O sinners! in his presence bow,
And all your guilt confess;
Accept the offered Savior now,
Nor trifle with his grace.

4 Soon will the awful trumpet sound,
And call you to his bar;
His mercy knows the appointed bound,
And yields to justice there.

Arlington, Key G. Ortonville, Key B♭. Brown, Key C.

THE GOSPEL—REMISSION OF SINS.

284 *He left us an example.* (382)

1 Buried beneath the yielding wave
  The great Redeemer lies;
  Faith views him in the watery grave,
  And thence beholds him rise.

2 With joy we in his footsteps tread,
  And would his cause maintain,
  Like him be numbered with the dead,
  And with him rise and reign.

3 Now, blest Redeemer, we to thee
  Our grateful voices raise:
  Washed in the fountain of thy blood,
  Our lives shall be thy praise.

285 *Not as the world giveth.* (402)

1 How happy is the Christian's state!
  His sins are all forgiven;
  A cheering ray confirms the grace,
  And lifts his hopes to heaven.

2 Though in the rugged path of life
  He heaves the pensive sigh;
  Yet, trusting in his God, he finds
  Delivering grace is nigh.

3 If, to prevent his wandering steps,
  He feels the chastening rod,
  The gentle stroke shall bring him back
  To his forgiving God.

4 And when the welcome message comes
  To call his soul away,
  His soul in raptures shall ascend
  To everlasting day.

286 *I was blind, but now I see.* (403)

1 Amazing grace! (how sweet the sound!)
  That saved a wretch like me!
  I once was lost, but now am found;
  Was blind, but now I see.

2 Through many dangers, toils, and snares
  I have already come;
  T is grace has brought me safe thus far,
  And grace will lead me home.

3 The Lord has promised good to me,
  His word my hope secures;
  He will my shield and portion be
  As long as life endures.

4 Yes, when this heart and flesh shall fail,
  And mortal life shall cease,
  I shall possess within the vail
  A life of joy and peace.

287 *Newness of life.* (404)

1 How happy every child of grace,
  Who knows his sins forgiven!
  This earth, he cries, is not my place—
  I seek my home in heaven.

2 A country far from mortal sight,
  Yet oh, by faith I see
  The land of rest, the saints delight,
  The heaven prepared for me.

3 Oh what a blessed hope is ours!
  While here on earth we stay,
  We more than taste the heavenly powers,
  And antedate that day.

4 We feel the resurrection near,
  Our life in Christ concealed,
  And with his glorious presence here,
  Our earthen vessels filled.

5 Oh, would he all of heaven bestow!
  Then like our Lord we'll rise;
  Our bodies, fully ransomed, go
  To take the glorious prize.

6 On him with rapture then I'll gaze,
  Who bought the bliss for me,
  And shout and wonder at his grace,
  Through all eternity.

288 *A plea for mercy.* (361)

1 Mercy alone can meet my case,
  For mercy, Lord, I cry;
  Jesus, Redeemer, show thy face
  In mercy, or I die.

2 I perish, and my doom were just;
  But wilt thou leave me? No!
  I hold thee fast, my hope, my trust;
  I will not let thee go.

3 To thee, thee only will I cleave;
  Thy word is all my plea;
  That word is truth, and I believe—
  Have mercy, Lord, on me.

Dunlap's Creek, Key F. Cambridge, Key B♭. Marlow, Key G. Peterboro, Key G.

108 THE GOSPEL—REMISSION OF SINS.

ST. THOMAS. S. M.

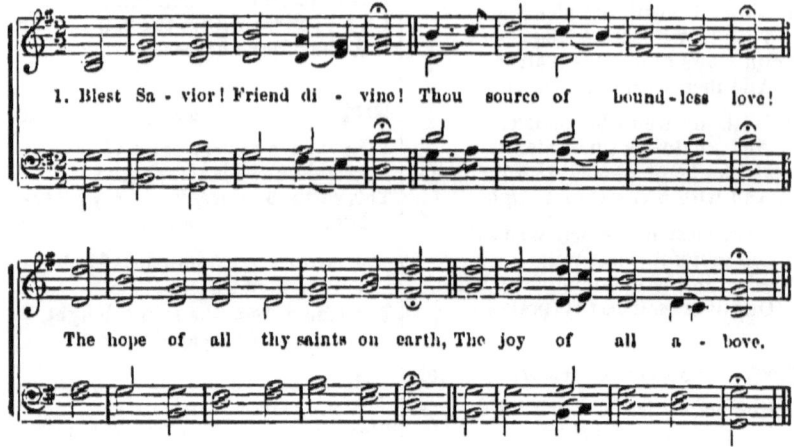

1. Blest Sa-vior! Friend di-vine! Thou source of bound-less love! The hope of all thy saints on earth, The joy of all a-bove.

289   Psalm 139: 6.   (406)

2 How can I tell thy worth!
  How make thy glories known!
No language can thy goodness speak,
  No tongue thy mercies own!

3 My words can not express
  The sweetness of thy name!
Nor can my feeble lips declare
  The wonders of thy fame!

4 Then take my trusting heart,
  I can not give thee more;
Make rich my soul's deep poverty,
  From thine unwasting store!

290   The same.   (387)

1 Savior, thy law we love,
  Thy pure example bless,
And with a firm, unwavering zeal,
  Would in thy footsteps press.

2 Not to the fiery pains
  By which the martyrs bled;
Not to the scourge, the thorn, the cross,
  Our favored feet are led—

3 But, at this peaceful tide,
  Assembled in thy fear,
The homage of obedient hearts,
  We humbly offer here.

291   Thus it becometh us.   (389)

1 With willing hearts we tread
  The path the Savior trod;
We love th' example of our Head,
  The glorious Lamb of God.

2 On thee, on thee alone,
  Our hope and faith rely;
Oh thou who didst for sin atone,
  Who didst for sinners die.

3 We trust thy sacrifice,
  To thy dear cross we flee,
Oh, may we die to sin, and rise
  To life and bliss in thee.

292   That they may be one in us.   (419)

1 Thy Spirit shall unite
  Our souls to thee, our Head;
Shall form us to thine image bright,
  That we thy paths may tread.

2 Death may our souls divide
  From these abodes of clay;
But love shall keep us near thy side
  Through all the gloomy way.

3 Since Christ and we are one,
  Why should we doubt or fear?
If he in heaven hath fixed his throne,
  He'll fix his members there.

Gerar, Key F.   Laban, Key C.   Boylston, Key C.

THE GOSPEL—REMISSION OF SINS.

CRANBROOK. S. M. — THOMAS CLARK.

1. Grace! 'tis a charming sound, Harmonious to the ear; Heaven with the echo shall resound, Heaven with the echo shall resound, And all the earth shall hear, And all the earth shall hear, And all the earth shall hear, And all the earth shall hear.

293 *By grace are ye saved.* (405)

2 Grace first contrived the way
To save rebellious man;
And all the steps that grace display,
Which drew the wondrous plan.

3 Grace led our wandering feet
To tread the heavenly road;
And new supplies each hour we meet
While pressing on to God.

4 Grace all the work shall crown
Through everlasting days;
It lays in heaven the topmost stone,
And well deserves our praise.

294 *His compassions fail not.* (652)

1 How various and how new
Are thy compassions, Lord!

Each morning shall thy mercies show,
Each night thy truth record.

2 Thy goodness, like the sun,
Dawned on our early days,
Ere infant reason had begun
To form our lips to praise.

3 Each object we beheld
Gave pleasure to our eyes;
And nature all our senses held
In bands of sweet surprise.

4 But pleasures more refined
Awaited that blest day,
When light arose upon our mind
And chased our sins away.

5 How new thy mercies, then!
How sovereign and how free!
Our souls, that had been dead in sin,
Were made alive to thee.

THE GOSPEL—REMISSION OF SINS.

MIGDOL. L. M. Dr. L. MASON, by permission.

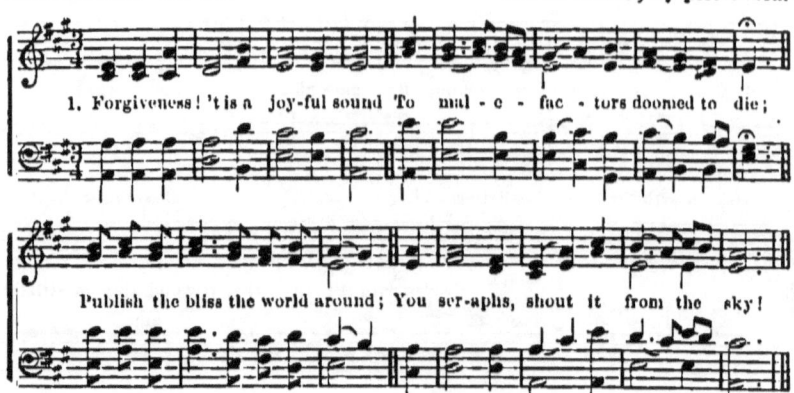

295 *The joys of pardon.* (395)

1 Forgiveness! 'tis a joyful sound
  To malefactors doomed to die:
Publish the bliss the world around;
  You seraphs, shout it from the sky!

2 'T is the rich gift of love divine;
  'T is full, outmeasuring every crime;
Unclouded shall its glories shine,
  And feel no change by changing time.

3 For this stupendous love of heaven,
  What grateful honors shall we show?
Where much transgression is forgiven,
  Let love in equal ardors glow.

4 By this inspired, let all our days
  With gospel holiness be crowned;
Let truth and goodness, prayer and praise,
  In all abide, in all abound.

296 *Rev. 11: 15.* (1269)

1 Soon may the last glad song arise
Through all the millions of the skies—
That song of triumph, which records
That all the earth is now the Lord's.

2 Let thrones and powers and kingdoms be
Obedient, mighty God! to thee;
And over land, and stream, and main,
Now wave the scepter of thy reign.

3 Oh let that glorious anthem swell!
Let host to host the triumph tell,
That not one rebel heart remains,
But over all the Savior reigns.

297 *Blessed is the man whose sin, etc.* (396)

1 Earth has a joy unknown in heaven—
The new-born joy of sins forgiven!
Tears of such pure and deep delight,
O angels! never dimmed your sight.

2 You saw of old on chaos rise
The beauteous pillars of the skies;
You know where morn exulting springs,
And evening folds her drooping wings.

3 Bright heralds of the Eternal Will,
Abroad his errands you fulfill;
Or, throned in floods of beamy day,
Symphonious in his presence play.

4 Loud is the song—the heavenly plain
Is shaken with the choral strain;
And dying echoes, floating far,
Draw music from each chiming star.

5 But I amid your choirs shall shine,
And all your knowledge shall be mine;
You on your harps must lean to hear
A secret chord that mine shall bear.

298 *His mercy endureth forever.* (637)

1 Oh render thanks to God above,
The fountain of eternal love!
Whose mercy firm through ages past
Has stood, and shall forever last.

2 Who can his mighty deeds express,
Not only vast, but numberless!
What mortal eloquence can raise
His tribute of immortal praise!

Hamburg, Key F.   Ward, Key B♭.   Gratitude, Key E♭.

THE GOSPEL—REMISSION OF SINS. 111

DICKINSON. L. M.   S. J. VAIL, by permission.

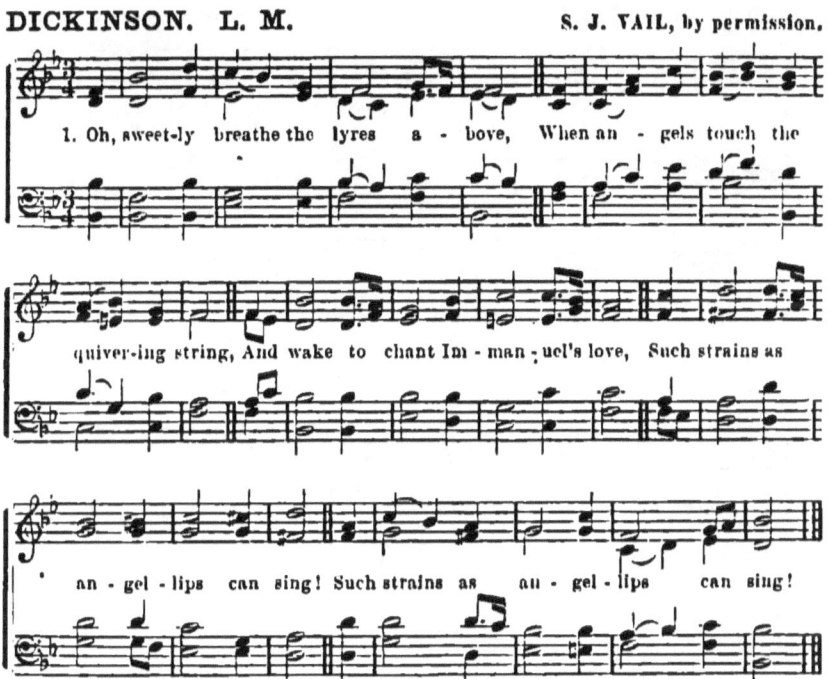

1. Oh, sweetly breathe the lyres above, When angels touch the quivering string, And wake to chant Immanuel's love, Such strains as angel-lips can sing! Such strains as angel-lips can sing!

299   *Joy of consecration to Christ.*   (399)
2 And sweet, on earth, the choral swell,
    From mortal tongues, of gladsome lays;
When pardoned souls their raptures tell,
    And, grateful, hymn Immanuel's praise.

3 Jesus, thy name our souls adore;
    We own the bond that makes us thine;
And carnal joys, that charmed before,
    For thy dear sake we now resign.

4 Our hearts, by dying love subdued,
    Accept thine offered grace to-day;
Beneath the cross, with blood bedewed,
    We bow, and give ourselves away.

300   *The beatitudes.*   (411)
1 Blessed are the humble souls that see
    Their emptiness and poverty;
Treasures of grace to them are given,
    And crowns of joy laid up in heaven.

2 Blessed are the men of broken heart,
    Who mourn for sin with inward smart;
The blood of Christ divinely flows,
    A healing balm for all their woes.

3 Blessed are the souls who thirst for grace,
    Hunger and thirst for righteousness;
They shall be well supplied and fed
    With living streams and living bread.

4 Blessed are the men of peaceful life,
    Who quench the glowing coals of strife;
They shall be called the heirs of bliss,
    The sons of God, the God of peace.

301   *The hour of worship.*   (679)
1 Blest hour, when mortal man retires
    To hold communion with his God,
To send to heaven his warm desires,
    And listen to the sacred word.

2 Blest hour, when earthly cares resign
    Their empire o'er his anxious breast,
While, all around, the calm divine,
    Proclaims the holy day of rest.

3 Blest hour when God himself draws nigh,
    Well pleased his people's voice to hear,
To hush the penitential sigh,
    And wipe away the mourner's tear.

Migdol, Key A.   Woodworth, Key E♭.   Sessions, Key C.

112 THE GOSPEL—REMISSION OF SINS.

ROWLEY. 11s & 9s. Arranged by Dr. L. MASON.

1. How happy are they who their Savior obey, And have laid up their treasures above! Tongue can not express the sweet comfort and peace Of a soul in its earliest love, Of a soul in its earliest love!
2. This comfort is mine, since the favor divine I have found in the blood of the Lamb! Since the truth I believed, what a joy I've received, What a heaven in Jesus' blest name, What a heaven in Jesus' blest name!

302 *Joy unspeakable and full of glory.* (408)

3 'Tis a heaven below my Redeemer to know,
  And the angels can do nothing more
Than to fall at his feet and the story repeat,
  And the lover of sinners adore!

4 Jesus all the day long is my joy and my song;
  Oh that all to this refuge may fly!
He has loved me, I cried, he has suffered and died
  To redeem such a rebel as I!

5 On the wings of his love I am carried above
  All my sin and temptation and pain;
Oh why should I grieve, while on him I believe!
  Oh why should I sorrow again!

6 Oh the rapturous height of that holy delight,
  Which I find in the life-giving blood!
Of my Savior possessed, I am perfectly blessed,
  Being filled with the fullness of God!

7 Now my remnant of days will I spend to his praise
  Who has died me from sin to redeem;
Whether many or few, all my years are his due;
  They shall all be devoted to him.

8 What a mercy is this? what a heaven of bliss!
  How unspeakably happy am I!
Gathered into the fold, with believers enrolled—
  With believers to live and to die!

NILLEN. 6s.

1. Cling to the Crucified! For thee, fast from his side,
His eye shall guard thee well— The crimson current fell.

303 *Cling to the Crucified.* (372)

2 Cling to the Crucified!
  My weary feet in peace
  dis tender hand shall guide
  Till all my wanderings cease.

3 Cling to the Crucified!
  His love the golden door
  For thee shall open wide,
  And bless thee evermore.

THE GOSPEL—REMISSION OF SINS. 113

HALLE. 7s, 6 lines. Arr. by Dr. HASTINGS.

1. Jesus, Lamb of God, for me
   Thou, the Lord of life, didst die;
   Whither—whither, but to thee,
   Can a trembling sinner fly?
   Death's dark waters o'er me roll;
   Save, oh, save my sinking soul.

304 *Lord, save me.* (390)

2 Never bowed a martyred head,
   Weighed with equal sorrow down;
Never blood so rich was shed,
   Never king wore such a crown!
To thy cross and sacrifice,
Faith now lifts her tearful eyes.

3 All my soul, by love subdued,
   Melts in deep contrition there;
By thy mighty grace renewed,
   New-born hope forbids despair;
Lord, thou canst my guilt forgive,
Thou hast bid me look and live.

4 While with broken heart I kneel,
   Sinks the inward storm to rest;
Life—immortal life—I feel
   Kindled in my throbbing breast;
Thine—forever thine—I am,
Glory to the bleeding Lamb!

305 *The soul panting for God.* (823)

1 As the hart, with eager looks,
   Panteth for the water-brooks,
So my soul, athirst for thee,
   Pants the living God to see:
When, oh when, with filial fear,
Lord, shall I to thee draw near?

2 Why art thou cast down, my soul?
   God, thy God, shall make thee whole:
Why art thou disquieted?
   God shall lift thy fallen head,
And his countenance benign
Be the saving health of thine.

306 *He is our peace.* (302)

1 Weary souls, that wander wide
   From the central point of bliss,
Turn to Jesus crucified:
   Fly to those dear wounds of his;
Sink into the purple flood,
Rise into the life of God.

2 Find in Christ the way of peace,
   Peace unspeakable, unknown;
By his pain he gives you ease,
   Life, by his expiring groan:
Rise, exalted by his fall;
Find in Christ your all in all.

3 Oh believe the record true,
   God to you his Son hath given!
You may now be happy too;
   Find on earth the life of heaven;
Live the life of heaven above,
All the life of glorious love.

307 *As a weaned child.* (920)

1 Quiet, Lord, my froward heart,
   Make me teachable and mild,
Upright, simple, free from art,
   Make me as a weaned child;
From distrust and envy free,
Pleased with all that pleases thee.

2 What thou shalt to-day provide,
   Let me as a child receive:
What to-morrow may betide,
   Calmly to thy wisdom leave;
'Tis enough that thou wilt care—
Why should I the burden bear?

Rosefield, Key B♭.   Alletta, Key F.   Rock of Ages, Key B♭.

114 THE GOSPEL—HOPE OF ETERNAL LIFE.

DESIRE. L. M.

1. How vain is all beneath the skies! How transient ev'ry earthly bliss! How slender all the fondest ties That bind us to a world like this!

308 *Our life is a vapor.* (426)

2 The evening cloud, the morning dew,
  The withering grass, the fading flower,
Of earthly hopes are emblems true—
  The glory of a passing hour.

3 But though earth's fairest blossoms die,
  And all beneath the skies is vain,
There is a brighter world on high,
  Beyond the reach of care and pain.

4 Then let the hope of joys to come
  Dispel our cares and chase our fears;
If God be ours, we're traveling home,
  Though passing through a vale of tears.

309 *In Christ.* (412)

1 God of my life! thy boundless grace
  Chose, pardoned, and adopted me:
My rest, my home, my dwelling-place—
  Father! I come, I come to thee.

2 Jesus, my Hope, my Rock, my Shield!
  Whose precious blood was shed for me,
Into thy hands my soul I yield—
  Savior! I come, I come to thee.

310 *The bread of life.* (518)

1 Away from earth my spirit turns—
  Away from every transient good;
With strong desire my bosom burns
  To feast on heaven's diviner food.

2 Thou, Savior, art the living bread;
  Thou wilt my every want supply;
By thee sustained, and cheered, and led,
  I'll press through dangers to the sky.

3 What though temptations oft distress,
  And sin assails and breaks my peace,
Thou wilt uphold, and save, and bless,
  And bid the storms of passion cease.

4 Then let me take thy gracious hand,
  And walk beside thee onward still,
Till my glad feet shall safely stand
  Forever firm on Zion's hill.

311 *Repose in God's wisdom.* (767)

1 Whither, oh whither should I fly
  But to my loving Father's breast!
Secure within thine arms to lie,
  And safe beneath thy wings to rest!

2 In all my ways thy hand I own,
  Thy ruling providence I see:
Assist me still my course to run,
  And still direct my paths to thee.

3 I have no skill the snare to shun;
  But thou, O God, my wisdom art!
I ever into ruin run;
  But thou art greater than my heart.

4 Foolish, and impotent, and blind,
  Lead me a way I have not known;
Bring me where I my heaven may find—
  The heaven of loving thee alone!

Hamburg, Key F.   Zephyr, Key C.   Gratitude, Key E♭.

THE GOSPEL—HOPE OF ETERNAL LIFE.

VARINA. C. M., Double. German.

1. There is a land of pure delight, Where saints immortal reign, Infinite day excludes the night, And pleasures banish pain. There everlasting spring abides, And never-with'ring flow'rs; Death, like a narrow sea, divides This heav'nly land from ours.

312 *The land of promise.* (428)

2 Sweet fields, beyond the swelling flood,
Stand dressed in living green;
So to the Jews old Canaan stood,
While Jordan rolled between.
But timorous mortals start and shrink
To cross this narrow sea,
And linger, shivering, on the brink,
And fear to launch away.

3 Oh could we make our doubts remove,
Those gloomy doubts that rise,
And see the Canaan that we love,
With unbeclouded eyes;
Could we but climb where Moses stood,
And view the landscape o'er,
Not Jordan's stream, nor death's cold flood,
Should fright us from the shore.

313 *We all shall meet in heaven.* (430)

1 Hail, sweetest, dearest tie! that binds
Our glowing hearts in one;
Hail, sacred hope! that tunes our minds
To harmony divine.
It is the hope, the blissful hope,
Which Jesus' grace has given—
The hope, when days and years are past,
We all shall meet in heaven.

2 What though the northern wintry blast
Shall howl around our cot;
What though beneath an eastern sun
Be cast our distant lot;
Yet still we share the blissful hope
Which Jesus' grace has given—
The hope, when days and years are past,
We all shall meet in heaven.

3 From eastern shores, from northern lands,
From western hill and plain,
From southern climes, the brother-bands
May hope to meet again.
It is the hope, the blissful hope,
Which Jesus' grace has given—
The hope, when life and time are o'er,
We all shall meet in heaven.

4 From Burmah's shores, from Afric's strand,
From India's burning plain,
From Europe, from Columbia's land,
We hope to meet again.
It is the hope, the blissful hope,
Which Jesus' grace has given—
The hope, when days and years are past,
We all shall meet in heaven.

5 No lingering look, nor parting sigh,
Our future meeting knows;
There friendship beams from every eye,
And love immortal glows.
O sacred hope! O blissful hope!
Which Jesus' grace has given—
The hope, when days and years are past,
We all shall meet in heaven.

Wayne, Key E.   Alida, Key C.   Fleming, Key G.

116 THE GOSPEL—HOPE OF ETERNAL LIFE.

HOUSTON. C. M., with Chorus.   Arr. from J. W. DADMUN.

1. On Jordan's stormy banks I stand, And cast a wishful eye To Canaan's fair and happy land, Where my possessions lie.

Chorus. There'll be no sorrowing there, There'll be no sorrowing there; In heaven above, where all is love, There'll be no sorrowing there.

314   *The heavenly Canaan.*   (431)

2 Oh the transporting, rapturous scene
That rises to my sight!
Sweet fields arrayed in living green,
And rivers of delight!

3 There generous fruits that never fail
On trees immortal grow;
There rocks and hills, and brooks and vales,
With milk and honey flow.

4 All o'er these wide-extended plains
Shines one eternal day;
There God, the Sun, forever reigns,
And scatters night away.

5 No chilling winds nor poisonous breath
Can reach that healthful shore;
Sickness and sorrow, pain and death,
Are felt and feared no more.

6 When shall I reach that happy place,
And be forever blest!
When shall I see my Father's face,
And in his bosom rest!

315   *The land that is afar off.*   (429)

1 Far from these narrow scenes of night,
Unbounded glories rise,
And realms of infinite delight
Unknown to mortal eyes.

2 Celestial land! could our weak eyes
But half thy charms explore,
How would our spirits long to rise,
And dwell on earth no more!

3 There pain and sickness never come,
And grief no place obtains;
Health triumphs in immortal bloom,
And endless pleasure reigns.

4 No cloud these blissful regions know,
Forever bright and fair!
For sin, the source of every woe,
Can never enter there.

5 There no alternate night is known,
Nor sun's faint, sickly ray;
But glory from the sacred throne
Spreads everlasting day.

Aspiration, Key A.   Mount Pisgah, Key A.   New Richmond, Key G.

THE GOSPEL—HOPE OF ETERNAL LIFE.

ASPIRATION. C. M., (Old.)

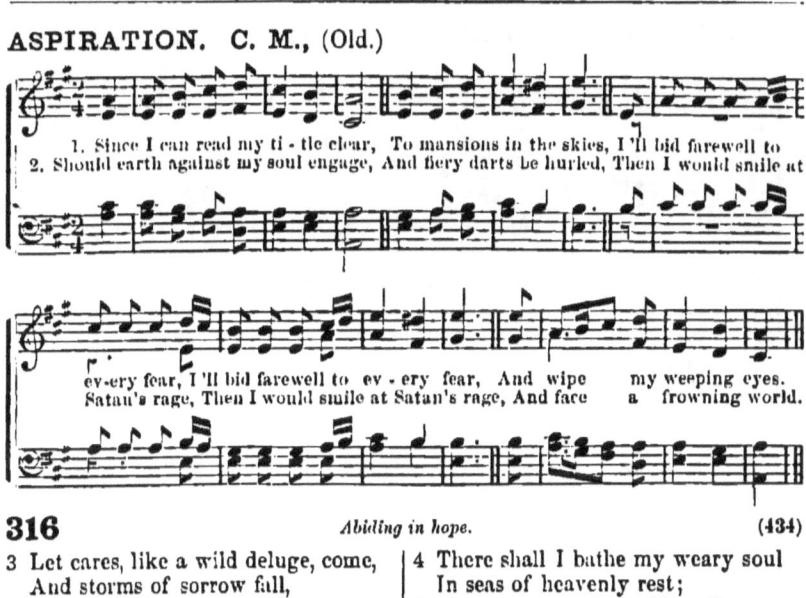

1. Since I can read my ti-tle clear, To mansions in the skies, I'll bid farewell to ev-ery fear, I'll bid farewell to ev-ery fear, And wipe my weeping eyes.
2. Should earth against my soul engage, And fiery darts be hurled, Then I would smile at Satan's rage, Then I would smile at Satan's rage, And face a frowning world.

316 *Abiding in hope.* (434)

3 Let cares, like a wild deluge, come,
  And storms of sorrow fall,
May I but safely reach my home,
  My God, my heaven, my all.

4 There shall I bathe my weary soul
  In seas of heavenly rest;
And not a wave of trouble roll
  Across my peaceful breast.

McCHESNEY. P. M. (New.)   T. J. COOK.

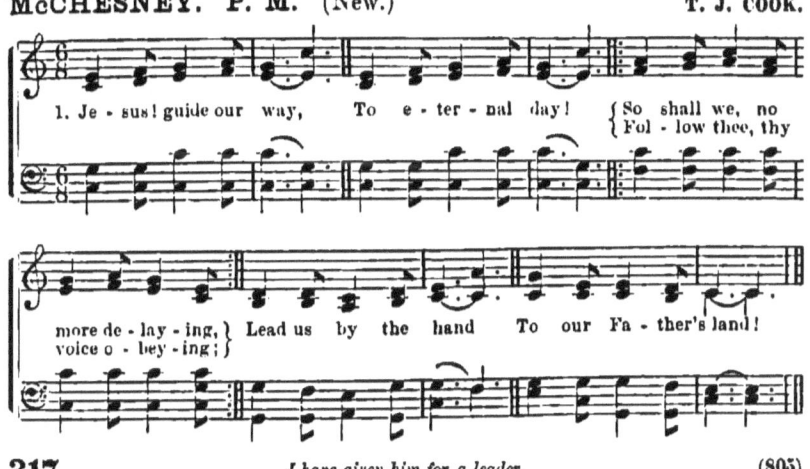

1. Je-sus! guide our way, To e-ter-nal day! { So shall we, no more de-lay-ing, } Lead us by the hand To our Fa-ther's land!
{ Fol-low thee, thy voice o-bey-ing; }

317 *I have given him for a leader.* (805)

2 When we danger meet,
  Steadfast make our feet,
Lord preserve us, uncomplaining,
'Mid the darkness round us reigning!
  Through adversity
  Lies our way to thee.

3 Order all our way
  Through this mortal day;
In our toil with aid be near us;
In our need with succor cheer us;
  When life's course is o'er,
  Open thou the door!

118 THE GOSPEL—HOPE OF ETERNAL LIFE.

VAIN WORLD, ADIEU. 8s & 4s. (New.)   S. J. VAIL.

1. When for e-ter-nal worlds we steer, And seas are calm and skies are clear, And faith, in live-ly ex-er-cise, Sees dis-tant fields of Ca-naan rise, The soul for joy then spreads her wings, And loud her lovely sonnet sings, Vain world a-dieu, Vain world a-dieu.

318   *Vain world, adieu.*   (437)

2 With cheerful hope her eyes explore
Each land-mark on the distant shore,
The trees of life, the pastures green,
The golden streets, the crystal stream;
Again for joy she spreads her wings,
And loud her lovely sonnet sings,
　I'm going home.

3 The nearer still she draws to land,
More eager all her powers expand;
With steady helm and free bent sail,
Her anchor drops within the vail;
And now for joy she folds her wings,
And her celestial sonnet sings,
　I'm safe at home.

CLING TO THE MIGHTY ONE. 6s & 4s. (New.)
(265)   W. H. DOANE.

Andante, with feeling.

319
1. Cling to the Mighty One, Cling in thy grief; Cling to the Holy One, He gives relief;
2. Cling to the Living One, Cling in thy woe; Cling to the Loving One, Thro' all below;
3. Cling to the Bleeding One, Cling to his side; Cling to the Risen One, In him abide;

Cling to the Gracious One, Cling in thy pain; Cling to the Faithful One, He will sustain.
Cling to the Pard'ning One, He speaketh peace; Cling to the Healing One, Anguish shall cease.
Cling to the Coming One, Hope shall arise; Cling to the Reigning One, Joy lights thine eyes.

THE GOSPEL—HOPE OF ETERNAL LIFE.

JESUS IS MINE. 6, 4, 6, 4, 6, 6, 6, 4.   T. E. PERKINS, by permission.

1. Now I have found a friend, Je-sus is mine; His love shall nev-er end,
D. S. Now I have last-ing peace;
Je-sus is mine; Tho' earthly joys decrease, Tho' human friendships cease,
Je-sus is mine.

320 *Jesus is mine.* (440)

2 Though I grow poor and old,
   Jesus is mine;
He will my faith uphold,
   Jesus is mine;
He shall my wants supply,
His precious blood is nigh,
Naught can my hope destroy,
   Jesus is mine!

3 When earth shall pass away,
   Jesus is mine.
In the great judgment day,
   Jesus is mine.
Oh! what a glorious thing
Then to behold my king,
On tuneful harp to sing,
   Jesus is mine.

4 Farewell, mortality!
   Jesus is mine;
Welcome, eternity!
   Jesus is mine.
He my redemption is,
Wisdom and Righteousness,
Life, Light, and Holiness,
   Jesus is mine,

321 *Glory to God in the highest.* (140)

1 Hark! from the world on high
   Glory to God!
Now swells along the sky
   Glory to God!
Songs, like sweet notes of praise,
Pour forth in rapturous lays,
As all the voices raise
   Glory to God!

2 Hear how the angels sing
   Glory to God!
Through all the heavens ring
   Glory to God!
Now let each heart on earth
Sing of the Savior's birth,
Telling his matchless worth,
   Glory to God!

322 *To him be glory.* (541)

1 Jesus has died for me,
   Glory to God!
From sin he set me free,
   Glory to God!
And, if I trust his grace,
I soon shall win the race;
Then see his lovely face,
   Glory to God!

2 Soon, I shall sing above,
   Glory to God!
Tell of his wondrous love,
   Glory to God:
Free from all death and wrong,
Then shall my notes prolong
One loud, triumphant song,
   Glory to God!

Oak, Key G.

120 THE CHURCH—DIVINE CONSTITUTION.

FEDERAL STREET. L. M.
H. K. OLIVER.

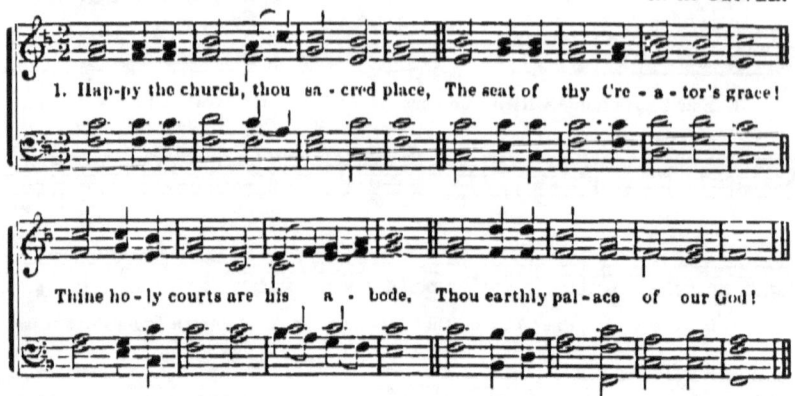

1. Happy the church, thou sa-cred place, The seat of thy Cre-a-tor's grace! Thine ho-ly courts are his a-bode, Thou earthly pal-ace of our God!

323   *God in the midst of her.*   (441)

1 Happy the church, thou sacred place,
The seat of thy Creator's grace!
Thine holy courts are his abode,
Thou earthly palace of our God!

2 Thy walls are strength, and at thy gates
A guard of heavenly warriors waits;
Nor shall thy deep foundations move,
Fixed on his counsels and his love.

3 Thy foes in vain designs engage;
Against his throne in vain they rage;
Like rising waves, with angry roar,
That dash and die upon the shore.

4 God is our shield, and God our sun;
Swift as the fleeting moments run,
On us he sheds new beams of grace,
And we reflect his brightest praise.

324   *God is our refuge.*   (442)

1 God is the refuge of his saints,
When storms of sharp distress invade;
Ere we can offer our complaints,
Behold him present with his aid.

2 Let mountains from their seats be hurled
Down to the deep, and buried there;
Convulsions shake the solid world;
Our faith shall never yield to fear.

3 Zion enjoys her monarch's love,
Secure against a threatening hour;
Nor can her firm foundations move,
Built on his truth, and armed with power.

325   *Go ye into all the world.*   (465)

1 Ye Christian heralds! go, proclaim
Salvation through Immanuel's name;
To distant climes the tidings bear,
And plant the rose of Sharon there.

2 He'll shield you with a wall of fire,
With holy zeal your hearts inspire,
Bid raging winds their fury cease,
And hush the tempest into peace.

3 And when our labors all are o'er,
Then we shall meet to part no more—
Meet with the blood-bought throng, to fall,
And crown our Jesus—Lord of all!

326   *Pray for us.*   (467)

1 Father of mercies, bow thine ear,
Attentive to our earnest prayer:
We plead for those who plead for thee;
Successful pleaders may they be.

2 How great their work! how vast their charge!
Do thou their anxious souls enlarge:
Their best endowments are our gain;
We share the blessings they obtain.

3 Oh, clothe with energy divine
Their words; and let those words be thine;
To them thy sacred truth reveal;
Suppress their fears, inflame their zeal.

4 Teach them to sow the precious seed;
Teach them thy chosen flock to feed;
Teach them immortal souls to gain—
And thus reward their toil and pain.

Gratitude, Key E♭.   Hamburg, Key F.   Sessions, Key C.

CHELMSFORD. C. M.

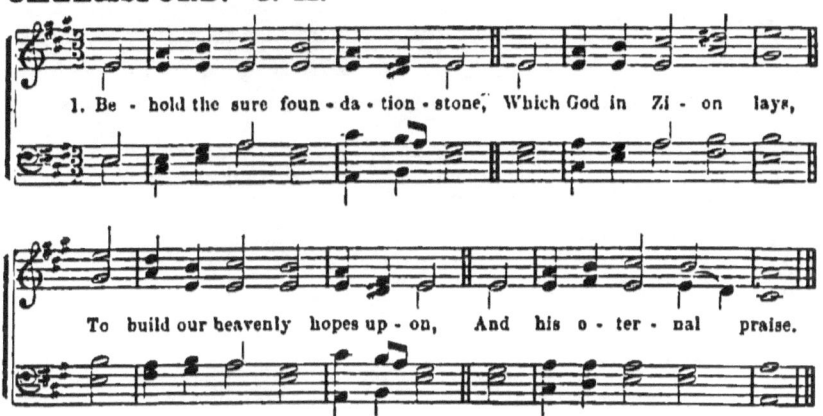

1. Behold the sure foundation-stone, Which God in Zion lays, To build our heavenly hopes upon, And his eternal praise.

327 *A sure foundation.* (444)

2 Chosen of God, to sinners dear,
And saints adore the name;
They trust their whole salvation here,
Nor shall they suffer shame.

3 The foolish builders, scribe and priest,
Reject it with disdain;
Yet on this rock the church shall rest,
And envy rage in vain.

4 What though the gates of hell withstood,
Yet must this building rise:
'Tis thy own work, almighty God,
And wondrous in our eyes.

328 *We have left all, etc.* (416)

1 There is a name I love to hear,
I love to speak its worth;
It sounds like music in mine ear,
The sweetest name on earth.

2 It tells me of a Savior's love,
Who died to set me free;
It tells me of his precious blood,
The sinner's perfect plea.

3 It tells me of a Father's smile,
Beaming upon his child;
It cheers me through this "little while,"
Through desert, waste, and wild.

4 It bids my trembling heart rejoice,
It dries each rising tear;
It tells me in "a still, small voice,"
To trust and never fear.

5 Jesus! the name I love so well,
The name I love to hear!
No saint on earth its worth can tell,
No heart conceive how dear.

6 This name shall shed its fragrance still,
Along this thorny road,
Shall sweetly smooth the rugged hill
That leads me up to God.

329 *Ordination.* (409)

1 With joy we own thy servant, Lord,
Thy minister below,
Ordained to spread thy truth abroad,
That all thy name may know.

2 Oh may he now, and ever, keep
His eye intent on thee;
Do thou, great Shepherd of the sheep,
His bright example be.

3 With plenteous grace his heart prepare
To execute thy will;
And give him patience, love, and care,
And faithfulness and skill.

4 Inflame his mind with ardent zeal,
Thy flock to feed and teach;
And let him live, and let him feel,
The truths he's called to preach.

5 As showers refresh the thirsty plain,
So let his labors prove:
By him extend thy righteous reign—
The reign of truth and love.

Balerma, Key B♭.   St. Martins, Key G.   Devizes, Key G.

THE CHURCH—CONSTITUTION.

BEALOTH. S. M., Double.

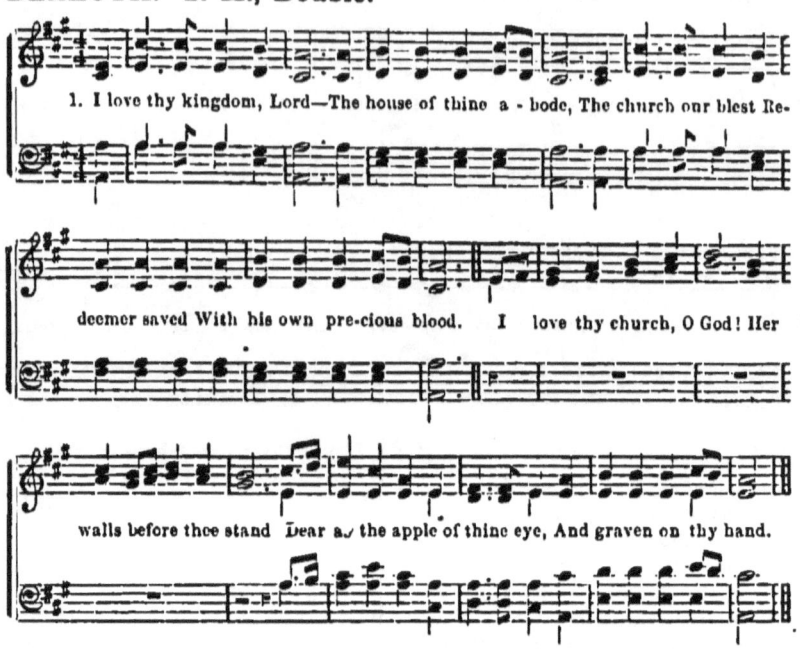

1. I love thy kingdom, Lord—The house of thine a-bode, The church our blest Redeemer saved With his own precious blood. I love thy church, O God! Her walls before thee stand Dear as the apple of thine eye, And graven on thy hand.

330 *I love thy kingdom, Lord.* (453)

2 For her my tears shall fall,
  For her my prayers ascend;
To her my cares and toils be given,
  Till toils and cares shall end.
Beyond my highest joy
  I prize her heavenly ways,
Her sweet communion, solemn vows,
  Her hymns of love and praise.

3 Jesus, thou Friend divine,
  Our Savior and our King!
Thy hand from every snare and foe
  Shall great deliverance bring.
Sure as thy truth shall last,
  To Zion shall be given
The brightest glories earth can yield,
  And brighter bliss of heaven.

331 *The church in the wilderness.* (459)

1 Far down the ages now,
  Much of her journey done,
The pilgrim church pursues her way,
  Until her crown be won.
The story of the past
  Comes up before her view:
How well it seems to suit her still—
  Old, and yet ever new!

2 It is the oft-told tale
  Of sin and weariness—
Of grace and love yet flowing down
  To pardon and to bless.
No wider is the gate,
  No broader is the way,
No smoother is the ancient path,
  That leads to life and day.

3 No sweeter is the cup,
  Nor less our lot of ill:
'T was tribulation ages since,
  'T is tribulation still.
No slacker grows the fight,
  No feebler is the foe,
Nor less the need of armor tried,
  Of shield, and spear, and bow.

Shirland, Key G. Gerar, Key F. Laban, Key C.

THE CHURCH—CONSTITUTION.

SHIRLAND. S. M.

1. How charm-ing is the place Where my Re-deem-er, God,
Un-veils the beau-ties of his face, And sheds his love a-broad!

332 *How amiable are thy tabernacles.* (454)

2 Not the fair palaces
  To which the great resort
Are once to be compared with this,
  Where Jesus holds his court.

3 Here on the mercy-seat,
  With radiant glory crowned,
Our joyful eyes behold him sit,
  And smile on all around.

4 To him their prayers and cries
  Each humble soul presents;
He listens to their broken sighs,
  And grants them all their wants.

5 Give me, O Lord, a place
  Within thy blessed abode,
Among the children of thy grace,
  The servants of my God.

333 *It shall stand forever.* (455)

1 Thy kingdom, gracious Lord,
  Shall never pass away;
Firm as thy truth it still shall stand,
  When earthly thrones decay.

2 Thy people here have found,
  Through many weary years,
The sweet communion, joy, and peace,
  To banish all their fears.

3 And now, while in thy courts,
  Do thou our love increase;
Give us the food our spirits need,
  And fill our hearts with peace.

334 *The Ark of God.* (456)

1 Like Noah's weary dove,
  That soared the earth around,
But not a resting-place above
  The cheerless waters found.

2 Oh cease, my wandering soul,
  On restless wing to roam!
All the wide world, to either pole,
  Has not for thee a home.

3 Behold the ark of God!
  Behold the open door!
Hasten to gain that dear abode,
  And rove, my soul, no more.

4 There safe thou shalt abide,
  There sweet shall be thy rest,
And every longing satisfied,
  With full salvation blest.

5 And when the waves of ire
  Again the earth shall fill,
The ark shall ride the sea of fire;
  Then rest on Zion's hill.

335 *Blessedness of the pure in heart.* (741)

1 Blest are the pure in heart,
  For they shall see our God;
The secret of the Lord is theirs;
  Their soul is his abode.

2 Still to the lowly soul
  He doth himself impart,
And for his temple and his throne
  Selects the pure in heart.

Gerar, Key F.   Olmutz, Key B♭.   Kentucky, Key A♭.

THE CHURCH—CONSTITUTION.

ALBERTE. S. M. (New.) — Dr. HASTINGS.

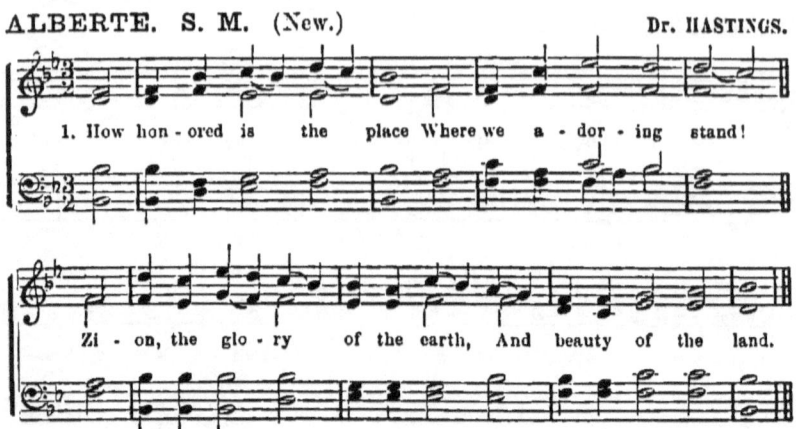

1. How honored is the place Where we adoring stand!
Zion, the glory of the earth, And beauty of the land.

336 *The Lord loveth the gates of Zion.* (457)

2 Bulwarks of grace defend
The city where we dwell;
While walls, of strong salvation made,
Defy the assaults of hell.

3 Lift up the eternal gates,
The doors wide open fling;
Enter, ye nations that obey
The statutes of our King.

4 Here taste unmingled joys,
And live in perfect peace—
You that have known Jehovah's name,
And ventured on his grace.

337 *Be ye, therefore, ready also.* (472)

1 Ye servants of the Lord,
Each in his office wait;
With joy obey his heavenly word,
And watch before his gate.

2 Let all your lamps be bright,
And trim the golden flame;
Gird up your loins, as in his sight;
For awful is his name.

3 Watch! 'tis the Lord's command;
And while we speak, he's near;
Mark the first signal of his hand,
And ready all appear.

4 Oh happy servant he,
In such a posture found!
He shall his Lord with rapture see,
And be with honor crowned.

338 *On the departure of a missionary.* (470)

1 You messengers of Christ,
His sovereign voice obey;
Arise and follow where he leads,
And peace attend your way.

2 The master whom you serve
Will needful strength bestow;
Depending on his promised aid,
With sacred courage go.

3 Mountains shall sink to plains,
And hell in vain oppose;
The cause is God's, and must prevail,
In spite of all his foes.

4 Go, spread a Savior's fame,
And tell his matchless grace,
To the most guilty and depraved
Of Adam's numerous race.

5 We wish you, in his name,
The most divine success,
Assured that he who sends you forth
Will your endeavors bless.

339 *God be merciful to us.* (737)

1 To bless thy chosen race,
In mercy, Lord, incline;
And cause the brightness of thy face
On all thy saints to shine,—

2 That so thy wondrous way
May through the world be known:
While distant lands their homage pay,
And thy salvation own.

Thatcher, Key G.   Shirland, Key G.   Boylston Key C.

THE CHURCH—CONSTITUTION. 125

CAMDEN. 8s & 7s. ✣

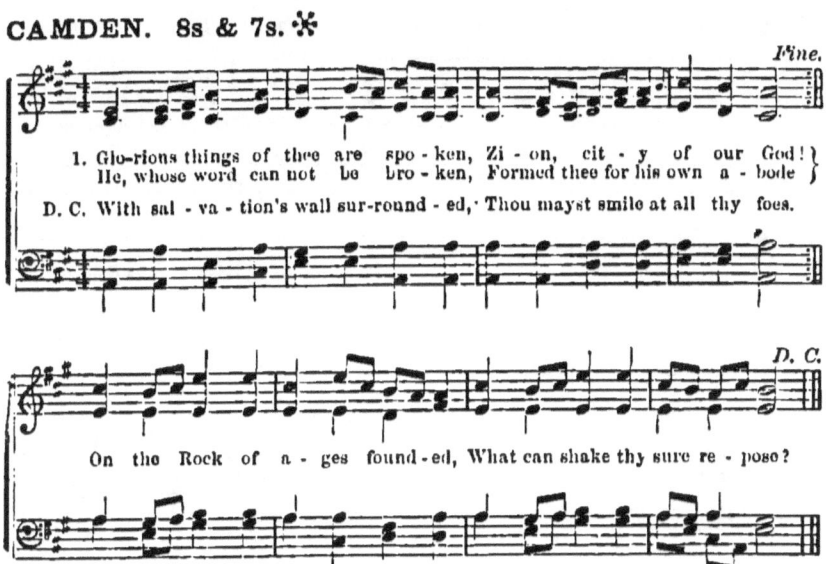

1. Glo-rious things of thee are spo-ken, Zi-on, cit-y of our God!
He, whose word can not be bro-ken, Formed thee for his own a-bode
D. C. With sal-va-tion's wall sur-round-ed, Thou mayst smile at all thy foes.

On the Rock of a-ges found-ed, What can shake thy sure re-pose?

340 *Glorious things are spoken of thee.* (460)

2 See the streams of living waters
Springing from Eternal Love,
Well supply thy sons and daughters,
And all fear of drought remove:
Who can faint while such a river
Ever flows their thirst t' assuage!
Grace, which like the Lord, the giver,
Never fails from age to age.

3 Round each habitation hovering,
See the cloud and fire appear,
For a glory and a covering,
Showing that the Lord is near:
Thus deriving from their banner
Light by night, and shade by day,
Safe they feed upon the manna
Which he gives them when they pray.

4 Blest inhabitants of Zion,
Washed in the Redeemer's blood,
Jesus, whom their souls rely on,
Makes them kings and priests to God:
'T is his love his people raises
With himself to reign as kings;
And, as priests, his solemn praises
Each for a thank-offering brings.

5 Savior, since of Zion's city
I through grace a member am,
Let the world deride or pity,
I will glory in thy name:
Fading is the worldling's treasure,
All his boasted pomp and show!
Solid joy and lasting pleasure
None but Zion's children know.

341 *Far from mortal cares retreating.* (700)

1 Far from mortal cares retreating,
Sordid hopes, and vain desires,
Here our willing footsteps meeting,
Every heart to heaven aspires.
From the fount of glory beaming,
Light celestial cheers our eyes,
Mercy from above proclaiming,
Peace and pardon from the skies.

2 Blessings all around bestowing,
God withholds his care from none;
Grace and mercy ever flowing
From the fountain of his throne.
Lord, with favor still attend us;
Bless us with thy wondrous love;
Thou, our Sun, our Shield, defend us;
All our hope is from above.

Bavaria, Key G.   Pleading Savior, Key G.   Nettleton, Key F.

THE CHURCH—CONSTITUTION.

WYMAN. 10s. B. WYMAN. From "Christian Heart Songs," by per.

1. Re-store, O Father! to our times re-store The peace which filled thine infant church of yore, Ere lust of power had sown the seeds of strife, And quenched the new-born char-i-ties of life.

342 *When the Lord shall bring again Zion.* (461)

2 Oh never more may different judgments part
From kindled sympathy a brother's heart!
But, linked in one, believing thousands kneel,
And share with each the sacred joy they feel.

3 From soul to soul, quick as the sunbeam's ray,
Let concord spread one universal day;
And faith by love lead all mankind to thee,
Parent of peace, and Fount of harmony!

343 *Communion of the body and blood of Christ.* (544)

1 Here, O my Lord, I see thee face to face;
  Here would I touch and handle things unseen;
Here grasp with firmer hand the eternal grace,
  And all my weariness upon thee lean.

2 Here would I feed upon the bread of God;
  Here drink with thee the royal wine of heaven;
Here would I lay aside each earthly load;
  Here taste afresh the calm of sin forgiven.

3 Too soon we rise; the symbols disappear;
  The feast, though not the love, is passed and gone;
The bread and wine remove, but thou art here—
  Nearer than ever—still my Shield and Sun.

4 Feast after feast thus comes and passes by;
  Yet, passing, points to the glad feast above—
Giving sweet foretaste of the festal joy—
  The Lamb's great bridal feast of bliss and love.

THE CHURCH—FUTURE TRIUMPHS.

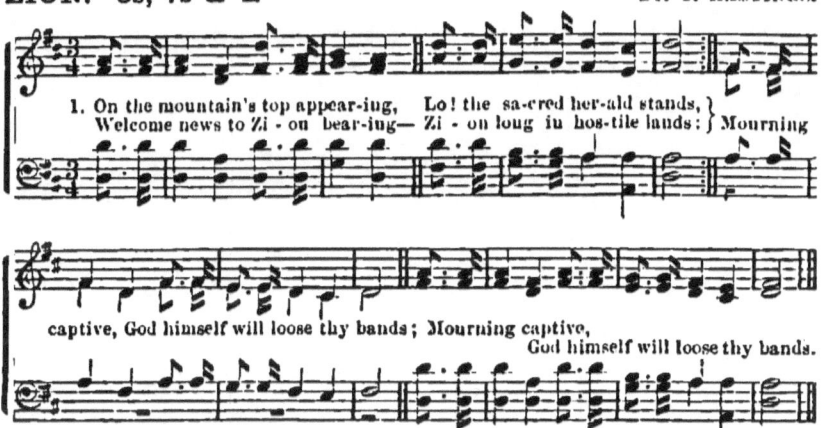

ZION. 8s, 7s & 4. Dr. T. HASTINGS.

1. On the mountain's top appear-ing, Lo! the sa-cred her-ald stands,
Welcome news to Zi-on bear-ing— Zi-on long in hos-tile lands: Mourning
captive, God himself will loose thy bands; Mourning captive,
God himself will loose thy bands.

344 *How beautiful on the mountains.* (604)

2 Has thy night been long and mournful?
Have thy friends unfaithful proved?
Have thy foes been proud and scornful,
By thy sighs and tears unmoved?
Cease thy mourning;
Zion still is well beloved.

3 God, thy God, will now restore thee:
He himself appears thy Friend:
All thy foes shall flee before thee;
Here their boasts and triumphs end:
Great deliverance
Zion's King will surely send.

4 Peace and joy shall now attend thee;
All thy warfare now be past;
God thy Savior will defend thee;
Victory is thine at last;
All thy conflicts
End in everlasting rest.

345 *Mount Zion, etc.* (464)

1 Zion stands with hills surrounded—
Zion kept by power divine;
All her foes shall be confounded,
Though the world in arms combine:
Happy Zion,
What a favored lot is thine!

2 Every human tie may perish,
Friend to friend unfaithful prove,

Mothers cease their own to cherish,
Heaven and earth at last remove,
But no changes
Can attend Jehovah's love.

3 In the furnace God may prove thee,
Thence to bring thee forth more bright,
But can never cease to love thee;
Thou art precious in his sight:
God is with thee—
God, thine everlasting light.

346 *Living waters.* (462)

1 See, from Zion's sacred mountain,
Streams of living water flow;
God has opened there a fountain
That supplies the world below:
They are blessed
Who its sovereign virtues know.

2 Through ten thousand channels flowing,
Streams of mercy find their way:
Life, and health, and joy bestowing,
Waking beauty from decay.
Oh ye nations,
Hail the long-expected day!

3 Gladdened by the flowing treasure,
All-enriching as it goes,
Lo! the desert smiles with pleasure,
Buds and blossoms as the rose;
Lo! the desert
Sings for joy where'er it flows.

Happy Zion, Key C. Marton, Key F. Peron, Key G.

THE CHURCH:

HEBRON. L. M.
Dr. L. MASON.

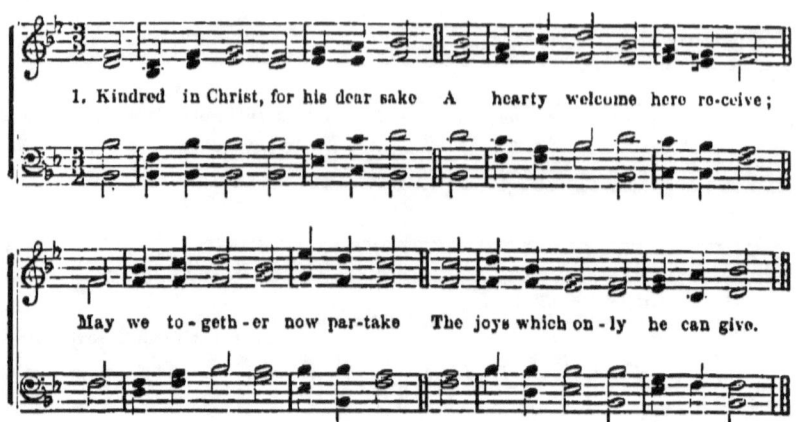

1. Kindred in Christ, for his dear sake A hearty welcome here re-ceive;
May we to-geth-er now par-take The joys which on-ly he can give.

347   *Christian fellowship.*   (477)

2 May he, by whose kind care we meet,
    Send his good Spirit from above;
  Make our communications sweet,
    And cause our hearts to burn with love.

3 Forgotten be each worldly theme,
    When Christians meet together thus:
  We only wish to speak of him
    Who lived, and died, and reigns for us.

4 We'll talk of all he did, and said,
    And suffered for us here below;
  The path be marked for us to tread,
    And what he's doing for us now.

5 Thus, as the moments pass away,
    We'll love, and wonder, and adore;
  And hasten on the glorious day
    When we shall meet to part no more.

348   *Welcome to young converts.*   (516)

1 Welcome, ye hopeful heirs of heaven,
    To this rich feast of gospel love!
  This pledge is but the prelude given
    To that immortal feast above.

2 How great the blessing, thus to meet
    According to our Savior's word,
  And hold by faith communion sweet
    With our unseen yet present Lord.

3 And if so sweet this feast below,
    What will it be to meet above,
  Where all we see, and feel, and know,
    Are fruits of everlasting love!

4 Soon shall we tune the heavenly lyre,
    While listening worlds the song approve;
  Eternity itself expire,
    Ere we exhaust the theme of love.

349   *I will lay me down in peace.*   (1190)

1 Thus far the Lord has led me on;
    Thus far his power prolongs my days;
  And every evening shall make known
    Some fresh memorial of his grace.

2 Much of my time has run to waste,
    And I, perhaps, am near my home;
  But he forgives my follies past;
    He gives me strength for days to come.

3 I lay my body down to sleep;
    Peace is the pillow for my head;
  While well-appointed angels keep
    Their watchful stations round my bed.

4 Thus, when the night of death shall come,
    My flesh shall rest beneath the ground.
  And wait thy voice to rouse my tomb,
    With sweet salvation in the sound.

Woodworth, Key E♭.   Gratitude, Key E♭.   Ernan, Key B♭.

LOVE, UNITY, AND FELLOWSHIP. 129

HAMBURG. L. M. Arranged by Dr. L. MASON.

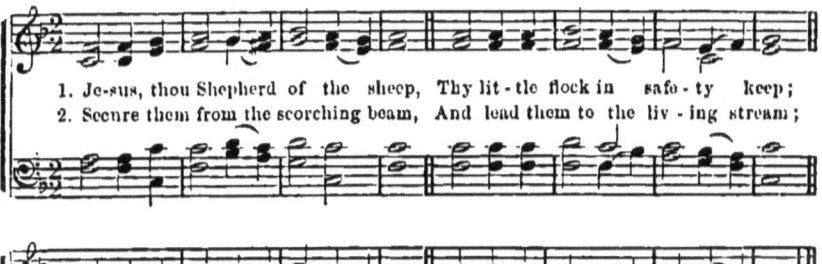

1. Je-sus, thou Shepherd of the sheep, Thy lit-tle flock in safe-ty keep;
2. Secure them from the scorching beam, And lead them to the liv-ing stream;

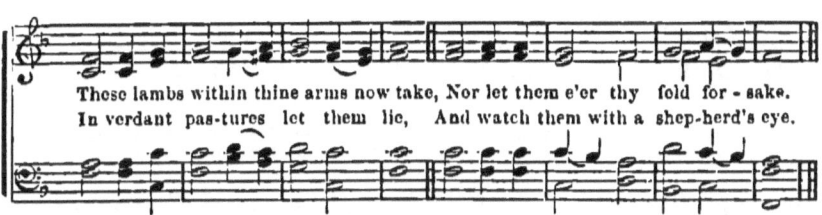

Those lambs within thine arms now take, Nor let them e'er thy fold for-sake.
In verdant pas-tures let them lie, And watch them with a shep-herd's eye.

350 *Thy little flock in safety keep.* (482)

3 Oh, teach them to discern thy voice,
  And in its sacred sound rejoice!
  From strangers may they ever flee,
  And know no other guide but thee.

4 Lord, bring thy sheep that wander yet,
  And let their number be complete;
  Then let the flock from earth remove,
  And reach the heavenly fold above.

351 *Delight in Christ.* (513)

1 Jesus, thou Joy of loving hearts!
  Thou Fount of Life! thou Light of men!
  From the best bliss that earth imparts,
  We turn unfilled to thee again.

2 Thy truth unchanged hath ever stood;
  Thou savest those that on thee call;
  To them that seek thee, thou art good,
  To them that find thee—All in All!

3 We taste thee, O thou Living Bread,
  And long to feed upon thee still;
  We drink of thee, the Fountain Head,
  And thirst our souls from thee to fill.

4 Our restless spirits yearn for thee,
  Where'er our changeful lot is cast;
  Glad, when thy gracious smile we see,
  Blest, when our faith can hold thee fast.

352 *You are all one in Christ Jesus.* (484)

1 Still one in life and one in death,
  One in our hope of rest above;
  One in our joy, our trust, our faith,
  One in each other's faithful love.

2 Yet must we part, and, parting, weep;
  What else has earth for us in store?
  Our farewell pangs, how sharp and deep!
  But soon we'll meet to part no more.

353 *Glorying only in the cross.* (512)

1 When I survey the wondrous cross
  On which the Prince of glory died,
  My richest gain I count but loss,
  And pour contempt on all my pride.

2 Forbid it, Lord, that I should boast,
  Save in the death of Christ, my Lord:
  All the vain things that charm me most,
  I sacrifice them to his blood.

3 See from his head, his hands, his feet,
  Sorrow and love flow mingled down;
  Did e'er such love and sorrow meet—
  Or thorns compose so rich a crown?

4 Were the whole realm of nature mine,
  That were a present far too small;
  Love so amazing, so divine,
  Demands my soul, my life, my all.

Zephyr, Key C.   Ward, Key B♭.   Olive's Brow, Key A♭.

THE CHURCH:

FRATERNITY. L. M.

1. Come in, thou bless-ed of our God, In Jesus' name we bid thee come;
No more thy feet shall roam a-broad, Henceforth a brother—wel-come home.

Chorus.

I'm go-ing home, I'm go-ing home, I'm go-ing home to die no more;
To die no more, to die no more, I'm go-ing home to die no more.

---

354 *Come in, thou blessed of the Lord.* (478)

1 Come in, thou blessed of our God,
In Jesus' name we bid thee come;
No more thy feet shall roam abroad,
Henceforth a brother—welcome home.

CHORUS.

I'm going home, I'm going home,
I'm going home to die no more;
To die no more, to die no more,
I'm going home to die no more.

2 Those joys which earth can not afford,
We'll seek in fellowship to prove,
Joined in one spirit to our Lord,
Together bound by mutual love.

3 And while we pass this vail of tears
We'll make our joys and sorrows known;
We'll share each other's hopes and fears,
And count a brother's cares our own.

4 Once more our welcome we repeat,
Receive assurance of our love;
Oh may we altogether meet
Around the throne of God above.

355 *The pilgrim band.* (481)

1 Come you that love the Lord indeed,
Who are from sin and bondage freed,
Submit to all the ways of God,
And walk the narrow, happy road.

2 Great tribulation you shall meet,
But soon shall walk the golden street;
Though hell may rage and vent its spite,
Yet Christ will save his heart's delight.

3 That happy day will soon appear
When Michael's trumpet you shall hear
Sound through the earth—yea, down to hell,
And call the nations, great and small.

4 Behold the righteous marching home,
And all the angels bid them come,
While Christ the Judge these words proclaims:
"Here come my saints—I own their names!"

5 "You everlasting gates, fly wide,
Make ready to receive my bride;
You harps of heaven, now sound aloud,
Here come the ransomed by my blood"

6 In grandeur see the royal line,
In glittering robes the sun outshine!
See saints and angels join in one,
And march in splendor to the throne.

7 They stand, and wonder, and look on,
They join in one eternal song,
Their great Redeemer to admire,
While rapture sets their souls on fire.

LOVE, UNITY, AND FELLOWSHIP.

PARTING HYMN. L. M., Double. ✱

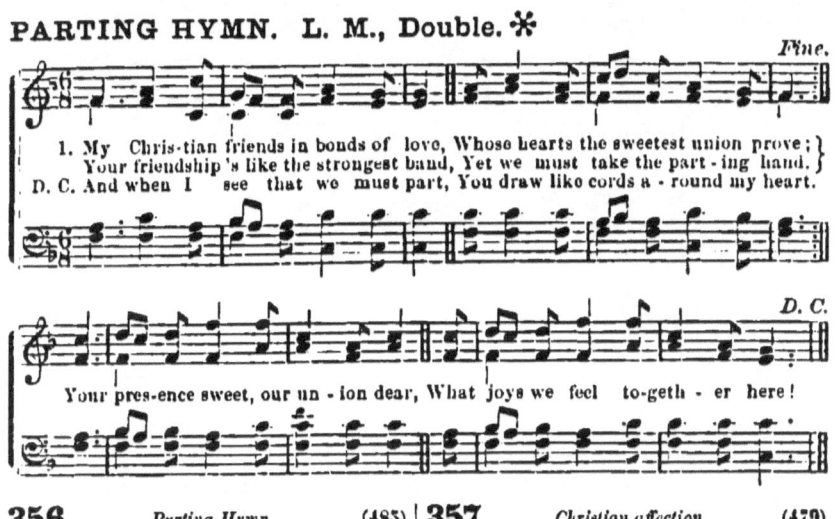

1. My Christian friends in bonds of love, Whose hearts the sweetest union prove;
Your friendship's like the strongest band, Yet we must take the parting hand.
D. C. And when I see that we must part, You draw like cords around my heart.

Your presence sweet, our union dear, What joys we feel together here!

356 *Parting Hymn.* (485)

2 How sweet the hours have passed away,
Since we have met to sing and pray;
How loath are we to leave the place
Where Jesus shows his smiling face!
Oh could I stay with friends so kind,
How would it cheer my fainting mind!
But pilgrims in a foreign land,
We oft must take the parting hand.

3 My Christian friends, both old and young,
I trust you will in Christ go on;
Press on, and soon you'll win the prize—
A crown of glory in the skies.
A few more days, or years, at most,
And we shall reach fair Canaan's coast:
When, in that holy, happy land,
We'll take no more the parting hand.

357 *Christian affection.* (479)

1 How blest the sacred tie that binds,
In sweet communion, kindred minds!
How swift the heavenly course they run,
Whose hearts, whose faith, whose hopes are one!
To each the soul of each how dear!
What tender love, what holy fear!
How doth the generous flame within
Refine from earth, and cleanse from sin!

2 Their streaming eyes together flow
For human guilt and mortal woe;
Their ardent prayers together rise
Like mingling flames in sacrifice.
Nor shall the glowing flame expire,
When dimly burns frail nature's fire;
Then shall they meet in realms above,
A heaven of joy, a heaven of love.

THY WILL BE DONE. Chant.

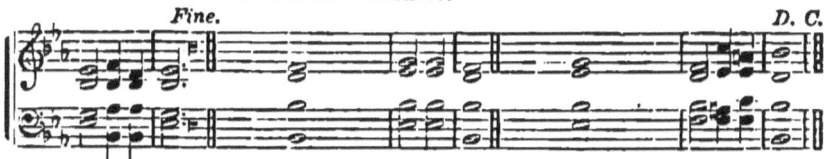

1 "Thy will be | done!" ‖ In devious way
The hurrying stream of | life may | run; ‖
Yet still our grateful hearts shall say, |
   "Thy will be | done."

2 "Thy will be | done!" ‖ if o'er us shine
A gladdening and a | prosperous | sun, ‖

This prayer will make it more divine; |
   "Thy will be | done."

3 "Thy will be | done!" ‖ though shrouded o'er
Our | path with | gloom, ‖ one comfort, one
Is ours; to breathe, while we adore, |
   "Thy will be | done."

BROWN. C. M.   WM. B. BRADBURY, by permission.

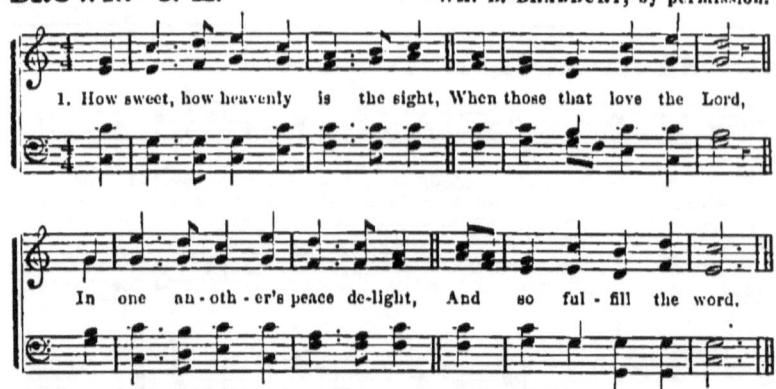

1. How sweet, how heavenly is the sight, When those that love the Lord, In one an-oth-er's peace de-light, And so ful-fill the word.

358   *The bond of perfectness.*   (498)

2 When each can feel his brother's sigh,
And with him bear a part;
When sorrow flows from eye to eye,
And joy from heart to heart;

3 When free from envy, scorn, and pride,
Our wishes all above,
Each can his brother's failing hide,
And show a brother's love;

4 When love, in one delightful stream,
Through every bosom flows;
When union sweet and dear esteem
In every action glows.

5 Love is the golden chain that binds
The happy souls above;
And he's an heir of heaven that finds
His bosom glow with love.

359   *The whole family in heaven, etc.* (494)

1 Come, let us join our friends above
Who have obtained the prize,
And, on the eagle wings of love,
To joy celestial rise.

2 Let saints below in concert sing
With those to glory gone;
For all the servants of our King
In heaven and earth are one:

3 One family—we dwell in him;
One church—above, beneath;
Though now divided by the stream—
The narrow stream of death.

4 One army of the living God,
To his command we bow;
Part of the host have crossed the flood,
And part are crossing now.

5 Even now to their eternal home
Some happy spirits fly;
And we are to the margin come,
Expecting soon to die.

6 Dear Savior! be our constant guide;
Then, when the word is given,
Bid Jordan's narrow stream divide,
And land us safe in heaven.

360   *Remembering Christ.* (520)

1 If human kindness meets return,
And owns the grateful tie—
If tender thoughts within us burn
To feel a friend is nigh—

2 Oh shall not warmer accents tell
The gratitude we owe
To him who died our fears to quell,
And save from endless woe!

3 While yet his anguished soul surveyed
Those pangs he would not flee,
What love his latest words displayed—
"Meet and remember me"!

4 Remember thee! thy death, thy shame,
The griefs which thou didst bear;
O memory, leave no other name
But his recorded there!

St. Martin's, Key G.   Avon, Key A♭.   Dedham, Key A.

LOVE, UNITY, AND FELLOWSHIP. 133

DEDHAM. C. M.   GARDNER.

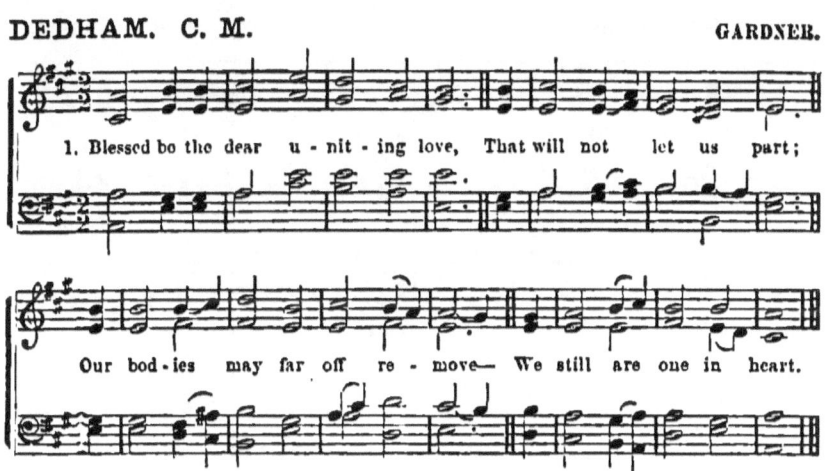

1. Blessed be the dear u-nit-ing love, That will not let us part;
Our bod-ies may far off re-move— We still are one in heart.

361   *The unity of the Spirit.*   (488)
2 Joined in one Spirit to our Head,
   Where he appoints, we go;
And still in Jesus' footsteps tread,
   And show his praise below.

3 Partakers of the Savior's grace,
   The same in mind and heart;
Nor joy, nor grief, nor time, nor place,
   Nor life, nor death, can part.

362   *Planting a church.*   (487)
1 Planted in Christ, the living vine,
   This day with one accord,
Ourselves, with humble faith and joy,
   We yield to thee, O Lord.

2 Joined in one body may we be;
   One inward life partake;
One be our heart; one heavenly hope
   In every bosom wake.

3 In prayer, in effort, tears, and toils,
   One wisdom be our guide;
Taught by one Spirit from above,
   In thee may we abide.

4 Around this feeble, trusting band,
   Thy sheltering pinions spread,
Nor let the storms of trial beat
   Too fiercely on our head.

5 Then, when among the saints in light
   Our joyful spirits shine,
Shall anthems of immortal praise,
   O Lamb of God, be thine.

363   *He was known of them, etc.*   (525)
1 Shepherd of souls, refresh and bless
   Thy chosen pilgrim flock,
With manna from the wilderness,
   With water from the rock.

2 Hungry and thirsty, faint and weak,
   As thou when here below,
Our souls the joys celestial seek,
   That from thy sorrows flow.

3 We would not live by bread alone,
   But by thy word of grace—
In strength of which we travel on
   To our abiding place.

4 Be known to us in breaking bread,
   But do not then depart—
Savior, abide with us, and spread
   Thy table in our heart.

5 Then sup with us in love divine;
   Thy body and thy blood,
That living bread and heavenly wine,
   Be our immortal food.

364   *In remembrance of me.*   (524)
1 In memory of the Savior's love,
   We keep the sacred feast,
Where every humble, contrite heart
   Is made a welcome guest.

2 Under his banner thus we sing
   The wonders of his love,
And thus anticipate by faith
   The heavenly feast above

Brown, Key C.   Dundee, Key F.   Edmeston, Key C.

THE CHURCH:

DENNIS. S. M.   H. G. NAGELI.

1. Blest be the tie that binds Our hearts in Chris-tian love;
The fel-low-ship of kin-dred minds Is like to that a-bove.

365   *Love as brethren.*   (495)

2 Before our Father's throne
We pour our ardent prayers;
Our fears, our hopes, our aims are one,
Our comforts and our cares.

3 We share our mutual woes,
Our mutual burdens bear;
And often for each other flows
The sympathizing tear.

4 Though often called to part,
Amid these scenes of pain;
Yet we shall still be joined in heart,
And hope to meet again.

5 This glorious hope revives
Our courage by the way;
While each in expectation lives,
And longs to see the day.

6 From sorrow, toil, and pain,
And sin, we shall be free;
And perfect love and friendship reign
Through all eternity.

366   *Whom the Lord loveth, etc.*   (1015)

1 How tender is thy hand,
Oh thou most gracious Lord!
Afflictions come at thy command,
And leave us at thy word.

2 How gentle was the rod
That chastened us for sin!
How soon we found a smiling God
Where deep distress had been!

3 A Father's hand we felt,
A Father's heart we knew,
'Mid tears of penitence we knelt,
And found his word was true.

4 Now we will bless the Lord,
And in his strength confide;
Forever be his name adored,
For there is none beside.

367   *God dealeth with you as with sons.*   (1018)

1 How gracious and how wise
Is our chastising God!
And, oh! how rich the blessings are
Which blossom from his rod!

2 He lifts it up on high,
With pity in his heart,
That every stroke his children feel
May grace and peace impart.

3 Instructed thus, they bow
And own his sovereign sway;
They turn their erring footsteps back
To his forsaken way.

4 His covenant love they seek,
And seek the happy bands
That closer still engage their hearts
To honor his commands.

5 Our Father, we consent
To discipline divine,
And bless the pain that makes our souls
Still more completely thine.

Gerar, Key F.   Shirland, Key G.   Thatcher, Key G.

LOVE, UNITY, AND FELLOWSHIP.

368 *Let there be no divisions among you.* (497)

1 Let party names no more
The Christian world o'erspread,
Gentile and Jew, and bond and free,
Are one in Christ, their Head.

2 Among the saints on earth
Let mutual love be found;
Heirs of the same inheritance,
With mutual blessings crowned.

3 Thus will the church below
Resemble that above,
Where streams of pleasure ever flow,
And every heart is love.

369 *After the Supper.* (527)

1 Now let each happy guest
The sacred concert raise,
To close the honors of the feast,
And sing the Master's praise.

2 His condescending love
First calls our wonder forth;
He left the blessed realms above
To dwell with men on earth.

3 His precepts, how divine!
How suited to our state!
How bright his acts of mercy shine!
His promises, how great!

4 Redemption's glorious plan,
How wondrous in our view!
The salutary source to man
Of peace and pardon too.

370 *Take this, etc.* (529)

1 Jesus invites his saints
To meet around his board:
Here pardoned rebels sit, and hold
Communion with their Lord.

2 This holy bread and wine
Maintain our fainting breath,
By union with our living Lord,
And interest in his death.

3 Let all our powers be joined
His glorious name to raise;
Let holy love fill every mind,
And every voice be praise.

371 *And when they had sung, etc.* (530)

1 A parting hymn we sing
Around thy table, Lord:
Again our grateful tribute bring,
Our solemn vows record.

2 Here have we seen thy face,
And felt thy presence here;
So may the savor of thy grace
In word and life appear.

3 The purchase of thy blood—
By sin no longer led—
The path our dear Redeemer trod
May we rejoicing tread.

4 In self-forgetting love
Be Christian union shown,
Until we join the church above,
And know as we are known.

372 *Behold the Lamb of God.* (531)

1 Not all the blood of beasts,
On Jewish altars slain,
Could give the guilty conscience peace,
Or wash away its stain.

2 But Christ, the heavenly Lamb,
Bears all our sins away—
A sacrifice of nobler name
And richer blood than they.

3 My faith would lay her hand
On that dear head of thine,
While like a penitent I stand,
And there confess my sin.

4 Believing, we rejoice
To see the curse remove;
We bless the Lamb with cheerful voice,
And sing his dying love.

373 *Peace I leave with you.* (735)

1 Lord, at this closing hour,
Establish every heart
Upon thy word of truth and power,
To keep us when we part.

2 Peace to our brethren give;
Fill all our hearts with love;
In faith and patience may we live,
And seek our rest above.

Dennis, Key F.   Kentucky, Key A♭.   Olmutz, Key B♭.

NUREMBURG. 7s.

1. Chil-dren of the heaven-ly King, As ye jour-ney, sweet-ly sing:
Sing your Sav-ior's wor-thy praise, Glo-rious in his works and ways.
2. Ye are trav-eling home to God, In the way the fa-thers trod;
They are hap-py now—and ye Soon their hap-pi-ness shall see.

374 *Strangers and pilgrims.* (498)

3 Shout, ye little flock, and blest;
You on Jesus' throne shall rest;
There your seat is now prepared—
There your kingdom and reward.

4 Fear not, brethren; joyful stand
On the borders of your land;
Jesus Christ, your Father's Son,
Bids you undismayed go on.

5 Lord, submissive make us go,
Gladly leaving all below;
Only thou our leader be,
And we still will follow thee.

375 *The memory of thy great goodness.* (1249)

1 Praise to God, immortal praise,
For the love that crowns our days!
Bounteous source of every joy,
Let thy praise our tongues employ.

2 For the blessings of the field,
For the stores the gardens yield;
For the vine's exalted juice,
For the generous olive's use:

3 Flocks that whiten all the plain;
Yellow sheaves of ripened grain;
Clouds that drop their fattening dews;
Suns that temperate warmth diffuse:

4 All that spring with bounteous hand
Scatters o'er the smiling land;
All that liberal autumn pours
From her rich, o'erflowing stores:

5 These to thee, my God, we owe,
Source whence all our blessings flow;
And for these my soul shall raise
Grateful vows and solemn praise.

376 *Prayer for deacons.* (475)

1 Son of God, our glorious Head!
On us now thy blessing shed;
From thy throne let mercy flow
To thy waiting flock below.

2 Taught by thee, with prayer sincere,
We have called thy servants here,
For thy needy ones to care,
And thy holy feast to bear.

3 May the Spirit from above
Fill their hearts with faith and love;
Make them humble, zealous, wise,
Strife to shun, and good devise.

4 When their earthly work is done,
When the crown of life is won,
May they, with thy favor blest,
Pass from labor into rest.

Amboy, Key D. Pleyel's Hymn, Key G. Hendon, Key G.

LOVE, UNITY, AND FELLOWSHIP.   137

ZEPHYR. L. M.   W. B. BRADBURY, by permission.

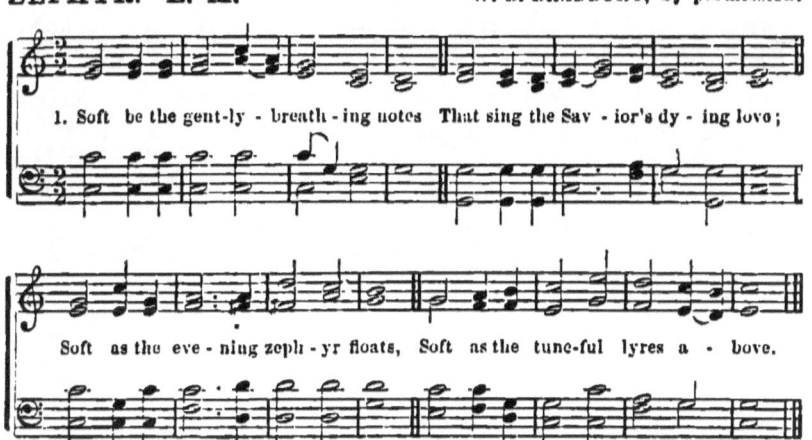

1. Soft be the gent-ly - breath-ing notes That sing the Sav-ior's dy-ing love;
Soft as the eve-ning zeph-yr floats, Soft as the tune-ful lyres a-bove.

377 *Soft be the gently breathing notes.* (514)

2 Soft as the morning dews descend,
  While warbling birds exulting soar;
So soft to our almighty Friend
  Be every sigh our bosoms pour.

3 Pure as the sun's enlivening ray,
  That scatters life and joy abroad,
Pure as the lucid orb of day,
  That wide proclaims its Maker, God;

4 Pure as the breath of vernal skies,
  So pure let our contrition be;
And purely let our sorrows rise
  To him who bled upon the tree.

378 *This is the gate of heaven.* (548)

1 How sweet to leave the world awhile
  And seek the presence of our Lord!
Dear Savior! on thy people smile,
  And come according to thy word!

2 From busy scenes we now retreat,
  That we may here converse with thee:
Ah! Lord! behold us at thy feet—
  Let this the "gate of heaven" be.

3 "Chief of ten thousand!" now appear,
  That we by faith may see thy face:
Oh! grant that we thy voice may hear,
  And let thy presence fill this place.

379   *Isaiah 57: 15.*   (551)

1 Jesus, where'er thy people meet,
  There they behold thy mercy-seat;
Where'er they seek thee, thou art found;
  And every place is hallowed ground.

2 For thou, within no walls confined,
  Inhabitest the humble mind;
Such ever bring thee where they come,
  And, going, take thee to their home.

3 Dear Shepherd of thy chosen few,
  Thy former mercies here renew;
Here to our waiting hearts proclaim,
  The sweetness of thy saving name.

4 Here may we prove the power of prayer
  To strengthen faith and banish care;
To teach our faint desires to rise,
  And bring all heaven before our eyes.

380   *The living temple.*   (087)

1 O Father! with protecting care,
  Meet us in this, our house of prayer;
Assembled in thy sacred name,
  Thy promised blessing here we claim.

2 But chiefest in the cleansed breast,
  Forever let thy Spirit rest,
And make the contrite heart to be
  A temple pure and worthy thee.

Oriel, Key A♭.   Ward, Key B♭.   Woodworth, Key E♭.

12

138　　　THE CHURCH:

THE FUTURE REST. P. M.✽(503)　　Arranged from S. J. VAIL.

381
1. We shall meet no more to part; Cease thy sorrows, mourning heart! Weary days will soon de-part— Then we may rest for-ev-er! When the work of life is done, When the vic-tor's crown is won, Then, im-mor-tal life be-gun,
2. In the house of peace and bliss, In the world where Jesus is, When we bid a-dieu to this, Then we may love for-ev-er! Pu-ri-fied from every stain, Thro' the Lamb that once was slain, Breth-ren, we shall meet a-gain,

Chorus.
We no more shall sever, And be part-ed never. We shall meet no more to part, We shall meet, etc. Cease thy sor-rows, mourning heart! Weary days will soon de-part, Then we may rest for-ev-er.

382　*Dedham, Key A.*　(1003)

1 Christ leads me through no darker rooms
　Than he went through before:
He that into God's kingdom comes
　Must enter by this door.

2 Come, Lord, when grace hath made me meet
　Thy blessed face to see;
For if thy work on earth be sweet,
　What must thy glory be?

383　*Naomi, Key D.*　(1006)

1 My times of sorrow and of joy,
　Great God! are in thy hand;
My choicest comforts come from thee,
　And go at thy command.

2 If thou shouldst take them all away,
　Yet would I not repine;
Before they were possessed by me,
　They were entirely thine.

LOVE, UNITY, AND FELLOWSHIP. 139

BENNETT. C. P. M.   S. J. VAIL, by permission.

1. O love divine, how sweet thou art! When shall I find my wand'ring heart All taken up in thee! Oh may I daily live to prove The sweetness of redeeming love, The love of Christ to me.

384   *He that dwelleth in love.*   (505)

2 God only knows the love of God,
Oh may it now be shed abroad
 To cheer my fainting heart!
I want to feel that love divine;
This heavenly portion, Lord, be mine—
 Be mine this better part.

3 Oh that I could forever sit
With Mary at the Master's feet!
 Be this my happy choice;
My only care, delight, and bliss,
My joy, my heaven on earth, be this,
 To hear the Bridegroom's voice.

4 Oh that I might, with happy John,
Recline my weary head upon
 The blessed Redeemer's breast!
From care, and fear, and sorrow free,
Give me, O Lord, to find in thee
 My everlasting rest.

385   *The great salvation.*   (672)

1 To him who did salvation bring,
Wake every tuneful power, and sing
 A song of sweetest praise:
His grace diffuses as the rains
Crown nature's flowery hills and plains,
 And spread a thousand ways.

2 Salvation is the noblest song,
Oh may it dwell on every tongue,
 And all repeat, Amen!
The Lord will come from heaven to earth
To give his people second birth,
 And make them one again.

3 We feel redemption drawing near;
We soon in glory shall appear,
 And be forever blessed:
His promise never can delay;
Our Jesus, on the appointed day,
 Will give his people rest.

4 By faith we view him coming down
With angels hovering all around;
 He smiles upon his saints:
He cries aloud in melting strains,
I come to save you from your pains,
 And end your sore complaints.

THE CHURCH:

FOLSOM. 10, 11, 10, 10. ✻   Arr. from MOZART.

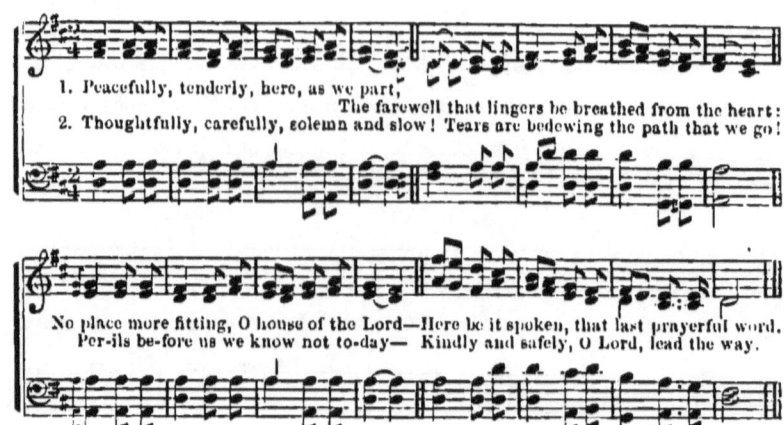

1. Peacefully, tenderly, here, as we part,
The farewell that lingers be breathed from the heart:
No place more fitting, O house of the Lord—Here be it spoken, that last prayerful word.

2. Thoughtfully, carefully, solemn and slow! Tears are bedewing the path that we go!
Per-ils be-fore us we know not to-day— Kindly and safely, O Lord, lead the way.

386   *A parting hymn.*   (506)

3 Upwardly, steadfastly, gaze on that brow;
Jesus, our Leader, reigns conqueror now;
His steps let us follow, his sufferings dare,
Go up to glory, his blessedness share.

4 Patiently, cheerfully, up, and depart
To labor and duty, with gladness of heart;
The ransomed, with triumph, to Zion we'll bring,
Shouting salvation to Jesus, our King.

VAN PELT. 6, 6, 8, 8, 6. (New.)   T. J. COOK.

1. To heaven I lift mine eye, To heaven, Jehovah's throne, For there my Savior
sits on high, And thence shall strength and aid supply To all he calls his own.

2. He will not faint nor fail, Nor cause thy feet to stray; For him no wea-ry
hours as-sail, Nor evening darkness spreads her veil O'er his e-ter-nal day.

387   *Psalm 121.*   (937)

3 Beneath that light divine,
  Securely shalt thou move;
The sun with milder beams shall shine,
And eve's still queen her lamp incline
  Benignant from above.

4 For he, thy God and Friend,
  Shall keep thy soul from harm,
In each sad scene of doubt attend,
And guide thy life, and bless thine end,
  With his almighty arm.

LOVE, UNITY, AND FELLOWSHIP. 141

DAYTON. 10s & 8s. ✱   A. D. FILLMORE, by permission.

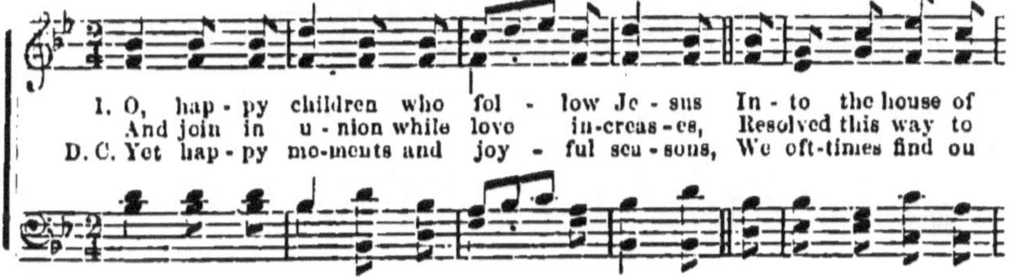

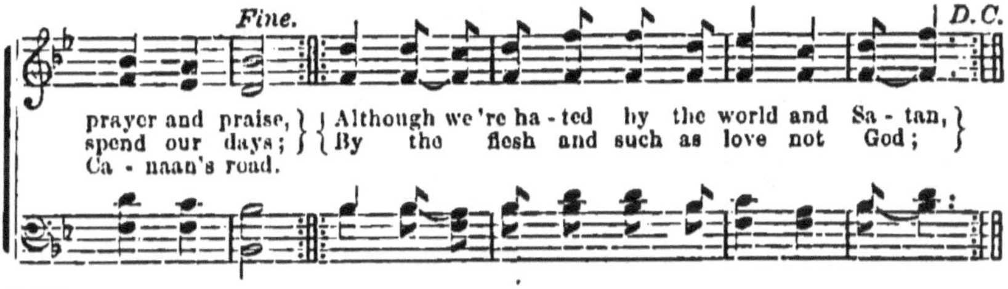

1. O, hap-py children who fol-low Je-sus In-to the house of prayer and praise,
And join in u-nion while love in-creas-es, Resolved this way to spend our days;
D.C. Yet hap-py mo-ments and joy-ful sea-sons, We oft-times find ou Ca-naan's road.

Although we're ha-ted by the world and Sa-tan,
By the flesh and such as love not God;

388   *Waiting on God.*   (508)

2 Since we've been waiting on lovely Jesus,
We've felt some strength come from above,
Our hearts have burned with holy rapture,
We long to be absorbed in love:
Let us sing praises for what is given,
And trust in God for time to come:
Sure we shall find the way to heaven;
So farewell, brethren—we're going home,

3 And as we go let us praise our Savior,
And pray for those who spurn his grace,
Lest they should lose love's richest treasure,
And ne'er enjoy his smiling face.
Now here's my hand, and my best wishes,
In token of my Christian love;
In hopes with you to praise my Jesus:
So farewell, brethren—we'll meet above.

PENDLETON. 9s, 8s & 4. ✱   (104)   A. D. FILLMORE.

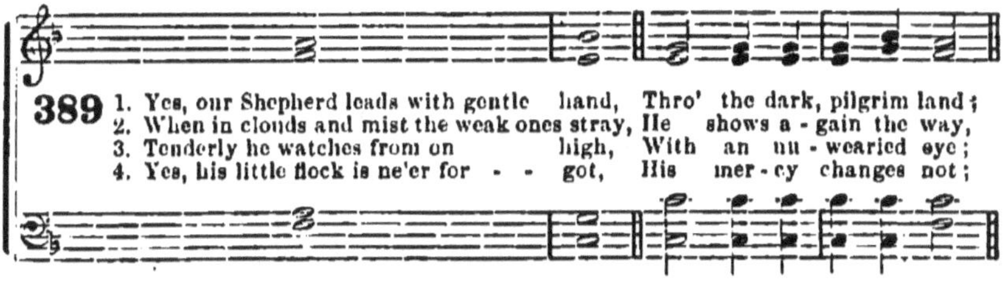

389
1. Yes, our Shepherd leads with gentle hand, Thro' the dark, pilgrim land;
2. When in clouds and mist the weak ones stray, He shows a-gain the way,
3. Tenderly he watches from on high, With an un-wearied eye;
4. Yes, his little flock is ne'er for-got, His mer-cy changes not;

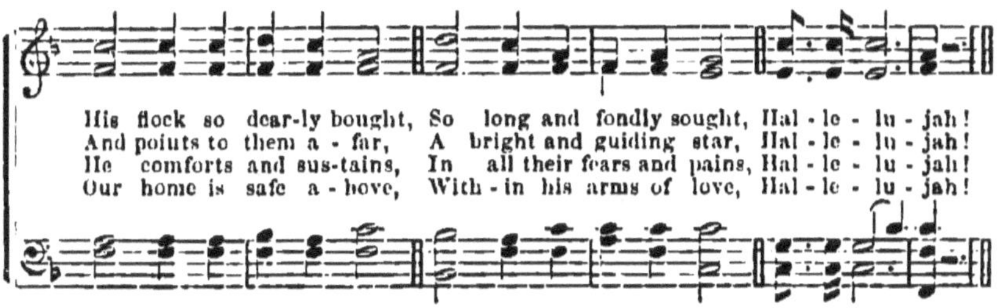

His flock so dear-ly bought, So long and fondly sought, Hal-le-lu-jah!
And points to them a-far, A bright and guiding star, Hal-le-lu-jah!
He comforts and sus-tains, In all their fears and pains, Hal-le-lu-jah!
Our home is safe a-bove, With-in his arms of love, Hal-le-lu-jah!

THE CHURCH:

HOME. 11s, with Chorus.

390 *Home.* (510)

2 Sweet bonds, that unite all the children of peace;
And thrice blessed Jesus, whose love can not cease;
Though oft from thy presence in sadness I roam,
I long to behold thee in glory at home.

3 While here in the valley of conflict I stray,
Oh give me submission and strength as my day;
In all my afflictions to thee would I come,
Rejoicing in hope of my glorious home.

4 I long, dearest Lord, in thy beauty to shine;
No more as an exile in sorrow to pine;
And in thy dear image arise from the tomb,
With glorified millions to praise thee at home.

391 *Strangers and pilgrims.* (838)

1 My rest is in heaven—my home is not here;
Then why should I murmur when trials appear?
Be hushed, my sad spirit, the worst that may come
But shortens thy journey and hastens thee home.

2 A pilgrim and stranger, I seek not my bliss,
Nor lay up my treasures in regions like this;
I look for a city which hands have not piled;
I pant for a country by sin undefiled.

3 Afflictions may try me, but can not destroy;
One vision of home turns them all into joy;
And the bitterest tear that flows from my eyes,
But sweetens my hope of that home in the skies.

4 Though foes and temptations my progress oppose,
They only make heaven more sweet at the close;
Come joy, or come sorrow—the worst may befall,
One moment in heaven will make up for all.

LOVE, UNITY, AND FELLOWSHIP.

MOORE. L. M.   T. E. PERKINS, by permission.

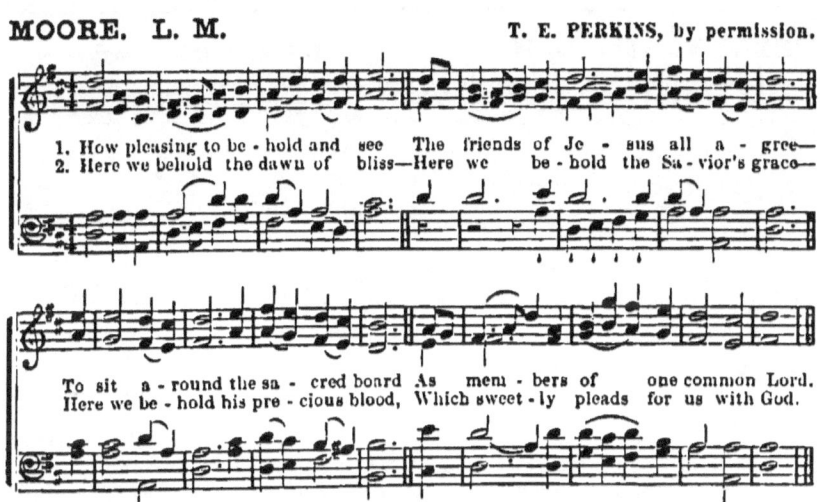

1. How pleasing to be-hold and see The friends of Je-sus all a-gree—
To sit a-round the sa-cred board As mem-bers of one common Lord.

2. Here we behold the dawn of bliss—Here we be-hold the Sa-vior's grace—
Here we be-hold his pre-cious blood, Which sweet-ly pleads for us with God.

---

392   *Communion in Christ.*   (515)

3 While here we sit, we would implore
That love may spread from shore to shore,
Till all the saints, like us, combine
To praise the Lord in songs divine.

4 To all we freely give our hand,
Who love the Lord in every land;
For all are one in Christ our Head,
To whom be endless honors paid.

393   *It is a good thing to give thanks.* (611)

1 Sweet is the work, my God! my King!
To praise thy name, give thanks and sing;
To show thy love by morning light,
And talk of all thy truth at night.

2 Sweet is the day of sacred rest,
No mortal care shall seize my breast;
Oh! may my heart in tune be found,
Like David's harp, of solemn sound.

3 My heart shall triumph in the Lord,
And bless his works, and bless his word;
Thy works of grace, how bright they shine!
How deep thy counsels! how divine.

4 Lord! I shall share a glorious part,
When grace hath well refined my heart;
And fresh supplies of joy are shed,
Like holy oil, to cheer my head.

5 Then shall I see, and hear, and know
All I desired or wished below:
And every power find sweet employ
In that eternal world of joy.

394   *Christ is risen.*   (614)

1 Hail! morning known among the blest!
Morning of hope, and joy, and love,
Of heavenly peace and holy rest;
Pledge of the endless rest above.

2 Blessed be the Father of our Lord,
Who from the dead has brought his Son!
Hope to the lost was then restored,
And everlasting glory won.

3 Scarce morning twilight had begun
To chase the shades of night away,
When Christ arose—unsetting Sun—
The dawn of joy's eternal day!

4 Mercy looked down with smiling eye
When our Immanuel left the dead;
Faith marked his bright ascent on high,
And Hope with gladness raised her head.

5 God's goodness let us bear in mind,
Who to his saints this day has given,
For rest and serious joy designed,
To fit us for the bliss of heaven.

Rockingham, Key G.   Ward, Key B♭.   Wells, Key E♭.

FELLOWSHIP. C. M.
T. E. PERKINS, by permission.

1. Lord, at thy ta-ble we be-hold The won-ders of thy grace;
. But most of all ad-mire that we Should find a wel-come place.

395   *Blessed are the poor in spirit.*   (523)

2 What strange, surprising grace is this,
That we, so lost, have room!
Jesus our weary souls invites,
And freely bids us come.

3 Ye saints below, and hosts of heaven,
Join all your sacred powers;
No theme is like redeeming love—
No Savior is like ours.

396   *Spiritual refreshment.*   (521)

1 O God! unseen, yet ever near,
Reveal thy presence now,
While we, in love that hath no fear,
Before thy glory bow.

2 Here may obedient spirits find
The blessings of thy love—
The streams that through the desert wind,
The manna from above.

FENELON. 8s & 7s, Peculiar.
C. C. CONVERSE.

1. Near the cross our station taking, Meet it is for us to mourn:
Earthly cares and joys forsaking,
'T was for us he came from heaven,
'T was for us his heart was riven; All his griefs for us were borne.

397   *It was for us.*   (536)

2 When no eye its pity gave us,
When there was no arm to save us,
He his love and power displayed:
By his stripes our help and healing,
By his death our life revealing,
He for us the ransom paid.

398   *I will draw all men unto me.*   (533)

1 It is finished! Man of Sorrows!
From thy cross our frailty borrows
Strength to bear and conquer thus
While extended there we view thee,
Mighty Sufferer! draw us to thee;
Sufferer victorious!

2 Not in vain for us uplifted,
Man of Sorrows, wonder-gifted!
May that sacred emblem be;
Lifted high amid the ages,
Guide of heroes, saints, and sages,
May it guide us still to thee!

LOVE, UNITY, AND FELLOWSHIP. 145

STEARNS. 8s & 7s. Arr. from MAZZINGHI.

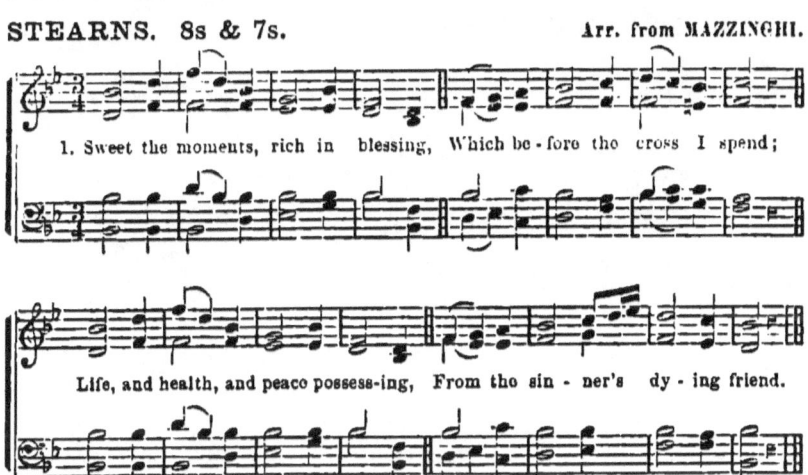

1. Sweet the moments, rich in blessing, Which be-fore the cross I spend;
Life, and health, and peace possess-ing, From the sin-ner's dy-ing friend.

399 *Looking to Jesus.* (538)

2 Here I'll sit, forever viewing
Mercy streaming in his blood;
Precious drops! my soul bedewing,
Plead they now my peace with God.

3 Truly blessed is this station,
Here unfolds his wondrous grace;
While I see divine compassion
Beaming in his lovely face.

4 Here it is I find my heaven,
While upon the cross I gaze;
Here the joy of sins forgiven
Shall inspire my songs of praise.

5 Love and grief my heart dividing,
While his feet I bathe with tears;
Constant still in faith abiding—
Hope triumphant o'er my fears.

6 Lord! in ceaseless contemplation,
Fix my trusting heart on thee,
Till I know thy full salvation,
And thy face in glory see.

400 *Thou art worthy.* (205)

1 Crown his head with endless blessing,
Who, in God the Father's name,
With compassion never ceasing,
Comes, salvation to proclaim.

2 Jesus, thee our Savior hailing,
Thee our God in praise we own;
Highest honors, never failing,
Rise eternal round thy throne.

3 Now, ye saints, his power confessing,
In your grateful strains adore;
For his mercy, never ceasing,
Flows, and flows for evermore.

401 *Hear and obey.* (393)

1 Humble souls, who seek salvation,
Through the Lamb's redeeming blood,
Hear the voice of revelation;
Tread the path that Jesus trod.

2 Hear the blest Redeemer call you;
Listen to his heavenly voice;
Dread no ills that can befall you,
While you make his way your choice.

402 *Closing hymn.* (751)

1 Israel's Shepherd, guide me, feed me,
Through my pilgrimage below,
And beside the waters lead me,
Where thy flock rejoicing go.

2 Lord, thy guardian presence ever,
Meekly kneeling, I implore;
I have found thee, and would never,
Never wander from thee more.

Dorrnance, Key F.   Sicily, Key F.   Autumn, Key A♭.

THE CHURCH:

JESUS, BREAD OF LIFE. P. M. (New.) (565)   W. H. DOANE.
Gently and Gliding.

403
1. Here I sink be-fore thee low-ly, Filled with gladness deep and ho-ly,
As with trembling awe and won-der
2. Sun, who all my life dost brighten! Light, who dost my soul en-light-en!
Joy, the sweetest man e'er knoweth!
3. Je-sus, Bread of Life, from heaven, Nev-er be thou vain-ly giv-en,
Nor I to my hurt in-vit-ed;

On thy mighty work I ponder—On this banquet's myster-y, On the depths we
Fount, whence all my being floweth, Humbly draw I near to thee; Grant that I may
Be thy love with love requited; Let me learn its depths indeed, While on thee my

can not see! Far be-yond all mor-tal sight Lie the se-crets of thy might.
wor-thi-ly Take this blessed, heavenly food, To thy praise, and to my good.
soul doth feed; Let me, here so rich-ly blest, Be here-af-ter, too, thy guest.

SILENT DEVOTION. P. M. ✻   Harmonized by J. P. POWELL.
(1032)

404
1. As down in the sunless retreats of the o-cean, Sweet flowers are springing no
So, deep in my heart the still prayer of devotion, Unheard by the world, rises
2. As still to the star of its worship, though clouded, The needle points faith-ful-ly
So, dark as I roam thro' this wintry world shrouded, The hope of my spi-rit turns

mor-tal can see,
si-lent to thee—   } My God! si-lent to thee—Pure, warm, silent to thee.
o'er the dim sea,
trembling to thee } My God! trembling to thee—True, fond, trembling to thee.

LOVE, UNITY, AND FELLOWSHIP. 147

OLIVET. 6s & 4s.   Dr. L. MASON.

1. My faith looks up to thee, Thou Lamb of Calvary, Savior di - vine! Now hear me while I pray; Take all my guilt away: Oh, let me, from this day, Be wholly thine.

405   *Christ our confidence.*   (542)

2 May thy rich grace impart
Strength to my fainting heart;
  My zeal inspire;
As thou hast died for me,
Oh may my love to thee
Pure, warm, and changeless be—
  A living fire.

3 While life's dark maze I tread,
And griefs around me spread,
  Be thou my guide;
Bid darkness turn to day,
Wipe sorrow's tears away,
Nor let me ever stray
  From thee aside.

4 When ends life's transient dream,
When death's cold, sullen stream
  Shall o'er me roll;
Blest Savior, then, in love,
Fear and distress remove;
Oh bear me safe above—
  A ransomed soul.

406   *Worthy the Lamb.*   (927)

1 Come, all ye saints of God,
Wide through the earth abroad,
  Spread Jesus' fame:
Tell what his love hath done;
Trust in his name alone;
Shout to his lofty throne,
  "Worthy the Lamb!"

2 Hence, gloomy doubts and fears!
Dry up your mournful tears;
  Swell the glad theme:
To Christ, our gracious King,
Strike each melodious string;
Join heart and voice to sing,
  "Worthy the Lamb!"

3 Hark! how the choirs above,
Filled with the Savior's love,
  Dwell on his name!
There, too, may we be found,
With light and glory crowned;
While all the heavens resound,
  "Worthy the Lamb!"

407   *The God of harvest praise.*   (1234)

1 The God of harvest praise;
In loud thanksgiving raise
  Hand, heart, and voice;
The valleys smile and sing,
Forests and mountains ring,
The plains their tribute bring,
  The streams rejoice.

2 Yea, bless his holy name,
And purest thanks proclaim
  Through all the earth;
To glory in your lot
Is duty—but be not
God's benefits forgot,
  Amidst your mirth.

3 The God of harvest praise;
Hands, hearts, and voices raise
  With sweet accord:
From field to garner throng,
Bearing your sheaves along,
And, in your harvest song,
  Bless ye the Lord.

New Haven, Key G.   America, Key F.   Dort, Key C.

RETREAT. L. M.   Dr. T. HASTINGS.

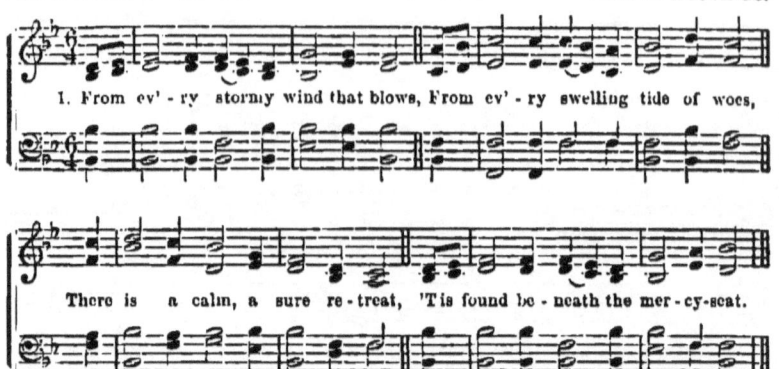

1. From ev'-ry stormy wind that blows, From ev'-ry swelling tide of woes,
There is a calm, a sure re-treat, 'Tis found be-neath the mer-cy-seat.

408   *The Mercy-Seat.*   (547)

2 There is a place where Jesus sheds
    The oil of gladness on our heads,
    A place than all besides more sweet—
    It is the blood-bought mercy-seat.

3 There is a scene where spirits blend,
    Where friend holds fellowship with friend;
    Though sundered far, by faith they meet
    Around one common mercy-seat.

4 Ah! whither could we flee for aid,
    When tempted, desolate, dismayed;
    Or how the host of hell defeat,
    Had suffering souls no mercy-seat?

5 There! there on eagle wings we soar,
    And sin and sense seem all no more,
    And heaven comes down our souls to greet,
    And glory crowns the mercy-seat!

6 Oh let my hand forget her skill,
    My tongue be silent, cold and still,
    This bounding heart forget to beat,
    Ere I forget the mercy-seat!

409   *Lord's-day evening.*   (615)

1 Sweet is the fading light of eve,
    And soft the sunbeams lingering there;
    For these blest hours the world I leave,
    Wafted on wings of praise and prayer.

2 The time, how lovely and how still!
    Peace shines and smiles on all below:
    The plain, the stream, the wood, the hill,
    All fair with evening's setting glow.

3 Season of rest! the tranquil soul
    Feels the sweet calm, and melts to love,
    And while these sacred moments roll,
    Faith sees a smiling heaven above.

4 Nor will our days of toil be long;
    Our pilgrimage will soon be trod;
    And we shall join the ceaseless song,
    The endless Sabbath of our God.

410   *The tranquil hour.*   (555)

1 Thou, Savior, from thy throne on high,
    Enrobed with light, and girt with power,
    Dost note the thought, the prayer, the sigh,
    Of hearts that love the tranquil hour.

2 Oft thou thyself didst steal away,
    At eventide, from labor done,
    In some still, peaceful shade to pray,
    Till morning watches were begun.

3 Thou hast not, dearest Lord, forgot
    Thy wrestlings on Judea's hills;
    And still thou lovest the quiet spot
    Where praise the lowly spirit fills.

4 Now to our souls, withdrawn awhile
    From earth's rude noise, thy face reveal,
    And, as we worship, kindly smile,
    And for thine own our spirits seal.

5 To thee we bring each grief and care,
    To thee we fly while tempests lower;
    Thou wilt the weary burdens bear
    Of hearts that love the tranquil hour.

Mercy-seat, Key E♭.   Zephyr, Key C.   Woodworth, Key E♭.

PRAYER AND SOCIAL MEETINGS. 149

MERCY-SEAT. L. M. ✶
Harmonized by J. P. POWELL.

1. What various hin-dran-ces we meet In com-ing to a mer-cy-seat!
Yet who, that knows the worth of prayer, But wish-es to be of-ten there?

411 *Exhortation to prayer.* (556)

2 Prayer makes the darkened clouds withdraw:
Prayer climbs the ladder Jacob saw,
Gives exercise to faith and love,
Brings every blessing from above.

3 Restraining prayer, we cease to fight;
Prayer makes the Christian's armor bright,
And Satan trembles, when he sees
The weakest saint upon his knees.

4 Have you no words? Ah, think again;
Words flow apace when we complain,
And fill a fellow-creature's ear
With the sad tale of all our care.

5 Were half the breath thus vainly spent,
To heaven in supplication sent,
Our cheerful song would oftener be,
"Hear what the Lord has done for me?"

412 *I pray—that thou shouldst keep, etc.* (952)

1 While others pray for grace to die,
O Lord, I pray for grace to live;
For every hour a fresh supply;
Oh see my need and freely give.

2 I do not dread the hour of death;
If I am thine, no fears remain:
I know that with my parting breath
I yield forever mortal pain.

3 E'en if the darkness should appear
Too deep for faith as well as sight,
If I am thine, thou wilt be near,
And take me to thy heavenly light.

4 But oh! my Lord, in life's highway
I crave the sunshine of thy face;
And every moment of the day
I need thy strong supporting grace.

5 I dare not—will not—Lord, deny
That heart and feet both go astray;
Therefore, the more to thee I cry
To keep me in the chosen way.

6 The more my sin and unbelief,
Keep me from walking near to thee:
The more, Lord Jesus, is my grief—
The more I long thy face to see.

413 *Retirement and meditation.* (982)

1 Return, my roving heart, return,
And chase these shadowy forms no more:
Seek out some solitude to mourn,
And thy forsaken God implore.

2 O thou, great God, whose piercing eye
Distinctly marks each deep recess;
In these sequestered hours draw nigh,
And with thy presence fill the place.

3 Through all the windings of my heart,
My search let heavenly wisdom guide;
And still its radiant beams impart
Till all be searched and purified.

4 Then with the visits of thy love,
Vouchsafe my inmost soul to cheer;
Till every grace shall join to prove
That God has fixed his dwelling there

Retreat, Key B♭.   Hebron, Key B♭.   Windham, Key F.

SWEET HOUR OF PRAYER. L. M. D.
W. B. BRADBURY, by per.

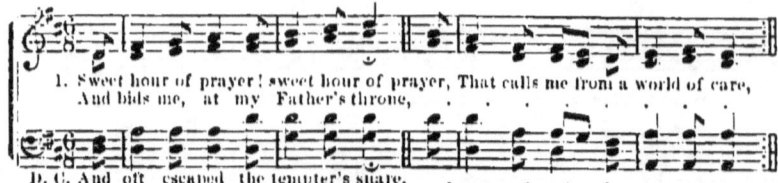

1. Sweet hour of prayer! sweet hour of prayer, That calls me from a world of care, And bids me, at my Father's throne,
D. C. And oft escaped the tempter's snare,

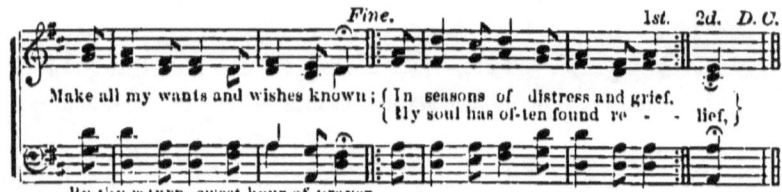

Make all my wants and wishes known; { In seasons of distress and grief.
{ My soul has of-ten found re - - lief, }
By thy return, sweet hour of prayer.

414 *Hour of prayer.* (550)

2 Sweet hour of prayer! sweet hour of prayer!
The joy I feel, the bliss I share,
Of those whose anxious spirits burn
With strong desires for thy return.

With such I hasten to the place
Where God my Savior shows his face,
And gladly take my station there,
And wait for thee, sweet hour of prayer.

UNITY. 6s & 5s. Peculiar. (504)
Dr. L. MASON, by permission.

415
1. When shall we meet again, Meet ne'er to sever? When will peace wreath her chain Round us for-ev - er? Our hearts will ne'er re - pose, Safe from each blast that blows In this dark vale of woes, Nev - er, no, nev - er.
2. When shall love freely flow, Pure as life's river? When shall sweet friendship glow, Changeless for-ev - er? Where joys celestial thrill, Where bliss each heart shall fill, And fears of part - ing chill, Nev - er, no, nev - er.
3. Up to that world of light Take us, dear Sav-ior; May we all there u - nite, Hap-py for-ev - er; Where kindred spir - its dwell, There may our mu-sic swell, And time our joys dis - pel, Nev - er, no, nev - er.

PRAYER AND SOCIAL MEETINGS. 151

NAOMI. C. M.   Dr. L. MASON, by permission.

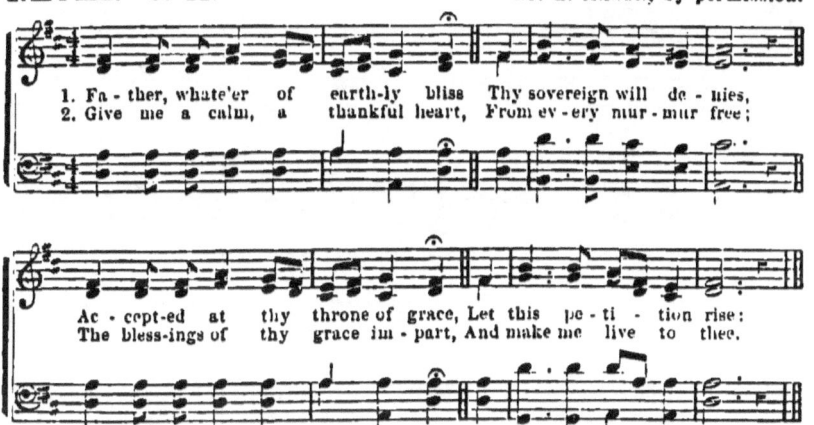

1. Fa-ther, whate'er of earth-ly bliss Thy sovereign will de-nies, Ac-cept-ed at thy throne of grace, Let this pe-ti-tion rise:
2. Give me a calm, a thankful heart, From ev-ery mur-mur free; The bless-ings of thy grace im-part, And make me live to thee.

416   *Prayer for contentment.*   (558)

3 Let the sweet hope that thou art mine,
   My life, and death attend;
Thy presence through my journey shine,
   And crown my journey's end.

417   *Thy will be done.*   (560)

1 How sweet to be allowed to pray
   To God, the Holy One;
With filial love and trust to say,
   "O God, thy will be done."

2 We in these sacred words can find
   A cure for every ill;
They calm and soothe the troubled mind,
   And bid all care be still.

3 Oh let that will which gave me breath,
   And an immortal soul,
In joy or grief, in life or death,
   My every wish control.

4 Oh, could my heart thus ever pray,
   Thus imitate thy Son!
Teach me, O God, with truth to say,
   Thy will, not mine, be done.

418   *Retirement and meditation.*   (562)

1 I love to steal awhile away
   From every cumbering care,
And spend the hours of setting day
   In humble, grateful prayer.

2 I love in solitude to shed
   The penitential tear:
And all his promises to plead,
   Where none but God can hear.

3 I love to think on mercies past,
   And future good implore,
And all my cares and sorrows cast
   On him whom I adore.

4 I love, by faith, to take a view
   Of brighter scenes in heaven;
The prospect doth my strength renew,
   While here by tempests driven.

419   *Prayer.*   (565)

1 Prayer is the soul's sincere desire,
   Unuttered or expressed;
The motion of a hidden fire
   That trembles in the breast.

2 Prayer is the burden of a sigh,
   The falling of a tear;
The upward glancing of an eye
   When none but God is near.

3 Prayer is the simplest form of speech
   That infant lips can try;
Prayer, the sublimest strains that reach
   The Majesty on high.

4 Prayer is the contrite sinner's voice,
   Returning from his ways,
While angels in their songs rejoice,
   And say—"Behold, he prays."

Dundee, Key F.   Balerma, Key B♭.   Mear, Key F.   Avon, Key A♭.

BALERMA. C. M.

1. Approach, my soul, the mer-cy-seat, Where Jesus an-swers prayer;
There hum-bly fall be-fore his feet, For none can per-ish there.

420 *Let us draw near.* (564)

2 Thy promise is my only plea,
 With this I venture nigh:
Thou callest burdened souls to thee,
 And such, O Lord, am I.

3 Bowed down beneath a load of sin,
 By Satan sorely pressed,
By war without, and fear within,
 I come to thee for rest.

4 Be thou my shield and hiding-place;
 That, sheltered near thy side,
I may my fierce accuser face,
 And tell him, "Thou hast died."

5 Oh, wondrous love, to bleed and die,
 To bear the cross and shame,
That guilty sinners, such as I,
 Might plead thy gracious name!

421 *A new heart.* (811)

1 Oh for a heart to praise my God,
 A heart from sin set free,
A heart that always feels the blood
 So freely shed for me.

2 A heart resigned, submissive, meek,
 My great Redeemer's throne,
Where only Christ is heard to speak,
 Where Jesus reigns alone.

3 Oh for a lowly, contrite heart,
 Confiding, true, and clean,
Which neither life nor death can part
 From him that dwells within;

4 A heart in every thought renewed,
 And full of love divine,
Perfect and right, and pure and good,
 A copy, Lord, of thine.

5 Thy Spirit, gracious Lord, impart;
 Direct me from above;
May thy dear name be near my heart,
 That dear, best name is Love.

422 *Oh, that I were as in months past.* (944)

1 Sweet was the time when first I felt
 The Savior's pardoning blood
Applied to cleanse my soul from guilt,
 And bring me home to God.

2 Soon as the morn the light revealed,
 His praises tuned my tongue;
And, when the evening shade prevailed,
 His love was all my song.

3 In prayer, my soul drew near the Lord,
 And saw his glory shine;
And when I read his holy word,
 I called each promise mine.

4 But now, when evening shade prevails,
 My soul in darkness mourns;
And when the morn the light reveals,
 No light to me returns.

5 Rise, Savior! help me to prevail,
 And make my soul thy care;
I know thy mercy can not fail;
 Let me that mercy share.

Prayer, Key C.   Asmon, Key A.   Fountain, Key E♭.

PRAYER AND SOCIAL MEETINGS.

PRAYER. C. M.   T. J. COOK, by permission.

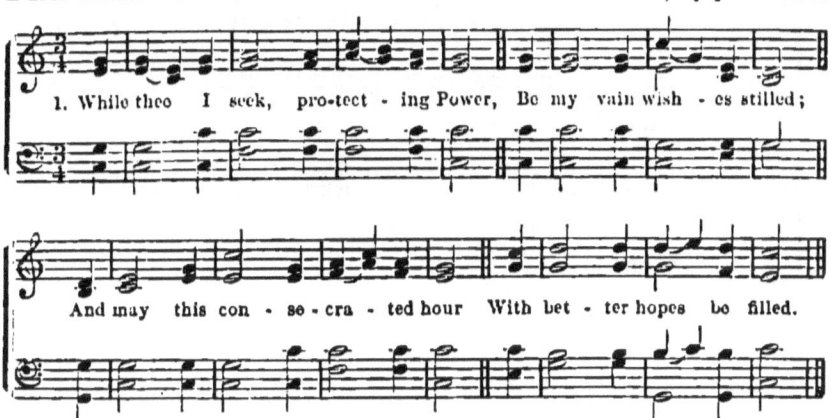

1. While thee I seek, pro-tect-ing Power, Be my vain wish-es stilled;
And may this con-se-cra-ted hour With bet-ter hopes be filled.

423   *Sanctify the Lord God, etc.*   (561)

2 Thy love the power of thought bestowed;
To thee my thoughts would soar;
Thy mercy o'er my life has flowed;
That mercy I adore.

3 In each event of life, how clear
Thy ruling hand I see!
Each blessing to my soul more dear,
Because conferred by thee.

4 In every joy that crowns my days,
In every pain I bear,
My heart shall find delight in praise,
Or seek relief in prayer.

5 When gladness wings my favored hour,
Thy love my thoughts shall fill;
Resigned, when storms of sorrow lower,
My soul shall meet thy will.

6 My lifted eye, without a tear,
The gathering storm shall see;
My steadfast heart shall banish fear;
That heart shall rest on thee.

424   *Oh for a closer walk with God!*   (943)

1 Oh for a closer walk with God!
A calm and heavenly frame!
A light to shine upon the road
That leads me to the Lamb!

2 Where is the blessedness I knew
When first I saw the Lord?
Where is the soul-refreshing view
Of Jesus and his word?

3 What peaceful hours I once enjoyed!
How sweet their memory still!
But they have left an aching void
The world can never fill.

4 Return, O holy Dove! return,
Sweet messenger of rest!
I hate the sins that made thee mourn,
And drove thee from my breast.

5 The dearest idol I have known,
Whate'er that idol be,
Help me to tear it from thy throne,
And worship only thee.

6 So shall my walk be close with God,
Calm and serene my frame;
So purer light shall mark the road
That leads me to the Lamb.

425   *Thy will be done.*   (908)

1 Father, I know thy ways are just,
Although to me unknown;
Oh grant me grace thy love to trust,
And cry, "Thy will be done."

2 If thou shouldst hedge with thorns my path,
Should wealth and friends be gone,
Still, with a firm and lively faith,
I'll cry, "Thy will be done."

3 Although thy steps I can not trace,
Thy sovereign right I'll own;
And, as instructed by thy grace,
I'll cry, "Thy will be done."

Balerma, Key B♭.   Memphis, Key A.   Ortonville, Key B♭.

OLMUTZ. S. M.
Arranged by Dr. L. MASON.

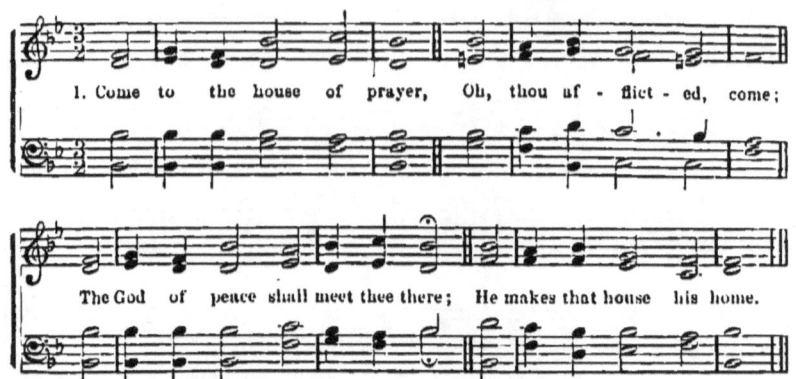

1. Come to the house of prayer, Oh, thou af-flict-ed, come; The God of peace shall meet thee there; He makes that house his home.

426 *Invitation to prayer.* (570)

2 Come to the house of praise,
Ye who are happy now;
In sweet accord your voices raise,
In kindred homage bow.

3 Ye aged, hither come,
For you have felt his love;
Soon shall your trembling tongues be dumb,
Your lips forget to move.

4 Ye young, before his throne
Come, bow; your voices raise;
Let not your hearts his praise disown
Who gives the power to praise.

5 Thou, whose benignant eye
In mercy looks on all—
Who seest the tear of misery,
And hearest the mourner's call—

6 Up to thy dwelling-place
Bear our frail spirits on,
Till they outstrip time's tardy pace,
And heaven on earth be won.

427 *Having all in Christ.* (770)

1 My spirit on thy care,
Blest Savior, I recline;
Thou wilt not leave me to despair,
For thou art love divine.

2 In thee I place my trust;
On thee I calmly rest;
I know thee good, I know thee just,
And count thy choice the best.

3 Whate'er events betide,
Thy will they all perform;
Safe in thy breast my head I hide,
Nor fear the coming storm.

4 Let good or ill befall,
It must be good for me—
Secure of having thee in all,
Of having all in thee.

428 *Not far from home.* (917)

1 Your harps, ye trembling saints!
Down from the willows take;
Loud to the praise of love divine,
Bid every string awake.

2 Though in a foreign land,
We are not far from home,
And, nearer to our house above,
We every moment come.

3 His grace will, to the end,
Stronger and brighter shine;
Nor present things, nor things to come,
Shall quench this spark divine.

4 When we in darkness walk,
Nor feel the heavenly flame,
Then will we trust our gracious God,
And rest upon his name.

5 Blest is the man, O God!
That stays himself on thee:
Who waits for thy salvation, Lord!
Shall thy salvation see.

Golden Hill, Key F.   St. Thomas, Key G.   Kentucky, Key A♭.

PRAYER AND SOCIAL MEETINGS. 155

WILBOR. 7s, Double. Subject by SCHICHT.

1. Sav-ior, when in dust to thee Low we bow th' a-dor-ing knee;
When, re-pent-ant, to the skies Scarce we lift our stream-ing eyes;
Oh, by all thy pains and woe, Suffered once for man be-low,
Bend-ing from thy throne on high, Hear us when to thee we cry.

429 *Hear us when to thee we cry.* (578)
2 By thy birth and early years,
By thy human griefs and fears,
By thy fasting and distress
In the lonely wilderness;
By thy victory in the hour
Of the subtle tempter's power;
Jesus, look with pitying eye,
Hear our humble, earnest cry.

3 By thine hour of dark despair,
By thine agony of prayer,
By thy purple robe of scorn,
By thy wounds, thy crown of thorn,
By thy cross, thy pangs, and cries,
By thy perfect sacrifice;
Jesus, look with pitying eye,
Listen to our humble cry.

4 By thy deep, expiring groan,
By the sealed sepulchral stone,
By thy triumph o'er the grave,
By thy power from death to save:
Dying, risen, ascended, Lord,
To thy throne in heaven restored,
Bending from thy throne on high,
Hear us when to thee we cry.

430 *Flee from the wrath to come.* (308)
1 Sinner, art thou still secure?
Wilt thou still refuse to pray?
Can thy heart or hands endure
In the Lord's avenging day?
See his mighty arm made bare!
Awful terrors clothe his brow!
For his judgment now prepare,
Thou must either break or bow.

2 At his presence nature shakes;
Earth, affrighted, hastes to flee;
Solid mountains melt like wax:
What will then become of thee?
Who his coming may abide?
You that glory in your shame,
Will you find a place to hide
When the world is wrapt in flame?

3 Then the great, the rich, the wise,
Trembling, guilty, self-condemned,
Must behold the wrathful eyes
Of the Judge they once blasphemed.
Where are now their haughty looks?
Oh! their horror and despair,
When they see the opened books,
And their dreadful sentence hear.

THE CHURCH:

HOUR OF PRAYER. 8, 8, 8, 4, or 8, 8, 8, 6. (New.)   J. P. POWELL.

1. My God! is an-y hour so sweet From blush of morn to evening star,
As that which calls me to thy feet—The hour of prayer.

431   *The hour of prayer.*   (581)

2 Blest is the tranquil hour of morn,
  And blest that hour of solemn eve,
When, on the wings of prayer up-borne,
  The world I leave.

3 Then is my strength by thee renewed;
  Then are my sins by thee forgiven;
Then dost thou cheer my solitude
  With hopes of heaven.

4 No words can tell what sweet relief
  There for my every want I find;
What strength for warfare, balm for grief,
  What peace of mind!

5 Hushed is each doubt, gone every fear;
  My spirit seems in heaven to stay;
And e'en the penitential tear
  Is wiped away.

432   *God is love.*   (86)

1 I can not always trace the way
  Where thou, almighty One, dost move;
But I can always, always say,
  That God is love.

2 When fear her chilling mantle flings
  O'er earth, my soul to heaven above,
As to her native home, upsprings;
  For God is love.

3 When mystery clouds my darkened path,
  I'll check my dread, my doubts reprove;
In this my soul sweet comfort hath,
  That God is love!

4 Oh may this truth my heart employ,
  And every gloomy thought remove;
It fills my soul with boundless joy,
  That God is love!

433   *Thy will be done.*   (900)

1 My God, my Father, while I stray
Far from my home, on life's rough way,
Oh, teach me from my heart to say,
  "Thy will be done!"

2 What though in lonely grief I sigh
For friends beloved no longer nigh;
Submissive still would I reply,
  "Thy will be done!"

3 If thou shouldst call me to resign
What most I prize—it ne'er was mine,
I only yield thee what was thine:
  "Thy will be done!"

4 If but my fainting heart be blest
With thy sweet Spirit for its guest,
My God, to thee I leave the rest:
  "Thy will be done!"

Oriel, Key A♭.   Delaware, Key A♭.

PRAYER AND SOCIAL MEETINGS. 157

THE HOUSE OF THE LORD. ✱ Harmonized by T. E. PERKINS.

1. You may sing of the beau-ty of mountain and dale,
Of the sil-ver-y streamlets and flowers of the vale; But the place most de-
light-ful this earth can af-ford, Is the place of de-votion, the house of the Lord.

2. You may boast of the sweetness of day's ear-ly dawn,
Of the sky's softening graces when day is just gone; But there's no oth-er
sea-son or time can compare With the hour of devotion, the sea-son of prayer.

434   *The house of the Lord.*   (403)

3 You may value the friendships of youth and of age,
And select for your comrades the noble and sage;
But the friends that most cheer me on life's rugged road
Are the friends of my Master, the children of God.

4 You may talk of your prospects, of fame, or of wealth,
And the hopes that oft flatter the favorites of health;
But the hope of bright glory, of heavenly bliss—
Take away every other, and give me but this.

5 Ever hail, blessed temple, abode of my Lord!
I will turn to thee often, to hear from his word;
I will walk to thine altar with those that I love,
And rejoice in the prospects revealed from above.

SING OF JESUS. 8s & 5, Peculiar. (260) From "Harp of Judah."

435
1. Sing of Je-sus, sing for-ev-er Of the love that chang-es
nev-er! Who, or what, from him can sev-er Those he makes his own?

2. With his blood the Lord hath bought them, When they knew him not he
sought them, And from all their wanderings bro't them: His the praise a-lone.

3. Through the des-ert Je-sus leads them, With the bread of heaven he
feeds them, And through all their way he speeds them To their home a-bove.

PORTUGUESE HYMN. 11s. (580)

436

1. Our Father in heaven, We hallow thy name! May thy kingdom ho-ly On earth be the same! Oh, give to us dai-ly Our portion of bread; It is from thy bounty That all must be fed, It is from thy boun-ty That all must be fed.

2. Forgive our transgressions, And teach us to know That humble compassion That pardons each foe; Keep us from temptation, From weakness and sin, And thine be the glo-ry For-ev-er—A-men, And thine be the glo-ry Forev-er—A-men.

437 *Faint, yet pursuing.* (583)

1 Though faint, yet pursuing, we go on our way;
The Lord is our Leader, his Word is our stay;
Though suffering, and sorrow, and trial be near,
The Lord is our refuge, and whom can we fear?

2 He raiseth the fallen, he cheereth the faint;
The weak and oppressed, he will hear their complaint;
The way may be weary, and thorny the road,
But how can we falter? our help is in God.

3 And to his green pastures our footsteps he leads;
His flock in the desert, how kindly he feeds!
The lambs in his bosom he tenderly bears,
And brings back the wanderers all safe from the snares.

4 Though clouds may surround us, our God is our light;
Though storms rage around us, our God is our might;
So faint, yet pursuing, still onward we come;
The Lord is our Leader, and heaven is our home.

Kimmel, Key E.   Expostulation, Key G.   How firm a foundation, Key A.

HOW FIRM A FOUNDATION. 11s.

1. How firm a foun-da-tion, you saints of the Lord, Is laid for your faith in his ex-cel-lent word! What more can he say than to you he has said,
D. S. You who un-to Je-sus for ref-uge have fled?

438 *Precious promises.* (792)

2 In every condition, in sickness, in health,
In poverty's vale, or abounding in wealth;
At home and abroad, on the land, on the sea,
As your days may demand, so your succor shall be.

3 Fear not—I am with you; oh be not dismayed!
I, I am your God, and will still give you aid;
I'll strengthen you, help you, and cause you to stand,
Upheld by my righteous, omnipotent hand.

4 When through the deep waters I cause you to go,
The rivers of sorrow shall not you o'erflow:
For I will be with you, your troubles to bless,
And sanctify to you your deepest distress.

5 When through fiery trials your pathway shall lie,
My grace, all-sufficient, shall be your supply:
The flame shall not hurt you; I only design
Your dross to consume, and your gold to refine.

6 E'en down to old age all my people shall prove
My sovereign, eternal, unchangeable love;
And when hoary hairs shall their temples adorn,
Like lambs they shall still in my bosom be borne.

439 *The house of prayer.* (585)

1 How honored, how dear, is that sacred abode
Where Christians draw near to their Father and God!
'Mid worldly commotion my wearied soul faints
For the house of devotion, the home of thy saints.

2 Thou hearer of prayer, oh still grant me a place
Where Christians repair to the courts of thy grace!
More blest beyond measure one day so employed,
Than years of vain pleasure by worldlings enjoyed.

Portuguese Hymn, Key G. Memory, Key E.

HENLEY. 11s & 10s.　　　　　　　Dr. L. MASON, by permission.

1. Come un-to me when shadows dark-ly gath-er, When the sad heart is
D. S. Come un-to me, and

wea-ry and distressed, Seek-ing for com-fort from your heavenly Father,
I will give you rest.

440　　　　　"Come unto me."　　　　　(1228)

2 Ye who have mourned when the spring flowers were taken;
When the ripe fruit fell richly to the ground;
When the loved slept, in brighter homes to waken,
Where their pale brows with spirit-wreaths are crowned.

3 Large are the mansions in thy Father's dwelling,
Glad are the homes that sorrows never dim;
Sweet are the harps in holy music swelling,
Soft are the tones which raise the heavenly hymn.

4 There, like an Eden, blossoming in gladness,
Bloom the fair flowers the earth too rudely pressed;
Come unto me, all ye who droop in sadness,
Come unto me, and I will give you rest.

441　　　　For divine strength.　　　　(584)

1 Father, in thy mysterious presence kneeling,
Fain would our souls feel all thy kindling love,
For we are weak, and need some deep revealing
Of trust, and strength, and calmness, from above.

2 Lord, we have wandered forth through doubt and sorrow,
And thou hast made each step an onward one;
And we will ever trust each unknown morrow—
Thou wilt sustain us till its work is done.

3 In the heart's depths, a peace serene and holy
Abides; and when pain seems to have her will,
Or we despair, oh may that peace rise slowly,
Stronger than agony, and we be still!

4 Now, Father, now, in thy dear presence kneeling,
Our spirits yearn to feel thy kindling love:
Now make us strong; we need thy deep revealing
Of trust, and strength, and calmness from above.

442   *A little while.*   (930)

1 Oh for the peace that floweth as a river,
   Making life's desert places bloom and smile!
Oh for that faith to grasp the glad Forever,
   Amid the shadows of earth's Little While!

2 A little while for patient vigil keeping,
   To face the storm, to wrestle with the strong;
A little while to sow the seed with weeping,
   Then bind the sheaves and sing the harvest-song.

3 A little while to wear the veil of sadness,
   To toil with weary step through miry ways,
Then to pour forth the fragrant oil of gladness,
   And clasp the girdle round the robe of Praise!

4 A little while, 'mid shadow and illusion,
   To strive by faith love's mysteries to spell,
Then read each dark enigma's bright solution,
   Then hail sight's verdict—he doeth all things well.

5 And he who is himself the Gift and Giver,
   The future glory and the present smile,
With the bright promise of the glad Forever,
   Will light the shadows of earth's Little While.

443   "*Sorrowful, yet always rejoicing.*"   (1031)

1 We will not weep, for God is standing by us,
   And tears will blind us to the blessed sight;
We will not doubt, if darkness still doth try us;
   Our souls have promise of serenest light.

2 We will not faint, if heavy burdens bend us;
   They press no harder than our souls can bear;
The thorniest way is lying still behind us;
   We shall be braver for the past despair.

3 Oh not in doubt shall be our journey's ending;
   Sin, with its fears, shall leave us at the last;
All its best hopes in glad fulfillment blending,
   Life shall be with us more when death is past.

4 Help us, O Father! when the world is pressing
   On our frail hearts, that faint without their friend;
Help us, O Father! let thy constant blessing
   Strengthen our weakness, till the joyful end.

444   *I, the Lord, will hasten it, etc.*   (978)

1 Down the dark future, through long generations,
   The sounds of war grow fainter, and then cease;
And like a bell with solemn, sweet vibrations,
   I hear once more the voice of Christ say, "Peace!

2 Peace! and no longer, from its brazen portals,
   The blast of war's great organ shakes the skies;
But beautiful as songs of the immortals,
   The holy melodies of love arise.

Henley, Key E.

SUPPLICATION. 6, 11, 11, 10, 6. (New.) Dr. T. HASTINGS.

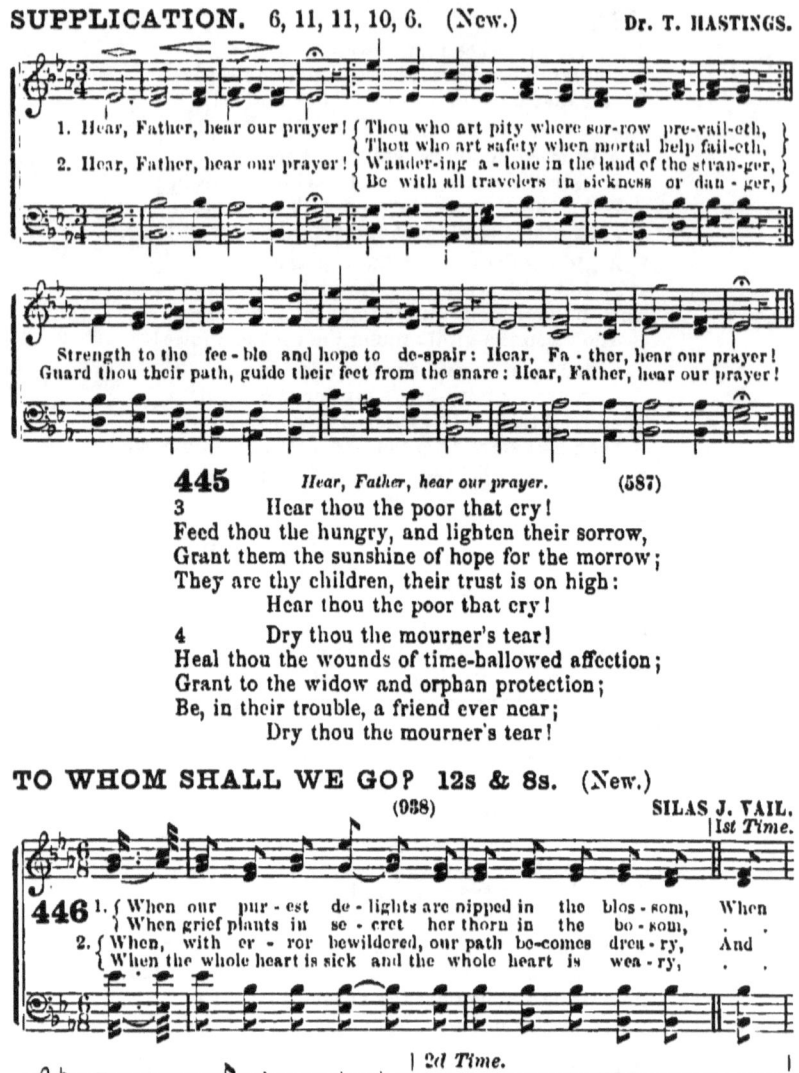

1. Hear, Father, hear our prayer! Thou who art pity where sorrow prevaileth,
Thou who art safety when mortal help faileth,
2. Hear, Father, hear our prayer! Wandering alone in the land of the stranger,
Be with all travelers in sickness or danger,
Strength to the feeble and hope to despair: Hear, Father, hear our prayer!
Guard thou their path, guide their feet from the snare: Hear, Father, hear our prayer!

445 *Hear, Father, hear our prayer.* (587)

3 Hear thou the poor that cry!
Feed thou the hungry, and lighten their sorrow,
Grant them the sunshine of hope for the morrow;
They are thy children, their trust is on high:
Hear thou the poor that cry!

4 Dry thou the mourner's tear!
Heal thou the wounds of time-hallowed affection;
Grant to the widow and orphan protection;
Be, in their trouble, a friend ever near;
Dry thou the mourner's tear!

TO WHOM SHALL WE GO? 12s & 8s. (New.)
(938) SILAS J. VAIL.

446
1. When our purest delights are nipped in the blossom,
When grief plants in secret her thorn in the bosom,
2. When, with error bewildered, our path becomes dreary,
And when the whole heart is sick and the whole heart is weary,
those we love best are laid low;
tears of despondency flow:
Deserted—"to whom shall we go?"
Despairing—"to whom shall we go?"

PRAYER AND SOCIAL MEETINGS. 163

COME, YE DISCONSOLATE. 11s & 10s. (386)   S. WEBBE.

Solo, Duet, or Trio.

447

1. Come, ye discon-so-late, wher-e'er you lan-guish, Come, at the shrine of God fer-vent-ly kneel; here tell your an-guish, Earth has no sor-row that heaven can not heal.
2. Joy of the des-o-late, light of the stray-ing, Hope of the pen-i-tent, fade-less and pure! ten-der-ly say-ing, Earth has no sor-row that heaven can not cure.
3. Here see the bread of life; see wa-ters flow-ing, Forth from the throne of God, pure from a-bove; come, ev-er know-ing, Earth has no sor-rows but heaven can remove.

1st time Duet; 2d time Chorus.

Here bring your wounded hearts,
Here speaks the Com-fort - er,
Come to the feast of love;

COME TO JESUS JUST NOW.

1. Come to Je-sus, come to Je-sus, Come to Je-sus, just now, just now; Come to Je-sus, come to Je-sus, just now.

448   *Come unto me.*

2. He will save you, etc.
3. Oh, believe him.
4. He is able.

5. He is willing, etc.
6. Only trust him.
7. He'll receive you.

THE CHURCH:

TRUST. 8s & 7s, with Chorus. ✢   W. T. MOORE.

1. Gently, Lord, oh, gently lead us
Thro' this gloomy vale of tears,
Thro' the changes thou 'st decreed us,
Till our last great change appears.
When temptation's darts assail us,
When in devious paths we stray,
Let thy goodness never fail us,
Lead us in thy perfect way.

D. S. May thy mercies, never ceasing,
Fit us for thy dwelling place.

Chorus.
Oh, refresh us with thy blessing,
Oh, refresh us with thy grace.

449   *For thy name's sake, lead me, etc.*   (1175)

2 In the hour of pain and anguish,
  In the hour when death draws near,
Suffer not our hearts to languish,
  Suffer not our souls to fear.
Let thy promise to be near us
  Fill our hearts with joy and peace;
May thy presence sweetly cheer us,
  Till our conflicts all shall cease.
    Oh, refresh us, etc.

3 When this mortal life is ended,
  Bid us in thy arms to rest,
Till, by angel hands attended,
  We awake among the blest.
Then, oh, crown us with thy blessing,
  Through the triumphs of thy grace;
Then shall praises never ceasing
  Echo through thy dwelling-place.
    Oh, refresh us, etc.

FROM THE DEPTHS. 11s & 5. (New.)   Dr. T. HASTINGS.

1. From the re-cess-es of a low - ly spir-it, Our humble prayer ascends; O Father!
2. We see thy hand: it leads us, it supports us; We hear thy voice: it counsels and it

hear it, Up-soar-ing on the wings of awe and meekness; Forgive its weak-ness!
courts us; And then we turn away; and still thy kindness Forgives our blind-ness.

450   *Prayer of the contrite.*   (588)

3 Oh, how long suffering, Lord! but thou delightest
To win with love the wandering; thou invitest
By smiles of mercy, not by frowns or terrors,
    Man from his errors.

LEAD THOU ME ON. 10s & 4s.

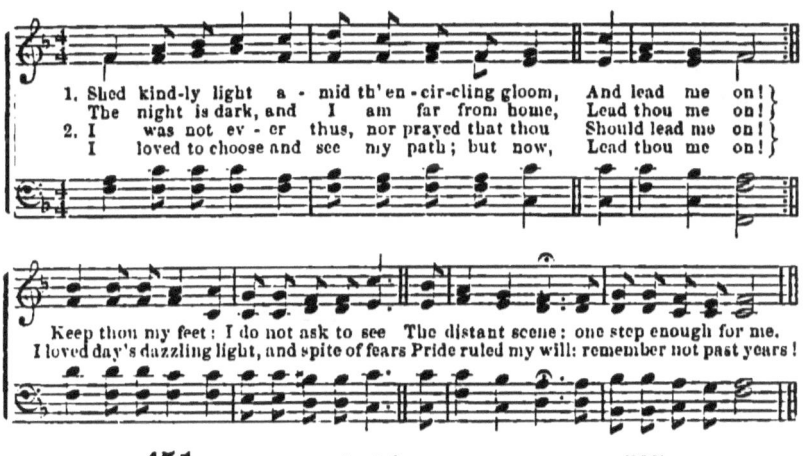

1. Shed kind-ly light a - mid th' en-cir-cling gloom, And lead me on!
   The night is dark, and I am far from home, Lead thou me on!
2. I was not ev - er thus, nor prayed that thou Should lead me on!
   I loved to choose and see my path; but now, Lead thou me on!

Keep thou my feet: I do not ask to see The distant scene: one step enough for me.
I loved day's dazzling light, and spite of fears Pride ruled my will: remember not past years!

451   *Lead thou me on.*   (590)

3 So long thy power hath blessed me, surely still
   'T will lead me on!
Through dreary doubt, through pain and sorrow, till
   The night is gone!
And with the morn those angel faces smile
Which I have loved long since and lost awhile.

THE CHURCH:

ANVERN. L. M.
Dr. L. MASON, by permission.

1. Triumphant Zion! lift thy head From dust, and darkness, and the dead! Tho' humbled long, awake at length, And gird thee with thy Savior's strength, And gird thee with thy Savior's strength.

452 *Put on thy strength, O Zion.* (591)

2 Put all thy beauteous garments on,
And let thy excellence be known;
Decked in the robes of righteousness,
The world thy glories shall confess.

3 No more shall foes unclean invade,
And fill thy hallowed walls with dread;
No more shall hell's insulting host
Their victory and thy sorrows boast.

4 God, from on high, has heard thy prayer:
His hand thy ruins shall repair;
Nor will thy watchful monarch cease
To guard thee in eternal peace.

453 *All nations shall serve him.* (592)

1 Eternal Lord! from land to land
Shall echo thine all-glorious name,
Till kingdoms bow at thy command,
And every lip thy praise proclaim.

2 Exalted high on every shore,
The banner of the cross unfurled,
Shall summon thousands to adore
The Savior of a ransomed world.

3 Thousands shall join thy pilgrim band,
And, by that sacred standard led,
Press forward to Immanuel's land,
Nor fear the thorny path to tread.

4 Triumphant over every foe,
Their ransomed hosts shall move along
To that blest world, where sin and woe
Shall never mingle with their song.

454 *Put on thy beautiful garments.* (593)

1 Zion, awake! thy strength renew;
Put on thy robes of beauteous hue;
Church of our God, arise and shine,
Bright with the beams of truth divine.

2 Soon shall thy radiance stream afar,
Wide as the heathen nations are;
Gentiles and kings thy light shall view;
All shall admire and love thee too.

455 *Isaiah 51 : 9.* (1268)

1 Arm of the Lord, awake! awake!
Put on thy strength, the nations shake,
And let the world, adoring, see
Triumphs of mercy wrought by thee.

2 Say to the heathen, from thy throne,
"I am Jehovah—God alone!"
Thy voice their idols shall confound,
And cast their altars to the ground.

3 No more let human blood be spilt—
Vain sacrifice for human guilt!
But to each conscience be applied
The blood that flowed from Jesus' side.

4 Let Zion's time of favor come;
Oh bring the tribes of Israel home!
And let our wondering eyes behold
Gentiles and Jews in Jesus' fold.

5 Almighty God, thy grace proclaim
In every land, of every name!
Let adverse powers before thee fall,
And crown the Savior Lord of all.

Ware, Key B♭.   Wells, Key E♭.

456 *All the ends of the world.* (1267)

1 Come from the east, with gifts, ye kings,
With gold, and frankincense, and myrrh,
Where'er the morning spreads her wings,
Let man to God his vows prefer.

2 Come from the west! the bond, the free;
His easy service make your choice;
Ye isles of the Pacific sea,
Like halcyon nests, in God rejoice.

3 Come from the south! through desert sands,
A highway for the Lord prepare!
Let Ethiopia stretch her hands,
And Libya pour her soul in prayer.

4 Come from the north! let Europe raise
In all her languages one song;
Give God the glory, power, and praise
That to his holy name belong.

457 *Prayer for general peace.* (951)

1 Thy footsteps, Lord, with joy we trace,
And mark the conquest of thy grace;
Complete the work thou hast begun,
And let thy will on earth be done.

2 Oh, show thyself the Prince of Peace;
Command the din of war to cease;
Oh, bid contending nations rest,
And let thy love rule every breast!

3 Then peace returns with balmy wing:
Glad plenty laughs, the valleys sing;
Reviving commerce lifts her head,
And want, and woe, and hate, have fled.

4 Thou good and wise, and righteous Lord,
All move subservient to thy word;
Oh, soon let every nation prove
The perfect joy of Christian love!

458 *A parting hymn.* (720)

1 Come, Christian brethren, ere we part,
Join every voice and every heart;
One solemn hymn to God we raise,
One final song of grateful praise.

2 Christians, we here may meet no more;
But there is yet a happier shore;
And there, released from toil and pain,
Dear brethren, we shall meet again.

459 *I will praise thee forever.* (635)

1 My God, my King, thy various praise
Shall fill the remnant of my days;
Thy grace employ my humble tongue,
Till death and glory raise the song.

2 The wings of every hour shall bear
Some thankful tribute to thine ear,
And every setting sun shall see
New works of duty done for thee.

3 Let distant times and nations raise
The long succession of thy praise;
And unborn ages make my song
The joy and labor of my tongue.

4 But who can speak thy wondrous deeds?
Thy greatness all my thoughts exceeds:
Vast and unsearchable thy ways,
Vast and immortal is thy praise.

460 *Condescension of Christ.* (638)

1 How sweet the praise, how high the theme,
To sing of him who rules supreme,
Who dwells at God's right hand on high,
Yet looks on us with tender eye.

2 The angelic host, in countless throngs,
Recount his glories in their songs,
And golden harps salute his ear;
Yet our weak praise he deigns to hear.

3 The planets roll their orbits round;
Unnumbered worlds, in space profound,
Are ruled by him, by him controlled;
Yet he's the Shepherd of our fold.

4 Exalted high upon his throne,
The universe is all his own:
Untold the honors he doth wear;
Yet we are objects of his care.

461 *Bid us all depart in peace.* (721)

1 Dismiss us with thy blessing, Lord;
Help us to feed upon thy word;
All that has been amiss, forgive,
And let thy truth within us live.

2 Though we are guilty, thou art good;
Cleanse all our sins in Jesus' blood;
Give every burdened soul release,
And bid us all depart in peace.

Rockingham, Key G.   Old Hundred, Key A.   Uxbridge, Key E.

DEVIZES. C. M.

1. Behold the mountain of the Lord In lat-ter days shall rise On mountain tops a-bove the hills, And draw the wondering eyes, And draw the wondering eyes.

462 *All nations shall flow unto it.* (507)

2 To this the joyful nations round,
All tribes and tongues shall flow;
Up to the hill of God, they'll say,
And to his house we'll go!

3 The beam that shines from Zion hill
Shall lighten every land!
The King who reigns in Salem's towers
Shall all the world command.

4 No strife shall vex Messiah's reign,
Or mar the peaceful years,
To plowshares men shall beat their swords,
To pruning-hooks their spears.

5 No longer hosts, encountering hosts,
Their millions slain deplore;
They hang the trumpet in the hall,
And study war no more.

6 Come, then—oh come from every land,
To worship at his shrine;
And, walking in the light of God,
With holy beauties shine.

463 *This is the day.* (618)

1 Come, let us join, with one accord,
In hymns around the throne;
This is the day our risen Lord
Hath made and called his own.

2 This is the day which God has blessed,
The brightest of the seven,
Type of the everlasting rest
The saints enjoy in heaven.

3 Then let us in his name sing on,
And hasten on that day,
When our Redeemer shall come down,
And shadows pass away.

4 Not one, but all our days below,
Our hearts his praise employ;
And in our Lord rejoicing go
To his eternal joy.

464 *The Savior died for me.* (643)

1 To our Redeemer's glorious name
Awake the sacred song;
Oh may his love (immortal flame!)
Tune every heart and tongue.

2 His love, what mortal thought can reach!
What mortal tongue display!
Imagination's utmost stretch
In wonder dies away.

3 He left his radiant throne on high,
Left the bright realms of bliss,
And came to earth to bleed and die!
Was ever love like this?

4 Blest Lord, while we adoring pay
Our humble thanks to thee,
May every heart with rapture say,
"The Savior died for me!"

5 Oh may the sweet, the blissful theme,
Fill every heart and tongue,
Till strangers love thy charming name,
And join the sacred song.

Arlington, Key G. Chimes, Key C. Brown, Key C.

GROWTH AND FUTURE TRIUMPHS. 169

HARK! THE SONG OF JUBILEE. 7s, Double. HANDEL.

1. Hark! the song of Jubilee, Loud as it
Or the full-ness of the sea When mighty thunders roar,
D. C. Hal-le-lu-jah! let the word Ech-o breaks up-on the shore!} Hal-le-lu-jah round the earth and main. for the Lord God om-nip-o-tent shall reign!

465 Rev. 19: 6. (600)

2 Hallelujah! Hark! the sound,
  From the depths unto the skies,
Wakes above, beneath, around,
  All creation's harmonies.
See Jehovah's banner furled,
  Sheathed his sword: he speaks—'t is done!
And the kingdoms of this world
  Are the kingdoms of his Son!

3 He shall reign from pole to pole,
  With illimitable sway;
He shall reign when, like a scroll,
  Yonder heavens have passed away.
Then the end: beneath his rod
  Man's last enemy shall fall:
Hallelujah! Christ in God,
  God in Christ, is all in all!

466 Let us not sleep, as do others. (884)

1 Sleep not, soldier of the cross!
  Foes are lurking all around;
Look not here to find repose;
  This is but thy battle-ground;
Up! and take thy shield and sword;
  Up! it is the call of heaven:
Shrink not faithless from the Lord:
  Nobly strive as he hath striven.

2 Break through all the force of ill;
  Tread the might of passion down—
Struggling onward, onward still,
  To thy conquering Savior's crown!
Through the midst of toil and pain,
  Let this thought ne'er leave thy breast;
Every triumph thou dost gain
  Makes more sweet thy coming rest.

Amboy, Key D. Eltham, Key G. Ives, Key E♭.

THE CHURCH:

DAUGHTER OF ZION. 11s. (605)

467
1. Daughter of Zion, awake from thy sadness; Awake, for thy foes shall oppress thee no more; Bright o'er the hills dawns the day-star of gladness, Arise, for the night of thy sorrow is o'er. Daughter of Zi-on, awake from thy sadness; Awake, for thy foes shall oppress thee no more, Shall oppress thee no more, no more, no more.
2. Strong were thy foes, but the arm that subdued them, And scattered their legions, was mightier far; They fled, like the chaff, from the scourge that pursued them, Vain were their steeds and their chariots of war. Daughter of Zi-on, etc.
3. Daughter of Zion, the power that hath saved thee, Extolled with the harp and the timbrel should be; Shout! for the foe is destroyed that enslaved thee, The oppressor is vanquished and Zi-on is free. Daughter of Zi-on, etc.

"OUR FATHER." Chant. Gregorian.

468 *The Lord's Prayer.*

1 Our Father, who art in heaven, | hallowed | be thy | name ; |
 Thy kingdom come, thy will be done on | earth,...as it | is in | heaven ; |
2 Give us this | day our | daily | bread ; |
 And forgive us our trespasses, as we forgive | them that || tres-...passa- | gainst us.
3 And lead us not into temptation, but de- | liver | us from || evil ; |
 For thine is the kingdom, and the power, and the glory, for- | ever. | A- || men.

GROWTH AND FUTURE TRIUMPHS. 171

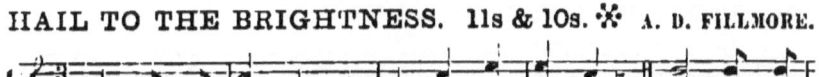

469 *Hail to the brightness.* (608)

2 Hail to the brightness of Zion's glad morning,
  Long by the prophets of Israel foretold!
Hail to the millions from bondage returning!
  Gentiles and Jews the blest vision behold.

3 Lo! in the desert rich flowers are springing;
  Streams ever copious are gliding along;
Loud from the mountain-tops echoes are ringing;
  Wastes rise in verdure and mingle in song.

4 See, from all lands—from the isles of the ocean—
  Praise to Jehovah ascending on high;
Fallen are the engines of war and commotion,
  Shouts of salvation are rending the sky.

470 *The day of joy.* (1284)

1 Wake thee, O Zion! thy mourning is ended;
  God—thine own God—hath regarded thy prayer;
Wake thee, and hail him in glory descended,
  Thy darkness to scatter—thy wastes to repair.

2 Wake thee, O Zion! his spirit of power
  To newness of life is awaking the dead;
Array thee in beauty, and greet the glad hour
  That brings thee salvation, through Jesus who bled.

3 Savior, we gladly, with voices resounding
  Loud as the thunder, our chorus would swell,
Till from rock, wood, and mountain, its echoes rebounding,
  To all the wide world of salvation shall tell.

MARTON. 8s, 7s & 4.

471 *The day-spring.* (602)

1 Christian, see! the orient morning
Breaks along the heathen sky;
Lo! the expected day is dawning—
Glorious day-spring from on high;
Hallelujah!—
Hail the day-spring from on high!

2 Heathens at the sight are singing;
Morning wakes the tuneful lays;
Precious offerings they are bringing—
First-fruits of more perfect praise;
Hallelujah!—
Hail the day-spring from on high!

3 Zion's Sun! salvation beaming,
Gilding now the radiant hills,
Rise and shine till, brighter gleaming,
All the world thy glory fills;
Hallelujah!—
Hail the day-spring from on high!

4 Lord of every tribe and nation!
Spread thy truth from pole to pole;
Spread the light of thy salvation
Till it shine on every soul;
Hallelujah!—
Hail the day-spring from on high!

472 *Encouraging prospects.* (603)

1 Yes, we trust the day is breaking;
Joyful times are near at hand;
God, the mighty God, is speaking,
By his word, in every land:
When he chooses,
Darkness flies at his command.

2 While the foe becomes more daring,
While he enters like a flood,
God, the Savior, is preparing
Means to spread his truth abroad:
Every language
Soon shall tell the love of God.

3 Oh 't is pleasant, 't is reviving
To our hearts, to hear, each day,
Joyful news, from far arriving,
How the gospel wins its way;
Those enlightening
Who in death and darkness lay.

4 God of Jacob! high and glorious,
Let thy people see thy hand;
Let the gospel be victorious,
Through the world, in every land;
Then shall idols
Perish, Lord, at thy command.

Zion, Key D.   Molucca, Key D.   Happy Zion, Key C.

GROWTH AND FUTURE TRIUMPHS. 173

BURLINGTON. 12s, 11 & 8. From NAGELI.

1. The Prince of Salvation in triumph is riding, And glory attends him along his bright way.
The news of his grace on the breezes is gliding, And nations are owning his sway.

2. And now through the darkness of earth's gloomy regions, The wheels of his chariot are rolling sublime;
His banners un-fold-ing his own true relig-ion, Dis-pell-ing the errors of time.

473 *In thy majesty, etc.* (606)

3 Behold a bright angel from heaven descending,
  High lifting his trumpet, hosannas to raise:
"Hail, Son of the Highest! let every knee, bending,
  Adore thee with off'rings of praise.

4 "Thy sword and thy buckler shall save and deliver
  The poor and the needy from foes that assail;
Thy bow and thy quiver shall vanquish forever
  The prince and the legions of hell.

5 "Ride on in thy greatness, thou conquering Savior!
  Let thousands of thousands submit to thy reign,
Acknowledge thy goodness, entreat for thy favor,
  And follow thy glorious train."

JESUS WAITS FOR THEE. HUBERT P. MAIN.

474
1. Come, come to Je-sus! He waits to wel-come thee, O Wan-d'rer! ea-ger-ly; Come, come to Je-sus;
2. Come, come to Je-sus! He waits to ran-som thee, O Slave! e-ter-nal-ly; Come, come to Je-sus;

3 Come, come to Jesus!
  He waits to lighten thee,
  O Burdened! graciously;
  Come, come to Jesus!

4 Come, come to Jesus!
  He waits to give to thee,
  O Blind! a vision free;
  Come, come to Jesus!

THE CHURCH:

TRUMPET. 10s, 11s & 12s.   I. B. WOODBURY, by permission.

*1. Shout the glad tidings! ex-ult-ing-ly sing, Je - ru - sa - lem triumphs! Mes-
D. C. Shout the glad tidings, etc.
si-ah is King! { Zi - on, the marvelous sto-ry be telling, The }
             { Son of the Highest, how lowly his birth! ... } The brightest of
angels in glo - ry ex - cell - ing, He stoops to redeem thee—he reigns upon earth.

* Chorus to precede and close each verse.

475   *Shout, inhabitant of Zion.*   (607)

2 Tell how he cometh from nation to nation,
  The heart-cheering news let the earth echo round,
  How free to the sinner he offers salvation!
  How his people with joy everlasting are crowned!

3 Mortals, your homage be gratefully bringing,
  And sweet let the gladsome hosanna arise;
  You angels, the full hallelujah be singing—
  One chorus resound through the earth and the skies!

476   *Lanesboro, Key C.*   (712)

1 Blest is the hour when cares depart,
    And earthly scenes are far—
  When tears of woe forget to start,
  And gently dawns upon the heart
    Devotion's holy star.

2 Blest is the place where angels bend
    To hear our worship rise,
  Where kindred hearts their musings blend,
  And all the soul's affections tend
    Beyond the veiling skies.

3 Blest are the hallowed vows that bind
    Man to his work of love—
  Bind him to cheer the humble mind,
  Console the weeping, lead the blind,
    And guide to joys above.

4 Sweet shall the song of glory swell,
    Savior divine, to thee,
  When they whose work is finished well,
  In thy own courts of rest shall dwell,
    Blest through eternity.

PUBLIC WORSHIP:

PETERBORO. C. M.

1. This is the day the Lord hath made, He calls the hours his own; Let heaven rejoice, let earth be glad, And praise sur-round the throne.

478 *We will rejoice and be glad in it.* (619)

2 To-day he rose and left the dead,
And Satan's empire fell,
To-day the saints his triumphs spread,
And all his wonders tell.

3 Hosanna to the anointed King,
To David's holy Son;
Help us, O Lord—descend and bring
Salvation from thy throne.

4 Blessed be the Lord who comes to men
With messages of grace;
Who comes in God his Father's name
To save our sinful race.

5 Hosanna in the highest strains
The church on earth can raise;
The highest heavens, in which he reigns,
Shall give him nobler praise.

479 *I will praise thee, etc.* (620)

1 O Father! though the anxious fear
May cloud to-morrow's way,
No fear nor doubt shall enter here;
All shall be thine to-day.

2 We will not bring divided hearts
To worship at thy shrine;
But each unworthy thought departs,
And leaves this temple thine.

3 Sleep, sleep to-day, tormenting cares,
Of earth and folly born;
Ye shall not dim the light that streams
From this celestial morn.

480 *Lev. 23: 11, and 1 Cor. 15: 20.* (621)

1 This is the day the first ripe sheaf
Before the Lord was waved,
And Christ, first fruits of them that slept,
Was from the dead received.

2 He rose for them for whom he died,
That, like to him, they may
Rise when he comes, in glory great,
That ne'er shall fade away.

3 This is the day the Spirit came
With us on earth to stay—
A Comforter, to fill our hearts
With joys that ne'er decay.

4 His comforts are the earnest sure
Of that same heavenly rest
Which Jesus entered on, when he
Was made forever blest.

5 This day the Christian Church began,
Formed by his wondrous grace;
This day the saints in concord meet,
To join in prayer and praise.

481 *Glory to God.* (734)

1 Glory to God! who deigns to bless
This consecrated day,
Unfolds his wondrous promises,
And makes it sweet to pray.

2 Glory to God! who deigns to hear
The humblest sigh we raise,
And answers every heartfelt prayer,
And hears our hymn of praise.

Howard, Key C.   Mear, Key F.   Heber, Key C.

THE LORD'S DAY.

FERGUSON. S. M.   G. KINGSLEY, by permission.

1. Welcome, sweet day of rest, That saw the Lord arise; Welcome to this reviving breast, And these rejoicing eyes.

482   *Welcome, sweet day of rest.*   (626)

2 The King himself comes near,
   And feasts his saints to-day:
Here may we sit and see him here,
   And love, and praise, and pray.

3 One day, amid the place
   Where Christ, my Lord, hath been,
Is sweeter than ten thousand days
   Within the tents of sin.

4 My willing soul would stay
   In such a frame as this,
And sit and sing herself away
   To everlasting bliss.

483   *This is the Lord's doing.*   (624)

1 This is the glorious day
   That our Redeemer made;
Let us rejoice, and sing, and pray,
   Let all the church be glad.

2 The work, O Lord, is thine,
   And wondrous in our eyes;
This day declares it all divine,
   This day did Jesus rise.

3 Hosanna to the King,
   Of David's royal blood:
Bless him, you saints, he comes to bring
   Salvation from your God.

4 We bless thy Holy Word,
   Which all this grace displays,
And offer on thine altar, Lord,
   Our sacrifice of praise.

484   *Redemption completed.*   (187)

1 "The Lord is risen indeed!"
   Then is his work performed;
The mighty Captive now is freed,
   And death, our foe, disarmed.

2 "The Lord is risen indeed!"
   He lives to die no more;
He lives, his people's cause to plead,
   Whose curse and shame he bore.

3 "The Lord is risen indeed!"
   The grave has lost his prey:
With him is risen the ransomed seed,
   To reign in endless day.

4 "The Lord is risen indeed!"
   Attending angels! hear:
Up to the courts of heaven with speed,
   The joyful tidings bear.

5 Then wake your golden lyres,
   And strike each cheerful chord;
Join, all ye bright, celestial choirs!
   To sing our risen Lord.

485   *The spread of truth.*   (740)

1 Thy name, almighty Lord,
   Shall sound through distant lands:
Great is thy grace, and sure thy word,
   Thy truth forever stands.

2 Far be thine honor spread,
   And long thy praise endure,
Till morning light and evening shade
   Shall be exchanged no more.

Laban, Key C.   Luther, Key F.   Gerar, Key F.

PUBLIC WORSHIP:

SABBATH. 7s, 6 lines.
Dr. L. MASON, by permission.

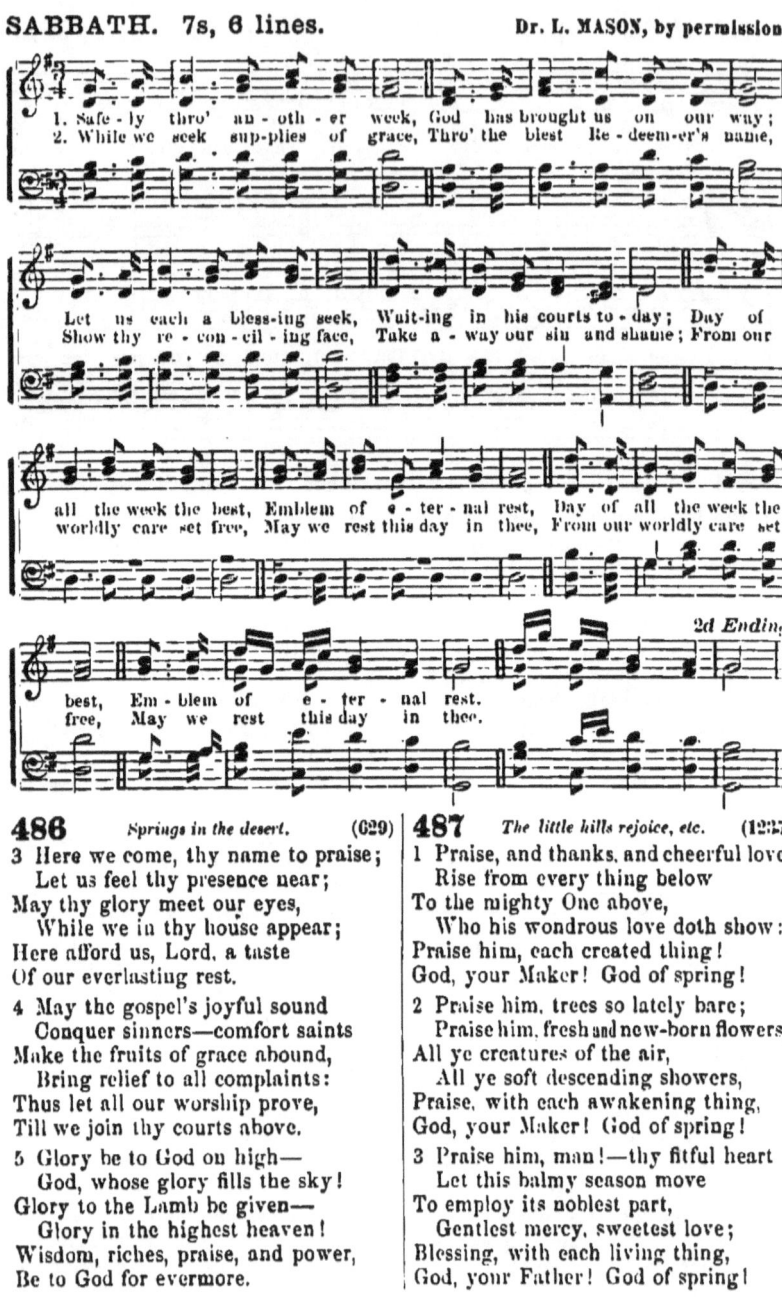

1. Safely thro' an-oth-er week, God has brought us on our way;
Let us each a blessing seek, Waiting in his courts to-day; Day of all the week the best, Emblem of e-ter-nal rest, Day of all the week the best, Em-blem of e-ter-nal rest.

2. While we seek supplies of grace, Thro' the blest Re-deem-er's name,
Show thy re-con-cil-ing face, Take a-way our sin and shame; From our worldly care set free, May we rest this day in thee, From our worldly care set free, May we rest this day in thee.

2d Ending.

---

486 *Springs in the desert.* (629)

3 Here we come, thy name to praise;
　Let us feel thy presence near;
May thy glory meet our eyes,
　While we in thy house appear;
Here afford us, Lord, a taste
Of our everlasting rest.

4 May the gospel's joyful sound
　Conquer sinners—comfort saints
Make the fruits of grace abound,
　Bring relief to all complaints:
Thus let all our worship prove,
Till we join thy courts above.

5 Glory be to God on high—
　God, whose glory fills the sky!
Glory to the Lamb be given—
　Glory in the highest heaven!
Wisdom, riches, praise, and power,
Be to God for evermore.

487 *The little hills rejoice, etc.* (1235)

1 Praise, and thanks, and cheerful love,
　Rise from every thing below
To the mighty One above,
　Who his wondrous love doth show:
Praise him, each created thing!
God, your Maker! God of spring!

2 Praise him, trees so lately bare;
　Praise him, fresh and new-born flowers;
All ye creatures of the air,
　All ye soft descending showers,
Praise, with each awakening thing,
God, your Maker! God of spring!

3 Praise him, man!—thy fitful heart
　Let this balmy season move
To employ its noblest part,
　Gentlest mercy, sweetest love;
Blessing, with each living thing,
God, your Father! God of spring!

GRATITUDE AND PRAISE. 179

HAPPY DAY. L. M., with Chorus.

488 *Happy day.* (398)

2 O happy bond, that seals my vows
To him who merits all my love!
Let cheerful anthems fill his house,
While to that sacred shrine I move.

3 'T is done; the great transaction's done,
I am my Lord's and he is mine;
He drew me, and I followed on,
Charmed to confess the voice divine.

4 Now rest, my long divided heart!
Fixed on this blissful center rest;
Here have I found a nobler part,
Here heavenly pleasures fill my breast.

489 *Self-dedication.* (397)

1 Lord, I am thine, entirely thine,
Purchased alone by blood divine;
With full consent I yield to thee,
And own thy sovereign right to me.

2 Grant me, in mercy, now a place
Among the children of thy grace;
A wretched sinner, lost to God,
But ransomed by Immanuel's blood.

490 *What shall I render unto thee?* (401)

1 Redeemed from guilt, redeemed from fears,
My soul enlarged, and dried my tears,
What can I do, O Love Divine,
What to repay such gifts as thine?

2 What can I do, so poor, so weak,
But from thy hands new blessings seek,
A heart to feel thy mercies more,
A soul to know thee and adore?

3 Oh teach me at thy feet to fall,
And yield thee up myself, my all!
Before thy saints my debts to own,
And live and die to thee alone!

491 *Christ the Redeemer.* (340)

1 Now to the Lord, who makes us know
The wonders of his dying love,
Be humble honors paid below,
And strains of nobler praise above.

2 'Twas he who cleansed us from our sins,
And washed us in his precious blood;
'T is he who makes us priests and kings,
And brings us, rebels, near to God.

PUBLIC WORSHIP:

LISCHER. H. M. ✻
Arranged by J. P. POWELL.

1. Welcome, delightful morn, Thou day of sacred rest;
I hail thy kind return— Lord, make these moments blest;
From the low train of mortal toys, I soar to reach immortal joys, I soar to reach immortal joys.

492 *Welcome, delightful morn.* (632)
2 Now may the King descend
  And fill his throne with grace;
The scepter, Lord, extend,
  While saints address thy face:
Let sinners feel thy quickening word,
And learn to know and fear the Lord.

493 *A day in thy courts, etc.* (631)
1 To spend one sacred day
  Where God and saints abide,
Affords diviner joy
  Than thousand days beside:
Where God resorts, I love it more
To keep the door, than shine in courts.

2 God is our sun and shield,
  Our light and our defense;
With gifts his hands are filled;
  We draw our blessings thence;
He will bestow on Israel's race
Peculiar grace, and glory too.

494 *The resurrection celebrated.* (630)
1 Awake, ye saints, awake,
  And hail the sacred day;
In loftiest songs of praise
  Your joyful homage pay;
Come bless the day that God hath blest,
The type of heaven's eternal rest.

2 On this auspicious morn
  The Lord of life arose,
And burst the bars of death,
  And vanquished all our foes;
And now he pleads our cause above,
And reaps the fruit of all his love.

3 All hail, triumphant Lord!
  Heaven with hosannas rings;
All earth, in humbler strains,
  Thy praise responsive sings;
Worthy the Lamb that once was slain,
Through endless years to live and reign.

Zebulon, Key F. Haddam, Key D. Lenox, Key B♭.

GRATITUDE AND PRAISE. 181

LOVING KINDNESS. L. M. (634)

495
1. Awake, my soul, to joy-ful lays, And sing the great Re-deem-er's praise;
2. He saw me ru-ined in the fall, Yet loved me, not-withstanding all;

He just-ly claims a song from me, His lov-ing kindness, oh, how free.
He saved me from my lost es-tate. His lov-ing kindness, oh, how great.

His lov-ing kindness, lov-ing kindness, His lov-ing kind-ness, oh, how free.
His lov-ing kindness, lov-ing kindness, His lov-ing kind-ness, oh, how great.

3 Tho' num'rous hosts of mighty foes,
Tho' earth and hell my way oppose,
He safely leads my soul along,
His loving kindness, oh, how strong.

4 When trouble, like a gloomy cloud,
Has gather'd thick and thunder'd loud,
He near my soul has always stood,
His loving kindness, oh, how good.

PETITION. 7s & 6s. ✶ (579) Harmonized by Miss BETTIE WILSON.

496
1. Go, when the morning shineth, Go, when the moon is bright; Go, when the eve de-
2. Remember all who love thee, All who are loved by thee; Pray, too, for those who

clin-eth, Go, in the hush of night; Go with pure mind and feel-ing, Put
hate thee, If a-ny such there be; Then, for thy-self in meekness, A

earthly thoughts away, And in God's presence kneeling, Do thou in secret pray.
blessing humbly claim; And blend with each petition Thy great Redeemer's name.

PUBLIC WORSHIP:

ST. MARTIN'S. C. M.   TANSUR.

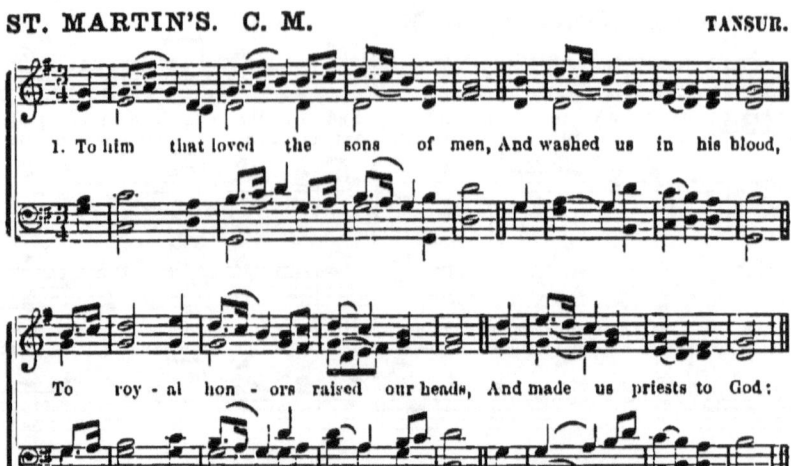

1. To him that loved the sons of men, And washed us in his blood,
To roy-al hon-ors raised our heads, And made us priests to God:

497 *Unto him that loved us.* (646)

2 To him let every tongue be praise,
And every heart be love;
All grateful honors paid on earth,
And nobler songs above.

3 Behold, on flying clouds he comes!
His saints shall bless the day;
While they that pierced him sadly mourn,
In anguish and dismay.

4 Thou art the First, and thou the Last;
Time centers all in thee;
Almighty Lord, who wast, and art,
And evermore shall be!

498 *I will bless thy name forever.* (645)

1 Long as I live, I'll praise thy name,
My King, my God of love!
My work and joy shall be the same
In the bright world above.

2 Great is the Lord, his power unknown,
And let his praise be great:
I'll sing the honors of thy throne,
Thy work of grace repeat.

3 Thy grace shall dwell upon my tongue;
And, while my lips rejoice,
The men that hear my sacred song
Shall join their cheerful voice.

4 Fathers to sons shall teach thy name,
And children learn thy ways;
Ages to come thy truth proclaim,
And nations sound thy praise.

5 Thy glorious deeds of ancient date
Shall through the world be known—
Thy arm of power, thy heavenly state
With public splendor shown.

6 The world is managed by thy hands,
Thy saints are ruled by love;
And thy eternal kingdom stands,
Though rocks and hills remove.

499 *The house of God.* (691)

1 My soul! how lovely is the place
To which thy God resorts!
'T is heaven to see his smiling face,
Though in his earthly courts.

2 There the great Monarch of the skies
His saving power displays,
And light breaks in upon our eyes
With kind and quickening rays.

3 There, mighty God! thy words declare
The secrets of thy will;
And still we seek thy mercy there,
And sing thy praises still.

Henry, Key C.   Howard, Key C.   Lanesboro, Key C.

GRATITUDE AND PRAISE.

183

HENRY. C. M.   S. B. POND.

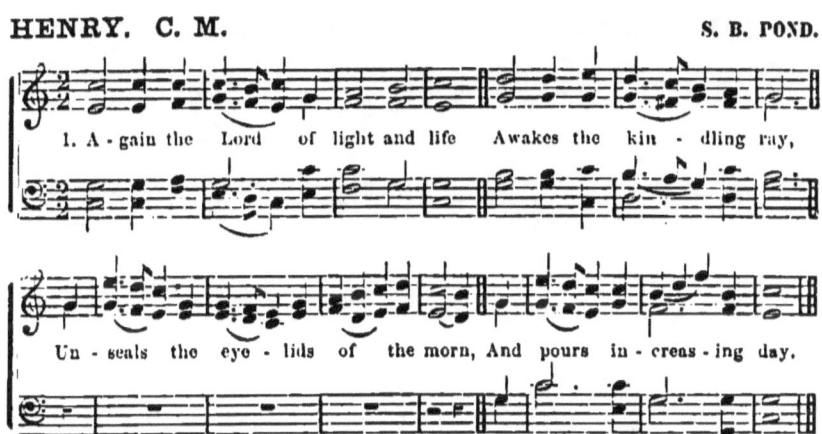

1. A-gain the Lord of light and life Awakes the kin-dling ray, Un-seals the eye-lids of the morn, And pours in-creas-ing day.

500 *Again the Lord of light and life.* (604)

2 Oh what a night was that which wrapt
   The heathen world in gloom!
Oh what a Sun which rose this day
   Triumphant from the tomb!

3 This day he grateful homage paid,
   And loud hosannas sung;
Let gladness dwell in every heart,
   And praise on every tongue.

4 Ten thousand different lips shall join
   To hail this welcome morn,
Which scatters blessings from its wings
   To nations yet unborn.

501 *Let us go up to the house, etc.* (606)

1 Again our earthly cares we leave,
   And to thy courts repair;
Again with joyful feet we come
   To meet our Savior here.

2 Within these walls let holy peace,
   And love and concord dwell;
Here give the troubled conscience ease,
   The wounded spirit heal.

3 The feeling heart, the melting eye,
   The humble mind, bestow;
And shine upon us from on high,
   To make our graces grow.

4 May we in faith receive thy word,
   In faith present our prayers,
And in the presence of our Lord
   Unbosom all our cares.

5 Show us some token of thy love,
   Our fainting hope to raise,
And pour thy blessings from above,
   That we may render praise.

502 *They shall speak of the glory, etc.* (230)

1 Come, you that love the Savior's name,
   And joy to make it known;
The Sovereign of your heart proclaim,
   And bow before his throne.

2 Behold your King, your Savior, crowned
   With glories all divine;
And tell the wondering nations round
   How bright these glories shine.

3 Infinite power and boundless grace
   In him unite their rays;
You that have seen his lovely face,
   Can you forbear his praise?

4 When in the earthly courts we view
   The beauties of our King,
We long to love as angels do,
   And wish like them to sing.

5 And shall we long and wish in vain?
   Lord, teach our songs to rise!
Thy love can animate our strain,
   And bid it reach the skies.

6 Oh for the day, the glorious day!
   When heaven and earth shall raise
With all their powers the raptured lay
   To celebrate thy praise.

St. Martin's, Key G.   Zanesville, Key G.   Peterboro, Key G.

LUTHER. S. M.

Dr. T. HASTINGS, by permission.

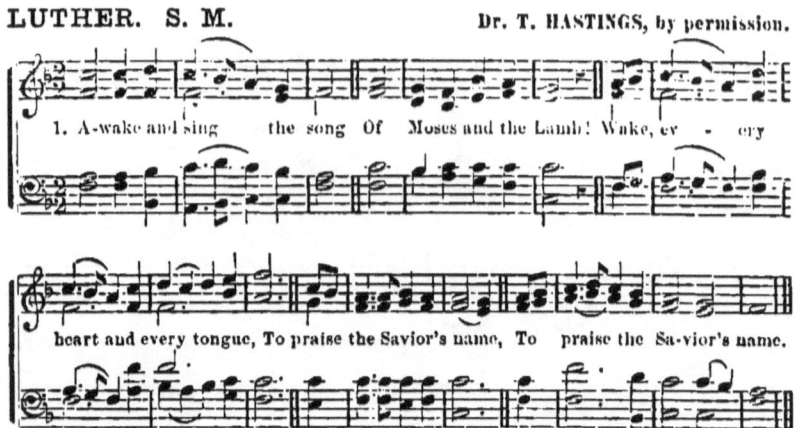

1. Awake and sing the song Of Moses and the Lamb! Wake, every heart and every tongue, To praise the Savior's name, To praise the Savior's name.

503 *The song of Moses and the Lamb.* (648)

2 Sing of his dying love!
 Sing of his rising power!
Sing how he intercedes above
 For those whose sins he bore!

3 Sing on your heavenly way,
 You ransomed sinners, sing;
Sing on, rejoicing every day
 In Christ, the glorious King.

4 Soon shall you hear him say,
 "You blessed children, come,"
Soon will he call you hence away,
 And take his pilgrims home.

504 *Break forth into joy.* (649)

1 Raise your triumphant songs
 To an immortal tune;
Let the wide earth resound the deeds
 Celestial grace has done.

2 Sing how Eternal Love,
 His Chief Beloved chose,
And bade him raise our wretched race
 From their abyss of woes.

3 His hand no thunder bears,
 Nor terror clothes his brow;
No bolts to drive our guilty souls
 To fiercer flames below.

4 He shows his Father's love,
 To raise our souls on high;
He came with pardon from above
 To rebels doomed to die.

5 Now, sinners, dry your tears;
 Let hopeless sorrow cease;
Bow to the scepter of his love,
 And take the offered peace.

6 Lord, we obey thy call;
 We lay an humble claim
To the salvation thou hast brought,
 And love and praise thy name.

505 *Psalm 103.* (650)

1 Oh bless the Lord, my soul!
 His grace to thee proclaim;
And all that is within me, join
 To bless his holy name.

2 Oh bless the Lord, my soul!
 His mercies bear in mind;
Forget not all his benefits;
 The Lord to thee is kind.

3 He will not always chide;
 He will with patience wait;
His wrath is ever slow to rise,
 And ready to abate.

4 He pardons all thy sins,
 Prolongs thy feeble breath:
He healeth thine infirmities,
 And ransoms thee from death.

5 Then bless his holy name
 Whose grace hath made thee whole,
Whose loving-kindness crowns thy days,
 Oh bless the Lord, my soul!

St. Thomas, Key G.   Gerar, Key F.   Silver Street, Key C.

GRATITUDE AND PRAISE. 185

HENDON. 7s.   Dr. L. MASON.

1. Now begin the heavenly theme; Sing aloud in Jesus' name; Ye who his salvation prove, Triumph in redeeming love, Triumph in redeeming love.

506   *Redeeming love.*   (653)
2 Ye who see the Father's grace
Beaming in the Savior's face,
As to Canaan on ye move,
Praise and bless redeemimg love.

3 Mourning souls, dry up your tears;
Banish all your guilty fears;
See your guilt and curse remove,
Canceled by redeeming love.

4 Welcome, all by sin oppressed,
Welcome to his sacred rest;
Nothing brought him from above,
Nothing but redeeming love.

5 Hither, then, your music bring;
Strike aloud each cheerful string;
Mortals, join the host above—
Join to praise redeeming love.

507   *Wait on the Lord, etc.*   (708)
1 Lord, we come before thee now;
At thy feet we humbly bow:
Oh do not our suit disdain,
Shall we seek thee, Lord, in vain?

2 Lord, on thee our souls depend,
In compassion now descend;
Fill our hearts with thy rich grace;
Tune our lips to sing thy praise.

3 In thine own appointed way,
Now we seek thee; here we stay;
Lord, from hence we would not go,
Till a blessing thou bestow.

4 Comfort those who weep and mourn;
Let the time of joy return;
Those that are cast down lift up;
Make them strong in faith and hope.

5 Grant that all may seek and find
Thee a God supremely kind;
Heal the sick; the captive free;
Let us all rejoice in thee.

508   *They shall come to Zion with songs.*   (654)
1 Songs of praise awoke the morn
When the Prince of Peace was born;
Songs of praise arose when he,
Captive, led captivity.

2 Heaven and earth must pass away,
Songs of praise shall crown the day:
God will make new heavens and earth,
Songs of praise shall hail their birth.

3 And will man alone be dumb,
Till that glorious kingdom come?
No; the church delights to raise
Psalms, and hymns, and songs of praise.

4 Saints below, with heart and voice,
Still in songs of praise rejoice;
Learning here, by faith and love,
Songs of praise to sing above.

5 Born upon the latest breath,
Songs of praise shall conquer death;
Then amidst eternal joy,
Songs of praise their powers employ.

Wilmot, Key C.   Nuremburg, Key A♭.   Pleyel, Key G.

PUBLIC WORSHIP:

DE FLEURY. 8s, Double.

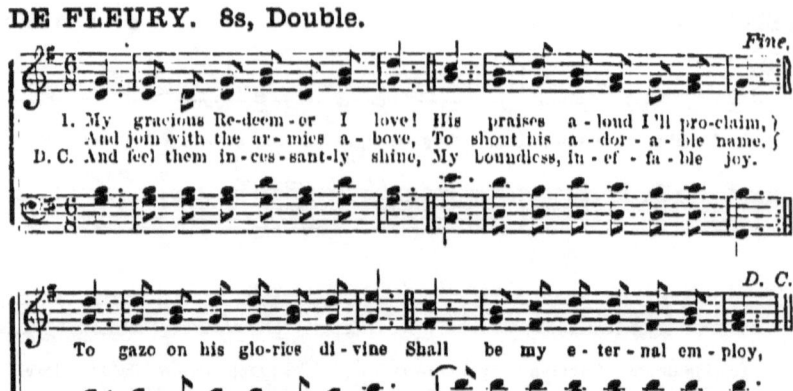

1. My gracious Redeemer I love! His praises aloud I'll proclaim,
And join with the armies above, To shout his adorable name.
D.C. And feel them incessantly shine, My boundless, ineffable joy.

To gaze on his glories divine Shall be my eternal employ,

509   *All things loss for Christ.*   (657)

2 You palaces, scepters, and crowns,
  Your pride with disdain I survey,
Your pomps are but shadows and sounds,
  And pass in a moment away.
The crown that my Savior bestows
  Yon permanent sun shall outshine;
My joy everlastingly flows—
  My God, my Redeemer, is mine.

510   *The unsearchable riches of Christ.*   (659)

1 How shall I my Savior set forth?
  How shall I his beauties declare?
Oh how shall I speak of his worth,
  Or what his chief dignities are?
His angels can never express,
  Nor saints who sit nearest his throne,
How rich are his treasures of grace;
  No; this is a secret unknown.

2 In him all the fullness of God
  Forever transcendently shines!
Though once like a mortal he stood
  To finish his gracious designs.
Though once he was nailed to the cross,
  Vile rebels like me to set free,
His glory sustained no loss,
  Eternal his kingdom shall be.

3 O sinners! believe and adore
  This Savior, so rich to redeem;
No creature can ever explore
  The treasures of goodness in him.

Come, all you who see yourselves lost,
  And feel yourselves burdened with sin,
Draw near, while with terror you're tossed,
  Obey, and your peace shall begin.

511   *Love is of God.*   (500)

1 Say, whence does this union arise,
  Where hatred is conquered by love?
It fastens our souls with such ties
  That distance nor time can remove.
It can not in Eden be found,
  Nor yet in a paradise lost;
It grows on Immanuel's ground,
  And Jesus' life's blood it has cost.

2 My friends so endeared unto me,
  Our souls so united in love,
Where Jesus is gone we shall be,
  In yonder blest mansions above.
Why then so unwilling to part,
  Since there we shall soon meet again;
Engraved on Immanuel's heart,
  At distance we can not remain.

3 And then we shall see that bright day
  And join with the angels above;
Set free from our prisons of clay,
  United in Jesus' kind love.
With Jesus we ever shall reign,
  And all his bright glory shall see;
Then sing hallelujahs—Amen!
  Amen! Even so let it be!

Clarington, Key A.   Somerset, Key F.   Enon's Isle, Key B♭.

GRATITUDE AND PRAISE. 187

NETTLETON. 8s & 7s, Double.

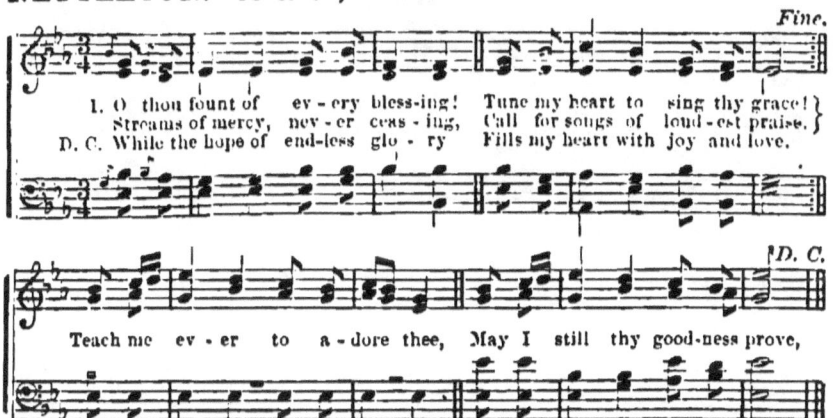

1. O thou fount of ev-ery bless-ing!
   Tune my heart to sing thy grace!
   Streams of mercy, nev-er ceas-ing,
   Call for songs of loud-est praise.
D. C. While the hope of end-less glo-ry
   Fills my heart with joy and love.

Teach me ev-er to a-dore thee, May I still thy good-ness prove,

512 *O thou Fount of every blessing.* (660)

2 Here I'll raise my Ebenezer,
 Hither by thy help I've come,
And I hope, by thy good pleasure,
 Safely to arrive at home.
Jesus sought me when a stranger,
 Wandering from thy fold, O God!
He, to rescue me from danger,
 Interposed his precious blood.

3 Oh to grace how great a debtor
 Daily I'm constrained to be!
Let thy goodness, like a fetter,
 Bind me closer still to thee.
Never let me wander from thee,
 Never leave thee, whom I love;
By thy Word and Spirit guide me,
 Till I reach thy courts above.

513 *The salutation of peace.* (750)

1 Peace be to this congregation!
 Peace to every heart therein!
Peace, the earnest of salvation;
 Peace, the fruit of conquered sin;
Peace, that speaks the heavenly Giver;
 Peace, to worldly minds unknown;
Peace that floweth as a river
 From the eternal Source alone.

2 O thou God of Peace! be near us,
 Fix within our hearts thy home;
With thy bright appearing cheer us,
 In thy blessed freedom come.

Come with all thy revelations,
 Truth which we so long have sought;
Come with thy deep consolations—
 Peace of God which passeth thought!

514 *Love divine, all love excelling.* (710)

1 Love divine, all love excelling,
 Joy of heaven to earth come down!
Fix in us thy humble dwelling;
 All thy faithful mercies crown.
Jesus, thou art all compassion,
 Pure, unbounded love thou art!
Visit us with thy salvation,
 Enter every trembling heart.

2 Breathe, oh breathe thy loving Spirit
 Into every troubled breast:
Let us all in thee inherit,
 Let us find thy promised rest.
Take away the love of sinning,
 Take our load of guilt away;
End the work of thy beginning,
 Bring us to eternal day.

515 *Apostolic benediction.* (752)

May the grace of Christ, our Savior,
 And the Father's boundless love,
With the Holy Spirit's favor,
 Rest upon us from above.
Thus may we abide in union
 With each other and the Lord;
And possess, in sweet communion,
 Joys which earth can not afford.

Greenville, Key F. Camden, Key A. Bavaria, Key G.

ADORATION. 11s.

1. O, Jesus, the giver of all we en-joy!
Our lives to thy hon-or we wish to em-ploy;
D. S. good-ness in-creas-ing thy love we'll pro-claim.

With prais-es un-ceas-ing we'll sing of thy name! Thy

516   *He hath put a new song in my mouth.*   (665)

2 The wonderful name of our Jesus we'll sing,
And publish the fame of our Captain and King;
With sweet exultation his goodness we prove;
His name is salvation—his nature is love.

3 And when to the regions of glory we rise,
And join the bright legions that shout through the skies,
We'll tell the glad story of Jesus' kind grace,
And give him the glory, and honor, and praise.

517   *Worthy is the Lamb.*   (666)

1 Come, saints! let us join in the praise of the Lamb,
The theme most sublime of the angels above;
They dwell with delight on the sound of his name,
And gaze on his glories with wonder and love.

2 They worship the Lamb who for sinners was slain;
But their loftiest songs never equal his love:
The claims of his mercy will ever remain,
Transcending the anthems in glory above.

3 Yet even our service he will not despise,
When we join in his worship and tell of his name;
Then let us unite in the song of the skies,
And, trusting his mercy, sing, "Worthy the Lamb."

518   *Acquaint now thyself with him.*   (780)

1 Acquaint thee, O mortal! acquaint thee with God,
And joy, like the sunshine, shall beam on thy road;
And peace, like the dew-drop, shall fall on thy head;
And sleep, like an angel, shall visit thy bed.

2 Acquaint thee, O mortal! acquaint thee with God,
And he shall be with thee when fears are abroad;
Thy safeguard in danger that threatens thy path;
Thy joy in the valley and shadow of death. . . .

GRATITUDE AND PRAISE. 189

NEW HAVEN. 6s & 4s.   Dr. T. HASTINGS.

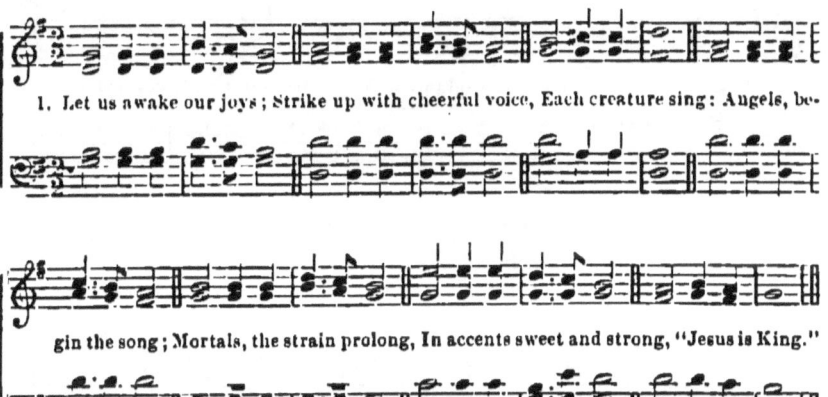

1. Let us awake our joys; Strike up with cheerful voice, Each creature sing: Angels, begin the song; Mortals, the strain prolong, In accents sweet and strong, "Jesus is King."

519   *Let us awake our joys.*   (667)

1 Let us awake our joys;
Strike up with cheerful voice,
Each creature sing:
Angels, begin the song;
Mortals, the strain prolong,
In accents sweet and strong,
"Jesus is King."

2 Proclaim abroad his name;
Tell of his matchless fame!
What wonders done;
Above, beneath, around,
Let all the earth resound,
Till heaven's high arch rebound,
"Victory is won."

3 He vanquished sin and hell,
And our last foe will quell;
Mourners, rejoice;
His dying love adore:
Praise him now raised in power;
Praise him for evermore
With joyful voice.

4 All hail the glorious day
When, through the heavenly way,
Lo! he shall come,
While they who pierced him wail;
His promise shall not fail:
Saints, see your King prevail;
Great Savior, come.

520   *Rev. 5: 12, 13.*   (668)

1 Glory to God on high!
Let heaven and earth reply;
Praise ye his name;
His love and grace adore,
Who all our sorrows bore,
And sing for evermore,
"Worthy the Lamb."

2 Ye who surround the throne,
Join cheerfully in one,
Praising his name;
Ye who have felt his blood
Sealing your peace with God,
Sound his dear name abroad:
"Worthy the Lamb."

3 Join, all ye ransomed race,
Our Lord and God to bless;
Praise ye his name;
In him we will rejoice,
And make a joyful noise,
Shouting with heart and voice,
"Worthy the Lamb."

4 Soon must we change our place;
Yet will we never cease
Praising his name;
To him our songs we'll bring,
Hail him our gracious King,
And through all ages sing,
"Worthy the Lamb."

Dort, Key C.   Olivet, Key E♭.   America, Key G.

OLD HUNDRED. L. M.

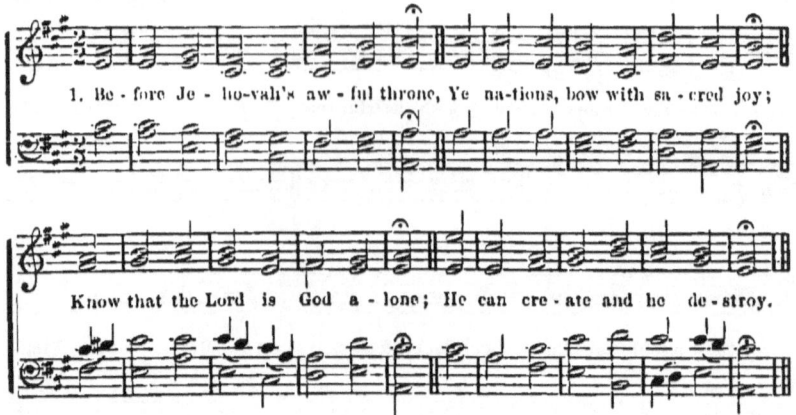

1. Be-fore Je-ho-vah's aw-ful throne, Ye na-tions, bow with sa-cred joy; Know that the Lord is God a-lone; He can cre-ate and he de-stroy.

521   Psalm 100.   (674)
2 His sovereign power, without our aid,
   Made us of clay, and formed us men;
   And when like wandering sheep we strayed,
   He brought us to his fold again.

3 We are his people—we his care—
   Our souls, and all our mortal frame:
   What lasting honors shall we rear,
   Almighty Maker, to thy name?

4 We'll crowd thy gates with thankful songs,
   High as the heavens our voices raise;
   And earth, with her ten thousand tongues,
   Shall fill thy courts with sounding praise.

5 Wide as the world is thy command!
   Vast as eternity thy love!
   Firm as a rock thy truth shall stand,
   When rolling years shall cease to move.

522   God exalted.   (675)
1 Be thou exalted, O my God!
   Above the heavens where angels dwell;
   Thy power on earth be known abroad,
   And land to land thy wonders tell.

2 My heart is fixed; my song shall raise
   Immortal honors to thy name;
   Awake my tongue, to sound his praise,
   My tongue, the glory of my frame.

3 High o'er the earth his mercy reigns,
   And reaches to the utmost sky;
   His truth to endless years remains,
   When lower worlds dissolve and die.

523   Psalm 100.   (29)
1 With one consent let all the earth
   To God their cheerful voices raise;
   Glad homage pay, with awful mirth,
   And sing before him songs of praise:

2 Convinced that he is God alone,
   From whom both we and all proceed;
   We, whom he chooses for his own,
   The flock that he vouchsafes to feed.

3 Oh, enter, then, his temple gate,
   Thence to his courts devoutly press;
   And still your grateful hymns repeat,
   And still his name with praises bless.

4 For he's the Lord supremely good,
   His mercy is forever sure;
   His truth, which always firmly stood,
   To endless ages shall endure.

524   Of him are all things.   (30)
1 Oh source divine, and life of all,
   The fount of being's wondrous sea!
   Thy depth would every heart appall,
   That saw not love supreme in thee.

2 We shrink before thy vast abyss,
   Where worlds on worlds eternal brood;
   We know thee truly but in this—
   That thou bestowest all our good.

3 And so, 'mid boundless time and space,
   Oh grant us still in thee to dwell,
   And through the ceaseless web ro trace
   Thy presence working all things well!

Duke Street, Key E♭.   Beethoven, Key C.   Mendon, Key C.

525 *Serve the Lord with gladness.* (681)
1 Ye nations round the earth, rejoice
  Before the Lord, your sovereign King:
  Serve him with cheerful heart and voice;
  With all your tongues his glory sing.

2 The Lord is God; 't is he alone
  Doth life, and breath, and being give;
  We are his work, and not our own;
  The sheep that on his pastures live.

3 Enter his gates with songs of joy;
  With praises to his courts repair;
  And make it your divine employ
  To pay your thanks and honors there.

4 The Lord is good, the Lord is kind;
  Great is his grace, his mercy sure;
  And the whole race of men shall find
  His truth from age to age endure.

526 *How amiable are thy tabernacles.* (680)
1 Great God, attend while Zion sings
  The joy that from thy presence springs;
  To spend one day with thee on earth,
  Exceeds a thousand days of mirth.

2 Might I enjoy the meanest place
  Within thy house, O God of grace,
  Not tents of ease, nor thrones of power,
  Should tempt my feet to leave thy door.

3 God is our sun, he makes our day;
  God is our shield, he guards our way
  From all th' assaults of hell and sin,
  From foes without and foes within.

4 All needful grace will God bestow,
  And crown that grace with glory too:
  He gives us all things, and withholds
  No real good from upright souls.

5 O God, our King, whose sovereign sway
  The glorious hosts of heaven obey,
  And devils at thy presence flee,
  Blest is the man that trusts in thee.

527 *Let all the people praise thee.* (718)
1 From all that dwell below the skies,
  Let the Creator's praise arise:
  Let the Redeemer's name be sung
  Through every land, by every tongue.

2 Eternal are thy mercies, Lord;
  Eternal truth attends thy word:
  Thy praise shall sound from shore to shore,
  Till suns shall rise and set no more.

528 *Sessions, Key of C.* (686)
1 How pleasant, how divinely fair,
  O Lord of hosts, thy dwellings are!
  With long desire my spirit faints
  To meet the assemblies of thy saints.

2 My soul would rest in thine abode,
  My panting heart cries out for God;
  My God! my King! why should I be
  So far from all my joys and thee?

3 Blest are the souls who find a place
  Within the temple of thy grace;
  There they behold thy gentler rays,
  And seek thy face, and learn thy praise.

4 Blest are the men whose hearts are set
  To find the way to Zion's gate;
  God is their strength, and through the road
  They lean upon their Helper, God.

529 *He shall go in and out, etc.* (715)
1 Now may the Lord our Shepherd lead
  To living streams his little flock;
  May he in flowery pastures feed;
  Shade us at noon beneath the rock!

2 Now may we hear our Shepherd's voice,
  And gladly answer to his call;
  Now may our hearts for him rejoice,
  Who knows, and names, and loves us all.

3 When the Chief Shepherd shall appear,
  And small and great before him stand,
  Oh, be the flock assembling here
  Found with the sheep on his right hand.

530 *Striving together for the faith, etc.* (728)
1 Lord, cause thy face on us to shine;
  Give us thy peace, and seal us thine;
  Teach us to prize the means of grace,
  And love thine earthly dwelling-place.

2 One is our faith, and one our Lord;
  One body, spirit, hope, reward;
  May we in one communion be
  One with each other, one with thee.

3 Bless all whose voice salvation brings,
  Who minister in holy things;
  Our pastors, rulers, deacons, bless;
  Clothe them with zeal and righteousness.

4 Let many in the judgment day,
  Turned from the error of their way,
  Their hope, their joy, their crown, appear:
  Save those who preach, and those who hear.

Uxbridge, Key E.   Wells, Key E♭.   Rothwell, Key E♭.

PUBLIC WORSHIP:

LANESBORO'. C. M. — English.

1. Early, my God, without delay, I haste to seek thy face; My thirsty spirit faints away, My thirsty spirit faints away, Without thy cheering grace,

531 *Early will I seek thee.* (698)

2 So pilgrims on the scorching sand,
Beneath a burning sky,
Long for a cooling stream at hand,
And they must drink or die.

3 Not life itself, with all its joys,
Can my best passions move,
Or raise so high my cheerful voice,
As thy forgiving love.

4 Thus, till my last expiring day,
I'll bless my God and King;
Thus will I lift my hands to pray,
And tune my lips to sing.

532 *Lift thou the light of thy countenance.* (690)

1 Within thy house, O Lord our God,
In glory now appear;
Make this a place of thine abode,
And shed thy blessings here.

2 When we thy mercy-seat surround,
Thy Spirit, Lord, impart;
And let thy gospel's joyful sound,
With power, reach every heart.

3 Here let the blind their sight obtain;
Here give the mourners rest;
Let Jesus here triumphant reign,
Enthroned in every breast.

4 Here let the voice of sacred joy
And humble prayer arise,
Till higher strains our tongues employ
In realms beyond the skies.

533 *So great a cloud of witnesses.* (817)

1 Give me the wings of faith, to rise
Within the vail, and see
The saints above, how great their joys,
How bright their glories be.

2 Once they were mourning here below,
And bathed their couch with tears;
They wrestled hard, as we do now,
With sins, and doubts, and fears.

3 I ask them whence their victory came;
They, with united breath,
Ascribe their conquest to the Lamb,
Their triumph to his death;

4 They marked the footsteps that he trod;
His zeal inspired their breast;
And, following their incarnate God,
Possessed the promised rest.

534 *Christ our refuge.* (1010)

1 In ev'ry trouble, sharp and strong
My soul to Jesus flies;
My anchor-hold is firm in him
When swelling billows rise.

2 His comforts bear my spirit up,
I trust a faithful God;
The sure foundation of my hope
Is in a Savior's blood.

3 Loud hallelujahs sing, my soul,
To thy Redeemer's name;
In joy and sorrow, life and death,
His love is still the same.

St. Martin's, Key G. Woodland, Key G. Fountain. Key E♭,

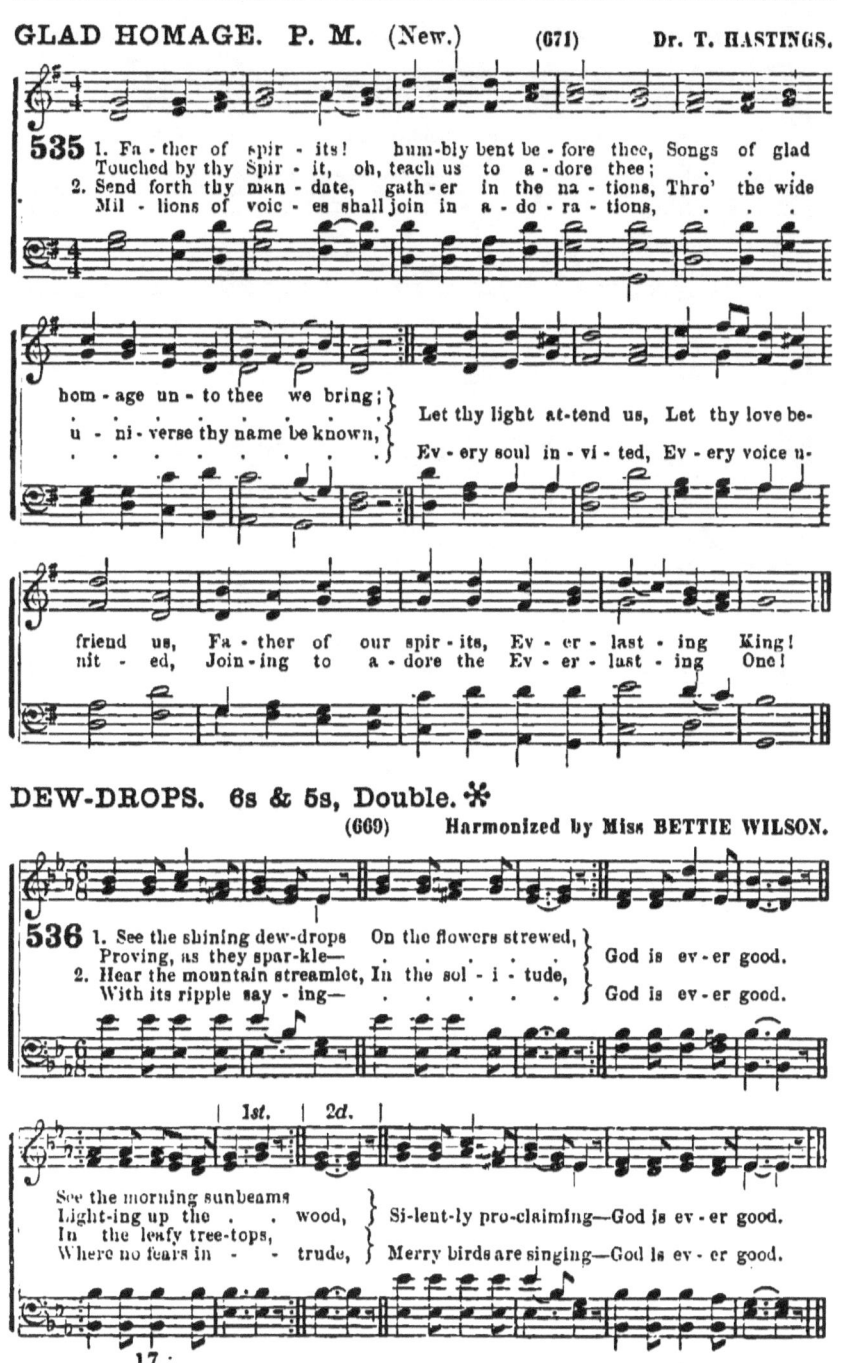

AIN. S. M., Double. From CORRELLI.

1. Come, we that love the Lord, And let our joys be known;
Join in a song with sweet ac-cord, And thus surround the throne.
The sor-rows of the mind Be banished from this place! Re-
lig — ion nev-er was de-signed To make our pleas-ures less.

537 *Come, we that love the Lord.* (701)
2 The hill of Zion yields
   A thousand sacred sweets,
Before we reach the heavenly fields,
   Or walk the golden streets.
Then let our songs abound,
   And every tear be dry;
We're marching o'er this hallowed ground
   To fairer worlds on high.

538 *A brighter day.* (822)
1 Lord, we expect a day
   Still brighter far than this,
When death shall bear our souls away
   To realms of light and bliss.
There rapturous scenes of joy
   Shall burst upon our sight;
And every pain, and tear, and sigh,
   Be drowned in endless night.

2 Beneath thy balmy wing,
   O Sun of Righteousness!
Our happy souls shall sit and sing
   The wonders of thy grace.
Nor shall the radiant day,
   So joyfully begun,
In evening shadows die away
   Beneath the setting sun.

539 *Establish thou the work, etc.* (006)
Oh praise our God to-day,
   His constant mercy bless,
Whose love hath helped us on our way,
   And granted us success.
Lord! may it be our choice
   This blessed rule to keep:
Rejoice with them that do rejoice,
   And weep with them that weep.

OPENING.

BOYLSTON. S. M.   Dr. L. MASON.

1. Hungry, and faint, and poor, Behold us, Lord, again
Assembled at thy mercy's door, Thy bounty to obtain.

540 *Blessed are they that hunger.* (703)

2 Thy word invites us nigh,
  Or we would starve indeed;
For we no money have to buy,
  Nor righteousness to plead.

3 The food our spirits want,
  Thy hand alone can give;
Oh! hear the prayer of faith, and grant
  That we may eat and live!

541 *To the only wise God, our Savior.* (736)

1 To God, the Only Wise,
  Our Savior and our King,
Let all the saints below the skies
  Their humble praises bring.

2 'Tis his almighty love,
  His counsel and his care,
Preserve us safe from sin and death
  And every hurtful snare.

3 He will present our souls,
  Unblemished and complete,
Before the glory of his face,
  With joys divinely great.

4 Then all the chosen seed
  Shall meet around the throne,
Shall bless the conduct of his grace,
  And make his wonders known.

5 To our Redeemer, God,
  Wisdom and power belong,
Immortal crowns of majesty,
  And everlasting song.

542 *At midnight there was a cry made.* (1070)

1 Servant of God, well done!
  Rest from thy loved employ;
The battle fought, the victory won,
  Enter thy Master's joy.

2 The voice at midnight came;
  He started up to hear;
A mortal arrow pierced his frame,
  He fell, but felt no fear.

3 Tranquil amid alarms,
  It found him on the field,
A veteran slumbering on his arms,
  Beneath his red-cross shield.

4 At midnight came the cry,
  "To meet thy God prepare!"
He woke—and caught his Captain's eye;
  Then, strong in faith and prayer,

5 His spirit with a bound,
  Left its encumbering clay;
His tent, at sunrise, on the ground
  A darkened ruin lay.

6 The pains of death are past,
  Labor and sorrow cease;
And life's long warfare, closed at last,
  His soul is found in peace.

543 *Absent in the flesh—present, etc.* (789)

And let our bodies part,
  To different climes repair;
Still and forever joined in heart
  The friends of Jesus are.

Thatcher, Key G.   **Golden Hill, Key F.**   **Shirland, Key G.**

PLEADING SAVIOR. 8s & 7s., Double.

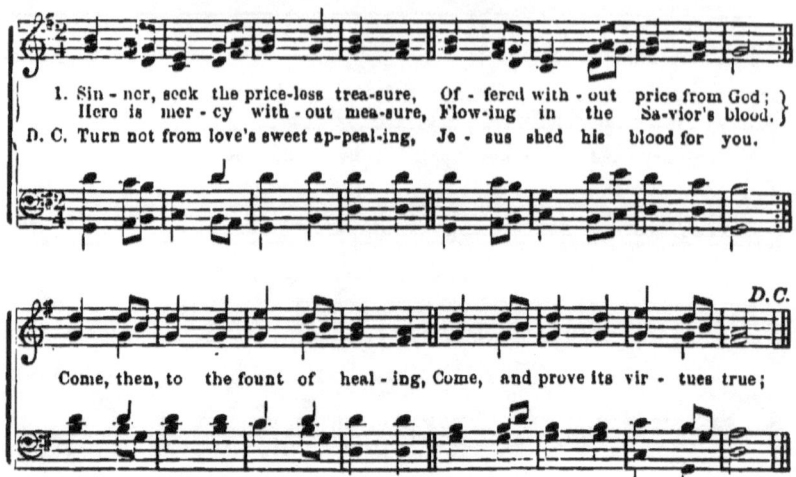

1. Sin-ner, seek the price-less trea-sure, Of-fered with-out price from God;
Here is mer-cy with-out mea-sure, Flow-ing in the Sa-vior's blood.
D. C. Turn not from love's sweet ap-peal-ing, Je-sus shed his blood for you.

Come, then, to the fount of heal-ing, Come, and prove its vir-tues true;

544 *The pearl of great price.* (311)

2 Come, begin the race for heaven;
  Start to-day, oh do not wait;
Now's the time that God has given;
  Sinner, do not be too late.
When the door of mercy closes,
  You will stand and knock in vain;
For, when justice interposes,
  Mercy will not call again!

545 *All thy waves and thy billows, etc.* (1024)

1 Full of trembling expectation,
  Feeling much and fearing more,
Mighty God of my salvation!
  I thy timely aid implore;
Suffering Son of Man, be near me,
  All my sufferings to sustain;
By thy sorer griefs to cheer me,
  By thy more than mortal pain.

2 Call to mind that unknown anguish,
  In thy days of flesh below;
When thy troubled soul did languish
  Under a whole world of woe;
When thou didst our curse inherit,
  Groan beneath our guilty load,
Burdened with a wounded spirit,
  Bruised by all the wrath of God.

3 By thy most severe temptation,
  In that dark, Satanic hour:
By thy last, mysterious passion,
  Screen me from the adverse power;
By thy fainting in the garden,
  By thy bloody sweat, I pray,
Write upon my heart the pardon,
  Take my sins and fears away.

546 *Blessed are the dead, etc.* (1077)

1 Happy soul! thy days are ended,
  All thy mourning days below;
Go, by angel guards attended,
  To the sight of Jesus go!
Waiting to receive thy spirit,
  Lo! the Savior stands above;
Shows the purchase of his merit,
  Reaches out the crown of love.

2 Struggling through thy latest passion
  To thy dear Redeemer's breast,
To his uttermost salvation,
  To his everlasting rest;
For the joy he sets before thee,
  Bear thy transitory pain;
Die to live a life of glory;
  Suffer, with thy Lord to reign.

Greenville, Key F.   Camden, Key A.   Nettleton, Key E♭.

OPENING. 197

ROCK OF SALVATION. P. M. (New.)   T. J. COOK.

1. If life's pleasures charm you, give them not your heart. Lest the gift ensnare you from your God to part; His favor seek, his praises speak—Fix here your hope's foundation; Serve him, and he will ev-er be The Rock of your Sal-va-tion.

547   *The rock of Salvation.*   (439)

2 If distress befall you, painful though it be,
Let not grief appall you—to your Savior flee;
He ever near, your prayer will hear,
And calm your perturbation;
The waves of woe shall ne'er o'erflow
The Rock of your Salvation.

3 When earth's prospects fail you, let it not distress;
Better comforts wait you—Christ will surely bless;
To Jesus flee—your prop he'll be,
Your heavenly consolation;
For griefs below can not o'erthrow
The Rock of your Salvation.

4 Dangers may approach you: let them not alarm:
Christ will ever watch you, and protect from harm;
He near you stands, with mighty hands,
To ward off each temptation;
To Jesus fly; he's ever nigh,
The Rock of your Salvation.

5 Let not death alarm you, shrink not from his blow;
For your God shall arm you, and victory bestow,
For death shall bring to you no sting,
The grave no desolation;
'T is sweet to die with Jesus nigh,
The Rock of your Salvation.

548   *Laban, Key of C.*   (1217)

1 Hail, gracious, heavenly Prince!
   To thee let children fly:
And on thy kindest providence,
   Oh may we all rely.

2 Jesus will take the young
   Beneath his special care;
And he will keep their youthful days
   From every woe and snare.

3 He knows their tender frame,
   Nor will their youth contemn;
For he a little child became,
   To love and pity them.

4 Nor does he now forget
   His youthful days on earth:
Nor would we ever cease our praise
   For the Redeemer's birth.

PUBLIC WORSHIP:

FLORIDA. 8s, 7s & 4s.   J. M. PELTON, by permission.

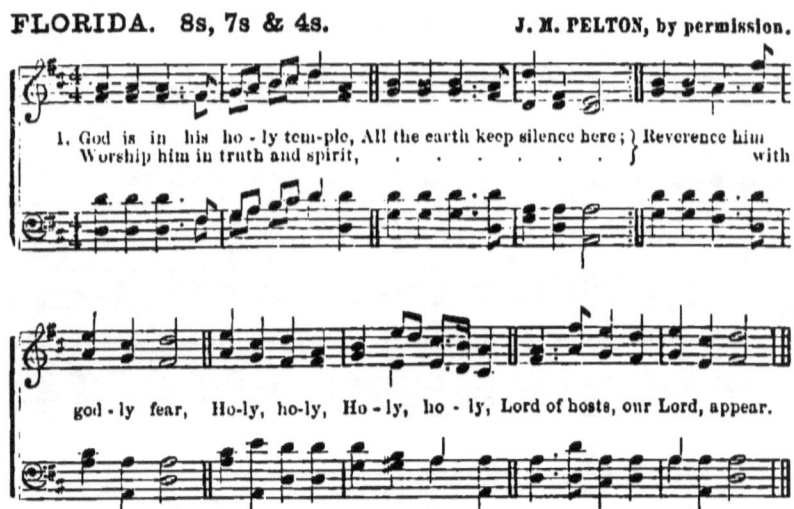

1. God is in his ho-ly tem-ple, All the earth keep silence here; Reverence him with godly fear, Ho-ly, ho-ly, Ho-ly, ho-ly, Lord of hosts, our Lord, appear.
Worship him in truth and spirit, ...

549   *The Lord is in his holy temple.*   (711)

2 God in Christ reveals his presence,
   Throned upon the mercy-seat:
Saints, rejoice! and sinners, tremble!
   Each prepare his God to meet:
     Lowly, lowly,
   Bow adoring at his feet.

3 Hail him here with songs of praises,
   Him with prayers of faith surround:
Hearken to his glorious gospel,
   While the preacher's lips expound;
     Blessed, blessed,
   They who know the joyful sound.

4 Though the heaven, and heaven of heavens,
   O thou Great Unsearchable!
Are too mean to comprehend thee,
   Thou with man art pleased to dwell;
     Welcome, welcome,
   God with us, Immanuel.

550   *Rejoice with trembling.*   (713)

1 In thy name, O Lord, assembling,
   We, thy people, now draw near;
Teach us to rejoice with trembling;
   Oh that we this day may hear—
     Hear with meekness—
   Hear thy word with godly fear.

2 While our days on earth are lengthened,
   May we give them, Lord, to thee!
Cheered by hope, and daily strengthened,
   We would run, nor weary be,
     Till thy glory,
   Without clouds, in heaven we see.

3 There, in worship, purer, sweeter,
   All thy people shall adore;
Tasting of enjoyment greater
   Than they could conceive before;
     Full enjoyment—
   Holy bliss for evermore.

551   *Calling on the name of the Lord.*   (894)

1 Gracious Savior, we adore thee!
   Purchased by thy precious blood;
We present ourselves before thee,
   Now to walk the narrow road:
     Savior, guide us—
   Guide us to our heavenly home.

2 Thou didst mark our path of duty;
   Thou wast laid beneath the wave;
Thou didst rise, in glorious beauty,
   From the semblance of the grave;
     May we follow
   In the same delightful way.

Happy Zion, Key C.   Alvan, Key F.   Siberia, Key D.

SIBERIA. 8s, 7s & 4s. S. B. POND.

1. Lord, dismiss us with thy blessing, Fill our hearts with joy and peace;
Let us each, thy love possessing, ... Triumph in redeeming grace; Oh, refresh us, Oh, refresh us, Trav'ling thro' this wilder-ness.

552   *Dismission.*   (754)

2 Thanks we give, and adoration,
For the gospel's joyful sound;
May the fruits of thy salvation
In our hearts and lives abound;
    May thy presence
With us evermore be found.

3 So, whene'er the signal's given
Us from earth to call away,
Borne on angel's wings to heaven,
Glad the summons to obey,
    May we, ready,
Rise and reign in endless day.

553   *All the kindreds of the nations.* (1280)

1 O'er the gloomy hills of darkness,
Look, my soul; be still and gaze;
All the promises do travail
With a glorious day of grace:
    Blessed Jubilee,
Let thy glorious morning dawn.

2 Let the Indian, let the negro,
Let the rude barbarian see
That divine and glorious conquest
Once obtained on Calvary:
    Let the gospel
Loud resound from pole to pole.

3 Kingdoms wide that sit in darkness,
Grant them, Lord, the glorious light:
And, from eastern coast to western,
May the morning chase the night!
    And redemption,
Freely purchased, win the day.

4 Fly abroad, thou mighty gospel!
Win and conquer! never cease!
May thy lasting, wide dominion
Multiply and still increase!
    Sway thy scepter,
Savior, all the world around.

554   *Keep us, Lord.*   (755)

1 Keep us, Lord, oh keep us ever!
Vain our hope, if left by thee;
We are thine; oh leave us never,
Till thy glorious face we see!
    Then to praise thee
Through a bright eternity.

2 Precious is thy word of promise,
Precious to thy people here;
Never take thy presence from us,
Jesus, Savior, still be near;
    Living, dying,
May thy name our spirits cheer.

Florida, Key D.   Peron, Key G.   Zion, Key D.

PUBLIC WORSHIP:

TRIUMPH. 7, 7, 8, 7, 7, 7, 8, 7. (742)　　W. B. BRADBURY, by permission.

555 Head of the Church triumphant! We joy-ful-ly a-dore thee; Till thou appear, thy members here Shall sing like those in . . glo-ry. We lift our hearts and voices In blest an-tic-i-pa-tion, And cry aloud, and give to God The praise of our sal-[vation.

CHESTNUT STREET. 8, 8, 8, 8, 7. ✻　　M. C. RAMSEY.

1. Rejoice, O earth! the Lord is King! To him your humble tribute bring; Let Jacob rise, and Zion sing, And all the world with praises ring, And give to Jesus glory!

556　　*To him be glory.*　　(640)

2 Oh may the saints of every name
Unite to serve the bleeding Lamb!
May jars and discords cease to flame,
And all the Savior's love proclaim,
　And give to Jesus glory!

3 We long to see the Christians join
In union sweet and love divine,
And glory through the churches shine,
And gentiles crowding to the sign,
　To give to Jesus glory!

4 Oh may the distant lands rejoice,
And sinners hear the Bridegroom's voice,
While praise their happy tongues employs,
And all obtain immortal joys,
　And give to Jesus glory!

5 Then tears shall all be wiped away,
And Christians never go astray;
When we are freed from cumbrous clay
We'll praise the Lord in endless day,
　And give to Jesus glory.

CLOSING. 201

PARTING IN HOPE. C. M., with Chorus.

1. Lord, when together here we meet, And taste thy heavenly grace,
Thy smiles are so divinely sweet, We're loath to leave the place.

We're loath to leave the place,.. We're loath to leave the place;
D. S. To meet to part no more,.. On Canaan's happy shore;

Thy smiles are so divinely sweet, We're loath to leave the place.
And sing the everlasting song With those who've gone before.

Chorus.
Oh, that will be joyful, joyful, joyful;
Oh, that will be joyful, To meet to part no more;

557   *Parting in hope.*   (732)

2 Yet, Father, since it is thy will
  That we must part again,
Oh let thy gracious presence still
  With every one remain!

3 Then let us all in Christ be one,
  Bound with the cords of love,
Till we, around thy glorious throne,
  Shall joyous meet above:

4 Where sin and sorrow from each heart
  Shall then forever fly,
And not one thought that we shall part
  Once interrupt our joy.

WELTON. L. M.

Dr. MADDEN.

1. Oh, peace of God, sweet peace of God, Where broods on earth this gen-tle dove, Where spread those pure and downy wings To shel-ter him whom God doth love?

558 *The peace of God.* (760)
1 Oh peace of God, sweet peace of God,
  Where broods on earth this gentle dove,
Where spread those pure and downy wings
  To shelter him whom God doth love?

2 Whence comes this blessing of the soul,
  This silent joy which can not fade?
This glory, tranquil, holy, bright,
  Pervading sorrow's deepest shade?

3 The peace of God, the peace of God!
  It shines as clear 'mid cloud and storm
As in the calmest summer day,
  'Mid chill as in the sunlight warm.

4 Oh peace of God! earth hath no power
  To shed thine unction o'er the heart;
Its smile can never bring it here—
  Its frown ne'er bid its light depart.

5 Calm peace of God, in holy trust,
  In love and faith thy presence dwells—
In patient suffering and toil
  Where mercy's gentle tear-drop swells.

6 Sweet peace! Oh let thy heavenly ray
  Shed its calm radiance o'er my road;
Its kindly light shall cheer me on—
  Guide to the endless peace of God.

559 *Submissiveness.* (898)
1 Be still, my heart! these anxious cares,
  To thee are burdens, thorns, and snares;
They cast dishonor on thy Lord,
  And contradict his gracious word.

2 Brought safely by his hand thus far,
  Why wilt thou now give place to fear?
How canst thou want if he provide,
  Or lose thy way with such a guide?

3 Did ever trouble yet befall,
  And he refuse to hear thy call?
And has he not his promise passed,
  That thou shalt overcome at last?

4 He who has helped me hitherto
  Will help me all my journey through,
And give me daily cause to raise
  New trophies to his endless praise.

560 *Far from my thoughts.* (977)
1 Far from my thoughts, vain world! begone,
  Let my religious hours alone:
Fain would mine eyes my Savior see;
  I wait a visit, Lord! from thee.

2 My heart grows warm with holy fire,
  And kindles with a pure desire;
Come, my dear Jesus! from above,
  And feed my soul with heavenly love.

3 Blest Savior, what delicious fare—
  How sweet thine entertainments are!
Never did angels taste above
  Redeeming grace and dying love.

4 Hail, great Immanuel, all divine!
  In thee thy Father's glories shine:
Thou brightest, sweetest, fairest One,
  That eyes have seen, or angels known!

Zephyr, Key C.   Woodworth, Key E♭.   Oriel, Key A♭.

BROWNE. 6s, 8s & 4s.* Miss BROWNE.

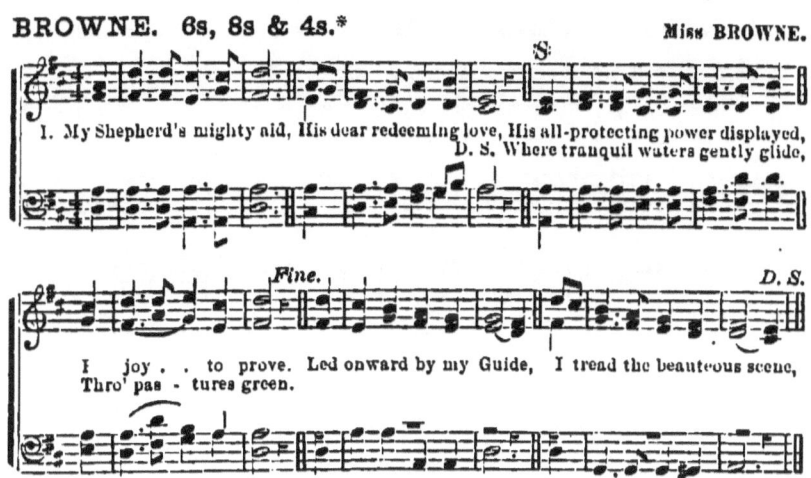

1. My Shepherd's mighty aid, His dear redeeming love, His all-protecting power displayed,
D. S. Where tranquil waters gently glide,
I joy . . to prove. Led onward by my Guide, I tread the beauteous scene,
Thro' pas - tures green.

* Or S. M. D., by omitting slur in 4th strain.

561 *Thou shalt guide me with thy counsel.* (781)
2 In error's maze my soul
 Shall wander now no more;
His Spirit shall, with sweet control,
 The lost restore.
My willing steps he 'll lead
 In paths of righteousness;
His power defend, his bounty feed,
 His mercy bless.

3 Affliction's deepest gloom
 Shall but his love display;
He will the vale of death illume
 With living ray.
I lean upon his rod,
 And thankfully adore;
My heart shall vindicate my God
 For evermore.

4 His goodness ever nigh,
 His mercy ever free,
Shall while I live, shall when I die,
 Still follow me.
For ever shall my soul
 His boundless blessings prove,
And, while eternal ages roll,
 Adore and love.

562 *Matt.* 13: 8. S. M. (1272)
1 God of the prophet's power!
 God of the gospel's sound!
Move glorious on—send out thy voice
 To all the nations round.

With hearts and lips unfeigned,
 We bless thee for thy word;
We praise thee for the joyful news,
 Which our glad ears have heard.

2 Oh may we treasure well
 The counsels that we hear,
Till righteousness and holy joy
 In all our hearts appear.
Water the sacred seed,
 And give it large increase;
May neither fowls, nor rocks, nor thorns,
 Prevent the fruits of peace.

563 *That Rock was Christ.* S. M. (778)
1 Israel the desert trod,
 Sustained by power divine,
While wondrous mercy marked the road
 With many a mystic sign.
When Moses gave the stroke
 From Horeb's flinty side
Issued a river, and the rock
 The Hebrew's thirst supplied.

2 But oh! what nobler themes
 Does gospel grace afford!
From Calvary spring superior streams—
 There hung the smitten Lord!
Of every hope bereft,
 Sinners to Jesus go;
Behold the Rock of Ages cleft,
 And living currents flow.

ALL WILL BE WELL. P. M.

From the "Golden Chain."

1. Thro' the love of God our Sav-ior, All will be well; Free and changeless is his fa-vor, All, all is well! { Pre-cious is the blood that healed us, Per-fect is the grace that sealed us, }

D. S. Strong the hand stretched out to shield us; All must be well!

564　　　　　*It is well.*　　　　　(787)

2 Though we pass through tribulation,
　All will be well:
Ours is such a full salvation;
　All, all is well:
Happy, still in God confiding,
Fruitful, if in Christ abiding,
Holy, through the Spirit's guiding,
　All must be well.

3 We expect a bright to-morrow;
　All will be well:
Faith can sing through days of sorrow,
　All, all is well:
On our Father's love relying,
Jesus every need supplying,
Or in living, or in dying,
　All must be well.

STILL WILL WE TRUST. (New.)

Dr. T. HASTINGS.

1. Still will we trust, tho' earth seem dark and dreary, And the heart faint beneath his chastening rod; Though rough and steep our pathway, worn and weary, Still will we trust in God.

565　　　　　*Still will we trust.*　　　　　(801)

2 Our eyes see dimly till by faith anointed,
　And our blind choosing brings us grief and pain;
Through him alone who hath our way appointed,
　We find our peace again.

(Concluded on page 205.)

TRUST AND JOY. 205

LEXINGTON. 8s & 4s.* (New.) T. J. COOK.

* The first and third lines may be sung as a duet, or by female voices only.

1. I know not if or dark or bright Shall be my lot; If that wherein my hopes de-light Be best, or not. It may be mine to drag for years Toil's hea-vy chain; Or day and night my meat be tears, On bed of pain.

566 *Trust.* (803)

2 Dear faces may surround my hearth
  With smiles and glee;
Or I may dwell alone, and mirth
  Be strange to me.
My bark is wafted to the strand
  By breath divine,
And on the helm there rests a hand
  Other than mine.

3 One who has known in storms to sail,
  I have on board;
Above the raving of the gale
  I hear my Lord.
His guiding hand will lead me o'er
  Life's darkest way,
To meet him where there's night no more,
  But endless day.

STILL WILL WE TRUST. (*Concluded from p. 204.*)

3 Choose for us, God; nor let our weak preferring
   Cheat our poor souls of good thou hast designed;
  Choose for us, God! thy wisdom is unerring,
   And we are fools and blind.

4 So from our sky the night shall furl her shadows,
   And day pour gladness through the golden gates;
  Our rough path leads through flowery-enameled meadows,
   Where joy our coming waits.

5 Let us press on in patient self-denial,
   Accept the hardship, shrinking not from loss—
  Our guerdon lies beyond the hour of trial;
   Our crown, beyond the Cross.

THE NEW LIFE:

JOYFULLY. 10s.

1. Joy-ful-ly, joy-ful-ly, on-ward I move, Bound to the land of bright spir-its a-bove;
An-gel-ic chor-is-ters sing as I come, Joy-ful-ly, joy-ful-ly, haste to thy home.
Soon with my pilgrim-age end-ed be-low, Home to the land of bright spirits I go; Pil-grim and stranger no more shall I roam, Joy-ful-ly, joy-ful-ly, rest-ing at home.

587   *Rejoicing in hope.*   (798)

2 Friends fondly cherished, but passed on before;
Waiting, they watch me approaching the shore;
Singing to cheer me through death's chilling gloom:
Joyfully, joyfully, haste to thy home.
Sounds of sweet melody fall on my ear;
Harps of the blessed, your voices I hear!
Rings with the harmony heaven's high dome—
Joyfully, joyfully, haste to thy home.

3 Death, with thy weapons of war, lay me low;
Strike, king of terrors! I fear not the blow;
Jesus hath broken the bars of the tomb!
Joyfully, joyfully, will I go home.
Bright will the morn of eternity dawn;
Death shall be banished, his scepter be gone;
Joyfully, then, shall I witness his doom,
Joyfully, joyfully, safely at home.

568   *Martyn, Key F.*   (781)

1 Savior! teach me, day by day,
Love's sweet lessons to obey;
Sweeter lessons can not be,
Loving him who first loved me.
With a child-like heart of love,
At thy bidding may I move;
Prompt to serve and follow thee,
Loving him who first loved me.

2 Teach me all thy steps to trace,
Strong to follow in thy grace;
Learning how to love from thee,
Loving him who first loved me.
Love in loving finds employ—
In obedience all her joy;
Ever new that joy will be,
Loving him who first loved me.

HALLEN. (New.)

SOLON WILDER.

1. Rest, weary heart, Rest weary heart, From all thy silent griefs, and se-cret pain, Thy pro-fit-less re-grets and long-ings vain! Wis-dom and love have or-dered all the past, All shall be bles-sed-ness and light at last; Cast off the cares that have so long oppressed, Rest, sweetly rest! Rest, sweetly rest!

2. Rest, weary head, Rest weary head! Lie down to slumber in the peace-ful tomb; Light from a-bove has bro-ken through its gloom; Here, in the place where once thy Savior lay, Where he shall wake thee on a fu-ture day, Like a tired child up-on its mother's breast, Rest, sweetly rest! Rest, sweetly rest!

569 *Rest, weary heart.* (796)

3 Rest, spirit free!
In the green pastures of the heavenly shore,
Where sin and sorrow can approach no more;
With all the flock by the Good Shepherd fed,
Beside the streams of life eternal led,
Forever with thy God and Savior blest,
Rest, sweetly rest!

570 *Hebron. Key B♭.* (549)

1 Benignant God of love and power,
Be with us in this solemn hour;
Smile on our souls; our plans approve,
By which we seek to spread thy love.

2 Let each discordant thought be gone,
And love unite our hearts in one;
Let all we have and are combine
To forward objects so divine.

571 *Hendon, Key G.* (706)

1 To thy temple we repair;
Lord, we love to worship there;
There, within the vail, we meet
Christ upon the mercy-seat.

2 While thy glorious name is sung,
Tune our lips, inspire our tongue;
Then our joyful souls shall bless
Christ, the Lord, our Righteousness.

THE NEW LIFE:

SHEPARD. 6, 6, 5, 5, 5, 5. (New.)   SOLON WILDER.

572   *The bright and morning star.*   (797)

1 Star of morn and even,
Sun of Heaven's heaven,
Savior high and dear,
Toward us turn thine ear;
Through whate'er may come,
Thou canst lead us home.

2 Though the gloom be grievous,
Those we leant on leave us,
Though the coward heart
Quit its proper part,
Though the tempter come,
Thou wilt lead us home.

3 Savior pure and holy,
Lover of the lowly,
Sign us with thy sign,
Take our hands in thine;
Take our hands and come,
Lead thy children home!

4 Star of morn and even,
Shine on us from heaven;
From thy glory-throne
Hear thy very own!
Lord and Savior, come,
Lead us to our home!

573   *Henley, Key F.*   (974)

1 Peace, peace on earth! the heart of man forever,
    Through all these weary strifes, foretells the day;
Blessed be God, the hope forsakes him never,
    That war shall end, and swords be sheathed for aye.

2 Peace, peace on earth! for men shall love each other;
    Hosts shall go forth to bless, and not destroy;
For man shall see in every man a brother,
    And peace on earth fulfill the angel's joy.

TRUST AND JOY.

574 *I will not let thee go.* (798)

2 I will not let thee go; should I forsake my bliss?
No, Lord, thou'rt mine,
And I am thine:
Thee will I hold when all things else I miss;
Though dark and sad the night,
Joy cometh with thy light,
Oh thou, my Sun; should I forsake my bliss?
I will not let thee go!

3 I will not let thee go, my God, my Life, my Lord!
Not death can tear
Me from his care,
Who for my sake his soul in death outpoured.
Thou diedst for love to me;
I say in love to thee,
E'en when my heart shall break, my God, my Life, my Lord,
I will not let thee go!

575 *Nillen, Key A♭.* (834)

1 My spirit longs for thee
Within my troubled breast,
Though I unworthy be
Of so divine a Guest.

2 Of so divine a Guest
Unworthy though I be,
Yet has my heart no rest
Unless it come from thee.

3 Unless it come from thee,
In vain I look around;
In all that I can see,
No rest is to be found.

4 No rest is to be found
But in thy blessed love:
Oh let my wish be crowned,
And send it from above!

GOD DOTH NOT LEAVE HIS OWN.

T. E. PERKINS, by per.

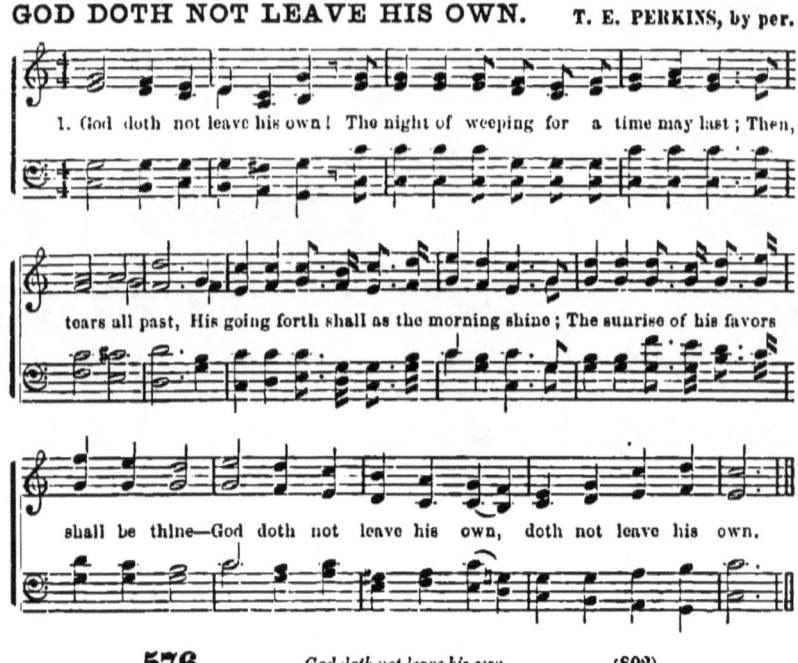

1. God doth not leave his own! The night of weeping for a time may last; Then, tears all past, His going forth shall as the morning shine; The sunrise of his favors shall be thine—God doth not leave his own, doth not leave his own.

576   *God doth not leave his own.*   (802)

2   God doth not leave his own!
Though "few and evil" all their days appear,
    Though grief and fear
Come in the train of earth and hell's dark crowd,
The trusting heart says, even in the cloud,
    God doth not leave his own.

3   God doth not leave his own!
This sorrow in their life he doth permit,
    Yea, useth it,
To speed his children on their heavenward way—
He guides the winds—Faith, Hope, and Love all say
    God doth not leave his own.

577   *Duke Street, Key E♭.*   (214)

1 The Lord is King! lift up thy voice,
O earth, and all ye heavens, rejoice!
From world to world the joy shall ring—
"The Lord omnipotent is King!"

2 The Lord is King! who then shall dare
Resist his will, distrust his care?
Holy and true are all his ways:
Let every creature speak his praise.

578   *Sessions, Key C.*   (216)

1 Savior, I lift my trembling eyes
To that bright seat, where, placed on high,
The great, the atoning sacrifice,
For me, for all, is ever nigh.

2 Be thou my guard on peril's brink;
Be thou my guide through weal or woe:
And teach me of thy cup to drink,
And make me in thy faith to go.

WYATT. 7s, Peculiar. (New.)
T. J. COOK.

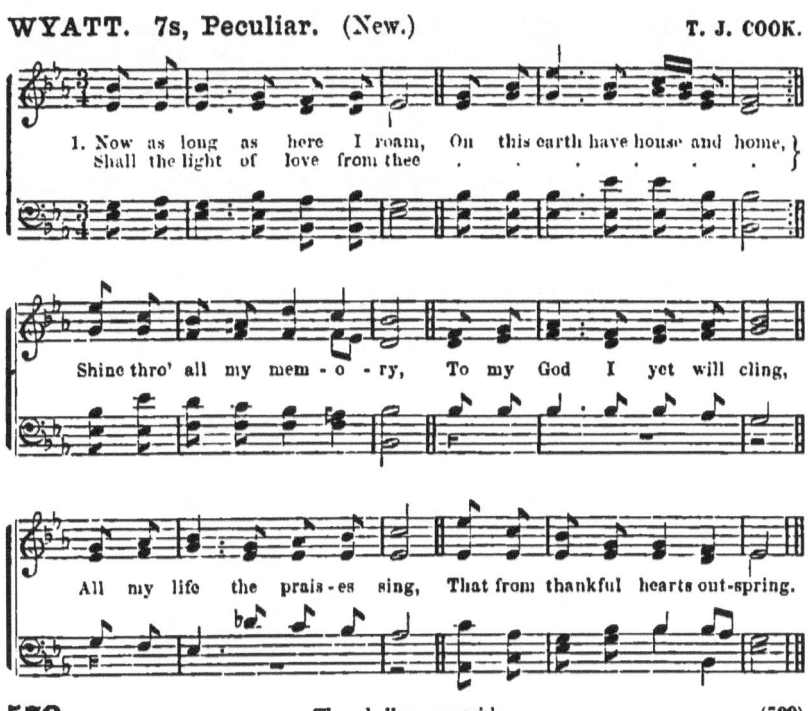

1. Now as long as here I roam, On this earth have house and home,
Shall the light of love from thee
Shine thro' all my mem-o-ry, To my God I yet will cling,
All my life the prais-es sing, That from thankful hearts out-spring.

579 *They shall never perish.* (799)

2 Every sorrow, every smart,
That the Father's loving heart
Hath appointed me of yore,
Or hath yet for me in store,
  As my life flows on I'll take;
  Calmly, gladly for his sake,
  No more faithless murmurs make.

3 I will meet distress and pain,
I will greet e'en death's dark reign,
I will lay me in the grave,
With a heart still glad and brave;
  Whom the strongest doth defend,
  Whom the highest counts his friend,
  Can not perish in the end.

580 *Naomi, Key E♭.* (521)

1 O God, unseen yet ever near!
Reveal thy presence now,
While we, in love that hath no fear,
Before thy glory bow.

2 Here may obedient spirits find
The blessings of thy love—
The streams that through the desert wind,
The manna from above.

3 Awhile beside the fount we stay,
And eat this bread of thine,
Then go, rejoicing, on our way,
Renewed with strength divine:

581 *Mear, Key F.* (231)

1 Thou dear Redeemer, dying Lamb,
I love to hear of thee;
No music's like thy charming name,
Nor half so sweet can be.

2 Oh may I ever hear thy voice
In mercy to me speak;
In thee, my Priest, will I rejoice,
And thy salvation seek.

3 My Jesus shall be still my theme
While on this earth I stay;
I'll sing my Jesus' lovely name
When all things else decay.

LONGING FOR REST. C. M. ✻

Harmonized by C.

1. Sweet land of rest, for thee I sigh; When will the moment come When I shall lay my armor by, And dwell in peace at home?

D. S. This world's a wilderness of woe, This world is not my home.

Oh, this is not my home, Oh, this is not my home;

582 *Longing for heaven.* (812)

2 No tranquil joy on earth I know,
   No peaceful, sheltering dome;
This world's a wilderness of woe,
   This world is not my home.

3 When by affliction sharply tried,
   I view the gaping tomb,
Although I dread death's chilling tide,
   Yet still I sigh for home.

4 Weary of wandering round and round
   This vale of sin and gloom,
I long to quit the unhallowed ground,
   And dwell with Christ at home.

583 *The true riches.* (813)

1 You glittering toys of earth, adieu!
   A nobler choice be mine;
A real prize attracts my view—
   A treasure all divine.

2 Away, unworthy of my cares,
   You specious baits of sense;
Inestimable worth appears,
   The pearl of price immense!

3 Jesus, to multitudes unknown—
   O name divinely sweet!
Jesus, in thee, in thee alone,
   Wealth, honor, pleasure, meet.

4 Should both the Indies, at my call,
   Their boasted stores resign,
With joy I would renounce them all,
   For leave to call thee mine.

5 Should earth's vain treasures all depart,
   Of this dear gift possessed,
I'd clasp it to my joyful heart,
   And be forever blest.

6 Blest Sovereign of my soul's desires,
   Thy love is bliss divine;
Accept the praise that love inspires,
   Since I can call thee mine!

584 *As a tale that is told.* (1052)

How short and hasty is our life:
How vast our soul's affairs!
Yet foolish mortals vainly strive
   To lavish out their years.

ASPIRATIONS. 213

GOING HOME. C. M. ✶
A. D. FILLMORE.

1. Je-ru-sa-lem, my happy home, Oh, how I long for thee!
   When will my sorrows have an end? . . . . . Thy joys, when shall I see?

Chorus.
We're go-ing home, we're going home, We're going home to live for-ev-er.

---

585   *The new Jerusalem.*   (820)

2 Thy walls are all of precious stones,
  Most glorious to behold!
Thy gates are richly set with pearl,
  Thy streets are paved with gold.

3 Thy gardens and thy pleasant greens
  My study long have been;
Such sparkling gems by human sight
  Have never yet been seen.

4 If heaven be thus glorious, Lord,
  Why should I stay from thence?
What folly 't is that I should dread
  To die and go from hence!

5 Reach down, reach down thine arms of grace,
  And cause me to ascend
Where congregations ne'er break up,
  And Sabbaths never end.

6 Jesus, my love, to glory's gone;
  Him will I go and see;
And all my brethren here below
  Will soon come after me.

586   *A city which hath foundations.*   (821)

1 Jerusalem, my glorious home,
  Name ever dear to me!
When shall my labors have an end,
  In joy, and peace, and thee?

2 When shall these eyes thy heaven-built walls
  And pearly gates behold?
Thy bulwarks with salvation strong,
  And streets of shining gold?

3 There happier bowers than Eden's bloom,
  Nor sin, nor sorrow know:
Blessed seats! thro' rude and stormy scenes,
  I onward press to you.

4 Why should I shrink at pain and woe,
  Or feel, at death, dismay?
I've Canaan's goodly land in view,
  And realms of endless day.

5 Apostles, martyrs, prophets there,
  Around my Savior stand;
And soon my friends in Christ below
  Will join the glorious band.

6 Jerusalem, my glorious home,
  My soul still pants for thee!
Then shall my labors have an end,
  When I thy joys shall see.

587   *Earnestly desiring.*   (1128)

1 Oh could our thoughts and wishes fly
  Above these gloomy shades,
To those bright worlds beyond the sky
  Which sorrow ne'er invades!

2 There joys, unseen by mortal eyes,
  Or reason's feeble ray,
In ever-blooming prospect rise,
  Unconscious of decay.

3 Lord, send a beam of light divine,
  To guide our upward aim!
With one reviving touch of thine
  Our languid hearts inflame.

THE NEW LIFE:

MESSIAH. 7s, Double.
Arr. by GEO. KINGSLEY.

1. Come, my Christian brethren, come, Let us onward to our home;
Though we many tri-als meet, ... Je-sus makes our tri-als sweet. Brother Christian, doubt no more, Christ your Savior's gone before;
D. S. We with Je-sus soon shall be, Hap-py in e-ter-ni-ty;
He himself has marked the way, Lead-ing to e - - ter-nal day.
By our Fa-ther's side sit down, They that conquer shall wear the crown.

588 *They that conquer shall wear, etc.* (824)
2 Let us never be afraid;
'Tis on Christ our help is laid:
He will all our foes o'ercome,
He will take his exiles home.
Though the world revile and mock,
We are built upon the Rock;
And, while thus we dwell secure,
Christ will make our goings sure.

589 *All things work together for good* (919)
1 Sovereign Ruler of the skies,
Ever gracious, ever wise!
All my times are in thy hand;
All events at thy command.
Times of sickness, times of health,
Times of penury and wealth—
All must come, at last, and end,
As shall please my heavenly Friend.

2 O thou gracious, wise and just!
In thy hands my life I trust;
Have I somewhat dearer still?
I resign it to thy will.

Thee at all times will I bless;
Having thee, I all possess;
Ne'er can I bereaved be,
While I do not part with thee

590 *That they go forward.* (882)
1 Oft in sorrow, oft in woe,
Onward, Christian, onward go;
Fight the fight, maintain the strife,
Strengthened with the bread of life.
Onward, Christian, onward go;
Join the war, and face the foe;
Will you flee in danger's hour?
Know you not your Captain's power?

2 Let your drooping heart be glad;
March, in heavenly armor clad;
Fight, nor think the battle long:
Soon shall victory tune your song.
Let not sorrow dim your eye;
Soon shall every tear be dry;
Let not fears your course impede;
Great your strength, if great your need.

Wilson, Key G.   Ives, Key E.   Martyn, Key F.

ASPIRATIONS. 215

SOMERSET. 8s. (New.) Arr. from J. G. ARCHER, by J. P. POWELL.

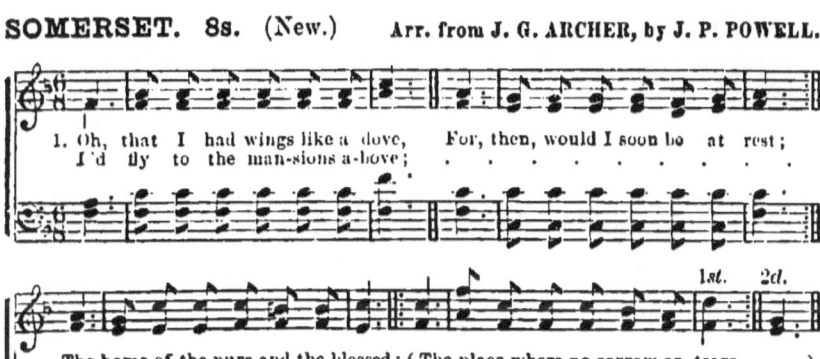

1. Oh, that I had wings like a dove, For, then, would I soon be at rest;
I'd fly to the mansions above; The home of the pure and the blessed; The place where no sorrow or tears Can ev-er my pleasures de - - stroy; But where, thro' e-ter-ni-ty's years, I'll drink from an o-cean of joy.

591   *Longing for rest.*   (S26)

2 The clouds that now hang o'er my soul,
  Make dark all the pathway of life;
While thunders unceasingly roll
  In storms of deep anger and strife;
I hope for some bright ray to beam
  From clouds where there yet may be light,
But only the lightning's red gleam
  Is seen through the darkness of night.

3 I try to be humble and meek,
  Leave all to my Savior's own will;
For, he to the tempest can speak,
  The winds will obey and be still;
But now my soul flutters and cries,
  And longs to be soaring away,
From darkness and gloom, to the skies,
  The regions of bright, endless day.

4 Dear Savior, oh let me come home,
  And rest on thy bosom in peace;
No more from thy presence to roam—
  Then tempests and storms shall all cease.
I'll sing of thy wonderful ways,
  With all of the glorified throng—
For ever and ever, thy praise
  Shall be the one theme of my song.

592   *Having a desire to depart.*   (S27)

1 To Jesus, the crown of my hope,
  My soul is in haste to be gone;
Oh bear me, ye cherubim, up,
  And waft me away to his throne.
My Savior, whom absent, I love,
  Whom, not having seen, I adore;
Whose name is exalted above
  All glory, dominion, and power!

2 Dissolve thou those bands that detain
  My soul from her portion in thee,
Ah! strike off this adamant chain,
  And make me eternally free.
When that happy era begins,
  When arrayed in thy glories I shine,
Nor grieve any more, by my sins,
  The bosom on which I recline;

3 Oh then shall the vail be removed!
  And round me thy brightness be opened;
I shall meet him, whom absent I loved;
  I shall see, whom unseen I adored.
And then, never more shall the fears,
  The trials, temptations, and woes,
Which darken this valley of tears,
  Intrude on my blissful repose.

LET ME GO. 8s & 7s, Double.
W. B. BRADBURY, by per.

1. Let me go: my soul is wea-ry Of the chain which binds me here;
Let my spir-it bend its pin-ion To a brighter, ho-lier sphere.
Earth, 't is true, hath friends that bless me With their fond and faithful love,
But the hands of an-gels beck-on On-ward to the climes a-bove.

2. Let me go: for earth hath sor-row, Sin, and pain, and bit-ter tears;
All its paths are dark and drear-y, All its hopes are fraught with fears.
Short-lived are its brightest flow-ers, Soon its cherished joys de-cay;
Let me go; I fain would leave it For the realms of end-less day.

593 *Prisoners of hope.* (825)

3 Let me go: my heart hath tasted
Of my Savior's wondrous grace;
Let me go, where I shall ever
See and know him face to face:
Let me go: the trees of heaven
Rise before me, waving bright,
And the distant crystal waters
Flash upon my failing sight.

4 Let me go: for songs seraphic
Now seem calling from the sky—
'T is the welcome of the angels,
Which e'en now are hovering nigh.
Let me go: they wait to bear me
To the mansions of the blest,
Where the spirit, worn and weary,
Finds at last its long-sought rest.

594 *I have led thee in right paths.* (922)

1 Oh how kindly hast thou led me,
Heavenly Father, day by day!
Found my dwelling, clothed and fed me,
Furnished friends to cheer my way!
Didst thou bless me, didst thou chasten,
With thy smile or with thy rod,
'T was that still my step might hasten
Homeward, heavenward, to my God.

2 Oh how slowly have I often
Followed where thy hand would draw!
How thy kindness failed to soften!
How thy chastening failed to awe!
Make me for thy rest more ready,
As thy path is longer trod;
Keep me in thy friendship steady,
Till thou call me home, my God!

ASPIRATIONS.

595 *Only waiting.* (1226)

1 Only waiting till the shadows
   Are a little longer grown;
Only waiting till the glimmer
   Of the day's last beam is flown;
Till the night of earth is faded
   From the heart once full of day;
Till the stars of heaven are breaking
   Through the twilight soft and gray.

2 Only waiting till the reapers
   Have the last sheaf gathered home;
For the summer-time is faded,
   And the autumn winds have come.
Quickly, reapers, gather quickly
   The last ripe hours of my heart,
For the bloom of life is withered,
   And I hasten to depart.

3 Only waiting till the shadows
   Are a little longer grown;
Only waiting till the glimmer
   Of the day's last beam is flown;
Then, from out the gathered darkness,
   Holy, deathless stars shall rise,
By whose light my soul shall gladly
   Tread its pathway to the skies.

596 *Suffer little children to come, etc.* (1074)

1 They are going—only going—
   Jesus called them long ago;
All the wintry time they're passing,
   Softly as the falling snow.
When the violets, in the spring-time,
   Catch the azure of the sky,
They are carried out to slumber
   Sweetly where the violets lie.

2 They are going—only going—
   When with summer earth is dressed,
In their cold hands holding roses
   Folded to each silent breast;
When the autumn hangs red banners
   Out above the harvest sheaves,
They are going—ever going—
   Thick and fast, like falling leaves.

3 All along the mighty ages,
   All adown the solemn time,
They have taken up their homeward
   March to that serener clime,

Where the watching, waiting angels
   Lead them from the shadow dim
To the brightness of his presence,
   Who has called them unto him.

4 They are going—only going—
   Out of pain and into bliss—
Out of sad and sinful weakness
   Into perfect holiness.
Snowy brows—no care shall shade them;
   Bright eyes—tears shall never dim;
Rosy lips—no time shall fade them:
   Jesus called them unto him.

5 Little hearts forever stainless—
   Little hands as pure as they—
Little feet by angels guided,
   Never a forbidden way!
They are going—ever going—
   Leaving many a lonely spot;
But 't is Jesus who has called them—
   Suffer and forbid them not.

597 *Shall we e'er forget the story?* (1156)

1 When we reach a quiet dwelling,
   On the strong, eternal hills,
And our praise to him is swelling,
   Who the vast creation fills;
When the paths of prayer and duty,
   And affliction all are trod,
And we wake to see the beauty
   Of our Savior and our God:

2 With the light of resurrection,
   When our changed bodies glow,
And we gain the full perfection
   Of the bliss begun below;
When the life that flesh obscureth
   In each radiant form shall shine,
And the joy that aye endureth
   Flashes forth in beams divine:

3 While we wave the palms of glory
   Through the long, eternal years,
Shall we e'er forget the story
   Of our mortal griefs and fears?
Shall we e'er forget the sadness,
   And the clouds that hung so dim,
When our hearts are filled with gladness,
   And our tears are dried by him?

Autumn, Key A.   Pleading Savior, Key G.   Trust, Key E♭.

THE NEW LIFE:

BONAR. S. M. Double. Dr. L. MASON, by permission.

1. A few more years shall roll, A few more seasons come, And we shall be with those that rest, A-sleep with-in the tomb; Then, O, my Lord, pre-pare My soul for that great day; Oh, wash me in thy pre-cious blood,
D. S. And take my sins a-way.

598 *A pilgrim's song.* (828)

2 A few more suns shall set
  O'er these dark hills of time;
And we shall be where suns are not,
  A far serener clime.
Then, O my Lord, prepare
  My soul for that blest day;
Oh wash me in thy precious blood,
  And take my sins away.

3 A few more storms shall beat
  On this wild rocky shore;
And we shall be where tempests cease,
  And surges swell no more.
Then, O my Lord, prepare
  My soul for that calm day,
Oh wash me in thy precious blood,
  And take my sins away.

4 A few more struggles here,
  A few more partings o'er,
A few more toils, a few more tears,
  And we shall weep no more.
Then, O my Lord, prepare
  My soul for that blest day;
Oh wash me in thy precious blood,
  And take my sins away.

599 *Come, Lord Jesus.* (1100)

1 The Church has waited long
  Her absent Lord to see;
And still in loneliness she waits,
  A friendless stranger she.
Age after age has gone,
  Sun after sun has set,
And still in weeds of widowhood
  She weeps, a mourner yet.

2 Saint after saint on earth
  Has lived, and loved, and died;
And as they left us, one by one,
  We laid them side by side;
We laid them down to sleep,
  But not in hope forlorn;
We laid them but to ripen there,
  Till the last glorious morn.

3 The whole creation groans,
  And waits to hear that voice
That shall restore her comeliness,
  And make her wastes rejoice.
Come, Lord, and wipe away
  The curse, the sin, the stain,
And make this blighted world of ours
  Thine own fair world again.

Browne, Key D.

ASPIRATIONS. 219

FOREVER WITH THE LORD. S. M., Double.

I. B. WOODBURY, by permission.

600 *Ever with the Lord.* (873)

2 My Father's house on high,
  Home of my soul, how near
At times, to faith's aspiring eye,
  Thy golden gates appear!
Ah, then my spirit faints,
  To reach the land I love,
The bright inheritance of saints,
  Jerusalem above, home above, etc.

3 Yet doubts still intervene,
  And all my comfort flies:
Like Noah's dove, I flit between
  Rough seas and stormy skies;
Anon the clouds depart,
  The winds and waters cease;
While sweetly o'er my gladdened heart
  Expands the bow of peace, bow of, etc.

601 *Bless his holy name.* (651)

1 Let every heart and tongue
  Proclaim the Savior's praise;
He is the source of all my joy,
  His mercy crowns my days.
He knows my feeble frame;
  Remembers I am dust;
And though he should my life destroy,
  In him I'll put my trust, put my, etc.

2 Each day he is my strength,
  My hope, my life, my all;
And, while upon his arm I lean,
  I surely can not fall.
Then, to my blessed Lord,
  Let grateful songs arise,
While angels bear the notes above
  And sound them thro' the skies, thro', etc.

THE NEW LIFE:

HERE AND YONDER. 8s & 7s. W. O. PERKINS, by permission.

1. Here we are but stray-ing pil-grims, Here our path is of-ten dim;
2. Here our feet are of-ten wea-ry, On the hills that throng our way;

But to cheer us on our jour-ney, Still we sing this way-side hymn:
Here the tem-pest dark-ly gath-ers, But our hearts with-in us say,

Chorus.
Yon-der, o-ver the rolling river, Where the shining mansions rise, Soon will be our home for-ev-er, And the smile of the blessed Giver Gladdens all our longing eyes.

602   *Here and yonder.*   (829)

3 Here, our souls are often fearful
   Of the pilgrim's lurking foe;
But the Lord is our defender,
   And he tells us we may know.

4 Here, our shadowed homes are transient,
   And we meet the stranger's frown;
So we'll sing with joy while going,
   E'en to death's dark billow down—

603   *Happy home.*   (1152)

1 In that world of ancient story,
   Where no storms can ever come,
Where the Savior dwells in glory,
   There remains for us a home.

2 There within the heavenly mansions,
   Where life's river flows so clear,
We shall see our blessed Savior,
   If we love and serve him here.

3 There with holy angels dwelling,
   Where the ransomed wander free,
Jesus' praises ever telling,
   Sing we through eternity.

4 There amid the shining numbers,
   All our toils and labors o'er,
Where the Guardian never slumbers,
   We shall dwell for evermore.

604   *St Martin's, Key G.*   (3S)

1 O God! my heart is fully bent
   To magnify thy name;
My tongue, with cheerful songs of praise,
   Shall celebrate thy fame.

2 Be thou, O God, exalted high
   Above the starry frame;
And let the world, with one consent,
   Confess thy glorious name.

ASPIRATIONS. 221

EXCELSIOR. 6s & 5s. Double.   S. J. VAIL, by permission.

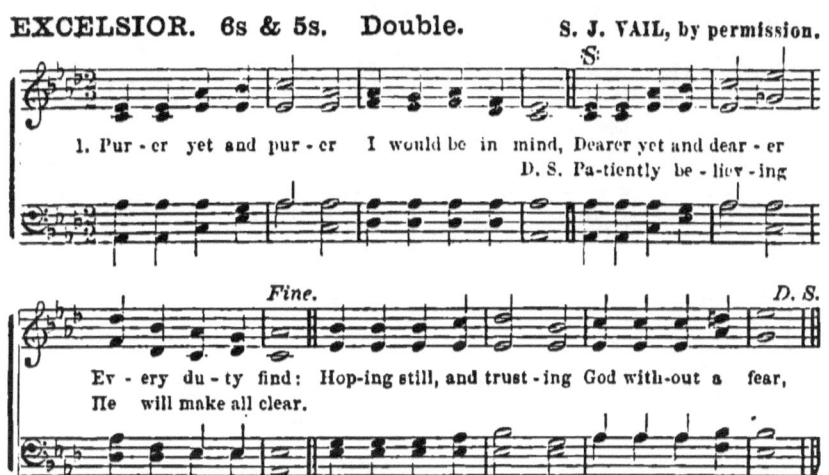

1. Pur-er yet and pur-er I would be in mind, Dearer yet and dear-er
D. S. Pa-tiently be-liev-ing

Fine.   *D. S.*

Ev-ery du-ty find: Hop-ing still, and trust-ing God with-out a fear,
He will make all clear.

605   *I have longed for thy salvation.* (835)

2 Calmer yet and calmer
Trial bear and pain,
Surer yet and surer
Peace at last to gain.
Suffering still and doing,
To his will resigned,
And to God subduing
Heart, and will, and mind;

3 Higher yet and higher,
Out of clouds and night,
Nearer yet and nearer
Rising to the light—
Oft these earnest longings
Swell within my breast;
Yet their inner meaning
Ne'er can be expressed.

606   *Psalm 91.* (897)

1 God of our salvation!
Unto thee we pray;
Hear our supplication,
Be our strength and stay.
Wretched and unworthy,
Poor and sick, and blind,
Prostrate we adore thee,
Call thy grace to mind.

2 He that dwelleth near thee,
Safely shall abide;
Ever love and fear thee,
In thy strength confide.
Sure is thy protection,
Safe is thy defense,
While in deep affliction,
Woe, or pestilence.

3 God of our salvation!
Savior, Prince of Peace,
Boundless thy compassion,
Infinite thy grace.
While with love unceasing,
Humbly we adore;
Grant us thy rich blessing,
And we ask no more.

607   *Dennis, Key F.* (1173)

1 In all my ways, O God!
I would acknowledge thee;
And seek to keep my heart and house
From all pollution free.

2 Where'er I have a tent,
An altar will I raise;
And thither my oblations bring
Of humble prayer and praise.

3 Could I my wish obtain,
My household, Lord, should be
Devoted to thyself alone,
A nursery for thee.

WEBB. 7s & 6s, Double.

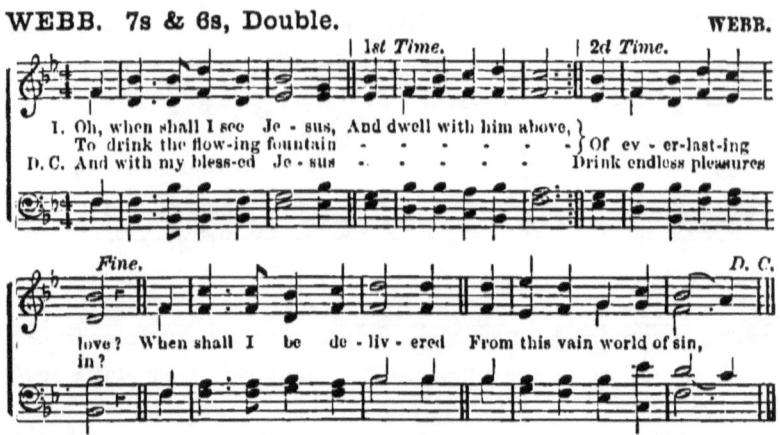

1. Oh, when shall I see Jesus, And dwell with him above,
To drink the flowing fountain Of everlasting
D. C. And with my blessed Jesus Drink endless pleasures

... love? When shall I be delivered From this vain world of sin,
... in?

608 *Song of our pilgrimage.* (830)

2 But now I am a soldier,
My Captain's gone before;
He's given me my orders,
And tells me not to fear.
And if I hold out faithful,
A crown of life he'll give,
And all his valiant soldiers
Eternal life shall have.

3 Through grace I am determined
To conquer, though I die;
And then away to Jesus
On wings of love I'll fly.
Farewell to sin and sorrow—
I bid them both adieu:
And you, my friends, prove faithful,
And on your way pursue.

4 And if you meet with troubles
And trials on the way,
Then cast your care on Jesus,
And don't forget to pray.
Gird on the heavenly armor
Of faith, and hope, and love,
And when your warfare's ended,
You'll reign with him above.

5 Oh! do not be discouraged,
For Jesus is your Friend,
And if you long for knowledge,
On him you may depend;
Neither will he upbraid you,
Though often you request;
He'll give you grace to conquer,
And take you home to rest.

609 *How long, O Lord.* (831)

1 How long, O Lord, our Savior,
Wilt thou remain away?
Our hearts are growing weary
Of thy so long delay;
Oh when shall come the moment,
When, brighter far than morn,
The sunshine of thy glory,
Shall on thy people dawn.

2 How long, O gracious Master,
Wilt thou thy household leave?
So long hast thou now tarried,
Few thy return believe.
Immersed in sloth and folly,
Thy servants, Lord, we see,
And few of us stand ready
With joy to welcome thee.

3 How long, O heavenly Bridegroom,
How long wilt thou delay?
And yet how few are grieving
That thou dost absent stay:
Thy very bride, her portion
And calling hath forgot,
And seeks for ease and glory
Where thou, her Lord, art not.

4 Oh wake thy slumbering virgins,
Send forth the solemn cry—
Let all thy saints repeat it—
The Bridegroom draweth nigh;
May all our lamps be burning,
Our loins well girded be,
Each longing heart preparing
With joy thy face to see.

ASPIRATIONS. 223

610 *All the rivers run into the sea.* (1088)

1 As flows the rapid river,
With channel broad and free,
Its waters rippling ever,
And hastening to the sea;
So life is onward flowing,
And days of offered peace,
And man is swiftly going
Where calls of mercy cease.

2 As moons are ever waning,
As hastes the sun away,
As stormy winds, complaining,
Bring on the wintry day;
So fast the night comes o'er us—
The darkness of the grave;
The death is just before us;
God takes the life he gave.

3 Say, hath thy heart its treasure
Laid up in worlds above?
And is it all thy pleasure
Thy God to praise and love?
Beware lest death's dark river
Its billows o'er thee roll,
And thou lament forever
The ruin of thy soul.

611 *Early piety.* (325)

1 Oh come in life's gay morning,
Ere in thy sunny way
The flowers of hope have withered,
And sorrow end thy day!
Come, while from joy's bright fountain
The streams of pleasure flow;
Come ere thy buoyant spirits
Have felt the blight of woe.

2 "Remember thy Creator"
Now in thy youthful days,
And he will guide thy footsteps
Through life's uncertain maze.
"Remember thy Creator,"
He calls in tones of love,
And offer deathless glories
In brighter worlds above.

3 And in the hour of sadness,
When earthly joys depart,
His love shall be thy solace,
And cheer thy drooping heart.

And when life's storm is over,
And thou from earth art free,
Thy God will be thy portion
Throughout eternity.

612 *Strangers and pilgrims.* (1155)

1 We have no home but heaven;
A pilgrim's garb we wear;
Our path is marked by changes,
And strewed with many a care;
Surrounded with temptation;
By varied ills oppressed;
Each day's experience warns us
That this is not our rest.

2 We have no home but heaven;
Then, wherefore seek one here?
Why murmur at privation,
Or grieve when trouble's near?
It is but for a season
That we as strangers roam,
And strangers must not look for
The comforts of a home.

3 We have no home but heaven;
We want no home beside;
O God, our Friend and Father,
Our footsteps thither guide!
Unfold to us its glory,
Prepare us for its joy,
Its pure and perfect friendship,
Its angel-like employ.

613 *Reunion in heaven.* (1144)

1 No seas again shall sever,
No desert intervene,
No deep, sad-flowing river
Shall roll its tide between.
Love and unsevered union
Of soul with those we love,
Nearness and glad communion,
Shall be our joy above.

2 No dread of wasting sickness,
No thought of ache or pain,
No fretting hours of weakness,
Shall mar our peace again.
No death our homes o'ershading
Shall e'er our harps unstring,
For all is life unfading
In presence of our King.

How long, O Lord, Key F.   Petition, Key A.   Western, Key G.

THE NEW LIFE:

FREDERICK. 11s. KINGSLEY.

1. I would not live always; I ask not to stay . . . Where storm after storm rises
D. C. Are enough for life's woes, full e - - - nough for its cheer.

dark o'er the way: The few cloudy mornings that dawn on us here,

614 *I would not live always.* (836)

2 I would not live always: no, welcome the tomb;
Since Jesus has lain there, I dread not its gloom;
There sweet be my rest, till he bid me arise
To hail him in triumph descending the skies.

3 Who, who would live always, away from his God,
Away from yon heaven, that blissful abode,
Where the rivers of pleasure flow o'er the bright plains,
And the noontide of glory eternally reigns;

4 Where the saints of all ages in harmony meet,
Their Savior and brethren transported to greet,
While the anthems of rapture unceasingly roll,
And the smile of the Lord is the feast of the soul!

615 Heb. 12: 2. (790)

1 O eyes that are weary, and hearts that are sore,
Look off unto Jesus; now sorrow no more!
The light of his countenance shineth so bright,
That here, as in heaven, there need be no night.

2 While looking to Jesus, my heart can not fear;
I tremble no more when I see Jesus near;
I know that his presence my safeguard will be,
For "Why are you troubled?" he saith unto me.

3 Still looking to Jesus, oh may I be found,
When Jordan's dark waters encompass me round!
They bear me away in his presence to be;
I see him still nearer whom always I see.

4 Then, then shall I know the full beauty and grace
Of Jesus, my Lord, when I stand face to face:
Shall know how his love went before me each day,
And wonder that ever my eyes turned away.

Memory, Key E.   Kimmel, Key E.   Home, Key E♭.

ASPIRATIONS. 225

KIMMEL. 11s, or 12, 12, 11, 11. ✱ W. T. MOORE.

1. I am wea-ry of straying; oh, fain would I rest In that far dis-tant
D. C. And tears and temptations for-ev-er are fled.

land of the pure and the blest; Where sin can no longer her blandishment spread,

616 *I am weary.* (837)

2 I am weary of hoping, where hope is untrue,
As fair but as fleeting as morning's bright dew;
I long for the land whose blest promise alone
Is as changeless and sure as eternity's throne.

3 I am weary of sighing o'er sorrows of earth,
O'er joy's glowing visions that fade at their birth,
O'er pangs of the loved, which we can not assuage,
O'er the blightings of youth, and the weakness of age.

4 I am weary of loving what passes away—
The sweetest and dearest, alas! may not stay;
I long for that land where those partings are o'er,
And death and the tomb can divide hearts no more.

617 *Psalm 23.* (103)

1 The Lord is my Shepherd, no want shall I know;
I feed in green pastures, safe folded I rest;
He leadeth my soul where the still waters flow,
Restores me when wandering, redeems when opprest.

2 Through the valley and shadow of death though I stray,
Since thou art my guardian, no evil I fear;
Thy rod shall defend me, thy staff be my stay;
No harm can befall, with my comforter near.

3 In the midst of affliction my table is spread;
With blessings unmeasured my cup runneth o'er;
With perfume and oil thou anointest my head;
Oh what shall I ask of thy providence more?

4 Let goodness and mercy, my bountiful God!
Still follow my steps till I meet thee above;
I seek, by the path which my forefathers trod,
Through the land of their sojourn, thy kingdom of love.

Frederick, Key F.   Memory, Key E.

A LITTLE WHILE. P. M.
SOLON WILDER, by Permission.

1. Be-yond the smil-ing and the weep-ing, I shall be soon; Be-yond the wak-ing and the sleeping, Be-yond the sowing and the reaping, I shall be soon. Love, rest, and home! Sweet home, sweet home! Lord, tar-ry not, but come.

618   *Lord, tarry not, but come.*   (840)

2 Beyond the blooming and the fading,
    I shall be soon;
Beyond the shining and the shading,
Beyond the hoping and the dreading,
    I shall be soon.
    Love, rest, and home, etc.

3 Beyond the rising and the setting,
    I shall be soon;
Beyond the calming and the fretting,
Beyond remembering and forgetting,
    I shall be soon.
    Love, rest, and home, etc.

4 Beyond the parting and the meeting,
    I shall be soon;
Beyond the farewell and the greeting,
Beyond the pulse's fever beating,
    I shall be soon.
    Love, rest, and home, etc.

5 Beyond the frost-chain and the fever,
    I shall be soon;
Beyond the rock-waste and the river,
Beyond the ever and the never,
    I shall be soon.
    Love, rest, and home, etc.

COME TO ME. Chant.
W. B. BRADBURY, by permission.

619   *Come unto me.*

With tearful eyes I look around;
    Life seems a dark and | stormy | sea;
Yet, 'midst the gloom, I hear a sound,
    A heavenly | whisper, | "Come to | me."

ASPIRATIONS. 227

SOON AND FOREVER. 10s & 11s. (New.)   Dr. T. HASTINGS.

1. Soon and for-ev-er the break-ing of day Shall chase all the night-clouds of sor-row a-way;
Soon and for-ev-er we'll see as we're seen, And know the deep meaning of things that have been,
2. Soon and for-ev-er—such promise our trust—Though ash-es to ash-es, and dust be to dust,
Soon and for-ev-er our un-ion shall be Made per-fect, our glo-rious Re-deem-er, in thee:

Where fightings without and con-flicts within Shall wea-ry no more in the warfare with sin—Where tears, and where fears, and where death shall be never, Christians with Christ shall be soon and for-ev - er.
When the cares and the sorrows of time shall be o'er, Its pangs and its part-ings re-mem-bered no more; Where life can not fail and where death can not sever, Christians with Christ shall be soon and for-ev - er.

620   *The night is far spent, etc.*   (844)
3 Soon and forever the work shall be done,
The warfare accomplished, the victory won;
Soon and forever the soldier lay down
The sword for a harp, and the cross for a crown:
Then droop not in sorrow, despond not in fear,
A glorious to-morrow is brightening and near,
When—blessed reward for each faithful endeavor—
Christians with Christ shall be soon and forever?

621   *Yoakley, Key E.*   (49)
1 Thou art, O God, the life and light
Of all the wondrous world we see;
Its glow by day, its smile by night,
Are but reflections caught from thee;
Where'er we turn, thy glories shine,
And all things fair and bright are thine.

2 When day, with farewell beam, delays
Among the opening clouds of even,
And we can almost think we gaze,
Through opening vistas, into heaven—
Those hues that mark the sun's decline,
So soft, so radiant, Lord, are thine.

THE NEW LIFE:

HAPPY ZION. 8s, 7s & 4s. I. B. WOODBURY, by permission.

1. Lead us, heav'nly Father, lead us O'er the world's tem-pestuous sea;
Guard us, guide us, keep us, feed us, For we have no help but thee.
Yet pos-sess-ing Ev'-ry bless-ing, If our God our Fa-ther be.

622 *Lead us, heavenly Father, lead us.* (842)
2 Savior! breathe forgiveness o'er us;
All our weakness thou dost know;
Thou didst tread this earth before us,
Thou didst feel its keenest woe.
Lone and dreary, faint and weary,
Through the desert thou didst go.

3 Spirit of our God descending!
Fill our hearts with heavenly joy,
Love with every passion blending,
Pleasure that can never cloy.
Thus provided, pardoned, guided,
Nothing can our peace destroy.

623 *Worthy is the Lamb, etc.* (604)
1 Glory, glory everlasting,
Be to him who bore the cross,
Who redeemed our souls by tasting
Death, the death deserved by us:
Sound his glory
While our heart with transport glows.

2 Jesus' love is love unbounded,
Without measure, without end:
Human thought is here confounded;
'Tis too vast to comprehend;
Praise the Savior;
Magnify the sinner's Friend.

3 While we hear the wondrous story
Of the Savior's cross and shame,
Sing we, "Everlasting glory
Be to God and to the Lamb!"
Saints and angels,
Give ye glory to his name.

624 *Songs for sighing.* (024)
1 Hallelujah! best and sweetest
Of the hymns of praise above!
Hallelujah! thou repeatest,
Angel-host, these notes of love;
This ye utter,
While your golden harps ye move.

2 Hallelujah! church victorious,
Join the concert of the sky;
Hallelujah! bright and glorious!
Lift, ye saints, the strains on high!
We, poor exiles,
Join not yet your melody.

3 Hallelujah! strains of gladness
Comfort not the faint and worn;
Hallelujah! sounds of sadness
Best become the heart forlorn;
Our offenses
We with bitter tears must mourn.

4 But our earnest supplication,
Holy God, we raise to thee;
Visit us with thy salvation,
Make us all thy peace to see!
Hallelujah!
Ours at length this strain shall be.

625 *God of our salvation, hear us.* (756)
God of our salvation, hear us;
Bless, oh bless us, ere we go;
When we join the world, be near us,
Lest we cold and careless grow;
Savior, keep us—
Keep us safe from every foe.

Alvan, Key G.   Siberia, Key D.   Osgood, Key E♭.

ASPIRATIONS. 229

626   *Oh, come quickly.*   (1102)

1 Savior, haste: our souls are waiting
For the long expected day,
When, new heavens and earth creating,
Thou shalt banish grief away;
   All the sorrow
Caused by sin and Satan's sway.

2 Haste, oh hasten thine appearing,
Take thy mourning people home;
'T is this hope our spirits cheering,
While we in the desert roam,
   Makes thy people
Strangers here till thou dost come.

3 Lord, how long shall the creation
Groan and travail sore in pain,
Waiting for its sure salvation
When thou shalt in glory reign,
   And like Eden
This sad earth shall bloom again?

4 Reign, oh reign, almighty Savior,
Heaven and earth in one unite;
Make it known, that in thy favor,
There alone is life and light;
   When we see thee
We shall have supreme delight.

627   *Adoration.*   (1323)

1 Let us sing the King Messiah,
King of Righteousness and Peace;
Hail him all his happy subjects,
Never let his praises cease!
   Ever hail him,
Let his honors still increase!

2 How transcendent are thy glories!
Fairer than the sons of men,
While thy blessed mediation
Brings us back to God again!
   Blessed Redeemer,
How we triumph in thy reign!

3 Gird thy sword on, Mighty Hero,
Make thy word of truth thy car,
Prosper in thy course triumphant,
All success attend thy war!
   Gracious Victor,
Let mankind before thee bow!

628   *Freely you have received, etc.*   (971)

1 With my substance I will honor
My Redeemer and my Lord;
Were ten thousand worlds my manor,
All were nothing to his word:
   Hallelujah!
Now we offer to the Lord.

2 While the heralds of salvation
His abounding grace proclaim,
Let his saints of every station
Gladly join to spread his fame:
   Hallelujah!
Gifts we offer to his name.

3 May his kingdom be promoted;
May the world the Savior know;
Be to him these gifts devoted,
For to him my all I owe:
   Hallelujah!
Run, ye heralds, to and fro.

4 Praise the Savior, all ye nations;
Praise him, all ye hosts above;
Shout with joyful acclamations
His divine, victorious love:
   Hallelujah!
By this gift our love we 'll prove.

629   *The Lord cometh, etc.*   (1103)

1 Lo! he cometh—countless trumpets
Wake to life the slumbering dead;
'Mid ten thousand saints and angels,
See their great exalted Head:
   Hallelujah!
Welcome, welcome, Son of God!

2 Full of joyful expectation,
Saints behold the Judge appear;
Truth and justice go before him—
Now the joyful sentence hear;
   Hallelujah!
Welcome, welcome, Judge divine!

3 "Come, ye blessed of my Father!
Enter into life and joy;
Banish all your fears and sorrows;
Endless praise be your employ;"
   Hallelujah!
Welcome, welcome, to the skies.

Peron, Key G.   Zion, Key D.   Molucca, Key D.

THE NEW LIFE:

ROTHWELL. L. M.

1. Awake, our souls; away, our fears; Let every trembling thought be gone; Awake and run the heavenly race, And put a cheerful courage on, And put a cheerful courage on.

630 *I press toward the mark.* (856)

2 True, 'tis a straight and thorny road,
  And mortal spirits tire and faint;
But they forget the mighty God,
  Who feeds the strength of every saint.

3 The mighty God, whose matchless power
  Is ever new and ever young,
And firm endures, while endless years
  Their everlasting circles run.

4 From thee, the overflowing spring,
  Our souls shall drink a full supply;
While those who trust their native strength,
  Shall melt away, and droop, and die.

5 Swift as an eagle cuts the air,
  We'll mount aloft to thine abode;
On wings of love our souls shall fly,
  Nor tire amid the heavenly road.

631 *Unchanging trust.* (65)

1 No change of time shall ever shock
  My firm affection, Lord, to thee;
For thou hast always been my rock,
  A fortress and defense to me.

2 Thou my deliverer art, my God;
  My trust is in thy mighty power;
Thou art my shield from foes abroad—
  At home my safeguard and my tower.

3 To thee I will address my prayer,
  To whom all praise I justly owe;
So shall I, by thy watchful care,
  Be guarded from my treacherous foe.

632 *Fight the good fight of faith.* (427)

1 Stand up, my soul, shake off thy fears,
  And gird the gospel armor on;
March to the gates of endless joy,
  Where Jesus, the great Captain's gone.

2 Hell and thy sins resist thy course;
  But hell and sin are vanquished foes;
Thy Savior nailed them to the cross,
  And sung the triumph when he rose.

3 Then let my soul march boldly on,
  Press forward to the heavenly gate;
There peace and joy eternal reign,
  And glittering robes for conquerors wait.

4 There shall I wear a starry crown,
  And triumph in almighty grace,
While all the armies of the skies
  Join in my glorious Leader's praise.

633 *And dying is but going home.* (806)

1 Now let our souls, on wings sublime,
  Rise from the vanities of time;
Draw back the parting vail, and see
  The glories of eternity.

2 Born by new, celestial birth,
  Why should we grovel here on earth?
Why grasp at vain and fleeting toys,
  So near to heaven's eternal joys?

3 Shall aught beguile us on the road,
  While we are walking back to God?
For strangers into life we come,
  And dying is but going home.

Duke Street, Key E♭.   Ware, Key B♭.   Anvern, Key F.

TEMPTATIONS AND CONFLICTS. 231

WINDHAM. L. M. DANIEL READ.

1. The billows swell, the winds are high; Clouds o-ver-cast my wint'ry sky; Out of the depths to thee I call; My fears are great, my strength is small.

634 *Lord, save us; we perish.* (857)

2 O Lord, the pilot's part perform,
And guide and guard me through the storm;
Defend me from each threatening ill:
Control the waves; say, "Peace! be still."

3 Amid the roaring of the sea,
My soul still hangs her hope on thee;
Thy constant love, thy faithful care,
Is all that saves me from despair.

4 Though tempest-tossed and half a wreck,
My Savior through the floods I seek:
Let neither winds nor stormy main
Force back my shattered bark again.

635 *Psalm 3.* (851)

1 The tempter to my soul hath said,
"There is no help in God for thee;"
Lord! lift thou up thy servant's head,
My glory, shield, and solace be.

2 Thus to the Lord I raised my cry;
He heard me from his holy hill;
At his command the waves rolled by;
He beckoned—and the winds were still.

3 I laid me down and slept—I woke—
Thou, Lord! my spirit didst sustain;
Bright from the east the morning broke—
Thy comforts rose on me again.

4 I will not fear, though armed throngs
'Compass my steps in all their wrath;
Salvation to the Lord belongs:
His presence guards his people's path.

636 *We walk by faith.* (855)

1 By faith in Christ I walk with God,
With heaven, my journey's end, in view;
Supported by his staff and rod,
My road is safe and pleasant too.

2 I travel through a desert wide,
Where many round me blindly stray;
But he vouchsafes to be my Guide,
And keep me in the narrow way.

3 The wilderness affords no food,
But God for my support prepares,
Provides me every needful good,
And frees my soul from wants and cares.

4 With him sweet converse I maintain;
Great as he is, I dare be free;
I tell him all my grief and pain,
And he reveals his love to me.

5 I pity all that worldlings talk
Of pleasures that will quickly end;
Be this my choice, O Lord! to walk
With thee, my Guide, my Guard, my Friend.

637 *Christ, all in all.* (554)

1 Oh thou pure light of souls that love,
True joy of every human breast,
Sower of life's immortal seed,
Our Savior and Redeemer blest!

2 Be thou our guide, be thou our goal;
Be thou our pathway to the skies;
Our joy when sorrow fills the soul;
In death our everlasting prize.

Forest, Key A.   Pilesgrove, Key G.   Hebron, Key B♭.

MOUNT PISGAH. C. M., with Chorus.

638 *Endure hardness as a good soldier.* (863)

1 Am I a soldier of the cross,
  A follower of the Lamb?
And shall I fear to own his cause,
  Or blush to speak his name?

2 Must I be carried to the skies
  On flowery beds of ease,
While others fought to win the prize,
  And sailed through bloody seas?

3 Are there no foes for me to face?
  Must I not stem the flood?
Is this vile world a friend to grace,
  To help me on to God?

4 Sure I must fight if I would reign;
  Increase my courage, Lord!
I'll bear the toil, endure the pain,
  Supported by thy word.

5 Thy saints, in all this glorious war,
  Shall conquer, though they die;
They see the triumph from afar,
  With Hope's exulting eye.

6 When that illustrious day shall rise,
  And all thy armies shine
In robes of victory through the skies,
  The glory shall be thine.

639 *With all boldness.* (865)

1 I'm not ashamed to own my Lord,
  Nor to defend his cause,
Maintain the honors of his word,
  The glory of his cross.

2 Jesus, my Lord, I know his name,
  His name is all my trust;
Nor will he put my soul to shame,
  Nor let my hope be lost.

3 Firm as his throne his promise stands,
  And he can well secure
What I've committed to his hands
  Till the decisive hour.

4 Then will he own my worthless name
  Before his Father's face,
And in the new Jerusalem
  Appoint for me a place.

Brown, Key C.   Aspiration, Key A.   Henry, Key C.

TEMPTATIONS AND CONFLICTS. 233

CHRISTMAS. C. M.   HANDEL.

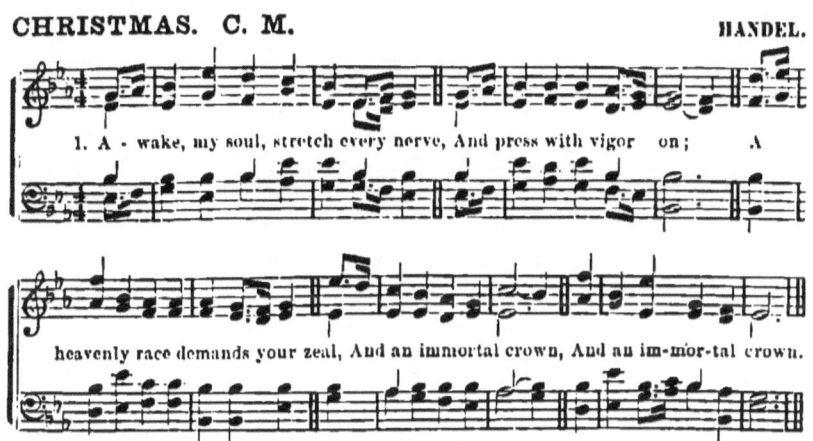

1. A-wake, my soul, stretch every nerve, And press with vigor on; A heavenly race demands your zeal, And an immortal crown, And an immortal crown.

640   *Run with patience.*   (866)

2 'Tis God's all-animating voice
That calls thee from on high:
'T is his own hand presents the prize
To thy aspiring eye.

3 A cloud of witnesses around,
Holds thee in full survey;
Forget the steps already trod,
And onward urge the way.

4 Blest Savior, introduced by thee,
Have we our race begun!
And crowned with victory at thy feet
We'll lay our honors down.

641   *So run that ye may obtain.*   (860)

1 Rise, O my soul! pursue the path
By ancient heroes trod;
Ambitious view those holy men
Who lived and walked with God.

2 Though dead they speak in reason's ear
And in example live;
Their faith, and hope, and mighty deeds,
Still fresh instruction give.

3 'T was through the Lamb's most precious blood
They conquered every foe:
And to his power, and matchless grace,
Their crowns and honors owe.

4 Lord, may we ever keep in view
The patterns thou hast given,
And ne'er forsake the blessed road
Which led them safe to heaven.

642   *Let me not wander, etc.*   (872)

1 Alas, what hourly dangers rise!
What snares beset my way!
To heaven, oh, let me fill mine eyes,
And hourly watch and pray.

2 How oft my mournful thoughts complain,
And melt in flowing tears!
My weak resistance, ah, how vain!
How strong my foes and fears!

3 O gracious God! in whom I live,
My feeble efforts aid;
Help me to watch, and pray, and strive,
Though trembling and afraid.

4 Increase my faith, increase my hope,
When foes and fears prevail;
And bear my fainting spirit up,
Or soon my strength will fail.

5 Oh, keep me in thy heavenly way,
And bid the tempter flee!
And let me never, never stray
From happiness and thee.

643   *The good Seed.*   (733)

1 Almighty God, thy word is cast
Like seed into the ground;
Now let the dew of heaven descend,
And righteous fruits abound.

2 Let not the foe of Christ and man
This holy seed remove;
But give it root in every heart,
To bring forth fruits of love.

Zerah, Key C.   Howard, Key C.   Peterboro, Key G.

LABAN. S. M.

Dr. L. MASON.

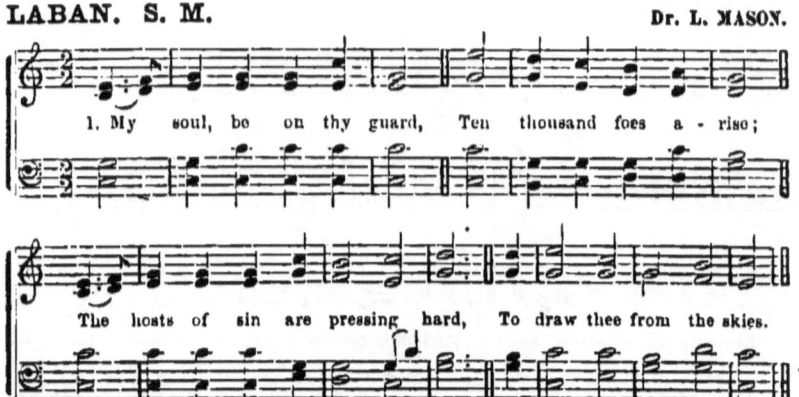

1. My soul, be on thy guard, Ten thousand foes a-rise;
The hosts of sin are pressing hard, To draw thee from the skies.

644 *Watch!* (875)

2 Oh watch, and fight, and pray;
  The battle ne'er give o'er;
Renew it boldly every day,
  And help divine implore.

3 Ne'er think the victory won,
  Nor lay thine armor down:
Thy arduous work will not be done
  Till thou obtain thy crown.

4 Fight on, my soul, till death
  Shall bring thee to thy God;
He'll take thee, at thy parting breath,
  To his divine abode.

645 *Occupy till I come.* (876)

1 A charge to keep I have,
  A God to glorify,
A never-dying soul to save,
  And fit it for the sky.

2 To serve the present age,
  My calling to fulfill;
Oh may it all my powers engage
  To do my Master's will.

3 Arm me with jealous care,
  As in thy sight to live;
And oh, thy servant, Lord, prepare
  A strict account to give!

4 Help me to watch and pray,
  And on thyself rely,
Assured, if I my trust betray,
  I shall forever die.

646 *To him that overcometh.* (877)

1 Arise, ye saints, arise!
  The Lord our Leader is;
The foe before his banner flies,
  For victory is his.

2 Lead on, almighty Lord,
  Lead on to victory!
Encouraged by the bright reward,
  With joy we'll follow thee.

3 We'll follow thee, our Guide,
  Our Savior, and our King;
We'll follow thee, through grace supplied
  From heaven's eternal spring.

4 We hope to see the day
  When all our toils shall cease;
When we shall cast our arms away,
  And dwell in endless peace.

5 This hope supports us here,
  It makes our burdens light;
'T will serve our drooping hearts to cheer,
  Till faith shall end in sight.

647 *Stand fast in the Lord.* (496)

1 All you that have confessed
  That Jesus is the Lord,
And to his people joined yourselves,
  According to his word;

2 In Zion you must dwell,
  Her altar ne'er forsake;
Must come to all her solemn feasts,
  Of all her joys partake.

Luther, Key F. Gerar, Key F. St. Thomas, Key G.

648 *Be strong in the Lord.* (879)

1 Soldiers of Christ, arise,
  And put your armor on!
Strong in the strength which God supplies
  Through his beloved Son.

2 Strong in the Lord of hosts,
  And in his mighty power;
Who in the strength of Jesus trusts,
  Is more than conqueror.

3 Stand, then, in his great might,
  With all his strength endued;
But take, to arm you for the fight,
  The panoply of God.

4 Leave no unguarded place,
  No weakness of the soul;
Take every virtue, every grace,
  And fortify the whole;

5 That, having all things done,
  And all your conflicts past,
You may o'ercome through Christ alone,
  And stand entire at last.

649 *Therefore will not we fear.* (880)

1 Give to the winds thy fears;
  Hope, and be undismayed;
God hears thy sighs, and counts thy tears;
  God shall lift up thy head.

2 Through waves, through clouds and storms,
  He gently clears thy way;
Wait thou his time; so shall this night
  Soon end in joyous day.

3 Still heavy is thy heart!
  Still sink thy spirits down!
Cast off the weight, let fear depart,
  Bid every care be gone.

4 Far, far above thy thought
  His counsel shall appear,
When fully he the work hath wrought
  That caused thy needless fear.

5 What, though thou rulest not!
  Yet heaven, and earth, and hell
Proclaim, God sitteth on the throne,
  And ruleth all things well!

650 *In the morning sow thy seed.* (967)

1 Sow in the morn thy seed;
  At eve hold not thy hand;
To doubt and fear, give thou no heed;
  Broadcast it o'er the land.

2 Thou knowest not which shall thrive—
  The late or early sown;
Grace keeps the precious germ alive,
  When and wherever strewn;

3 The good, the fruitful ground
  Expect not here nor there;
On hillside and in dale 't is found;
  Go forth, then, every-where!

4 And duly shall appear,
  In verdure, beauty, strength,
The tender blade, the stalk, the ear,
  And the full corn at length.

5 Thou canst not toil in vain;
  Cold, heat, the moist and dry,
Shall foster and mature the grain
  For garners in the sky.

6 Thence, when the glorious end—
  The day of God—is come,
The angel-reapers shall descend,
  And heaven cry, Harvest-home.

651 *Not hurt in all my holy mountain.* (965)

1 Hush the loud cannon's roar,
  The frantic warrior's call,
Why should the earth be drenched with gore?
  Are we not brothers all?

2 Want, from the wretch depart;
  Chains, from the captive fall;
Sweet mercy, melt the oppressor's heart:
  Sufferers are brothers all.

3 Churches and sects, strike down
  Each mean partition wall;
Let love each harsher feeling drown:
  Christians are brothers all.

4 Let love and truth alone
  Hold human hearts in thrall,
That heaven its work at length may own,
  And men be brothers all.

Laban, Key C. Silver Street, Key C. Boylston, Key C. Thatcher, Key G.

HASTINGS. 8s & 7s, Double.

Dr. T. HASTINGS.

1. Dark and thorny is the desert Thro' which pilgrims make their way,
But be-yond this vale of sor-row,
D. C. Meet the tempest, fight with courage—
Lie the
Never
realms of endless day. Dear young soldiers, do not murmur At the troubles of the way; faint, but often pray.

652 *Beyond this vail of sorrow.* (888)

2 He whose thunder shakes creation;
He that bids the planets roll;
He that rides upon the tempest,
And whose scepter sways the whole—
Jesus, Jesus, will defend you!
Trust in him and him alone;
He has shed his blood to save you,
And will bring you to his throne.

3 There on flowery fields of pleasure,
And the hills of endless rest,
Joy, and peace, and love, shall ever
Reign and triumph in your breast.
There ten thousand flaming seraphs
Fly across the heavenly plain;
There they sing immortal praises!
Glory, glory is their theme.

4 But, methinks, a sweeter concert
Makes the crystal arches ring,
And a song is heard in Zion
Which the angels can not sing;
Who can paint those sons of glory,
Ransomed souls that dwell on high,
Who with golden harps, forever,
Sound redemption through the sky.

5 See the heavenly host in rapture
Gazing on these shining bands;
Wondering at their costly garments,
And the laurels in their hands;
There upon the golden pavement,
See the ransomed march along!
While the splendid courts of glory
Sweetly echo with their song!

6 Here I see the under shepherds,
And the flocks they fed below,
Here with joy they dwell together,
Jesus is their shepherd now.
Hail! you happy, happy spirits!
Welcome to the blissful plain—
Glory, honor, and salvation;
Reign, sweet Shepherd, ever reign.

653 *Receive ye one another.* (501)

1 Come, dear friends, we all are brethren,
Bound for Canaan's happy land;
Come, unite and walk together,
Christ, our Leader, gives command.
Cease to boast of party merit,
Wound the cause of God no more,
Be united by his Spirit,
Zion's peace again restore.

2 Now our hand, our heart and spirit,
Here in fellowship we give;
Let us love and peace inherit,
Show the world how Christians live.
We'll be one in Christ our Savior,
Male and female, bond and free!
Christ is all in all forever,
In him we shall blessed be.

Pleading Savior, Key G.   Faith, Key G.   Camden, Key A.

TEMPTATIONS AND CONFLICTS. 237

FAITH. 8s & 7s, Double. W. B. BRADBURY, by permission.

1. Jesus, I my cross have taken, All to leave and follow thee;
I am poor, despised, forsaken— Thou henceforth my all shalt be:
Perish every fond ambition— All I've sought, or hoped, or known;
Yet how rich is my condition— God and heaven are still my own.

654 *Jesus, I my cross have taken.* (923)
2 Let the world despise and leave me,
   It has left my Savior too;
Human hearts and looks deceive me,
   Thou art not like them, untrue;
Whilst thy graces shall adorn me,
   God of wisdom, love, and might—
Foes may hate, and friends may scorn me,
   Show thy face, and all is bright.

3 Go, then—earthly fame and treasure,
   Come disaster, scorn, and pain;
In thy service, pain is pleasure—
   With thy favor loss is gain.
I have called thee, Abba Father!
   I have set my heart on thee;
Storms may howl, and clouds may gather,
   All will work for good to me.

4 Man may trouble and distress me,
   'T will but drive me to thy breast;
Life with trials hard may press me,
   Heaven will bring me sweeter rest.

Oh, 't is not in grief to harm me
   While thy love is left to me;
Oh, 't were not in joy to charm me,
   Were that joy unmixed with thee.

5 Soul—then know thy full salvation,
   Rise o'er sin, and fear, and care;
Joy to find, in every station,
   Something still to do or bear;
Think what spirit dwells within thee,
   Think what Father's smiles are thine;
Think that Jesus died to save thee;
   Child of heaven, canst thou repine?

6 Haste thee on from grace to glory,
   Armed by faith, and winged by prayer,
Heaven's eternal day's before thee,
   God's own hand shall guide thee there.
Soon shall close thy earthly mission;
   Soon shall pass thy pilgrim's days;
Hope shall change to glad fruition,
   Faith to sight, and prayer to praise!

Mozart, Key G.   Invitation, Key A.   Florenza, Key D

HOPE. 8s, 7s & 4s.

W. B. BRADBURY, by permission.

1. O my soul! what means this sadness? Wherefore art thou thus cast down?
Let thy griefs be turned to glad-ness, Bid thy rest-less fears be gone;
Look to Je-sus, Look to Je-sus, And re-joice in his dear name;
Look to Je-sus, Look to Je-sus, And re-joice in his dear name.

655 *Hope thou in God.* (890)

2 What though Satan's strong temptations
 Vex and grieve thee day by day,
And thy sinful inclinations
 Often fill thee with dismay;
  Thou shalt conquer,
Through the Lamb's redeeming blood.

3 Though ten thousand ills beset thee
 From without and from within,
Jesus saith he'll ne'er forget thee,
 But will save from hell and sin.
  He is faithful
To perform his gracious word.

4 Though distresses now attend thee,
 And thou tread'st the thorny road,
His right hand shall still defend thee;
 Soon he'll bring thee home to God.
  Therefore praise him,
Praise the great Redeemer's name.

5 Oh that I could now adore him
 Like the heavenly host above,
Who forever bow before him,
 And unceasing sing his love.
  Happy songsters!
When shall I your chorus join?

656 *Under clouds.* (891)

1 Here behold me, as I cast me
 At thy throne, O glorious King!
Tears fast thronging, child-like longing,
 Son of man, to thee I bring.
  Let me find thee—
Me, a poor and worthless thing.

2 Look upon me, Lord, I pray thee;
 Let thy Spirit dwell in mine;
Thou hast sought me, thou hast bought me,
 Only thee to know I pine:
  Let me find thee—
Take my heart and grant me thine.

3 Naught I ask for, naught I strive for,
 But thy grace, so rich and free,
That thou givest whom thou lovest,
 And who truly cleave to thee;
  Let me find thee—
He hath all things who hath thee.

4 Earthly treasure, mirth and pleasure,
 Glorious name or richest hoard,
Are but weary, void and dreary,
 To the heart that longs for God:
  Let me find thee—
I am ready, mighty Lord.

TEMPTATIONS AND CONFLICTS. 239

SICILY. 8s & 7s. — MOZART.

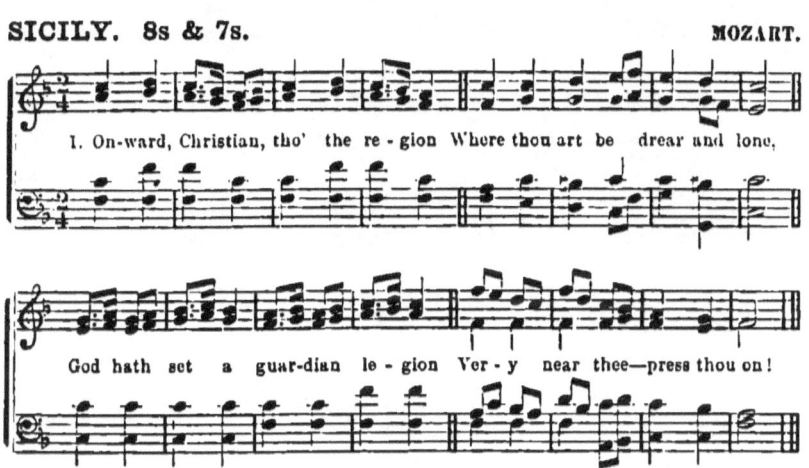

1. On-ward, Christian, tho' the re-gion Where thou art be drear and lone, God hath set a guar-dian le-gion Ver-y near thee—press thou on!

657 *Onward, Christian.* (885)

2 Listen, Christian, their hosanna
Rolleth o'er thee—"God is love,"
Write upon thy red-cross banner,
"Upward ever—heaven's above."

3 By the thorn-road, and none other,
Is the mount of vision won;
Tread it without shrinking, brother!
Jesus trod it—press thou on!

4 By thy trustful, calm endeavor,
Guiding, cheering, like the sun,
Earth-bound hearts thou shalt deliver;
Oh, for their sake, press thou on!

5 Be this world the wiser, stronger,
For thy life of pain and peace;
While it needs thee, oh no longer
Pray thou for thy quick release;

6 Pray thou, Christian, daily, rather
That thou be a faithful son;
By the prayer of Jesus—"Father,
Not my will, but thine, be done!"

658 *Father, take me.* (949)

1 Take me, O my Father! take me—
Take me, save me, through thy Son;
That which thou wouldst have me, make me;
Let thy will in me be done.

2 Long from thee my footsteps straying,
Thorny proved the way I trod;
Weary come I now, and praying—
Take me to thy love, my God!

3 Fruitless years with grief recalling,
Humbly I confess my sin!
At thy feet, O Father, falling,
To thy household take me in.

4 Freely now to thee I proffer
This relenting heart of mine;
Freely, life and soul I offer,
Gift unworthy love like thine.

5 Once the world's Redeemer, dying,
Bore our sins upon the tree;
On that sacrifice relying,
Now I look in hope to thee.

6 Father, take me! all forgiving,
Fold me to thy loving breast;
In thy love forever living,
I must be forever blest.

659 *Give me thy heart.* (1219)

1 Take my heart, O Father! mold it
In obedience to thy will;
And as ripening years unfold it,
Keep it true and childlike still.

2 Father, keep it pure and lowly,
Strong and brave, yet free from strife,
Turning from the paths unholy
Of a vain or sinful life.

3 Ever let thy might surround it;
Strengthen it with power divine;
Till thy cords of love have bound it,
Father, wholly unto thine.

Stockwell, Key B♭. Talmar, Key F. Yates, Key G.

THE NEW LIFE:

BEARING THE CROSS. ✱

Harmonized by J. P. POWELL.

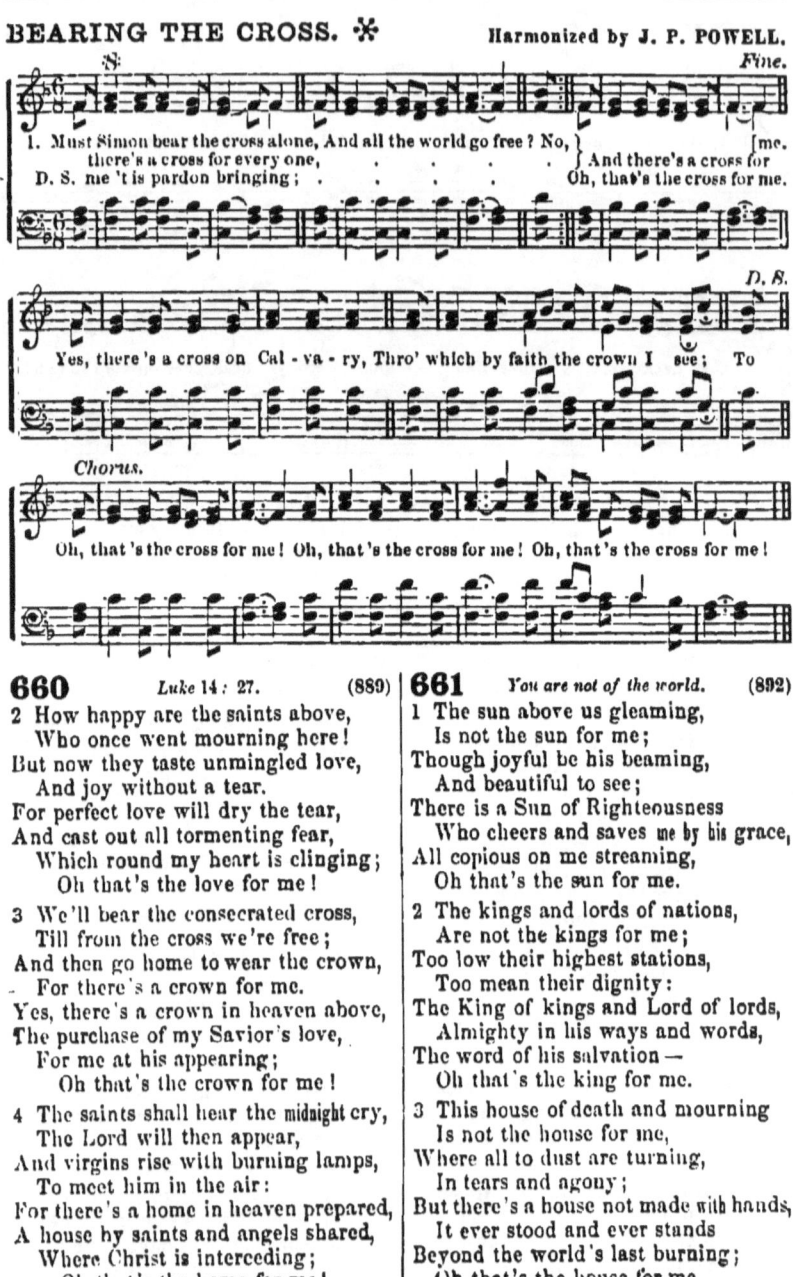

1. Must Simon bear the cross alone, And all the world go free ? No, there's a cross for every one, And there's a cross for me.
D. S. me 't is pardon bringing ; . . . . Oh, that's the cross for me.

Yes, there 's a cross on Cal - va - ry, Thro' which by faith the crown I see ; To

Chorus.

Oh, that 's the cross for me ! Oh, that 's the cross for me ! Oh, that's the cross for me !

660 *Luke 14: 27.* (889)

2 How happy are the saints above,
Who once went mourning here !
But now they taste unmingled love,
And joy without a tear.
For perfect love will dry the tear,
And cast out all tormenting fear,
Which round my heart is clinging;
Oh that 's the love for me !

3 We'll bear the consecrated cross,
Till from the cross we 're free ;
And then go home to wear the crown,
For there 's a crown for me.
Yes, there's a crown in heaven above,
The purchase of my Savior's love,
For me at his appearing;
Oh that 's the crown for me !

4 The saints shall hear the midnight cry,
The Lord will then appear,
And virgins rise with burning lamps,
To meet him in the air :
For there 's a home in heaven prepared,
A house by saints and angels shared,
Where Christ is interceding ;
Oh that 's the home for me !

661 *You are not of the world.* (892)

1 The sun above us gleaming,
Is not the sun for me ;
Though joyful be his beaming,
And beautiful to see ;
There is a Sun of Righteousness
Who cheers and saves me by his grace,
All copious on me streaming,
Oh that 's the sun for me.

2 The kings and lords of nations,
Are not the kings for me ;
Too low their highest stations,
Too mean their dignity :
The King of kings and Lord of lords,
Almighty in his ways and words,
The word of his salvation —
Oh that 's the king for me.

3 This house of death and mourning
Is not the house for me,
Where all to dust are turning,
In tears and agony ;
But there 's a house not made with hands,
It ever stood and ever stands
Beyond the world's last burning ;
Oh that 's the house for me.

PAUL. 10s, 11s & 12s.
From "Sabbath Hymn and Tune Book."

1. Breast the wave, Christian, when it is strongest; Watch for day, Christian, when night is [longest;
Onward and upward still be thine endeavor; The rest that remaineth endureth forever.

662   *Be thou faithful unto death.*   (895)

2 Fight the fight, Christian; Jesus is o'er thee;
Run the race, Christian; heaven is before thee;
He who hath promised, faltereth never;
Oh trust in the love that endureth forever!

3 Lift the eye, Christian, just as it closeth;
Raise the heart, Christian, ere it reposeth:
Thee from the love of Christ nothing shall sever;
Mount, when the work is done—praise God forever!

LYNCH. 6s & 4s.
From "Sabbath Hymn and Tune Book."

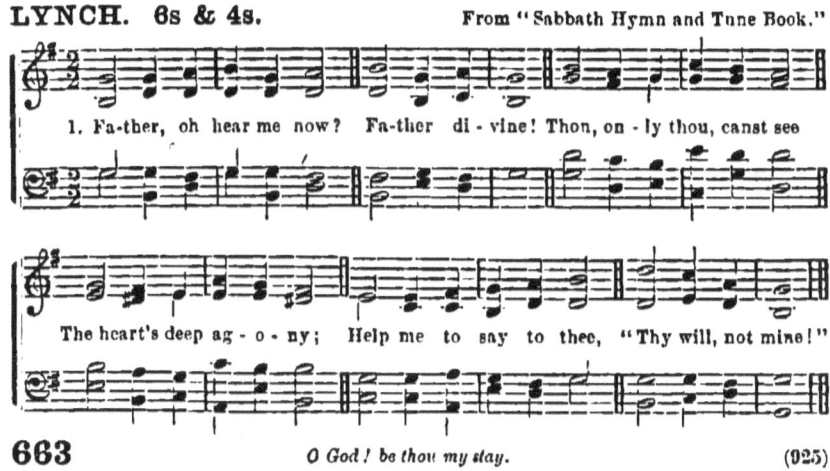

1. Fa-ther, oh hear me now? Fa-ther di-vine! Thou, on-ly thou, canst see
The heart's deep ag-o-ny; Help me to say to thee, "Thy will, not mine!"

663   *O God! be thou my stay.*   (925)

2 O God! be thou my stay
In this dark hour;
Kindly each sorrow hear,
Hush every troubled fear,
Thee let me still revere,
  Still own thy power.

4 In thee alone I trust,
Thou Holy One!
Humbly to thee I pray
That, through each troubled day
Of life, I still may say,
  "Thy will be done!"

MEAR. C. M.   English.

1. Our souls are in the Sav-ior's hand, And he will keep them still; And you and I shall sure-ly stand With him on Zi-on's hill.

664 *Our souls are in the Savior's hand.* (907)

2 Him eye to eye we there shall see,
   Our face like his shall shine;
Oh! what a glorious company,
   When saints and angels join!

3 Oh! what a joyful meeting there,
   In robes of white array!
Palms in our hands we all shall bear,
   And crowns that ne'er decay!

4 When we've been there ten thousand years,
   Bright shining as the sun,
We've no less days to sing God's praise,
   Than when we first begun!

5 Then let us hasten to the day
   When all shall be brought home:
Come, O Redeemer! come away!
   O Jesus! quickly come!

665   *Increase our faith.* (353)

1 Oh for a faith that will not shrink,
   Though pressed by every foe,
That will not tremble on the brink
   Of any earthly woe!

2 That will not murmur nor complain
   Beneath the chastening rod,
But, in the hour of grief or pain,
   Will lean upon its God;

3 A faith that shines more bright and clear
   When tempests rage without;
That, when in danger, knows no fear,
   In darkness feels no doubt;

4 That bears, unmoved, the world's dread frown,
   Nor heeds its scornful smile;
That seas of trouble can not drown,
   Nor Satan's arts beguile.

5 A faith that keeps the narrow way
   Till life's last hour is fled,
And with a pure and heavenly ray,
   Lights up a dying bed.

6 Lord, give us such a faith as this;
   And then, whate'er may come,
We'll taste e'en here the hallowed bliss
   Of an eternal home.

666   *Victory over death.* (1063)

1 Oh for an overcoming faith
   To cheer my dying hours,
To triumph o'er the monster death,
   And all his frightful powers.

2 Joyful, with all the strength I have,
   My quivering lips shall sing,
Where is thy boasted victory, grave?
   And where the monster's sting?

3 If sin be pardoned I'm secure—
   Death has no sting beside;
The law gives sin its damning power,
   But Christ my ransom died.

4 Now to the God of victory
   Immortal thanks be paid,
Who makes us conquerors while we die,
   Through Christ our living Head.

Balerma, Key B♭.   Dundee, Key F.   Notting Hill, Key B♭.

SUBMISSION AND DELIVERANCE. 243

LANMAN. 6s, Double.   W. B. BRADBURY, by permission.

1. My Jesus, as thou wilt! Oh, may thy will be mine!
   Into thy hand of love I would my all resign.
   Through sorrow, or through joy, Conduct me as thine own,
   And help me still to say, My Lord, thy will be done!

667   *As thou wilt.*   (921)

2 My Jesus, as thou wilt!
  If needy here and poor,
  Give me thy people's bread,
   Their portion rich and sure.
  The manna of thy word,
   Let my soul feed upon;
  And if all else should fail—
   My Lord, thy will be done!

3 My Jesus, as thou wilt!
  If among thorns I go,
  Still sometimes here and there
   Let a few roses blow.
  But thou, on earth, along
   The thorny path hast gone;
  Then lead me after thee;
   My Lord, thy will be done!

4 My Jesus, as thou wilt!
  Though seen through many a tear,
  Let not my star of hope
   Grow dim or disappear.
  Since thou on earth hast wept
   And sorrowed oft alone,
  If I must weep with thee,
   My Lord, thy will be done!

5 My Jesus, as thou wilt!
  If loved ones must depart,
  Suffer not sorrow's flood
   To overwhelm my heart;
  For they are blest with thee,
   Thy race and conflict won;
  Let me but follow them;
   My Lord, thy will be done!

6 My Jesus, as thou wilt!
  When death itself draws nigh,
  To thy dear wounded side
   I would for refuge fly.
  Leaning on thee, to go
   Where thou before hast gone;
  The rest as thou shalt please;
   My Lord, thy will be done!

668   *Changed from glory to glory.*   (926)

1 I did thee wrong, my God;
  I wronged thy truth and love;
  I fretted at the rod—
   Against thy power I strove.
  Come nearer, nearer still;
   Let not thy light depart;
  Bend, break this stubborn will;
   Dissolve this iron heart!

2 Less wayward let me be,
   More pliable and mild;
  In glad simplicity,
   More like a trustful child.
  Less, less of self each day,
   And more, my God, of thee;
  Oh keep me in the way,
   However rough it be!

3 Less of the flesh each day,
   Less of the world and sin;
  More of thy Son, I pray,
   More of thyself within.
  More molded to thy will,
   Lord, let thy servant be;
  Higher and higher still,
   More, and still more, like thee!

THE NEW LIFE:

BETHANY. 6s & 4s. Dr. L. MASON.

1. Near-er, my God, to thee, Near-er to thee; E'en tho' it be a cross That rais-eth me; Still all my song shall be, Near-er, my God, to thee, Near-er, my God, to thee, Near-er to thee!

2. Tho' like the wan-der-er, Day-light all gone, Dark-ness be o-ver me, My rest a stone; Yet in my dreams I'd be Near-er, etc.

669 *Nearer to thee.* (928)

3 There let the way appear
  Steps unto heaven;
All that thou sendest me,
  In mercy given;
Angels to beckon me
Nearer, my God, to thee!
  Nearer to thee.

4 Then, with my waking thoughts
  Bright with thy praise,
Out of my stony griefs
  Bethel I'll raise;
So by my woes to be
Nearer, my God, to thee—
  Nearer to thee.

5 Or, if on joyful wing,
  Cleaving the sky—
Sun, moon, and stars forgot,
  Upward I fly;
Still all my song shall be—
Nearer, my God, to thee,
  Nearer to thee.

670 1 Pet. 1: 8. (656)

1 Savior! thy gentle voice
  Gladly we hear;
Author of all our joys,
  Be ever near;
Our souls would cling to thee,
Let us thy fullness see,
  Our life to cheer.

2 Fountain of life divine!
  Thee we adore;
We would be wholly thine
  For evermore;
Freely forgive our sin,
Grant heavenly peace within,
  Thy light restore.

3 Though to our faith unseen,
  While darkness reigns,
On thee alone we lean
  While life remains;
By thy free grace restored,
Our souls shall bless the Lord
  In joyful strains!

Oak, Key G.

SUBMISSION AND DELIVERANCE. 245

WE ARE TOO FAR FROM THEE. (New.)   T. E. PERKINS.

1. We are too far from thee, our Savior, Too far from thee. Before our eyes, Dark
2. We are too far from thee, our Savior, Too far from thee. Fierce pains oppress, Dark

mists a-rise, And vail the glories from the skies; We are too far from thee.
cares distress, Made dark-er by our lone-li-ness; We are too far from thee.

671   *Nearer.*   (804)

3 We are too far from thee, our Savior,
    Too far from thee.
    Dark waters roll
    Above the soul;
Striving to reach the heavenly goal,
    We are too far from thee.

4 We are too far from thee, our Savior,
    Too far from thee.
    Alone afraid,
    Our path is laid
In darkness; send thy heavenly aid;
    We are too far from thee.

5 We are too far from thee, our Savior,
    Too far from thee.
    E'en if thy rod
    Bring us to God,
In meekness be the pathway trod,
    If it but lead to God.

6 Draw us more close to thee, our Savior,
    More close to thee.
    Let come what will
    Of good or ill,
'T is one to us, well knowing still
    Thou drawest us to thee.

672   *Sessions, Key C.*   (978)

1 Sun of my soul! thou Savior dear,
It is not night if thou be near:
Oh, may no earth-born cloud arise
To hide thee from thy servant's eyes!

2 When soft the dews of kindly sleep
My wearied eyelids gently steep,
Be my last thought—how sweet to rest
Forever on my Savior's breast!

3 Abide with me from morn till eve,
For without thee I can not live;
Abide with me when night is nigh,
For without thee I dare not die.

4 Be near to bless me when I wake,
Ere through the world my way I take;
Abide with me till in thy love
I lose myself in heaven above.

AFTER THE TOIL. (New.)

Dr. T. HASTINGS.

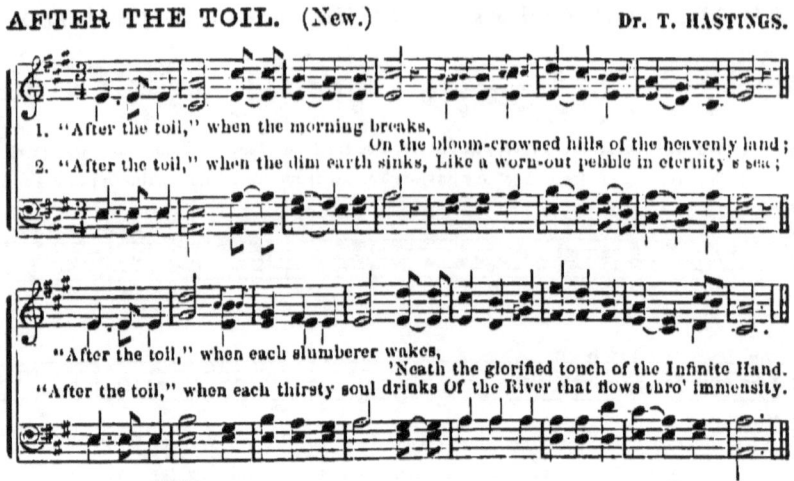

1. "After the toil," when the morning breaks,
On the bloom-crowned hills of the heavenly land;
2. "After the toil," when the dim earth sinks, Like a worm-out pebble in eternity's sea;

"After the toil," when each slumberer wakes,
'Neath the glorified touch of the Infinite Hand.
"After the toil," when each thirsty soul drinks Of the River that flows thro' immensity.

673 *After the toil.* (933)

3 "After the toil," O shadowing cloud
Of time o'er the face of the Infinite!
When thou shalt be dropped like a worm-eaten shroud,
What a morning will dawn on us after the night!

4 "After the toil," and the cross that we bear,
Way-worn and weary, through life's creeping years,
Angels will smile on the crown we shall wear,
And the songs of salvation will follow our tears.

5 "After the toil," O thou who art faint!
Rise from the shadows that darken thy way—
Rise while thy faith's raptured pencil shall paint
All its glorified dream of the Infinite Day.

674 *Go to the grave, Key B♭.* (950)

1 A weak and weary dove, with drooping wing,
And tired of wandering o'er this watery waste,
Jesus, my ark! once more, a worthless thing,
To thee I fly, thy pardoning love to taste.

2 For since I left thy sweet, secure retreat,
In search of pleasures fair, though false and vain,
My peace—my joy have flown; no rest my feet
Have found; and now I turn to thee again!

3 I've sought for rest in friendship's hallowed shrine,
But loved ones change, and earth's endearments **end**:
No love is true and lasting, Lord, but thine;
Henceforth, Incarnate Love, be thou my friend.

4 I've sought to find a place to rest my feet
In fame's alluring temple, bright and gay;
In health, and competence, and pleasures sweet,
But short and transient as the passing day.

SUBMISSION AND DELIVERANCE.

BEACON LIGHT. 9s & 8s., Double. (New.) J. P. POWELL.

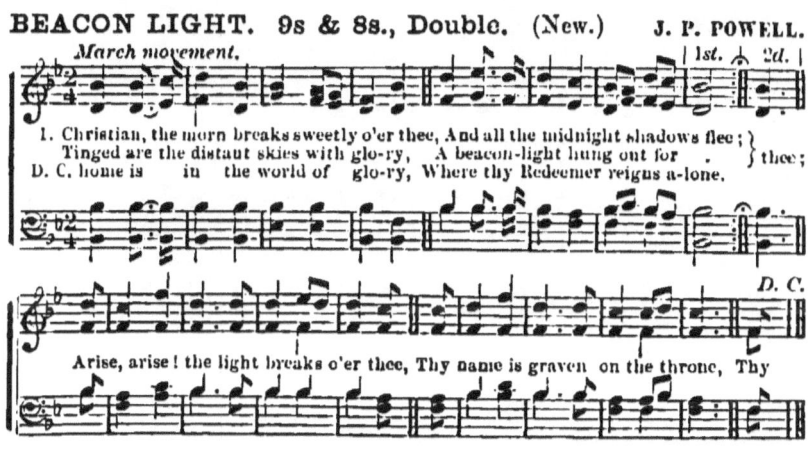

1. Christian, the morn breaks sweetly o'er thee, And all the midnight shadows flee;
Tinged are the distant skies with glo-ry, A beacon-light hung out for thee;
D. C. home is   in   the world of   glo-ry, Where thy Redeemer reigns a-lone.

Arise, arise! the light breaks o'er thee, Thy name is graven on the throne, Thy

675 *The day is at hand.* (934)

2 Tossed on time's rude, relentless surges,
  Calmly, composed, and dauntless stand;
For, lo! beyond those scenes emerges
  The heights that bound the promised land.
Behold! behold! the land is nearing,
  Where the wild sea-storm's rage is o'er;
Hark! how the heavenly hosts are cheering;
  See in what throngs they range the shore.

3 Cheer up! cheer up! the day breaks o'er thee,
  Bright as the summer's noontide ray,
The star-gemmed crowns and realms of glory
  Invite thy happy soul away;
Away! away! leave all for glory,
  Thy name is graven on the throne;
Thy home is in that world of glory,
  Where thy Redeemer reigns alone.

SIDMOUTH. 7s, Double. (968) Dr. MALAN.

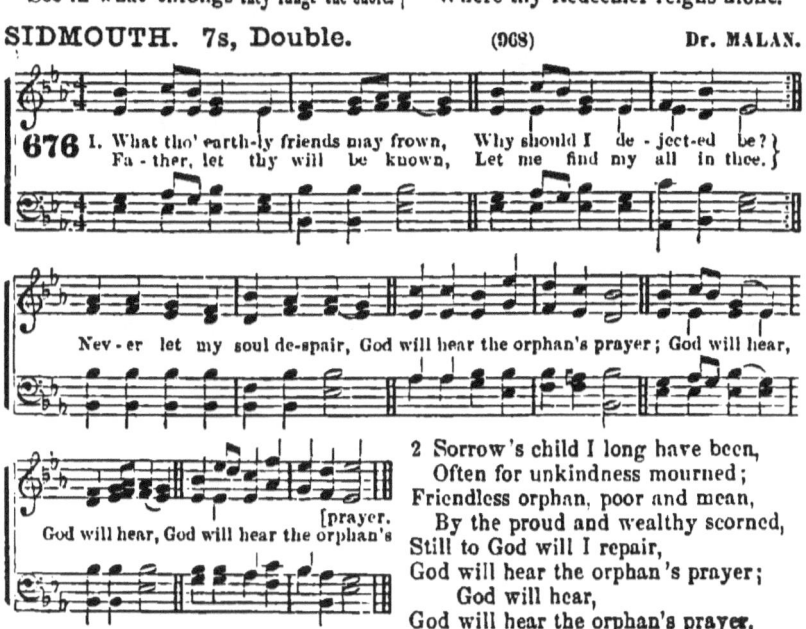

676 1. What tho' earth-ly friends may frown, Why should I de - ject-ed be?
Fa - ther, let thy will be known, Let me find my all in thee.

Nev-er let my soul de-spair, God will hear the orphan's prayer; God will hear,

God will hear, God will hear the orphan's [prayer.]

2 Sorrow's child I long have been,
  Often for unkindness mourned;
Friendless orphan, poor and mean,
  By the proud and wealthy scorned,
Still to God will I repair,
God will hear the orphan's prayer;
  God will hear,
God will hear the orphan's prayer.

THE NEW LIFE:

CLURE. 8, 6, 8, 6, 4, 4, 8, 8.

677 *Whate'er my God ordains is right.* (935)

2 Whate'er my God ordains is right;
  He never will deceive;
  He leads me by the proper path,
  And so to him I cleave,
    And take content
    What he hath sent;
  His hand can turn my griefs away,
  And patiently I wait his day.

3 Whate'er my God ordains is right;
  Though I the cup must drink
  That bitter seems to my faint heart,
  I will not fear or shrink;
    Tears pass away
    With dawn of day;
  Sweet comfort yet shall fill my heart,
  And pain and sorrow all depart.

AYLESBURY. S. M.

678 *Lead me to the Rock, etc.* (1016)

2 Oh lead me to the Rock
    That's high above my head,
  And make the covert of thy wings
    My shelter and my shade.

3 Within thy presence, Lord,
    Forever I'll abide;
  Thou art the tower of my defense,
    The refuge where I hide.

SUBMISSION AND DELIVERANCE.

THE PEACE OF GOD. (New.) — KNOWLES SHAW.

1. We ask for peace, O Lord! Thy children ask thy peace; Not what the world calls rest,
2. We ask for peace, O Lord! Yet not to stand se-cure, Girt round with iron pride,

That toil and care should cease, That thro' bright sunny hours Calm life should fleet away,
Con-tent-ed to endure, Crushing the gentle strings, That human hearts should know,

And tranquil night should fade In smiling day; It is not for such peace that we would pray.
Untouched by others' joys, Or others' woe; Thou, O dear Lord, wilt never teach us so.

679   *The peace of God.*   (423)

3 We ask thy peace, O Lord!
  Through storm, and fear, and strife,
To light and guide us on
  Through a long struggling life;
While no success or gain
  Shall cheer the desperate fight,
Or nerve, what the world calls,
  Our wasted might:
Yet pressing thro' the darkness to the light.

4 It is thine own, O Lord!
  Who toil while others sleep;
Who sow with loving care
  What other hands shall reap:
They lean on thee entranced,
  In calm and perfect rest:
Give us that peace, O Lord!
  Divine and blest,
Thou keepest for those hearts who love thee best.

SUNSET. 7s & 6s.   (1200)   From the "Jubilee."

680
1. The mellow eve is gliding   Se-rene-ly down the west;   So, every care sub-sid-ing, My soul would sink to rest.
2. The woodland hum is ringing The daylight's gentle close; May angels, round me sing-ing, Thus hymn my last re-pose.

3 The evening star has lighted
  Her crystal lamp on high;
So, when in death benighted,
  May hope illume the sky.

4 In golden splendor dawning,
  The morrow's light shall break;
Oh, on the last bright morning
  May I in glory wake!

COVENTRY. C. M.

1. Lord, lead the way the Saviour went, By lane and cell obscure,
And let our treasures still be spent, Like his, upon the poor.

681 *Ye have the poor always with you.* (955)
2 Like him, through scenes of deep distress,
    Who bore the world's sad weight,
We, in their gloomy loneliness,
    Would seek the desolate.

3 For thou hast placed us side by side
    In this wide world of ill;
And, that thy followers may be tried,
    The poor are with us still.

4 Small are the offerings we can make;
    Yet thou hast taught us, Lord,
If given for the Savior's sake,
    They lose not their reward.

682 *Scorn not the slightest word or deed.* (957)
1 Scorn not the slightest word or deed,
    Nor deem it void of power;
There's fruit in each wind-wafted seed,
    That waits its natal hour.

2 A whispered word may touch the heart,
    And call it back to life;
A look of love bid sin depart,
    And still unholy strife.

3 No act falls fruitless, none can tell
    How vast its powers may be,
Nor what results infolded dwell
    Within it silently.

4 Work on, despair not, bring thy mite,
    Nor care how small it be,
God is with all that serve the right,
    The holy, true, and free.

683 *Make channels for streams of love.* (958)
1 Make channels for the streams of love,
    Where they may broadly run;
And love has overflowing streams,
    To fill them every one.

2 But if at any time we cease
    Such channels to provide,
The very founts of love for us
    Will soon be parched and dried.

3 For we must share, if we would keep
    That blessing from above;
Ceasing to give, we cease to have:
    Such is the law of love.

684 *I delivered the poor, etc.* (851)
1 Bright Source of everlasting love,
    To thee our souls we raise,
And to thy sovereign bounty rear
    A monument of praise.

2 Thy mercy gilds the path of life
    With every cheering ray,
Kindly restrains the rising tear,
    Or wipes that tear away.

3 To tents of woe, to beds of pain,
    Our cheerful feet repair,
And with the gifts thy hand bestows,
    Relieve the mourners there.

4 The widow's heart shall sing for joy;
    The orphan shall be fed;
The hungering soul we'll gladly point
    To Christ, the living Bread.

Remsen, Key A♭. Maitland, Key A. Denfield, Key A♭.

SYMPATHIES AND ACTIVITIES. 251

PATIENCE. 8s & 5s. (New.)   W. T. MOORE.

1. Ev - ery day hath toil and trou-ble, Ev - ery heart hath care;
Meek-ly bear thine own full measure,   And thy
D. C. God shall fill thy mouth with gladness,   And thy

broth-er's share. Fear not, shrink not, though the burden Heavy to thee prove;
heart with love.

685   *Work on, hope on.*   (976)

2 Patiently enduring, ever
Let thy spirit be
Bound, by links that can not sever,
To humanity.
Labor, wait! thy master labored
Till his task was done;
Count not lost thy fleeting moments—
Life hath but begun.

3 Labor, wait! though midnight shadows
Gather round thee here,
And the storm above thee lowering
Fill thy heart with fear—
Wait in hope! the morning dawneth
When the night is gone,
And a peaceful rest awaits thee
When thy work is done.

THE DAY IS ENDED. 10s & 6. (New.)   PHILIP PHILLIPS.

1. The day is end-ed. Ere I sink to sleep, My wea-ry spir-it seeks repose in thine;
2. With loving-kindness curtain thou my bed, And cool in rest my burning pilgrim feet;

Fa - ther, for-give my tres-pass-es, and keep This lit - tle life of mine.
Thy par-don be the pil - low for my head—So shall my sleep be sweet.

686   *At peace with all the world, etc.*   (1208)

3 At peace with all the world, dear Lord, and thee,
No fears my soul's unwavering faith can shake;
All's well, whichever side the grave for me
The morning light may break!

PLEYEL. 7s. J. PLEYEL.

1. Praise the Lord, his glories show, Saints with-in his courts be-low;
An-gels round his throne a-bove, All that see and share his love.

687 *Let every thing that hath breath, etc.* (58)

2 Earth to heaven, and heaven to earth,
Tell his wonders, sing his worth:
Age to age, and shore to shore,
Praise him, praise him, evermore!

3 Praise the Lord, his mercies trace;
Praise his providence and grace—
All that he for man hath done,
All he sends us through his Son.

4 Strings and voices, hands and hearts,
In the concert bear your parts;
All that breathe, your Lord adore;
Praise him, praise him, evermore!

688 *The Lord make his face shine, etc.* (577)

1 Stealing from the world away,
 We are come to seek thy face:
Kindly meet us, Lord, we pray;
 Grant us thy reviving grace.

2 Yonder stars that gild the sky
 Shine but with a borrowed light.
We, unless thy light be nigh,
 Wander, wrapt in gloomy night.

3 Sun of Righteousness, dispel
 All our darkness, doubts, and fears;
May thy light within us dwell,
 Till eternal day appears.

689 *All the earth doth worship thee.* (60)

1 God eternal, Lord of all!
 Lowly at thy feet we fall:
All the earth doth worship thee;
 Wo amid the throng would be.

2 All the holy angels cry,
Hail, thrice holy, God Most High!
Glorified apostles raise,
Night and day, continual praise.

690 *Thou, God, seest me.* (991)

1 God is in the loneliest spot
Present, though thou know it not;
Morning vows and evening prayer
Make a Bethel every-where.

2 Go where duty guides thy feet;
There good angels thou shalt meet;
Hosts of God thou canst not see,
Watch thy steps and wait on thee.

691 *My voice shalt thou hear, etc.* (1186)

1 Now the shades of night are gone;
Now the morning light is come;
Lord, may I be thine to-day—
Drive the shades of sin away.

2 Fill my soul with heavenly light,
Banish doubt, and cleanse my sight;
In thy service, Lord, to-day,
Help me labor, help me pray.

3 Keep my haughty passions bound—
Save me from my foes around;
Going out, and coming in,
Keep me safe from every sin.

4 When my work of life is past,
Oh receive me then at last!
When I reach the heavenly shore,
Night of sin will be no more.

AFFLICTIONS. 253

CHINA. C. M.

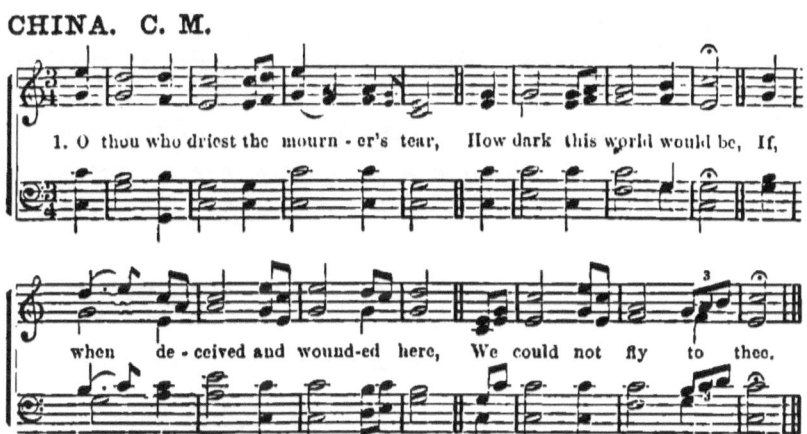

1. O thou who driest the mourn-er's tear, How dark this world would be, If, when de-ceived and wound-ed here, We could not fly to thee.

692 *Songs in the night.* (1005)

2 But thou wilt heal the broken heart,
Which, like the plants that throw
Their fragrance from the wounded part,
Breathes sweetness out of woe.

3 When joy no longer soothes or cheers,
And e'en the hope that threw
A moment's sparkle o'er our tears
Is dimmed and vanished too;

4 Oh, who would bear life's stormy doom,
Did not thy wing of love
Come brightly wafting through the gloom,
Our peace-branch from above?

5 Then sorrow, touched by thee, grows bright
With more than rapture's ray;
The darkness shows us worlds of light
We never saw by day.

693 *Why mourn departing friends.* (1057)

1 Why do we mourn departing friends,
Or shake at death's alarms?
'T is but the voice that Jesus sends
To call them to his arms.

2 Are we not tending upward, too,
As fast as time can move?
Nor would we wish the time more slow
To keep us from our Love.

3 Why should we tremble to convey
Their bodies to the tomb?
'T was there the flesh of Jesus lay,
Amid its silent gloom.

4 The graves of all the saints he blest,
And softened every bed;
Where should the dying members rest,
But with their dying Head?

5 Thence he arose, ascending high,
And showed our feet the way;
Up to the Lord our souls shall fly,
At the great rising day.

6 Then let the last loud trumpet sound,
And bid our kindred rise:
Awake, ye nations under ground;
Ye saints, ascend the skies.

694 *The Lord will strengthen, etc.* (1008)

1 When languor and disease invade
This trembling house of clay,
'T is sweet to look beyond my pains,
And long to fly away:

2 Sweet to look inward, and attend
The whispers of his love;
Sweet to look upward to the place
Where Jesus pleads above:

3 Sweet to look back and see my name
In life's fair book set down;
Sweet to look forward, and behold
Eternal joys my own:

4 Sweet to rejoice in lively hope,
That when my change shall come,
Angels shall hover round my bed,
And waft my spirit home.

Balerma, Key B♭.   Naomi, Key D.   Edmeston, Key C.

THE NEW LIFE:

ARDON. 11s & 8s.

1. O thou in whose presence my soul takes delight, On whom in affliction I call;
My comfort by day and my song in the night, My hope, my salvation, my all!

695   *I sought him whom my soul loveth.*   (1030)

2 Where dost thou at noontide resort
   with thy sheep
 To feed on the pastures of love?
 For why in the valley of death should
   I weep,
 Or alone in the wilderness rove?

3 Oh why should I wander an alien from
   thee,
 And cry in the desert for bread?
 Thy foes will rejoice when my sorrows
   they see,
 And smile at the tears I have shed.

4 You daughters of Zion, declare have
   you seen
 The star that on Israel shone?
 Say if in your tents my beloved has
   been,
 And where with his flock he is gone?

5 This is my beloved; his form is di-
   vine,
 His vestments shed odors around,
 The locks on his head are as grapes on
   the vine
 When autumn with plenty is crowned.

6 The roses of Sharon, the lilies that
   grow
 In the vales, on the banks of the streams,
 On his cheeks in the beauty of excel-
   lence glow,
 And his eyes are as quivers of beams.

7 His voice, as the sound of the dulci-
   mer sweet,
 Is heard through the shadows of death;
 The cedars of Lebanon bow at his
   feet,
 The air is perfumed with his breath.

8 His lips as a fountain of righteousness
   flow
 That water the garden of grace;
 From which their salvation the Gentiles
   shall know,
 And bask in the smiles of his face.

9 Love sits on his eyelids, and scatters
   delight
 Through all the bright mansions on high;
 Their faces the cherubim veil in his
   sight,
 And tremble with fullness of joy.

10 He looks, and ten thousands of angels
    rejoice,
  And myriads wait for his word;
  He speaks, and eternity, filled with his
    voice,
  Re-echoes the praise of her Lord.

PRESENT AND FUTURE. 255

DUNLAP'S CREEK. C. M.

1. Death can not make our souls a-fraid, If God be with us there;
We may walk thro' its dark-est shade, And nev-er yield to fear.

696 *And Moses went up to the top, etc.* (1054)

2 I could renounce my all below,
  If my Redeemer bid;
And run, if I were called to go,
  And die as Moses did.

3 Might I but climb to Pisgah's top,
  And view the promised land,
My flesh itself would long to drop,
  And welcome the command.

4 Clasped in my heavenly Father's arms,
  I would forget my breath,
And lose my life among the charms
  Of so divine a death.

697 *What is your life?* (1055)

1 Life is a span—a fleeting hour;
  How soon the vapor flies!
Man is a tender, transient flower
  That, even in blooming, dies.

2 The once-loved form, now cold and dead,
  Each mournful thought employs;
And nature weeps her comforts fled,
  And withered all her joys.

3 Hope looks beyond the bonds of time,
  When what we now deplore
Shall rise in full, immortal prime,
  And bloom to fade no more.

4 Cease, then, fond nature, cease thy tears;
  Religion points on high;
There everlasting spring appears,
  And joys that can not die.

698 *Weep not.* (1056)

1 Dear as thou wast, and justly dear,
  We would not weep for thee:
One thought shall check the starting tear;
  It is that thou art free.

2 And thus shall faith's consoling power
  The tears of love restrain;
Oh who that saw thy parting hour
  Could wish thee here again!

3 Gently the passing spirit fled,
  Sustained by grace divine;
Oh may such grace on us be shed,
  And make our end like thine!

699 *I will cause the sun to go, etc.* (1058)

1 When blooming youth is snatched away
  By death's resistless hand,
Our hearts the mournful tribute pay,
  Which pity must demand.

2 While pity prompts the rising sigh,
  Oh may this truth, impressed
With awful power, "I, too, must die,"
  Sink deep in every breast.

3 Let this vain world engage no more;
  Behold the opening tomb:
It bids us seize the present hour;
  To-morrow death may come.

4 Oh let us fly—to Jesus fly,
  Whose powerful arm can save;
Then shall our hopes ascend on high,
  And triumph o'er the grave.

Mear, Key F.   China, Key C.   Barby, Key A.

PRESENT AND FUTURE:

REST. L. M.
W. B. BRADBURY, by permission.

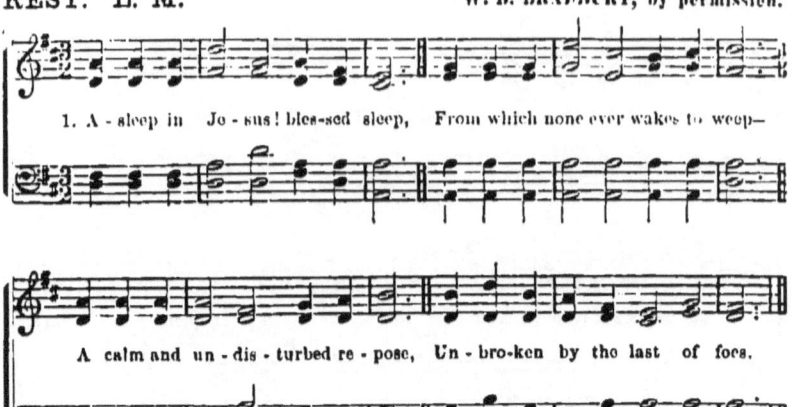

1. Asleep in Jesus! blessed sleep, From which none ever wakes to weep— A calm and un-dis-turbed re-pose, Un-bro-ken by the last of foes.

700 *Them which sleep in Jesus.* (1038)

2 Asleep in Jesus! oh how sweet
To be for such a slumber meet!
With holy confidence to sing,
That death has lost its venomed sting.

3 Asleep in Jesus! peaceful rest,
Whose waking is supremely blest:
No fear, no woe, shall dim the hour
That manifests the Savior's power.

4 Asleep in Jesus! oh for me
May such a blissful refuge be;
Securely shall my ashes lie,
And wait the summons from on high.

5 Asleep in Jesus! time nor space
Affects this precious hiding-place;
On Indian plains, or Lapland snows,
Believers find the same repose.

6 Asleep in Jesus! far from thee
Thy kindred and their graves may be;
But thine is still a blessed sleep
From which none ever wake to weep.

701 *Num. 23: 10.* (1039)

1 How blest the righteous when he dies!
When sinks a weary soul to rest!
How mildly beam the closing eyes!
How gently leaves the expiring breast!

2 So fades a summer cloud away;
So sinks the gale when storms are o'er;
So gently shuts the eye of day;
So dies a wave along the shore.

3 A holy quiet reigns around,
A calm which life nor death destroys:
And naught disturbs that peace profound
Which his unfettered soul enjoys.

4 Life's labor done, as sinks the clay,
Light from its load the spirit flies,
While heaven and earth combine to say,
"How blest the righteous when he dies!"

702 *Death of an infant.* (1040)

1 As the sweet flower that scents the morn,
But withers in the rising day—
Thus lovely seemed the infant's dawn;
Thus swiftly fled his life away!

2 Ere sin could blight, or sorrow fade,
Death timely came with friendly care:
The opening bud to heaven conveyed,
And bade it bloom forever there.

3 He died to sin, and all its woes,
But for a moment felt the rod—
On love's triumphant wing he rose,
To rest forever with his God!

Ward, Key B♭.   Meroe, Key G.   Olive's Brow, Key A♭.

LIFE AND DEATH. 257

703 *Death is the gate of endless joy.* (1043)

1 Why should we start and fear to die?
What timorous worms we mortals are!
Death is the gate of endless joy,
And yet we dread to enter there.

2 The pains, the groans, and dying strife,
Fright our approaching souls away;
Still we shrink back again to life,
Fond of our prison and our clay.

3 Oh if my Lord would come and meet,
My soul would stretch her wings in haste,
Fly fearless through death's iron gate,
Nor feel the terrors as she passed!

4 Jesus can make a dying bed
Feel soft as downy pillows are,
While on his breast I lean my head,
And breathe my life out sweetly there.

704 *That I may know how frail I am.* (1045)

1 Almighty Maker of my frame,
Teach me the measure of my days;
Teach me to know how frail I am,
And spend the remnant to thy praise.

2 My days are shorter than a span;
A little point my life appears;
How frail at best is dying man!
How vain are all his hopes and fears!

3 Vain his ambition, noise, and show,
Vain are the cares which rack his mind;
He heaps up treasures mixed with woe,
And dies, and leaves them all behind.

4 Oh be a nobler portion mine;
My God, I bow before thy throne;
Earth's fleeting treasures I resign,
And fix my hope on thee alone.

705 *Unvail thy bosom, faithful tomb.* (1050)

1 Unvail thy bosom, faithful tomb;
Take this new treasure to thy trust,
And give these sacred relics room
To slumber in the silent dust.

2 Nor pain, nor grief, nor anxious fear,
Invade thy bounds; no mortal woes
Can reach the peaceful sleeper here,
While angels watch the soft repose.

3 So Jesus slept; God's dying Son
Passed through the grave, and bless'd the bed;
Rest here, blest saint, till from his throne
The morning break, and pierce the shade.

4 Break from his throne, illustrious morn;
Attend, O earth, his sovereign word;
Restore thy trust; a glorious form
Shall then arise to meet the Lord.

706 *The small and great are there.* (1044)

1 The glories of our birth and state
Are shadows; not substantial things;
There is no armor against fate;
Death lays his icy hand on kings.

2 Princes and magistrates must fall,
And in the dust be equal made;
The high and mighty with the small,
Scepter and crown with scythe and spade.

3 The laurel withers on our brow;
Then boast no more your mighty deeds;
Upon death's purple altar now
See where the victor victim bleeds!

707 *The early dead.* (1042)

1 How blest are they whose transient years
Pass like an evening meteor's flight:
Not dark with guilt, nor dim with tears:
Whose course is short, unclouded, bright.

2 Oh, cheerless were our lengthened way:
But heaven's own light dispels the gloom,
Streams downward from eternal day,
And casts a glory round the tomb.

3 Oh, stay thy tears; the blest above
Have hailed a spirit's heavenly birth,
And sung a song of joy and love;
Then why should anguish reign on earth?

708 *I will fear no evil.* (1047)

1 Though I walk through the gloomy vale,
Where death and all its terrors are,
My heart and hope shall never fail,
For God my shepherd's with me there.

2 Amid the darkness and the deeps,
Thou art my comfort, thou my stay;
Thy staff supports my feeble steps,
Thy rod directs my doubtful way.

Zephyr, Key C.   Oriel, Key A♭.   Judgment Hymn, Key G

BANKOKE. S. M.

1. Go to thy rest, fair child! Go to thy dream-less bed;
While yet so gen-tle, un-de-filed, With blessings on thy head.

709 *Go to thy rest, fair child.* (1069)

2 Fresh roses in thy hand,
Buds on thy pillow laid,
Haste from this dark and fearful land,
Where flowers so quickly fade.

3 Before thy heart had learned,
In waywardness to stray;
Before thy feet had ever turned
The dark and downward way;

4 Ere sin had seared the breast,
Or sorrow woke the tear;
Rise to thy throne of changeless rest,
In yon celestial sphere.

5 Because thy smile was fair,
Thy lip and eye so bright,
Because thy loving cradle care
Was such a dear delight;

6 Shall love, with weak embrace,
Thy upward wing detain?
No! gentle angel, seek thy place
Amid the cherub train.

710 *Your fathers, where are they?* (1067)

1 Our fathers! where are they,
With all they called their own?
Their joys and griefs, their hopes and cares,
Their wealth and honor, gone!

2 But joy or grief succeeds,
Beyond our mortal thought,
While still the remnant of their dust
Lies in the grave, forgot.

3 God of our fathers, hear,
Thou everlasting Friend,
While we, as on life's utmost verge,
Our souls to thee commend.

711 *Inheritance of the saints in light.* (1133)

1 And is there, Lord, a rest
For weary souls designed,
Where not a care shall stir the breast,
Or sorrow entrance find?

2 Is there a blissful home,
Where kindred minds shall meet,
And live, and love, nor ever roam
From that serene retreat?

3 Are there bright, happy fields,
Where naught that blooms shall die;
Where each new scene fresh pleasure yields,
And healthful breezes sigh?

4 Are there celestial streams,
Where living waters glide,
With murmurs sweet as angel dreams,
And flowery banks beside?

5 Forever blessed they
Whose joyful feet shall stand,
While endless ages waste away,
Amid that glorious land!

6 My soul would thither tend
While toilsome years are given;
Then let me, gracious Lord, ascend
To sweet repose in heaven!

Shawmut, Key D.   Lottie, Key D.   Penitence, Key B♭.

PRESENT AND FUTURE. 259

BRATTLE STREET. C. M., Double.   Arr. from PLEYEL.

1. Fallen—on Zi-on's bat-tle-field, A sol-dier of re-nown,
Armed in the pa-no-ply of God,
In con-flict clo-ven down! His hel-met on, his ar-mor bright,
D. S. His dy-ing hour to cheer.
His cheek unblanched with fear— While round his head there gleamed a light,

712   *A soldier of renown.*   (1073)

2 Fallen—while cheering with his voice
The sacramental host,
With banners floating on the air—
Death found him at his post;
In life's high prime the warfare closed,
But not ingloriously;
He fell beyond the outer wall,
And shouted, victory!

3 Fallen—a holy man of God,
An Israelite indeed,
A standard-bearer of the cross,
Mighty in word and deed—
A master spirit of the age,
A bright and burning light,
Whose beams across the firmament
Scattered the clouds of night.

4 Fallen—as sets the sun at eve,
To rise in splendor where
His kindred luminaries shine,
Their heaven of bliss to share;
Beyond the stormy battle-field
He reigns in triumph now,
Sweeping a harp of wondrous song,
With glory on his brow!

713   *Help thou mine unbelief.*   (860)

1 Father, when o'er our trembling hearts
Doubt's shadows gathering brood;
When faith in thee almost departs,
And gloomiest fears intrude,
Forsake us not, O God of grace,
But send those fears relief;
Grant us again to see thy face;
Lord, help our unbelief.

2 When sorrow comes, and joys are flown,
And fondest hopes be dead,
And blessings, long esteemed our own,
Are now forever fled—
When the bright promise of our spring
Is but a withering leaf—
Lord, to thy truth still let us cling;
Help thou our unbelief.

3 And when the powers of nature fail
Upon the couch of pain,
Nor love, nor friendship can avail
The spirit to detain;
Then, Father, be our closing eyes
Undimmed by tears of grief,
And, if a trembling doubt arise,
Help thou our unbelief.

PRESENT AND FUTURE:

HOMEWARD (Originally, Beautiful River). 8s & 7s. R. LOWRY.

1. Dropping down the troubled river To the tranquil, tranquil shore, Where the sweet light shineth ever, ... And the sun goes down no more. Yes, we'll gather at the riv-er, The beautiful, the beautiful riv-er, Gather with the saints at the riv-er That flows by the throne of God.

714 *Homeward.* (1075)

2 Dropping down the winding river
To the wide and welcome sea.
Where no tempest wrecketh ever,
Where the sky is fair and free.

3 Dropping down the rapid river,
To the dear and deathless land,
Where the living live forever
At the Father's own right hand.

MOUNT VERNON. 8s & 7s. (1076) Dr. L. MASON.

715
1. Sister, thou wast mild and love-ly, Gen-tle as the sum-mer breeze,
2. Peaceful be thy si-lent slum-ber— Peaceful in the grave so low.
3. Dear-est sis-ter, thou hast left us; Here thy loss we deep-ly feel;
4. Yet a-gain we hope to meet thee, When the day of life is fled;

Pleas-ant as the air of eve-ning, When it floats a-mong the trees.
Thou no more wilt join our num-ber: Thou no more our songs shalt know
But 'tis God that hath be-reft us; He can all our sor-rows heal,
Then in heaven with joy to greet thee, Where no fare-well tear is shed.

LIFE AND DEATH.

ORIEL. L. M., or 8s & 4. W. B. BRADBURY, by permission.

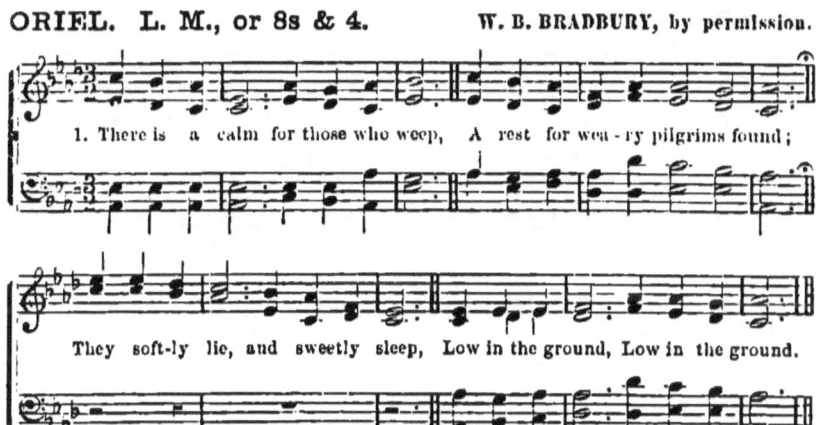

1. There is a calm for those who weep, A rest for weary pilgrims found;
They softly lie, and sweetly sleep, Low in the ground, Low in the ground.

716 *There remaineth a rest.* (1086)
2 The storm that racks the wintery sky
No more disturbs their deep repose,
Than summer evening's latest sigh,
 That shuts the rose.

3 Thou traveler in this vale of tears,
To realms of everlasting light,
Through time's dark wilderness of years,
 Pursue thy flight.

4 Whate'er thy lot—whate'er thou be—
Confess thy folly—kiss the rod;
And in thy chastening sorrows see
 The hand of God.

5 Though long of winds and waves the sport,
Condemned in wretchedness to roam,
Thou soon shall reach a sheltering port,
 A quiet home.

717 *In the night watches.* (980)
1 In silence of the voiceless night,
When chased by dreams, the slumbers flee,
Whom, in the darkness, do I seek,
 O God, but thee?

2 And if there weigh upon my breast
Vague memories of the day foregone,
Scarce knowing why, I fly to thee,
 And lay them down.

3 Or, if it be the gloom that comes,
In token of impending ill,
My bosom heeds not what it is,
 Since 't is thy will.

4 For, O! in spite of constant care,
Or aught beside, how joyfully
I pass that solitary hour,
 My God, with thee!

5 More tranquil than the stilly night,
More peaceful than the voiceless hour,
Supremely blest, my bosom lies
 Beneath thy power.

6 For what on earth can I desire,
Of all it hath to offer me?
Or whom in heaven do I seek,
 O God, but thee?

718 *Psalm 69: 15.* (905)
1 God of my life, to thee I call;
Afflicted at thy feet I fall;
When the great water floods prevail
Leave not my trembling heart to fail.

2 Friend of the friendless and the faint,
Where should I lodge my deep complaint?
Where, but with thee, whose open door
Invites the helpless and the poor?

3 He who has helped me hitherto,
Will help me all the journey through,
And give me daily cause to raise
New trophies to his endless praise.

4 Though rough and thorny be the road,
It leads thee home, apace, to God;
Then count thy present trials small,
For heaven will make amends for all.

Rest, Key E♭.   Hour of Prayer, Key A♭.   Zephyr, Key C.

PRESENT AND FUTURE:

GO TO THE GRAVE. 10s. (New.)   T. J. COOK.

1. Go to the grave in all thy glorious prime,
   A Christian can not die before his time;
   In full activity of zeal and power;
   The Lord's appointment is the servant's hour.
2. Go to the grave: at noon from labor cease;
   Come from the heat of battle, and in peace,
   Rest on thy sheaves; the harvest task is done;
   Soldier, go home; with thee the fight is won.

719   *His eye was not dim, etc.*   (1082)

3 Go to the grave; for thee thy Savior lay
    In death's embrace, ere he arose on high;
And all the ransomed, by that narrow way,
    Pass to eternal life beyond the sky.

4 Go to the grave—no; take thy seat above;
    Be thy pure spirit present with the Lord,
Where thou for faith and hope hast perfect love,
    And open vision for the written word.

720   *Faint, yet pursuing.*   (843)

1 My feet are worn and weary with the march
    O'er the rough road, and up the steep hillside;
O city of our God! I fain would see
    Thy pastures green, where peaceful waters glide.

2 My hands are worn and weary toiling on,
    Day after day, for perishable meat;
O city of our God! I fain would rest—
    I sigh to gain thy glorious mercy-seat.

3 My garments, travel-worn and stained with dust,
    Oft rent by briers and thorns that crowd my way,
Would fain be made, O Lord, my righteousness!
    Spotless and white in heaven's unclouded ray.

4 My eyes are weary looking at the sin,
    Impiety, and scorn upon the earth;
O city of our God! within thy walls
    All—all are clothed again with thy new birth.

5 My heart is weary of its own deep sin—
    Sinning, repenting, sinning still again;
When shall my soul thy glorious presence feel,
    And find, dear Savior, it is free from stain?   *(Concluded on p. 263.)*

ALL'S WELL. 8s & 3s.

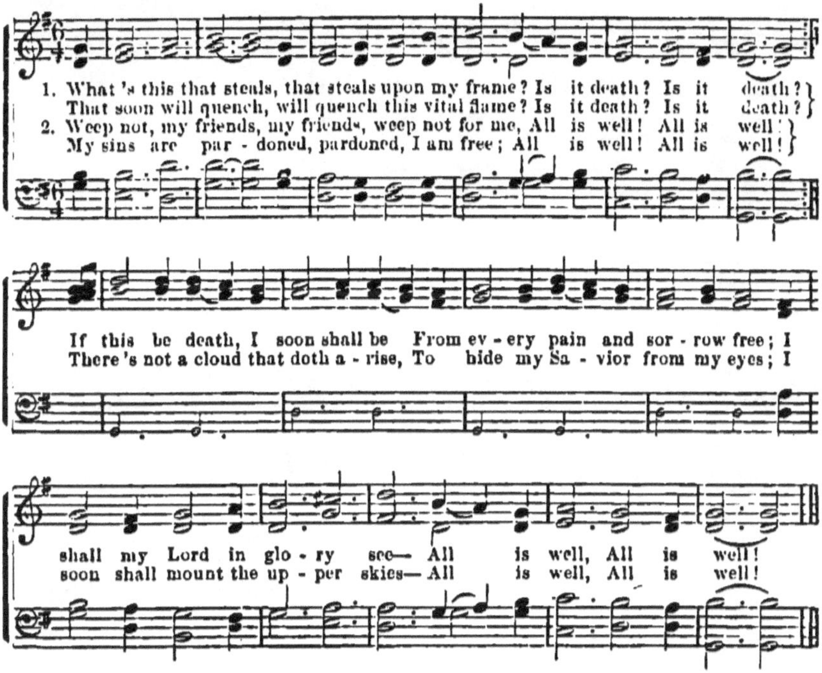

1. What's this that steals, that steals upon my frame? Is it death? Is it death?
That soon will quench, will quench this vital flame? Is it death? Is it death?
2. Weep not, my friends, my friends, weep not for me, All is well! All is well!
My sins are par-doned, pardoned, I am free; All is well! All is well!

If this be death, I soon shall be From ev-ery pain and sor-row free; I
There's not a cloud that doth a-rise, To hide my Sa-vior from my eyes; I

shall my Lord in glo-ry see— All is well, All is well!
soon shall mount the up-per skies— All is well, All is well!

721   *All is well.*   (1084)

3 Tune, tune your harps, ye saints in glory;
    All is well;
I will rehearse the pleasing story,
    All is well.
Bright angels have from glory come;
They're round my bed, they're in my room,
They wait to waft my spirit home—
    All is well.

4 Hark, hark! my Lord and Master calls me;
    All is well;
I soon shall see his face in glory;
    All is well.
Farewell, dear friends; adieu, adieu!
I can no longer stay with you—
My glittering crown appears in view;
    All is well.

5 Hail, hail, all hail, ye blood-washed throng,
    Saved by grace,
I've come to join your rapturous song,
    Saved by grace.
All, all is peace and joy divine,
All heaven and glory now are mine;
Oh, hallelujah to the Lamb!
    All is well.

FAINT, YET PURSUING. (*Concluded from p. 262.*)

6 Patience, poor soul! the Savior's feet were worn;
    The Savior's heart and hands were weary, too;
His garments stained, and travel-worn, and old;
    His vision blinded with a pitying dew.

7 Love thou the path of sorrow that he trod;
    Toil on, and wait in patience for thy rest:
O city of our God! we soon shall see
    Thy glorious walls—home of the loved and blest!

PRESENT AND FUTURE:

WEEP NOT FOR ME. 8s & 4s. (1091) S. J. VAIL, by permission.

722
1. When the spark of life is wan-ing, Weep not for me;
   When the languid eye is stream-ing, ...
2. When the pangs of death as-sail me, Weep not for me;
   Christ is mine—he can not fail me, ...

Weep not for me; When the fee-ble pulse is ceas-ing, Start not at its
Weep not for me; Yes, tho' sin and doubt en-deav-or From his love my

swift de-creas-ing, 'Tis the fet-tered soul's re-leas-ing, Weep not for me!
soul to sev-er, Je-sus is my strength for-ev-er, Weep not for me!

ENPAR. 6s & 4s.

1. Lowly and solemn be Thy children's cry to thee, Fa-ther di-vine;
2. O Father, in that hour, When earthly help and power Are all in vain,

A hymn of suppliant breath, Owning that life and death A-like are thine.
When spear, and shield, and crown, In faintness are cast down, Do thou sus-tain.

723   *Forsake me not.*   (1087)

3 By him who bowed to take
The death cup for our sake,
  The thorn, the rod—
From whom the last dismay
Was not to pass away—
  Aid us, O God!

4 Trembling beside the grave,
We call on thee to save,
  Father divine;
Hear, hear our suppliant breath;
Keep us, in life and death,
  Thine, only thine.

LIFE AND DEATH.

FADING. 11s & 12s. ✱ Harmonized by B. W.

724 *Vanity of vanities.* (1098)

2 Now through the charmed air, on the winds stealing,
List to the mourner's prayer, solemnly bending:
  Hark, hark, it seems to say, turn from those joys away
  To those which ne'er decay, for life is ending.

3 So when our mortal ties death shall dissever,
Lord, may we reach the skies, where care comes never,
  And in eternal day, joining the angel's lay,
  To our Creator pay homage forever.

POMEROY. 7s & 6s, Peculiar. ✱ GANZBACH.

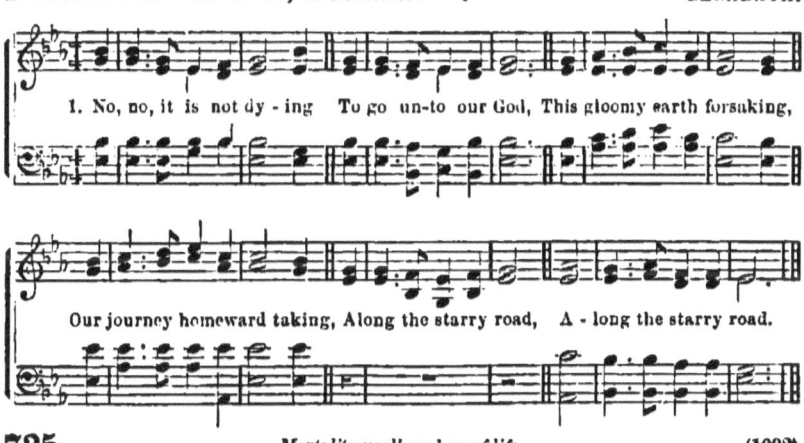

725 *Mortality swallowed up of life.* (1092)

2 No, no, it is not dying
  Heaven's citizen to be;
A crown immortal wearing,
And rest unbroken sharing,
  From care and conflict free.

3 No, no, it is not dying
  The Shepherd's voice to know;
His sheep he ever leadeth,
His peaceful flock he feedeth,
  Where living pastures grow.

4 No, no, it is not dying
  To wear a heavenly crown,
Among God's people dwelling,
The glorious triumph swelling,
  Of him whose sway we own.

5 Oh no, this is not dying,
  Thou Savior of mankind!
There, streams of love are flowing,
No hindrance ever knowing;
  Here, only drops we find.

266 — PRESENT AND FUTURE:

GO TO THY REST IN PEACE. 6, 6, 8, 8, 6.
J. M. PELTON, by permission.

1. Go to thy rest in peace, And soft be thy re-pose; Thy toils are o'er, thy troubles cease; From earthly cares, in sweet re-lease, Thine eye-lids gent-ly close, gent-ly close, Thine eye-lids gent-ly close.

726   *Go to thy rest in peace.*   (1094)

2 Go to thy peaceful rest;
  For thee we need not weep,
Since thou art now among the blest—
No more by sin and sorrow pressed,
  But hushed in quiet sleep.

3 Go to thy rest; and while
  Thy absence we deplore,
One thought our sorrow shall beguile;
For soon, with a celestial smile,
  We meet to part no more.

THE BURIAL. 10s, 6 & 4. (1093)

727
1. Thou God of love! beneath thy sheltering wings We leave our ho-ly dead, To rest in hope! From this world's suffer-ings Their souls have fled!
2. Oh! when our souls are burdened with the weight Of life, and all its woes, Let us re-mem-ber them, and calm-ly wait For our life's close.

SECOND ADVENT.

JOYFUL DAY. P. M. ✣ Harmonized by J. P. POWELL.

728 *When the King of kings comes.* (1101)

2 When the trump of God calls.
When the last of foes falls;
We shall have a joyful day,
   When the King of kings comes:
To see the saints raised from the dead,
And all together gathered,
And made like to their glorious Head,
   When the King of kings comes.

3 When the foe's distress comes,
When the church's rest comes;
We shall have a joyful day,
   When the King of kings comes:
To see the New Jerusalem,
Its fullness and its matchless frame,
Surpassing all report and fame,
   When the King of kings comes.

4 When the world's course is run,
When the judgment is begun!
We shall have a joyful day,
   When the King of kings comes
To see the sons of God well known,
All spotless to their Father shown,
And Jesus all his brethren own,
   When the King of kings comes.

5 When our Lord in clouds comes,
When he with great power comes;
We shall have a joyful day,
   When the King of kings comes:
To see all things by him restored,
And God himself alone adored,
By all the saints with one accord,
   When the King of kings comes.

THE GUIDING HAND. Chant. S. J. VAIL, by permission.

729 *The Guiding Hand.*

1 "Is this the way, my Father?" | "'Tis, my | child. |
Thou must pass through this tangled, | dreary | wild, |
If thou wouldst reach the city | unde- | filed, |
   Thy | peaceful | home a- | bove."

2 "But enemies are round." "Yes, child, I | know, |
Where least expecting, there thou 'lt find a | foe; |
But victor thou shalt prove o'er | all below, |
   On- | ly seek | strength a- | bove."

PRESENT AND FUTURE:

WE WAIT FOR THEE. (New.)   T. E. PERKINS.

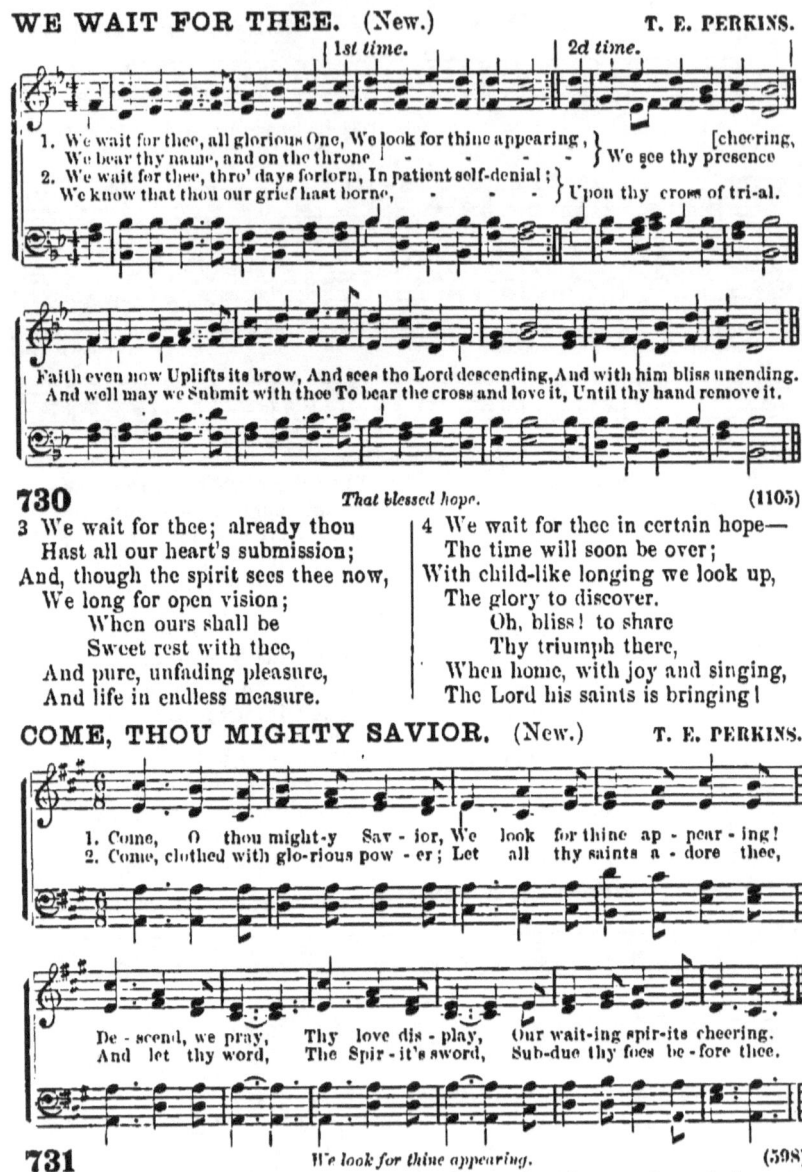

1. We wait for thee, all glorious One, We look for thine appearing,
We bear thy name, and on the throne - - - We see thy presence [cheering,
2. We wait for thee, thro' days forlorn, In patient self-denial;
We know that thou our grief hast borne, - - - Upon thy cross of tri-al.

Faith even now Uplifts its brow, And sees the Lord descending, And with him bliss unending.
And well may we Submit with thee To bear the cross and love it, Until thy hand remove it.

730   *That blessed hope.*   (1105)

3 We wait for thee; already thou
  Hast all our heart's submission;
And, though the spirit sees thee now,
  We long for open vision;
    When ours shall be
    Sweet rest with thee,
And pure, unfading pleasure,
And life in endless measure.

4 We wait for thee in certain hope—
  The time will soon be over;
With child-like longing we look up,
  The glory to discover.
    Oh, bliss! to share
    Thy triumph there,
When home, with joy and singing,
The Lord his saints is bringing!

COME, THOU MIGHTY SAVIOR. (New.)   T. E. PERKINS.

1. Come, O thou might-y Sav-ior, We look for thine ap-pear-ing!
2. Come, clothed with glo-rious pow-er; Let all thy saints a-dore thee,

De-scend, we pray, Thy love dis-play, Our wait-ing spir-its cheering.
And let thy word, The Spir-it's sword, Sub-due thy foes be-fore thee.

731   *We look for thine appearing.*   (598)

3 May every heart with gladness,
  Thine offered grace receiving,
    Now cease from sin,
    And, pure within,
Have peace, in thee believing.

4 Then when thou com'st to judgment,
  On flying clouds descending,
    May we rejoice
    When, at thy voice,
The solid earth is rending.

SECOND ADVENT. 269

JUDGMENT HYMN. L. M.
LUTHER.

1. The Lord will come, the earth shall quake, The hills their fix-ed seat forsake;
D. S. The stars withdraw their feeble light.

And withering, from the vault of night, The stars withdraw their feeble light,

732 *The day of the Lord will come.* (1106)

2 The Lord will come, but not the same
As once in lowly form he came;
A silent Lamb to slaughter led,
The bruised, the suffering, and the dead.

3 The Lord will come—a dreadful form,
With wreath of flame, and robe of storm,
On cherub wings, and wings of wind,
Anointed Judge of human kind.

4 While sinners in despair shall call,
"Rocks, hide us! mountains, on us fall!"
The saints, ascending from the tomb,
Shall joyful sing — " The Lord is come!"

733 *Public humiliation.* (1255)

1 Great maker of unnumbered worlds,
And whom unnumbered worlds adore,
Whose goodness all thy creatures share,
While nature trembles at thy power,—

2 Thine is the hand that moves the spheres,
That wakes the wind, and lifts the sea;
And man who moves, the lord of earth,
Acts but the part assigned by thee.

3 While suppliant crowds implore thy aid,
To thee we raise the humble cry;
Thy altar is the contrite heart,
Thy incense the repentant sigh.

4 Oh may our land, in this her hour,
Confess thy hand and bless the rod,
By penitence make thee her Friend,
And find in thee a guardian God.

734 *The great day of his wrath.* (1107)

1 That day of wrath! that dreadful day,
When heaven and earth shall pass away!
What power shall be the sinner's stay?
How shall he meet that dreadful day?

2 When shriveling like a parched scroll,
The flaming heavens together roll;
When, louder yet, and yet more dread,
Swells the high trump that wakes the dead;

3 Oh, on that day, that dreadful day,
When man to judgment wakes from clay,
Be thou, O God, the sinner's stay,
Though heaven and earth shall pass away.

735 *The Lord reigneth.* (28')

1 Jehovah reigns; his throne is high;
His robes are light and majesty;
His glory shines with beams so bright
No mortal can sustain the sight.

2 His terrors keep the world in awe;
His justice guards his holy law:
His love reveals a smiling face;
His truth and promise seal the grace.

3 Through all his works his wisdom shines,
And baffles Satan's deep designs;
His power is sovereign to fulfill
The noblest counsels of his will.

4 And will this glorious Lord descend
To be my father and my friend?
Then let my songs with angels join:
Heaven is secure, if God be mine.

Old Hundred, Key A.   Duke Street, Key E♭.   Sessions, Key C.

PRESENT AND FUTURE:

THATCHER. S. M. W. B. BRADBURY, by permission.

1. In expectation sweet, We wait, and sing, and pray,
Till Christ's triumphal car we meet, And see an endless day.

736 *And to wait for his Son, etc.* (1109)

2 He comes! the Conqueror comes!
Death falls beneath his sword;
The joyful prisoners burst their tombs,
And rise to meet their Lord.

3 The trumpet sounds—Awake!
Ye dead, to judgment come!
The pillars of creation shake,
While hell receives her doom.

4 Thrice happy morn for those
Who love the ways of peace;
No night of sorrow e'er shall close
Upon its perfect bliss.

737 *Awake and sing, etc.* (1110)

1 Rest for the toiling hand,
Rest for the anxious brow,
Rest for the weary, way-worn feet,
Rest from all labor now;

2 Soon shall the trump of God
Give out the welcome sound
That shakes thy silent chamber-walls,
And breaks the turf-sealed ground.

3 Ye dwellers in the dust,
Awake! come forth and sing;
Sharp has your frost of winter been,
But bright shall be your spring.

4 'T was sown in weakness here;
'T will then be raised in power;
That which was sown an earthly seed
Shall rise a heavenly flower.

738 *A morning without clouds.* (1184)

1 See how the rising sun
Pursues his shining way;
And wide proclaims his Maker's praise
With every brightening ray.

2 Thus would my rising soul
Its heavenly parent sing;
And to its great Original
An humble tribute bring.

3 Oh may I grateful use
The blessings I receive!
And ne'er in thought, in word, or deed,
His Holy Spirit grieve.

739 *I will sing of thy mercy, etc.* (1185)

1 The morning light returns,
The sun begins to shine;
Now let our souls in haste arise,
To run the race divine.

2 We praise the Father's love,
Who kept us through the night;
Oh may his kindness be our song,
His pleasure our delight!

3 While passing through this day,
Lord, we implore thy care,
To guide us on the heavenly way,
And guard from every snare.

4 And when our life shall close,
Oh may it be in peace!
May we lie down in sweet repose,
And wake in endless bliss.

Bankoke, Key G.   Kentucky, Key A♭.   Golden Hill, Key F.

SECOND ADVENT.

THE CHARIOT. 11s & 12s.   J. WILLIAMS.

1. The chariot! the chariot! its wheels roll in fire;
As the Lord cometh down in the pomp of his ire;
2. The glory! the glory! around him are poured
Mighty hosts of the angels that wait on the Lord;

Lo! self-moving, it drives on its pathway of cloud;
And the heavens with the burden of God-head are bowed.
And the glorified saints, and the martyrs are there,
And there, all who the palm-wreaths of victory wear.

740   *At the last trump.*   (1111)

3 The trumpet! the trumpet! the dead have all heard;
Lo! the depths of the stone-covered charnel are stirred!
From the sea, from the earth, from the south, from the north,
All the vast generations of men are come forth.

4 The judgment! the judgment! the thrones are all set,
Where the Lamb and the bright-crowned elders are met!
There all flesh is at once in the sight of the Lord,
And the doom of eternity hangs on his word.

VICTORY. 8s & 7s, Peculiar. (New.)   O. A. BARTHOLOMEW.

1. Lo; the seal of death is breaking; Those who slept its sleep are waking;
[Heaven opes its portals fair!

Hark! the harps of God are ringing; Hark! the seraph's hymn is flinging
[Music on im-mor-tal air.

741   *He will swallow up death in victory.*   (1112)

2 There, no more at eve declining,
Suns without a cloud are shining
O'er the land of life and love;
There the founts of life are flowing,
Flowers unknown to time are blowing,
In that radiant scene above.

PRESENT AND FUTURE:

BREST. 8s, 7s & 4.

1. Day of judgment, day of wonders! Hark! the trumpet's awful sound, Louder than a thousand thunders, Shakes the vast creation round! How the summons Will the sinner's heart confound!

742 *Every eye shall see him.* (1117)

2 See the Judge, our nature wearing,
Clothed in majesty divine!
You who long for his appearing,
Then shall say, "This Lord is mine!"
Gracious Savior,
Own me, in that day, for thine!

3 At his call the dead awaken,
Rise to life from earth and sea;
All the powers of nature, shaken
By his looks, prepare to flee:
Careless sinner,
What will then become of thee?

4 Horrors past imagination
Will surprise your trembling heart,
When you hear your condemnation—
"Hence, accursed wretch! depart!
Hence, with Satan
And his angels have your part."

5 But to those who have confessed,
Loved, and served the Lord below,
He will say, "Come near, you blessed;
See the kingdom I bestow:
You forever
Shall my love and glory know."

6 Under sorrows and reproaches,
May this thought our courage raise!
Swiftly God's great day approaches;
Sighs shall then be changed to praise:
May we triumph,
When the world is in a blaze!

743 *Behold, he cometh with clouds.* (1104)

1 Lo! he comes, with clouds descending,
Once for favored sinners slain,
Thousand thousand saints attending,
Swell the triumph of his train!
Hallelujah!
Jesus now shall ever reign!

2 Every eye shall now behold him
Robed in dreadful majesty;
Those who set at naught and sold him,
Pierced and nailed him to the tree,
Deeply wailing,
Shall the true Messiah see.

3 Every island, sea, and mountain,
Heaven and earth, shall flee away;
All who hate him, must, confounded,
Hear the trump proclaim the day,
Come to judgment!
Come to judgment! come away!

4 Now redemption, long expected,
See in solemn pomp appear!
All his saints by man rejected
Now shall meet him in the air:
Hallelujah!
See the day of God appear!

5 Lord, thy Bride says by thy Spirit,
Hasten thou the general doom!
Promised glory to inherit,
Take thy weary pilgrims home!
All creation
Travails, groans, and bids thee come.

SECOND ADVENT. 273

MERIBAH. C. P. M.   Dr. L. MASON.

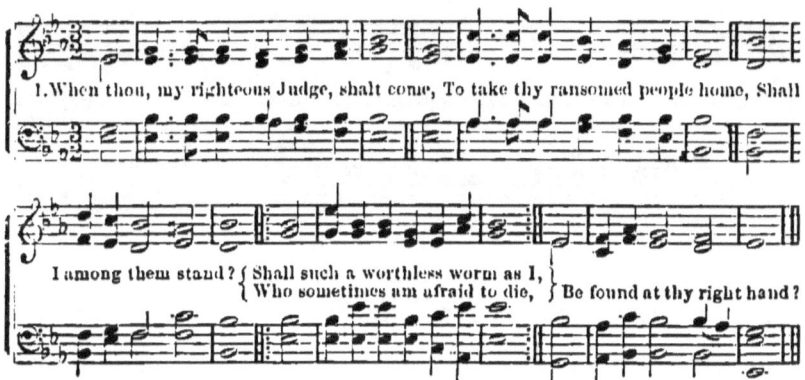

1. When thou, my righteous Judge, shalt come, To take thy ransomed people home, Shall I among them stand? { Shall such a worthless worm as I, } { Who sometimes am afraid to die, } Be found at thy right hand?

744   *That he may find mercy, etc.* (1114)

2 I love to meet thy people now,
Before thy feet with them to bow,
  Though vilest of them all;
But—can I bear the piercing thought—
What if my name should be left out
  When thou for them shalt call?

3 O Lord, prevent it by thy grace:
Be thou my only hiding-place,
  In this, the accepted day;
Thy pardoning voice, oh, let me hear,
To still my unbelieving fear,
  Nor let me fall, I pray.

4 And when the final trump shall sound,
Among thy saints let me be found,
  To bow before thy face;
Then in triumphant strains I'll sing,
While heaven's resounding mansions ring
  With praise of sovereign grace.

745   *Christ our only hope.* (363)

1 Desponding soul, oh cease thy woe;
Dry up thy tears; to Jesus go,
  In faith's appointed way;
Let not thy unbelieving fears
Still hold thee back—thy Savior hears—
  From him no longer stay.

2 No works of thine can e'er impart
A balm to heal thy wounded heart,
  Or solid comfort give;
Turn, then, to him who freely gave
His precious blood thy soul to save;
  E'en now he bids thee live.

3 Helpless and lost, to Jesus fly!
His power and love are ever nigh
  To those who seek his face;
Thy deepest guilt on him was laid;
He bore thy sins, thy ransom paid;
  Oh, haste to share his grace.

746   *They desire a better country.* (1061)

1 How happy is the pilgrim's lot!
How free from every anxious thought
  From worldly hope and fear!
Confined to neither court nor cell,
His soul disdains on earth to dwell—
  He only sojourns here.

2 This happiness in part is mine,
Already saved from low design,
  From every creature-love;
Blest with the scorn of finite good,
My soul is lightened of its load,
  And seeks the things above.

3 There is my house and portion fair;
My treasure and my heart are there,
  And my abiding home;
For me my elder brethren stay,
And angels beckon me away,
  And Jesus bids me come.

4 I come, thy servant, Lord, replies;
I come to meet thee in the skies,
  And claim my heavenly rest!
Soon will the pilgrim's journey end;
Then, oh my Savior, Brother, Friend,
  Receive me to thy breast!

Advent, Key E♭.   Ariel, Key E♭.   Bennett, Key E♭.

PRESENT AND FUTURE:

DOOM. 11s & 5s. (New.)   J. ZUNDEL.

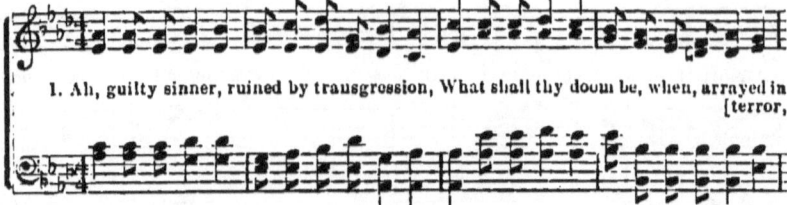

1. Ah, guilty sinner, ruined by transgression, What shall thy doom be, when, arrayed in [terror,

God shall command thee, covered with pollution, Up to the judgment? Up to the judgment?

747   *Where shall the ungodly, etc.*   (1118)

2 Stop, thoughtless sinner, stop awhile and ponder,
Ere death arrest thee, and the Judge, in vengeance,
Hurl from his presence thy affrighted spirit,
      Swift to perdition.

3 Oft has he called thee, but thou wouldst not hear him;
Mercies and judgments have alike been slighted;
Yet he is gracious, and, with arms unfolded,
      Waits to embrace thee.

4 Come, then, poor sinner, come away this moment,
Just as you are, come, filthy and polluted,
Come to the fountain open for the guilty;
      Jesus invites you.

5 But if you trifle with his gracious message,
Cleave to the world and love its guilty pleasures,
Mercy, grown weary, shall, in righteous judgment,
      Leave you forever.

6 O guilty sinner! hear the voice of warning;
Fly to the Savior, and embrace his pardon;
So shall your spirit meet, with joy triumphant,
      Death and the judgment.

---

748   *Horton, Key Bb.*   (1187)

1 Thou that dost my life prolong,
Kindly aid my morning song;
Thankful let my offerings rise
To the God that rules the skies.

2 Gently, with the dawning ray,
On my soul thy beams display;
Sweeter than the smiling morn,
Let thy cheering light return.

SECOND ADVENT. 275

THE LAST LOVELY MORNING. Harmonized by J. P. POWELL.

1. The last love-ly morn-ing, All blooming and fair,
   Is fast on-ward fleet-ing, And soon will ap-pear.
D. C. Oh, let us be read-y To hail the glad day.

While tho might-y, might-y, might-y trump Sounds, Come, come a-way;

749 *For the trumpet shall sound.* (1113)

2 And when that bright morning
  In splendor shall dawn,
  Our tears shall be ended,
  Our sorrows all gone.

3 The Bridegroom from glory
  To earth shall descend,
  Ten thousand bright angels
  Around him attend.

4 The grave shall be opened,
  The dead shall arise,
  And with the Redeemer
  Mount up to the skies.

5 The saints, then immortal,
  In glory shall reign,
  The Bride with the Bridegroom
  Forever remain.

NATURE AND LIFE. 8, 8, 8, 4, 8, 4. (New.) T. E. PERKINS.

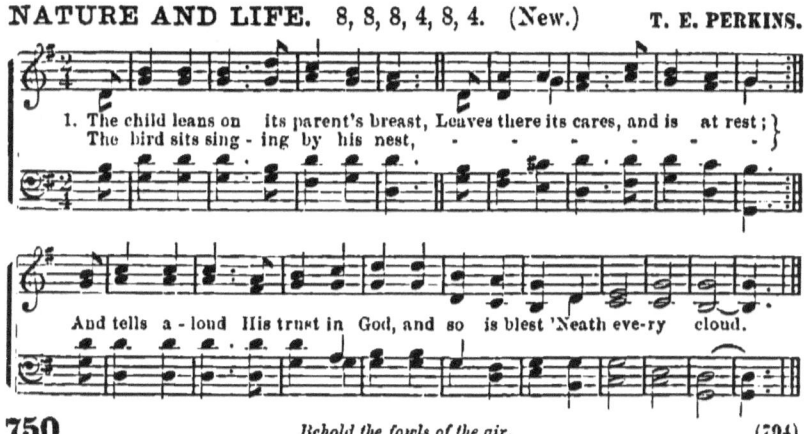

1. The child leans on its parent's breast, Leaves there its cares, and is at rest;
   The bird sits sing-ing by his nest,
   And tells a-loud His trust in God, and so is blest 'Neath eve-ry cloud.

750 *Behold the fowls of the air.* (704)

2 He has no store, he sows no seed;
  Yet sings aloud and doth not heed;
  By flowing stream, or grassy mead,
  He sings to shame
  Men, who forget, in fear of need,
  A Father's name.

3 The heart that trusts forever sings,
  And feels as light as it had wings;
  A well of peace within it springs:
  Come good or ill,
  Whate'er to-day, to-morrow brings,
  It is his will!

PRESENT AND FUTURE:

EFFINGHAM. L. M.

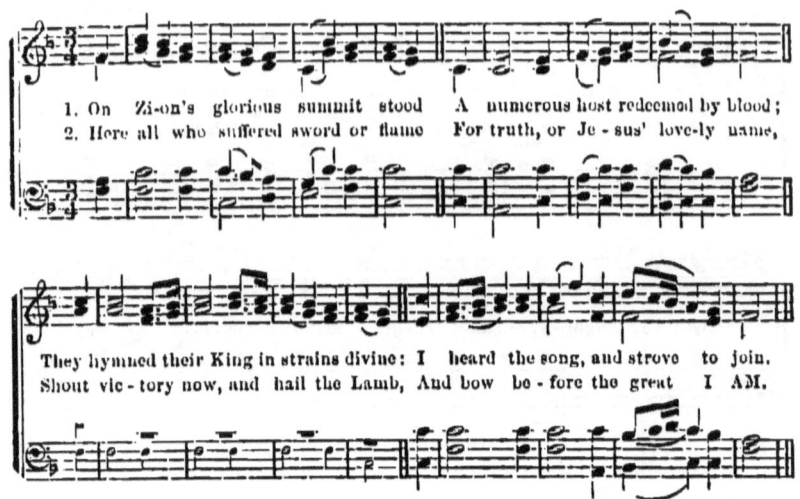

1. On Zion's glorious summit stood A numerous host redeemed by blood;
2. Here all who suffered sword or flame For truth, or Jesus' lovely name,

They hymned their King in strains divine: I heard the song, and strove to join.
Shout victory now, and hail the Lamb, And bow before the great I AM.

751   *Rev. 14: 1–3.*   (1120)

3 While everlasting ages roll,
Eternal love shall feast their soul,
And scenes of bliss, forever new,
Rise in succession to their view.

4 Oh sweet employ! to sing and trace
The amazing heights and depths of grace;
And spend, from sin and sorrow free,
A blissful, vast eternity!

5 Oh what a sweet, exalted song,
When every tribe and every tongue,
Redeemed by blood, with Christ appear,
And join in one full chorus there!

6 My soul anticipates the day—
Would stretch her wings and soar away,
To aid the song, the palm to bear,
And praise my great Redeemer there.

752   *Rev. 22: 4.*   (1121)

1 Lo! round the throne, a glorious band,
The saints in countless myriads stand;
Of every tongue redeemed to God,
Arrayed in garments washed in blood.

2 Through tribulation great they came;
They bore the cross, despised the shame;
But now from all their labors rest,
In God's eternal glory blest.

3 They see the Savior face to face;
They sing the triumph of his grace;
And day and night, with ceaseless praise,
To him their loud hosannas raise.

4 Oh may we tread the sacred road
That holy saints and martyrs trod;
Wage to the end the glorious strife,
And win, like them, a crown of life.

753 *The former things are passed away.* (1119)

1 There is a land mine eye hath seen,
In visions of enraptured thought,
So bright that all which spreads between
Is with its radiant glory fraught;

2 A land upon whose blissful shore
There rests no shadow, falls no stain;
There those who meet shall part no more,
And those long parted, meet again.

3 Its skies are not like earthly skies,
With varying hues of shade and light;
It hath no need of suns to rise
To dissipate the gloom of night.

4 There sweeps no desolating wind
Across that calm, serene abode;
The wanderer there a home may find,
Within the paradise of God.

Rockingham, Key E♭.   Rothwell, Key F.   Ware, Key B♭.

THE HEAVENLY MANSION. L. M., Peculiar.

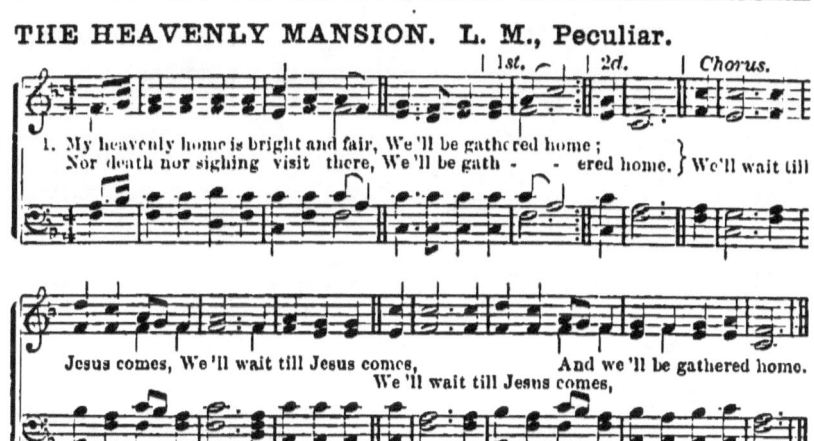

754   *The heavenly mansion.*   (1124)

2 Its glittering towers the sun outshine,
That heavenly mansion shall be mine.
3 My Father's house is built on high,
Above the arched and starry sky.
4 When from this earthly prison free,
That heavenly mansion mine shall be.
5 While here, a stranger far from home,
Affliction's waves may round me foam.

6 Let others seek a home below,
Which flames devour or waves o'erthrow;
7 Be mine the happier lot to own,
A heavenly mansion near the throne.
8 Then, fail this earth, let stars decline,
And sun and moon refuse to shine;
9 All nature sink and cease to be,
That heavenly mansion stands for me.

SING TO ME OF HEAVEN. S. M. ✱

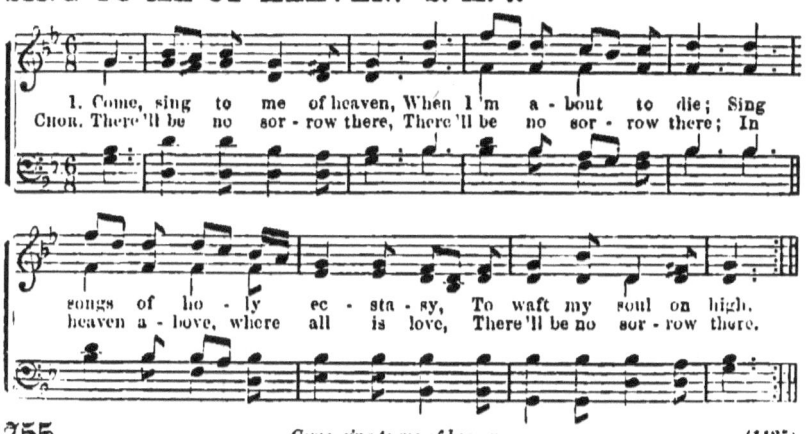

755   *Come, sing to me of heaven.*   (1135)

2 When the last moment comes,
  Oh watch my dying face,
To catch the bright, seraphic glow
  Which on each feature plays!

3 Then to my raptured ear
  Let one sweet song be given;
Let music charm me last on earth,
  And greet me first in heaven!

PRESENT AND FUTURE:

WOODLAND. C. M.
N. D. GOULD.

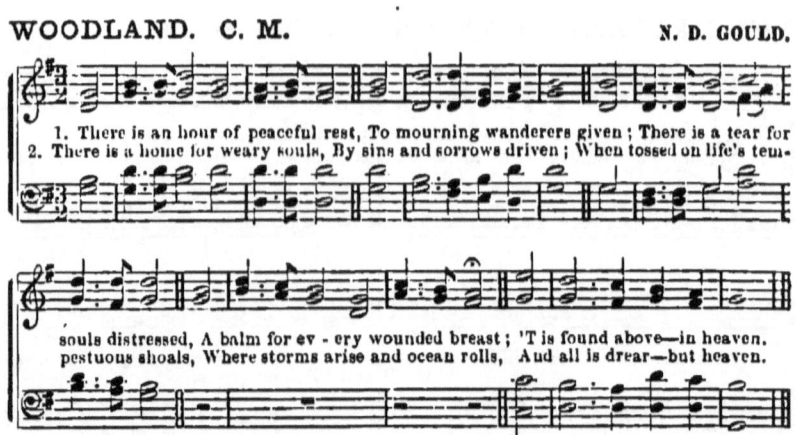

1. There is an hour of peaceful rest, To mourning wanderers given; There is a tear for
souls distressed, A balm for ev-ery wounded breast; 'T is found above—in heaven.
2. There is a home for weary souls, By sins and sorrows driven; When tossed on life's tempestuous shoals, Where storms arise and ocean rolls, And all is drear—but heaven.

756 *The hope—laid up for you in heaven.* (1130)

3 There faith lifts up the tearless eye,
The heart with anguish riven;
It views the tempest passing by,
Sees evening shadows quickly fly,
And all serene—in heaven.

4 There fragrant flowers immortal bloom,
And joys supreme are given;
There rays divine disperse the gloom;
Beyond the dark and narrow tomb
Appears the dawn—of heaven.

THERE IS A LAND IMMORTAL. 7s & 6s.

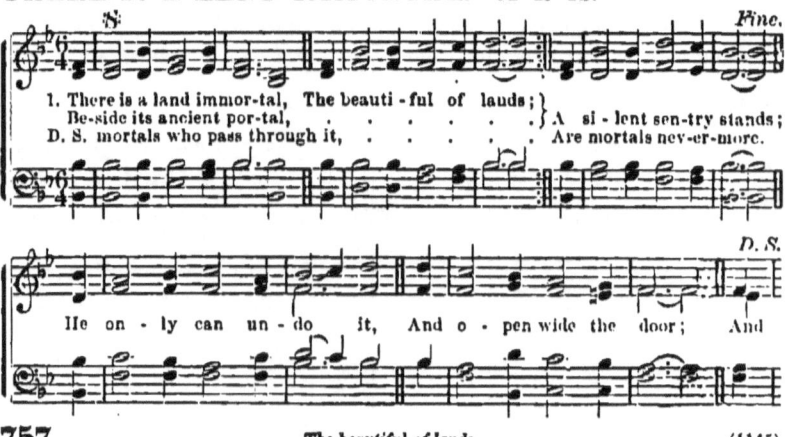

1. There is a land immor-tal, The beauti-ful of lands;
Be-side its ancient por-tal, ... A si-lent sen-try stands;
D. S. mortals who pass through it, ... Are mortals nev-er-more.

He on-ly can un-do it, And o-pen wide the door; And

757 *The beautiful of lands.* (1145)

2 Though dark and drear the passage
That leadeth to the gate,
Yet grace comes with the message
To souls that watch and wait;
And, at the time appointed,
A messenger comes down,
And leads the Lord's anointed
From cross to glory's crown.

3 Their sighs are lost in singing,
They're blessed in their tears;
Their journey heavenward winging,
They leave on earth their fears:
Death like an angel seemeth;
"We welcome thee," they cry;
Their face with glory beameth—
'T is life for them to die!

HEAVEN.

THE LAND OF BEULAH. C. M., with Chorus.
W. B. BRADBURY, by permission.

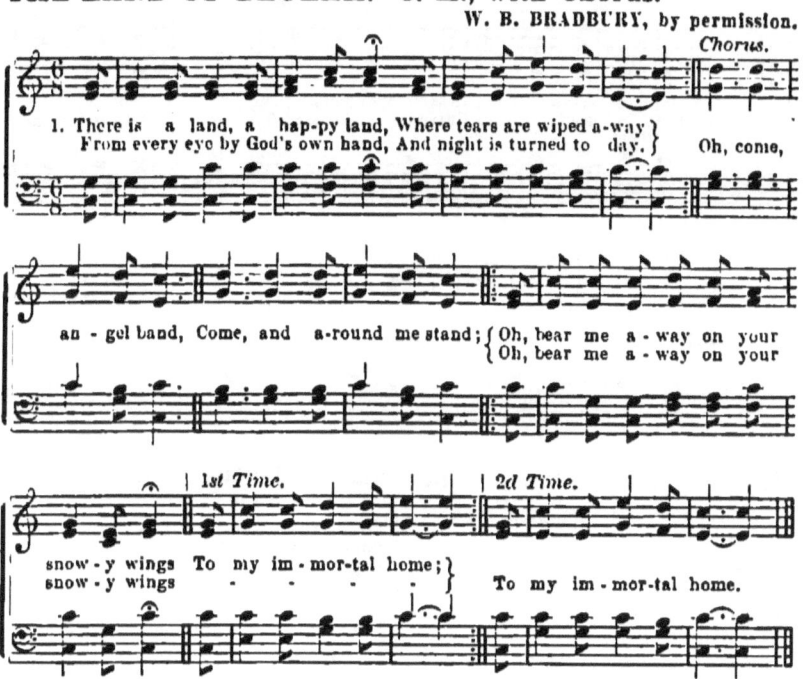

758 *There is a land, a happy land.* (1129)

1 There is a land, a happy land,
  Where tears are wiped away
From every eye by God's own hand,
  And night is turned to day.

2 There is a home, a happy home,
  Where way-worn travelers rest,
Where toil and languor never come,
  And every mourner's blest.

3 There is a port, a peaceful port,
  A safe and quiet shore,
Where weary mariners resort
  And fear the storms no more.

4 There is a crown, a dazzling crown,
  Bedecked with jewels fair;
And priests and kings of high renown
  That crown of glory wear.

5 That land be mine, that calm retreat,
  That crown of glory bright;
Then I'll esteem each bitter sweet,
  And every burden light.

759 *Far up the everlasting hills.* (1132)

1 There is a fold where none can stray,
  And pastures ever green,
Where sultry sun, or stormy day,
  Or night, is never seen.

2 Far up the everlasting hills,
  In God's own light it lies;
His smile its vast dominion fills
  With joy that never dies.

3 One narrow vale, one darksome wave,
  Divides that land from this;
I have a Shepherd pledged to save,
  And bear me home to bliss.

4 Soon at his feet my soul shall lie,
  In life's last struggling breath;
But I shall only seem to die,
  I shall not taste of death.

5 Far from this guilty world to be,
  Exempt from toil and strife;
To spend eternity with thee—
  My Savior, this is life!

PRESENT AND FUTURE:

OAK. 6s & 4s. — Dr. L. MASON, by permission.

1. I'm but a stranger here, Heaven is my home;
Earth is a desert dreary, Heaven is my home;
Danger and sorrow stand
Round me on every hand; Heaven is my fatherland—Heaven is my home.

760 *Heaven is my home.* (1146)

2 What though the tempests rage!
Heaven is my home;
Short is my pilgrimage;
Heaven is my home.
And time's wild wintry blast
Soon will be overpast,
I shall reach home at last;
Heaven is my home.

3 There at my Savior's side,
Heaven is my home;
I shall be glorified;
Heaven is my home.
There with the good and blest,
Those I loved most and best,
I shall forever rest;
Heaven is my home.

4 Therefore I'll murmur not;
Heaven is my home;
Whate'er my earthly lot,
Heaven is my home.
For I shall surely stand,
There at my Lord's right hand,
Heaven is my fatherland—
Heaven is my home.

761 *Hebrews 11 : 16.* (1136)

1 Know ye that better land
Where care's unknown?
Know ye that blessed band
Around the throne?
There, there is happiness,
There, streams of purest bliss;
There, there are rest and peace—
There, there alone.

2 Yes, yes, we know that place—
We know it well;
Eye hath not seen his face,
Tongue can not tell;
There are the angels bright,
There saints enrobed in white—
All, all are clothed in light—
There, there they dwell.

3 Oh! we are weary here,
A little band,
Yet soon in glory there
We hope to stand;
Then let us haste away,
Speed o'er this world's dark way,
Unto that land of day—
That better land.

4 Come! hasten that sweet day,
Let time begone;
Come! Lord, make no delay,
On thy white throne;
Thy face we wish to see,
To dwell and reign with thee,
And thine forever be—
Thine, thine alone.

Bethany, Key G.

HEAVEN.

IVES. 7s, Double.

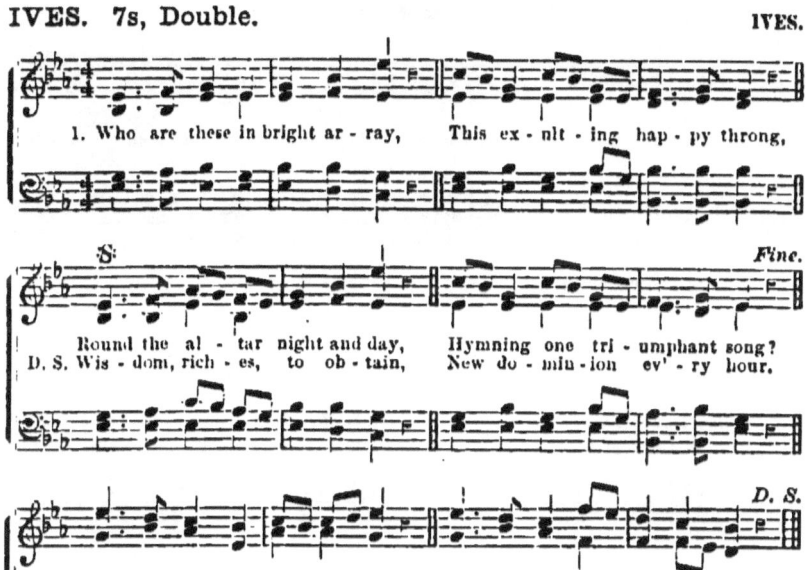

1. Who are these in bright ar-ray, This ex-ult-ing hap-py throng,
Round the al-tar night and day, Hymning one tri-umphant song?
D. S. Wis-dom, rich-es, to ob-tain, New do-min-ion ev'-ry hour.
"Worthy is the Lamb once slain, Blessing, hon-or, glo-ry, power,

762 *Who are these—and whence, etc.* (1137)

2 These through fiery trials trod;
These from great affliction came;
Now, before the throne of God,
Sealed with his almighty name.
Clad in raiment pure and white,
Victor-palms in every hand,
Through their great Redeemer's might,
More than conquerors they stand.

3 Hunger, thirst, disease unknown,
On immortal fruits they feed;
Them the Lamb, amidst the throne,
Shall to living fountains lead;
Joy and gladness banish sighs;
Perfect love dispels all fears;
And forever from their eyes
God shall wipe away their tears.

763 *They rest from their labors.* (1138)

1 High in yonder realms of light,
Dwell the raptured saints above;
Far beyond our feeble sight,
Happy in Immanuel's love:
Once they knew, like us below,
Pilgrims in this vale of tears,
Torturing pain and heavy woe,
Gloomy doubts, distressing fears.

2 'Mid the chorus of the skies,
'Mid the angelic lyres above,
Hark, their songs melodious rise,
Songs of praise to Jesus' love!
Happy spirits, ye are fled
Where no grief can entrance find,
Lulled to rest the aching head,
Soothed the anguish of the mind.

3 All is tranquil and serene,
Calm and undisturbed repose;
There no cloud can intervene,
There no angry tempest blows;
Every tear is wiped away,
Sighs no more shall heave the breast,
Night is lost in endless day,
Sorrow—in eternal rest.

Wilson, Key G. Amboy, Key D.

MT. BLANC. 7s & 6s, or 6s & 4s.*

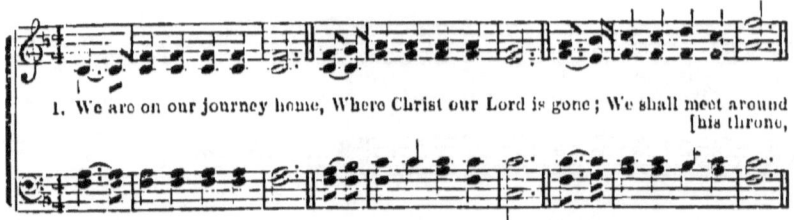

1. We are on our journey home, Where Christ our Lord is gone; We shall meet around [his throne,

* Use slurs throughout for second hymn, and when necessary for first hymn.

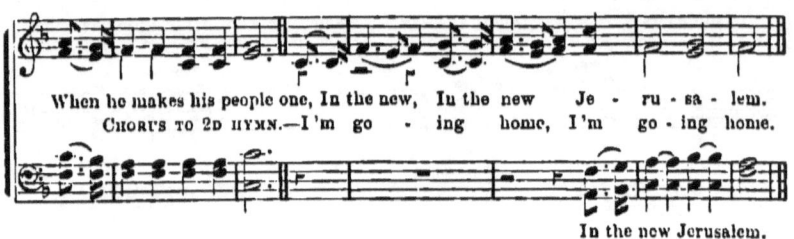

When he makes his people one, In the new, In the new Je-ru-sa-lem.
CHORUS TO 2D HYMN.—I'm go - ing home, I'm go-ing home.
In the new Jerusalem.

764 *He hath prepared for them a city.* (1141)

2 We can see that distant home,
Though clouds rise dark between;
Faith views the radiant dome,
And a luster flashes keen
From the new Jerusalem.

3 O glory shining far
From the never-setting sun!
O trembling morning star!
Our journey's almost done
To the new Jerusalem.

4 O holy! heavenly home!
O rest eternal there!
When shall the exiles come,
Where they cease from earthly care,
In the new Jerusalem.

5 Our hearts are breaking now
Those mansions fair to see:
O Lord! thy heavens bow,
And raise us up with thee
To the new Jerusalem.

765 *I'm going home.* (1154)

1 I am a stranger here;
No home, no rest I see;
Not all earth counts most dear
Can win a sigh from me.
I'm going home.

2 Jesus, thy home is mine,
And I thy Father's child;
With hopes and joys divine,
The world's a dreary wild.
I'm going home.

3 Home! oh! how soft and sweet
It thrills upon the heart!
Home! where the brethren meet,
And never, never part.
I'm going home.

4 Home! where the Bridegroom takes
The purchase of his love:
Home! where the Father waits
To welcome saints above.
I'm going home.

5 Yes! when the world looks cold,
Which did my Lord revile,
A Lamb within the fold,
I can look up and smile.
I'm going home.

6 When earth's delusive charms
Would snare my pilgrim feet,
I fly to Jesus' arms,
And yet again repeat,
I'm going home.

NO NIGHT IN HEAVEN. S. M., with Chorus.

S. J. VAIL, by permission.

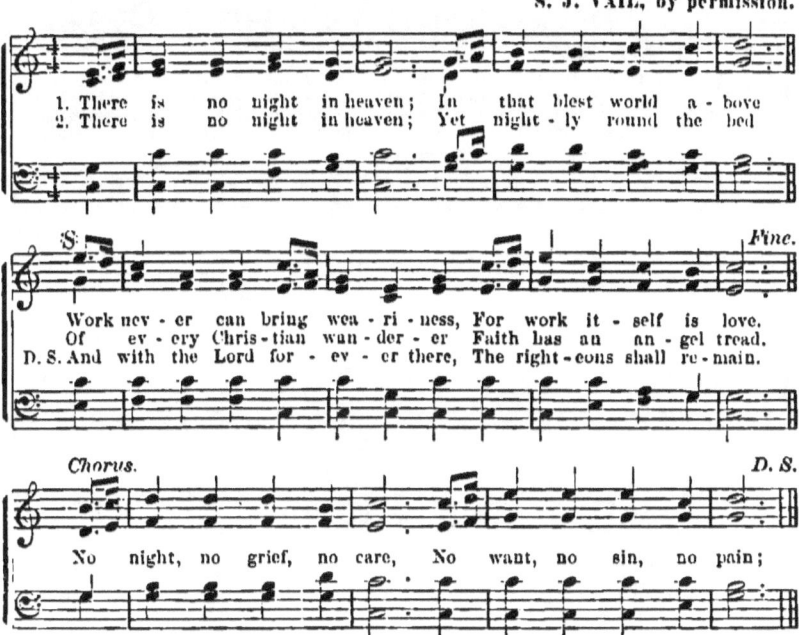

1. There is no night in heaven; In that blest world above
2. There is no night in heaven; Yet nightly round the bed

Work never can bring weariness, For work itself is love.
Of every Christian wanderer Faith has an angel tread.
D.S. And with the Lord forever there, The righteous shall remain.

Chorus.

No night, no grief, no care, No want, no sin, no pain;

766   Rev. 21: 25.   (1143)

3 There is no grief in heaven:
For life is one glad day,
And tears are of those former things
Which all have passed away.

4 There is no grief in heaven:
Yet angels from on high,
On golden pinions earthward glide,
The Christian's tears to dry.

5 There is no want in heaven:
The Lamb of God supplies
Life's tree of twelvefold fruitage still,
Life's spring which never dries.

6 There is no want in heaven:
Yet in a desert land

The fainting prophet was sustained
And fed by angel's hand.

7 There is no sin in heaven!
Behold that blessed throng;
All holy is their spotless robes,
All holy is their song.

8 There is no sin in heaven:
Here who from sin is free?
Yet angels aid us in our strife
For Christ's true liberty.

9 There is no death in heaven:
For they who gain that shore
Have won their immortality,
And they can die no more.

767   Fraternity, Key G.   (1125)

1 There is a region lovelier far
Than sages tell or poets sing—
Brighter than summer's beauties are,
And softer than the tints of spring.

Cho. I'm going home, I'm going home,
I'm going home to die no more,

To die no more, to die no more,
I'm going home to die no more.

2 It is all holy and serene,
The land of glory and repose;
No cloud obscures the radient scene;
There not a tear of sorrow flows.

SHALL WE SING IN HEAVEN.

WM. B. BRADBURY, by per.

770   *Shall we sing in heaven?*   (1164)

2 Shall we know each other ever
  In that land?
Shall we know each other ever
  In that happy land?
Yes! oh yes! in that land, that happy land,
  They that meet shall know each other, etc.

3 Shall we sing with holy angels
  In that land?
Shall we sing with holy angels
  In that happy land?
Yes! oh yes! in that land, that happy land,
  Saints and angels sing forever, etc.

4 Shall we rest from care and sorrow
  In that land?
Shall we rest from care and sorrow
  In that happy land?
Yes! oh yes! in that land, that happy land,
  They that meet shall rest forever, etc.

5 Shall we meet our dear lost children
  In that land?
Shall we meet our dear lost children
  In that happy land?

Yes! oh yes! in that land, that happy land,
  Children meet and sing forever, etc.

6 Shall we meet our Christian parents
  In that land?
Shall we meet our Christian parents
  In that happy land?
Yes! oh yes! in that land, that happy land,
  Parents and children meet together, etc.

7 Shall we meet our faithful teachers
  In that land?
Shall we meet our faithful teachers
  In that happy land?
Yes! oh yes! in that land, that happy land,
  Teachers and scholars meet together, etc.

8 Shall we know our blessed Savior
  In that land?
Shall we know our blessed Savior
  In that happy land?
Yes! oh yes! in that land, that happy land,
  We shall know our blessed Savior,
  Far beyond the rolling river,
  Love and serve him there forever,
  In that happy land.

HEAVEN. 287

KENDRICK. P. M. (New.)   T. J. COOK.

773   *Behold, I make all things new.*   (1165)

2 That sky is not, like this sad sky of ours,
    Tinged with earth's change and care;
No shadow dims it, and no rain-cloud lowers;
    No broken sunshine there:
One everlasting stretch of azure pours
Its stainless splendor o'er those sinless shores:
For there Jehovah shines with heavenly ray,
And Jesus reigns, dispensing endless day.

3 The dwellers there are not like those of earth,
    No mortal stain they bear;
And yet they seem of kindred blood and birth;
    Whence and how came they there?
Earth was their native soil, from sin and shame,
Through tribulation, they to glory came;
Bond-slaves delivered from sin's crushing load;
Brands plucked from burning by the hand of God.

4 Yon robes of theirs are not like those below;
    No angel's half so bright;
Whence came that beauty, whence that living glow,
    And whence that radiant white?
Washed in the blood of the atoning Lamb,
Fair as the light these robes of theirs became;
And now, all tears wiped off from every eye,
They wander where the freshest pastures lie.

PRESENT AND FUTURE:

SHALL WE KNOW EACH OTHER? 8s & 7s, with Chorus.
(1151)   Rev. R. LOWRY.

(*Concluded on page 289.*)

COME TO THY REST. P. M.

S. J. VAIL, by permission.

1. Is it a long way off? Oh, no! a few more years, A few more bitter tears—We shall be there.
2. O, brethren, dear, how weak, How faint and weak we are! Yet Jesus leads us far Through [tangled ways.

Sometimes the way seems long, Our comforters all go, Woe follows after woe, Care after care. Into the very heart Of this dark wilderness Where dangers thickest press, And Satan strays.

Chorus.
Spread thy bright wings, and soar Spotless for evermore, Sin stained no longer, but white and forgiven; Heir of in-fi-ni-ty, Robed in di-vin-i-ty, Come a-way, hap-py one! come up to heaven! Come away, hap-py one, come up to heaven!

775 *Almost home.* (1153)

3 But he is strong and wise,
And we, his children blind,
Must trust his gentle mind
  And tender care.
So gentle is his love,
We may be sure that sight
Would show us all is right,
  And answered prayer.

4 'T is no uncertain way
We tread, for Jesus still
Leads with unerring skill
  Where'er we roam;
And from the desert wild
Soon shall our path emerge,
And land us on the verge
  Of our dear home.

SHALL WE KNOW EACH OTHER THERE? (*Concluded from p. 288.*)

3 Yes, my earth-worn soul rejoices,
  And my weary heart grows light,
For the sweet and cheerful voices,
  And the forms so pure and bright,
That shall welcome us in heaven,
  Are the loved of long ago;
And to them 't is kindly given,
  Thus their mortal friends to know.

4 O ye weary, sad, and tossed ones,
  Droop not, faint not by the way;
Ye shall join the loved and just ones
  In the land of perfect day.
Harp-strings, touched by angel fingers,
  Murmured in my raptured ear—
Evermore their sweet song lingers—
  We shall know each other there.

HEAVEN.

FRONTIER. P. M. (New.)   Dr. T. HASTINGS.

1. Up-on the fron-tier of this shadowy land, We, pil-grims from e-ter-nal sorrow stand; What realm lies forward, with its happier store Of forests green and sensual dream—Its woods, unruffled by the wild wind's roar: Yet does the turbulent deep, Of valleys hushed in sleep, And lakes most peaceful? 'Tis the land of Evermore.

2. Ver-y far off its marble cit-ies seem—Ver-y far off—be-yond our surge Howl on its ver-y verge. One moment—and we breathe within the Evermore.

778   *Within the vail.*   (1168)

3 They whom we loved and lost so long ago,
Dwell in those cities far from mortal woe—
Haunt those fresh woodlands, whence sweet carolings soar.
Eternal peace have they:
God wipes their tears away:
They drink that river of life which flows for Evermore.

4 Thither we hasten through these regions dim;
But, lo! the wide wings of the seraphim
Shine in the sunset! On that joyous shore
Our lightened hearts shall know
The life of long ago:
The sorrow-burdened path shall fade for Evermore.

PILGRIM. (*Concluded from p. 290.*)

2 Pilgrim, thou dost justly call me,
Wand'ring o'er this waste so wide;
Yet no harm will e'er befall me,
While I'm blest with such a guide.

3 Such a guide—no guide attends thee:
Hence for thee my fears arise;
If some guardian power befriend thee,
'T is unseen by mortal eyes.

4 Yes, unseen—but still believe me,
Such a guide my steps attends;

He'll in every strait relieve me,
He from every harm defends.

5 Pilgrim! see that stream before thee,
Darkly winding through the vale;
Should its deadly waves roll o'er thee,
Would not then thy courage fail?

6 No, that stream has nothing frightful;
To its banks my steps I bend;
There to plunge will be delightful,
Then my pilgrimage will end.

PRESENT AND FUTURE:

THE HOME IN HEAVEN. (New.) — A. SQUIRE.

1. No sickness there, No sickness there, No wea-ry wasting of the frame a - way,
2. No hidden grief, No hidden grief, No wild and cheerless vision of de-spair,

No fearful shrinking from the midnight air, No dread of summer's bright and fervid ray.
No vain pe-ti-tion for a swift re-lief, No tearful eye, no broken hearts are there.

779   *The former things are passed away.*   (1160)

3   Care has no home
Within that realm of ceaseless praise and song;
Its tossing billows break and melt in foam,
Far from the mansions of the spirit throng.

4   No parted friends
O'er mournful recollections have to weep!
No bed of death enduring love attends,
To watch the coming of a pulseless sleep.

5   No blasted flower
Or withered bud celestial gardens grow!
No scorching blast or fierce descending
    shower
Scatters destruction like a ruthless foe!

6   No battle-word
Startles the sacred host with fear and dread!
The song of peace creation's morning heard,
Is sung wherever angel minstrels tread.

7   Let us depart
If scenes like these await the weary soul!
Look up, thou stricken one! thy wounded
    heart
Shall bleed no more at sorrows stern control!

8   With faith our guide,
White-robed and innocent, to lead the way,
Why fear to plunge in Jordan's rolling tide,
And find the ocean of eternal day!

HAPPY CLIME. P. M. *   (1162)   Harmonized by A. SQUIRE.

780 1. Have you heard, have you heard { Undimmed by sorrow, unhurt by time
    [of that sun-bright clime, { Where age hath no power o'er the fadeless frame,

Where the eye is fire, and the heart is flame—Have you heard of that sun-bright clime?

(Concluded on page 293.)

HEAVEN.

SHINING SHORE. 8s & 7s.   GEO. F. ROOT, by permission.

1. My days are gli-ding swift-ly by, And I, a pil-grim stranger,
2. We'll gird our loins, my brethren dear, Our dis-tant home dis-cern-ing;

Would not de-tain them as they fly, Those hours of toil and dan-ger.
Our ab-sent Lord has left us word, Let ev'-ry lamp be burn-ing.
D. S. just be-fore, the shin-ing shore We may al-most dis-cov-er.

Chorus.
For, oh! we stand on Jordan's strand, Our friends are passing o-ver; And

781   *The shining shore.*   (800)

3 Should coming days be cold and dark,
We need not cease our singing;
That perfect rest naught can molest,
Where golden harps are ringing.

4 Let sorrow's rudest tempest blow,
Each cord on earth to sever;
Our King says, "Come," and there's our home,
Forever! oh, forever!

HAPPY CLIME. *(Concluded from p. 293.)*

2 A river of water gushes there,
'Mid flowers of beauty strangely fair,
And a thousand wings are hovering o'er
The dazzling wave and the golden shore,
That are seen in that sun-bright clime.

3 Millions of forms, all clothed in white,
In garments of beauty, clear and bright,
There dwell in their own immortal bowers,
'Mid fadeless hues of countless flowers,
That bloom in that sun-bright clime.

4 Ear hath not heard, and eye hath not seen,
Their swelling songs, and their changeless sheen;
Their ensigns are waving, their banners unfurl,
O'er jasper walls and gates of pearl,
That are fixed in that sun-bright clime.

5 But far, far away is that sinless clime,
Undimmed by sorrow, unhurt by time,
Where, amid all things bright and fair, is given,
The home of the just, and its name is heaven—
The name of that sun-bright clime.

PRESENT AND FUTURE:

THE BETTER LAND. P. M. Harmonized by T. E. PERKINS.

1. I hear thee speak of the bet-ter land, Thou call-est its children a hap-py band;
2. Is it where the feath-er-y palm trees rise, And the date grows ripe un-der sun-ny skies,

Moth-er! oh, where is that ra-di-ant shore, Shall we not seek it and weep no more?
Or, 'midst the green islands of glit-ter-ing seas, Where fragrant forests perfume the breeze,

Is it where the flower of the orange blows, And the fire-flies dance in the myrtle boughs?
And strange, bright birds on their starry wings Bear the rich hues of all glorious things?

Not there, not there, not there! Not there, not there, not there!

782   *The better land.*   (1158)

3 Is it far away in some region old,
Where the rivers wander o'er sands of gold,
And the burning rays of the rubies shine,
And the diamond lights up the secret mine,
And the pearl glows forth from the coral strand?
Is it there, sweet mother, that better land?
  Not there! not there!

4 Eye hath not seen it, my gentle boy,
Ear hath not heard its sweet song of joy!
Dreams can not picture a world so fair,
Sorrow and death may not enter there,
Time may not breathe on its fadeless bloom;
Far beyond the clouds and beyond the tomb!
  'T is there! 't is there!

784 *Horton, Key B♭.* (1199)

1 Softly, now, the light of day
Fades upon my sight away;
Free from care, from labor free,
Lord! I would commune with thee.

2 Soon, for me, the light of day
Shall forever pass away;
Then, from sin and sorrow free,
Take me, Lord! to dwell with thee.

785 *Hendon, Key G.* (742)

1 All ye nations, praise the Lord;
All ye lands, your voices raise;
Heaven and earth, with loud accord,
Praise the Lord forever praise.

2 For his truth and mercy stand,
Past, and present, and to be,
Like the years of his right hand,
Like his own eternity.

BEAUTIFUL WORLD. Quartet. ✱
Arranged from the "Oriola," by Miss BETTIE WILSON.

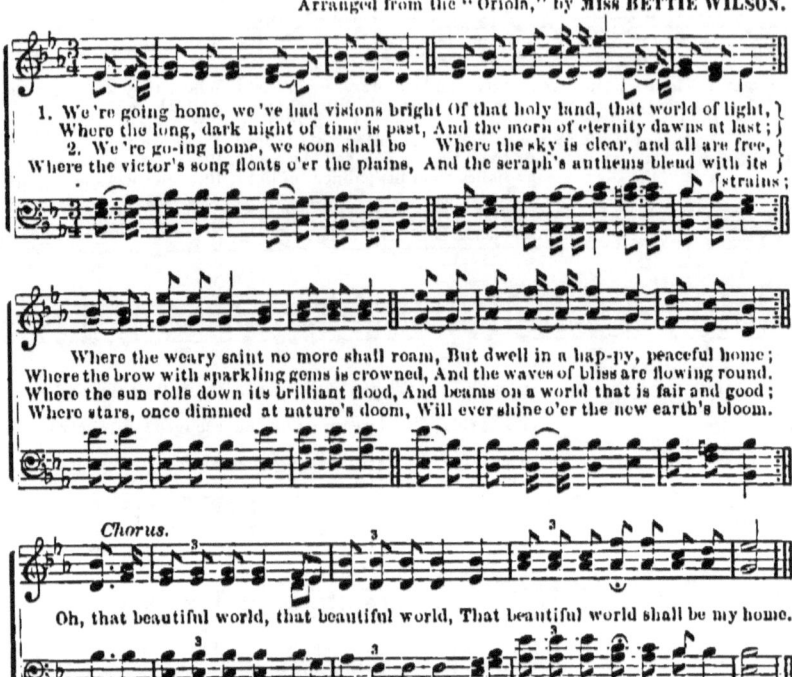

1. We're going home, we've had visions bright Of that holy land, that world of light,
Where the long, dark night of time is past, And the morn of eternity dawns at last;
2. We're go-ing home, we soon shall be Where the sky is clear, and all are free,
Where the victor's song floats o'er the plains, And the seraph's anthems blend with its strains;

Where the weary saint no more shall roam, But dwell in a hap-py, peaceful home;
Where the brow with sparkling gems is crowned, And the waves of bliss are flowing round.
Where the sun rolls down its brilliant flood, And beams on a world that is fair and good;
Where stars, once dimmed at nature's doom, Will ever shine o'er the new earth's bloom.

Chorus.
Oh, that beautiful world, that beautiful world, That beautiful world shall be my home.

786 *That beautiful world.* (1161)

3 'Mid the ransomed throng, 'mid the seas of bliss,
'Mid the holy city's gorgeousness;
'Mid the verdant plains, 'mid angels' cheer,
'Mid the saints that round the throne appear;
Where the conqueror's song, as it sounds afar,
Is wafted on the ambrosial air;
Through endless years we then shall prove
The worth of a Savior's matchless love.
Oh, that beautiful world! that beautiful world, etc.

787 *Sing to me of heaven,* Key G Minor. (1134)

1 I love to think of heaven,
 Where white-robed angels are,
Where many a friend is gathered, safe
 From fear, and toil, and care.

2 I love to think of heaven,
 Where my Redeemer reigns,
Where rapturous songs of triumph rise,
 In endless, joyous strains.

3 I love to think of heaven,
 The saints' eternal home,
Where palms, and robes, and crowns ne'er fade,
 And all our joys are one.

4 I love to think of heaven,
 The greetings there we'll meet,
The harps—the songs forever ours—
 The walks—the golden streets.

HOME—EVENING HYMNS.

OAKLAND. 7, 7, 7, 7, 7, 6, or 7s, 6 lines. (1188) SOLON WILDER.

788
1. Jesus, Sun of Righteousness, Brightest beam of love divine,
With the early morning rays Do thou on our darkness shine,
And dispel with purest light All our night, all our night.

2. Like the sun's reviving ray, May thy love with tender glow,
All our coldness melt away, Warm and cheer us forth to go,
Gladly serve thee and obey All the day, all the day.

3. Thou, our only Life and Guide! Never leave us nor forsake;
In thy light may we abide, Till th' eternal morning break,
Moving on to Zion's hill, Homeward still, homeward still.

OZREM. S. M. I. B. WOODBURY, by per.

1. A sweetly solemn thought Comes to me o'er and o'er;
To-day I'm nearer to my home, Than e'er I've been before.

2. Nearer my Father's house, Where many mansions be,
And nearer to the great white throne, Nearer tho crystal sea.

3. Nearer the bound of life, Where falls my burden down;
Nearer to where I leave my cross, And where I gain my crown.

789 *Now is our salvation nearer, etc.* (1195)

4 Savior, confirm my trust,
Complete my faith in thee;
And let me feel as if I stood
Close on eternity;

5 Feel as if now my feet
Were slipping o'er the brink;
For I may now be nearer home,
Much nearer than I think.

AUTUMN. 8s & 7s.   LUDOVICH NICHOLSON.

1. Faint-ly flow, thou fall-ing riv-er, Like a dream that dies a-way;
Down to o-cean gli-ding ev-er, Keep thy calm, un-ruf-fled way:
D. S. To e-ter-ni-ty's dark o-cean, Burying all its treas-ure there.
Time, with such a si-lent mo-tion, Floats a-long on wing's of air,

790 . *Fleeting moments.* (1205)
2 Roses bloom, and then they wither;
  Cheeks are bright, then fade and die;
Shapes of life are wafted hither,
  Then, like visions, hurry by;
Quick as clouds at evening driven
  O'er the many-colored west,
Years are bearing us to heaven—
  Home of happiness and rest.

791 *Savior! breathe, etc.* (1202)
1 Savior! breathe an evening blessing.
  Ere repose our eyelids seal;
Sin and want, we come confessing;
  Thou canst save, and thou canst heal.
Though destruction walk around us,
  Though the arrows past us fly,
Angel-guards from thee surround us—
  We are safe, if thou art nigh.

2 Though the night be dark and dreary,
  Darkness can not hide from thee:
Thou art he who, never weary,
  Watcheth where thy people be.
Should swift death this night o'ertake us,
  And our couch become our tomb,
May the morn in heaven awake us,
  Clad in bright and deathless bloom.

792 *Psalm 126: 6.* (963)
1 He that goeth forth with weeping,
  Bearing precious seed in love,
Never tiring, never sleeping,
  Findeth mercy from above.
Soft descend the dews of heaven;
  Bright the rays celestial shine;
Precious fruits will thus be given,
  Through the influence all divine.

2 Sow thy seed; be never weary;
  Let no fears thy soul annoy;
Be the prospect ne'er so dreary,
  Thou shalt reap the fruits of joy.
Lo! the scene of verdure brightening,
  In the rising grain appear;
Look again, the fields are whitening,
  For the harvest-time is near.

793 *For old age.* (1229)
Gracious Source of every blessing!
  Guard our breast from anxious fears;
Let us, each thy care possessing,
  Sink into the vale of years.
All our hopes on thee reclining,
  Peace companion of our way,
May our sun, in smiles declining,
  Rise in everlasting day.

STOCKWELL. 8s & 7s. JONES.

1. Si - lent-ly the shades of eve - ning Gath-er round my low-ly door;
2. Oh! the lost, the un - for - got - ten, Though the world be oft for - got;

Si - lent - ly they bring be-fore me Fa - ces I shall see no more.
Oh! the shrouded and the lone - ly— In our hearts they per - ish not.

794   *While I was musing.*   (1204)

3 Living in the silent hours,
 Where our spirits only blend—
They, unlinked with earthly trouble;
 We, still hoping for its end.

4 How such holy memories cluster,
 Like the stars when storms are past;
Pointing up to that far heaven
 We may hope to gain at last!

795   *Abide with us.*   (1203)

1 Tarry with me, O my Savior,
 For the day is passing by!
See the shades of evening gather,
 And the night is drawing nigh.

2 Many friends were gathered round me,
 In the bright days of the past;
But the grave has closed above them,
 And I linger here at last.

3 Deeper, deeper grow the shadows;
 Paler now the glowing west;
Swift the night of death advances;
 Shall it be the night of rest?

4 Feeble, trembling, fainting, dying,
 Lord, I cast myself on thee;
Tarry with me through the darkness!
 While I sleep, still watch by me.

5 Tarry with me, O my Savior!
 Lay my head upon thy breast
Till the morning; then awake me—
 Morning of eternal rest!

796   *A child's prayer.*   (1207)

1 Jesus, tender Shepherd, hear me;
 Bless thy little lamb to-night;
Through the darkness be thou near me;
 Keep me safe till morning light.

2 All this day thy hand has led me,
 And I thank thee for thy care;
Thou hast clothed me, warmed me, fed me,
 Listen to my evening prayer!

3 May my sins be all forgiven;
 Bless the friends I love so well;
Take me, when I die, to heaven,
 Happy there with thee to dwell.

797   *From my youth up.*   (1218)

1 Lord, a little band, and lowly,
 We are come to sing to thee;
Thou art great, and high, and holy,
 Oh how solemn should we be!

2 Fill our hearts with thoughts of Jesus,
 And of heaven, where he is gone;
And let nothing ever please us
 He would grieve to look upon.

3 For we know the Lord of glory
 Always sees what children do,
And is writing now the story
 Of our thoughts and actions too.

4 Let our sins be all forgiven;
 Make us fear whate'er is wrong;
Lead us on our way to heaven,
 There to sing a nobler song.

799

I will sing of the mercies, etc. (1209)

2 From age to age unchanging, still the same,
All good thou art;
Hallowed forever be thy reverend name
In every heart!

3 When the glad morn upon the hills was
Thy smile was there; [spread,
Now as the darkness gathers overhead,
We feel thy care.

4 Night spreads her shade upon another day
Forever past;
So, o'er our faults, thy love, we humbly pray,
A veil may cast.

5 Silence and calm, o'er hearts by earth dis-
Now sweetly steal; [tressed,
So every fear that struggles in the breast
Shall faith conceal.

6 Thou, thro' the dark, wilt watch above our
With eye of love; [sleep,
And thou wilt wake us, when the sunbeams
The hills above. [leap

7 Oh, may each heart its gratitude express
As life expands,
And find the triumph of its happiness
In thy commands!

THE LAST BEAM. (1210)

800
1. Fading, still fad-ing, the last beam is shin-ing, Fa-ther in heav-en! the day is de-clin-ing. Safe-ty and in-no-cence flee with the light, Temp-ta-tion and dan-ger walk forth with the night; From the fall of the shade till the morning bells chime, Shield us from dan-ger, keep us from crime. Fa-ther, have mer-cy, Fa-ther, have mer-cy,

2. Fa-ther in heav-en! oh, hear when we call; Hear, for Christ's sake, who is Sav-ior of all; Fee-ble and fainting, we trust in thy might, In doubt-ing and dark-ness thy love be our light; Let us sleep on thy breast while the night ta-per burns, Wake in thy arms when morn-ing re-turns. Fa-ther, etc.

For 2d verse.
Fa-ther, have mer-cy, thro' Je-sus Christ our Lord. A-men.

SILOAM. C. M.

I. B. WOODBURY, by permission.

801 *By cool Siloam's shady rill.* (1211)

2 Lo! such the child, whose early feet
   The paths of peace have trod,
Whose secret heart, with influence sweet,
   Is upward drawn to God.
3 By cool Siloam's shady rill
   The lily must decay;
The rose that blooms beneath the hill,
   Must shortly fade away.

4 And soon, too soon, the wintry hour
   Of man's maturer age
Will shake the soul with sorrow's power,
   And stormy passions rage.
5 O thou who givest life and breath,
   We seek thy grace alone,
In childhood, manhood, age, and death,
   To keep us still thine own!

CAMBRIDGE. C. M. (1231)

802

(Concluded on p. 303.)

FLEE, AS A BIRD. (1316)

803
1. Flee, as a bird, to your moun-tain, Thou who art wea-ry of sin;
Go to the clear flowing foun-tain,
2. He will pro-tect thee for-ev-er, Wipe ev-ery sad, fall-ing tear;
He will for-sake thee, oh nev-er,.

Where you may wash and be clean! Fly, for th' a-ven-ger is near thee;
Sheltered so ten-der-ly there; Haste, then, the hours now are fly-ing,

Call, and the Sa-vior will hear thee, He on his bo-som will bear thee, Oh,
Spend not the moments in sigh-ing, Cease from your sorrow and cry-ing, The

thou who art wea-ry of sin, Oh, thou who art wea-ry of sin.
Sav-ior will wipe ev-ery tear, The Sav-ior will wipe ev-ery tear.

CAMBRIDGE. C. M. (*Concluded from p. 302.*)

1 With songs and honors sounding loud,
  Address the Lord on high;
  Over the heavens he spreads his cloud,
  And waters veil the sky.

2 He sends his showers of blessings down,
  To cheer the plains below;
  He makes the grass the mountains crown,
  And corn in valleys grow.

3 His steady counsels change the face
  Of the declining year;
  He bids the sun cut short his race,
  And wintry days appear.

4 His hoary frost, his fleecy snow,
  Descend and clothe the ground;
  The liquid streams forbear to flow,
  In icy fetters bound.

5 He sends his word, and melts the snow,
  The fields no longer mourn;
  He calls the warmer gales to blow,
  And bids the spring return.

6 The changing wind, the flying cloud,
  Obey his mighty word;
  With songs and honors sounding loud,
  Praise ye the sovereign Lord.

HOME.

SWEET STORY. 11s & 8s.

1. I think when I read that sweet story of old, When Jesus was here among men, How he called little children as lambs to his fold, I should like to have been with them then.
2. I wish that his hands had been placed on my head, That his arm had been thrown around me, And that I might have seen his kind look when he said, "Let the little ones come unto me."

804 *I think when I read, etc.* (1220)

3 Yet still to his footstool in prayer I may go,
And ask for a share in his love;
And if I thus earnestly seek him below,
I shall see him and hear him above—

4 In that beautiful place he is gone to prepare
For all who are washed and forgiven,
And many dear children are gathering there—
"For of such is the kingdom of heaven."

5 But thousands and thousands who wander
Never heard of that heavenly home; [and fall,
I should like them to know there is room for
them all,
And that Jesus has bid them to come.

6 I long for the joy of that glorious time,
The sweetest, and brightest, and best,
When the dear little children of every clime
Shall crowd to his arms and be blessed.

FAREWELL HYMN. 6s, 7s & 4s. (New.) (1283)   J. ZUNDEL.

Rather slow.

805
1. E-ter-nal Lord! whose power Can calm the heaving ocean; Exalted thou, Yet gracious bow; Accept our warm devotion,
2. For thee, our all we leave, Nor drop a tear of sadness; As on we glide, Be thou our guide, And fill our hearts with gladness,
3. We go 'mid pagan gloom To spread the truth victorious; Thy blessing send, Thy word attend, And make its triumph glorious,

ABIDE WITH ME. 10s.

English.

1. Abide with me! fast falls the eventide; The darkness thickens; Lord, with me abide! When other helpers fail, and comforts flee, Help of the helpless! oh, abide with me!

807   *Abide with me.*   (1227)

2 Swift to its close ebbs out life's little day;
Earth's joys grow dim, its glories pass away;
Change and decay in all around I see;
O thou! who changest not, abide with me.

3 I need thy presence every passing hour;
What but thy grace can foil the tempter's power?
Who like thyself my guide and stay can be?
Through cloud and sunshine, oh abide with me!

4 Hold thou thy cross before my closing eyes;
Shine through the gloom, and point me to the skies;
Heaven's morning breaks, and earth's vain shadows flee;
In life, in death, O Lord! abide with me.

WINCHESTER. L. M. (1302)

Dr. CROFT.

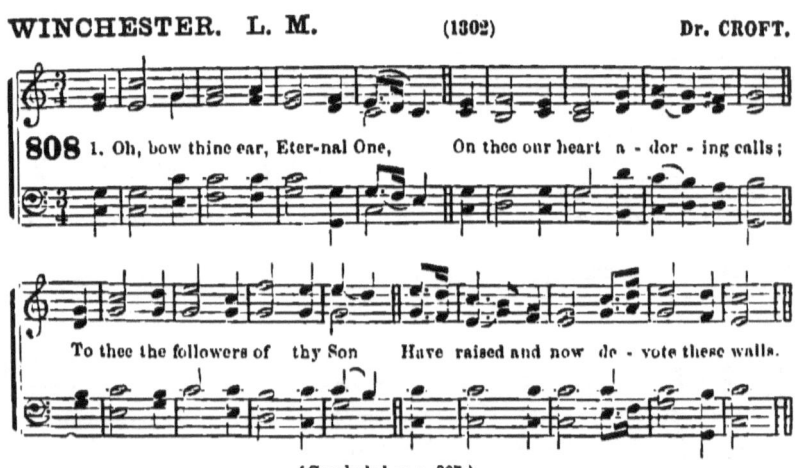

808 1. Oh, bow thine ear, Eter-nal One, On thee our heart a-dor-ing calls; To thee the followers of thy Son Have raised and now de-vote these walls.

(Concluded on p. 307.)

SHOUT THE TIDINGS. ✶

Arranged by J. P. POWELL.

1. Shout the ti-dings of sal-va-tion, To the a-ged and the young;
2. Shout the ti-dings of sal-va-tion, O'er the prai-ries of the West;

Till the pre-cious in-vi-ta-tion Wa-ken ev-ery heart and tongue.
Till each gath'ring congre-ga-tion, With the gos-pel sound is blest.

Chorus.
Send the sound The earth around, From the rising to the set-ting of the sun,
Till each gathering crowd, Shall proclaim a-loud, The glo-rious work is done.

809   *Shout the tidings of salvation.*   (1276)

3 Shout the tidings of salvation,
  Mingling with the ocean's roar,
Till the ships of every nation
  Bear the news from shore to shore.

4 Shout the tidings of salvation
  O'er the islands of the sea,
Till, in humble adoration,
  All to Christ shall bow the knee.

WINCHESTER. L. M. (*Concluded from p. 306.*)

2 Here let thy holy days be kept;
  And be this place to worship given,
Like that bright spot where Jacob slept,
  The house of God, the gate of heaven.

3 Here may thine honor dwell; and here,
  As incense, let thy children's prayer,
From contrite hearts and lips sincere,
  Rise on the still and holy air.

4 Here be thy praise devoutly sung;
  Here let thy truth beam forth to save,
As when, of old, thy Spirit hung,
  On wings of light, o'er Jordan's wave.

5 And when the lips, that with thy name
  Are vocal now, to dust shall turn,
On others may devotion's flame
  Be kindled here, and purely burn!

ZANESVILLE. C. M.

1. E-ter-nal Source of life and light! Su-preme-ly good and wise! To thee we bring our grate-ful vows, To thee lift up our eyes.

810 *Prayer for divine direction.* (730)

2 Our dark and erring minds illume
With truth's celestal rays;
Inspire our hearts with sacred love,
And tune our lips to praise.

3 Safely conduct us, by thy grace,
Through life's perplexing road;
And place us, when that journey's o'er,
At thy right hand, O God!

PAXAN. 7s, 6s & 4s.   C. E. PAX.

1. Come, come, come to the Sa-vior, Rich, rich mer-cy re-ceive;
Here, here, you will find par-don, Christ, Christ calls thee to come;
2. Come, come la-den and wea-ry,
Leave, leave paths dark and drea-ry,

Jesus from sin will relieve; Come, come, come, come, Come to the Savior and live.
Cease from the Savior to roam; Come, come, come, come, Jesus will guide thee safe home.

811 *Come.* (324)

3 Come—come seek his salvation,
Now—now hear and obey;
Hark—hark the sweet invitation,
Angels invite you away;
Come—come—come—come,
Sinner, believe and obey.

4 Hark—hark, angels are singing,
Love—love—love is their theme;
Peace—peace joyfully bringing,
Mercy from God the Supreme:
Come—come—come—come,
Jesus is rich to redeem.

ELTHAM. 7s, Double.
Dr. L. MASON.

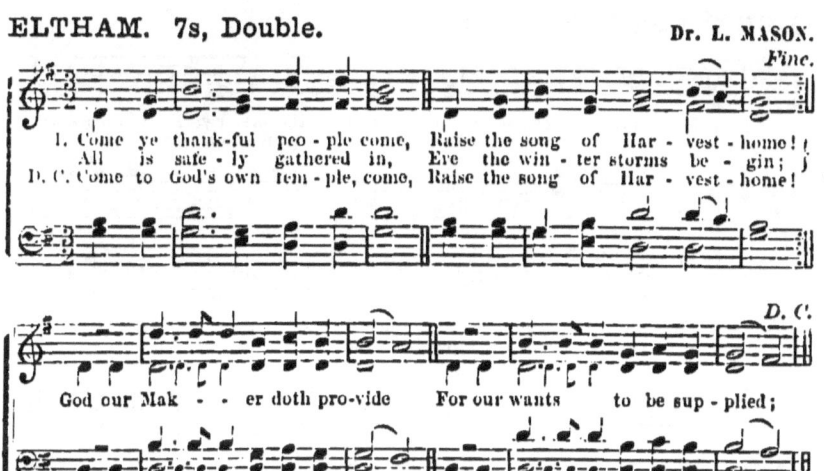

1. Come ye thankful people come,
   Raise the song of Harvest-home!
   All is safely gathered in,
   Ere the winter storms begin;
   God our Maker doth provide
   For our wants to be supplied;
   Come to God's own temple, come,
   Raise the song of Harvest-home!

812 *Harvest-Home.* (1236)

2 We ourselves are God's own field,
Fruit unto his praise to yield;
Wheat and tares together sown,
Unto joy our sorrow grown:
First the blade, and then the ear,
Then the full corn shall appear:
Lord of harvest, grant that we
Wholesome grain and pure may be!

3 For the Lord our God shall come,
And shall take his harvest home!
From his field shall purge away
All that doth offend, that day:
Give his angels charge at last
In the fires the tares to cast,
But the fruitful ears to store
In his garner evermore.

4 Then, thou Church triumphant, come,
Raise the song of Harvest-home!
All are safely gathered in,
Free from sorrow, free from sin;
There forever, purified,
In God's garner to abide;
Come, ten thousand angels, come,
Raise the glorious Harvest-home!

813 *Praise for deliverance and peace.* (1247)

1 Peace! the welcome sound proclaim;
Dwell with rapture on the theme;
Loud, still louder swell the strain;
Peace on earth, good-will to men!

Breezes, whispering soft and low,
Gently murmur as ye blow,
Now, when war and discord cease,
Praises to the God of peace.

2 Ocean's billows, far and wide,
Rolling in majestic pride!
Loud, still louder swell the strain;
Peace on earth, good-will to men!
Vocal songsters of the grove,
Sweetly chant in notes of love,
Now, when war and discord cease,
Praises to the God of peace.

814 *Guide us, Lord.* (745)

1 Guide us, Lord, while, hand in hand,
Journeying toward the better land;
Foes we know are to be met,
Snares the pilgrim's path beset;
Clouds upon the valley rest,
Rough and dark the mountain's breast;
And our home can not be gained,
Save through trials well sustained.

2 Guide us while we onward move,
Linked in closest bonds of love,
Striving for the holy mind.
And the soul from sense refined;
That when life no longer burns,
And the dust to dust returns,
With the strength which thou hast given,
We may rise to thee and heaven.

BENEVENTO. 7s, Double.

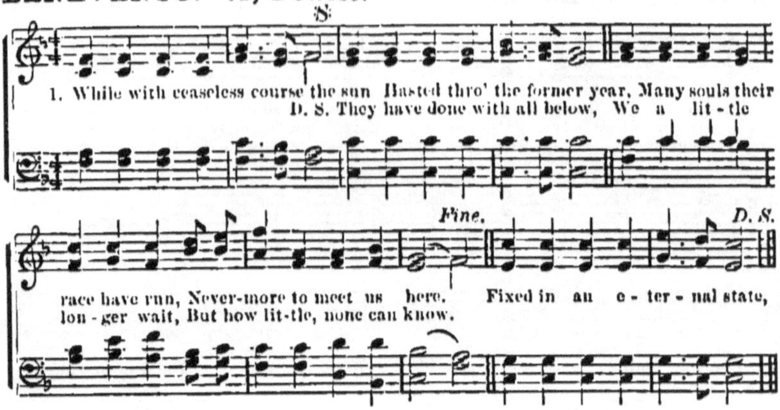

1. While with ceaseless course the sun Hasted thro' the former year, Many souls their race have run, Never-more to meet us here. Fixed in an e-ter-nal state, They have done with all below, We a lit-tle lon-ger wait, But how lit-tle, none can know.

815   *All below is but a dream.*   (1243)

2 As the winged arrow flies
Speedily the mark to find ;
As the lightning from the skies
Darts, and leaves no trace behind—
Swiftly thus our fleeting days
Bear us down life's rapid stream ;
Upward, Lord, our spirits raise,
All below is but a dream.

3 Thanks for mercies past receive,
Pardon of our sins renew ;
Teach us henceforth how to live,
With eternity in view ;
Bless thy word to old and young,
Fill us with a Savior's love ;
When our life's short race is run,
May we dwell with thee above.

WATCHWORD. C. H. M.   Dr. T. HASTINGS.

1. Go, watch and pray! thou canst not tell How near thine hour may be;
Thou canst not know how soon the bell May toll its notes for thee.
2. Fond youth, while free from blight-ing care, Does thy firm pulse beat high?
Do hope's glad vis-ions, bright and fair, Di-late be-fore thine eye?

Death's countless snares beset thy way ; Frail child of dust, go watch and pray.
Soon these must change, must pass away ; Frail child of dust, go watch and pray.

816   *Watch and pray.*   (1224)

3 Thou aged man, life's wintry storm
Hath seared thy vernal bloom ;
With trembling limbs, and wasting form,
Thou 'rt bending o'er the tomb ;
And can vain hope lead thee astray ?
Go, weary pilgrim, watch and pray.

4 Ambition, stop thy panting breath ;
Pride, sink thy lifted eye !
Behold the caverns, dark with death,
Before you open lie !
The heavenly warning now obey ;
Ye sons of pride, go watch and pray.

817 *Come, let us anew.* (1242)

2 Our life is a dream;
Our time, as a stream,
Glides swiftly away,
And the fugitive moment refuses to stay:
The arrow is flown;
The moment is gone;
The millennial year
Rushes on to our view, and eternity's near.

3 Oh that each, in the day
Of his coming, may say,
"I have fought my way through;
I have finished the work thou didst give me to do;"
Oh that each from his Lord
May receive the glad word,
"Well and faithfully done;
Enter into my joy and sit down on my throne."

THANKSGIVING. 13s & 14s. (New.)   A. SQUIRE.

1. When spring unlocks the flowers to paint the laughing soil, When summer's balmy show-ers re-fresh the mower's toil; When win-ter binds in frost-y chains the fallow and the flood, In God the earth re-joic-eth still, and owns its Maker good.

820   *All thy works praise thee.*   (1238)

2 The birds that wake the morning, and those that love the shade;
The winds that sweep the mountain, or lull the drowsy glade;
The sun that from his amber bower rejoiceth on his way,
The moon and stars their Maker's name in silent pomp display.

3 Shall man, the lord of nature, expectant of the sky—
Shall man, alone unthankful, his little praise deny!
No; let the year forsake his course, the seasons cease to be,
Thee, Father, must we always love—Creator! honor thee.

4 The flowers of spring may wither, the hope of summer fade,
The autumn droop in winter, the bird forsake the shade;
The winds be lulled—the sun and moon forget their old decree;
But we, in nature's latest hour, O Lord, will cling to thee!

I COME TO THEE. P. M. (*Concluded from p. 312.*)

4 Father! my soul would be
Pure as the drops of eve's unsullied dew—
And as the stars whose nightly course is true,
So would I be to thee.

5 Not for myself alone
Would I the blessings of thy love implore;
But for each penitent the wide earth o'er,
Whom thou hast called thine own.

6 And for my heart's best friends.
Whose steadfast kindness o'er my painful years
Has watched, to soothe affliction's griefs and tears,
My warmest prayer ascends.

7 And now, O Father! take
The heart I cast with humble faith on thee,
And cleanse its depths from each impurity,
For my Redeemer's sake.

GOD SPEED THE RIGHT. P. M.

From the German.

1. Now to heaven our prayer ascending, God speed the right!
In a no-ble cause ex-tend-ing, God speed the right!
Be their zeal in heaven recorded, With success on earth rewarded; God speed the right, God speed the right!

2. Be that prayer again re-peat-ed, God speed the right!
Ne'er despair-ing, tho' de-feat-ed, God speed the right!
Like the good and great in story, If they fail, they fail with glory; God speed the right, God speed the right!

821 *God speed the right!* (1278)

3 Patient, firm, and persevering,
God speed the right!
Ne'er the event or danger fearing,
God speed the right!
Pains, nor toils, nor trials heeding,
And in heaven's own time succeeding;
God speed the right!

4 Still their onward course pursuing,
God speed the right!
Every foe at length subduing,
God speed the right!
Truth thy cause, whate'er delay it,
There's no power on earth can stay it;
God speed the right!

AMERICA. 6s & 4s. (1251)

CAREY.

822
1. My country! 'tis of thee, Sweet land of liberty, Of thee I sing; Land where my fathers died; Land of the pilgrim's pride; From every mountain side Let freedom ring.
2. My native country! thee, Land of the no-ble free, Thy name I love; I love thy rocks and rills, Thy woods and templed hills; My heart with rapture thrills Like that above.

(*Concluded on p. 315.*)

ROCKVALE. 7s & 5s.

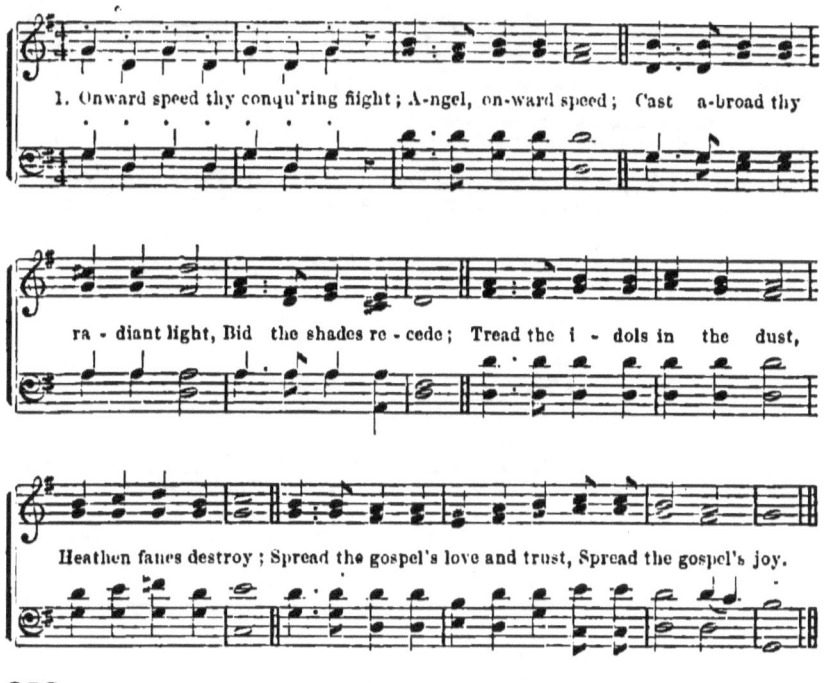

1. Onward speed thy conqu'ring flight; Angel, onward speed; Cast abroad thy radiant light, Bid the shades recede; Tread the idols in the dust, Heathen fanes destroy; Spread the gospel's love and trust, Spread the gospel's joy.

823   Rev. 14: 6.   (1286)

2 Onward speed thy conquering flight,
  Angel, onward haste!
Quickly on each mountain height
  Be thy standard placed;
Let thy blissful tidings float
  Far o'er vale and hill,
Till the sweetly-echoing note
  Every bosom thrill.

3 Onward speed thy conquering flight,
  Angel, onward fly!
Long has been the reign of night;
  Bring the morning nigh:

Unto thee earth's sufferers lift
  Their imploring wail;
Bear them heaven's holy gift,
  Ere their courage fail.

4 Onward speed thy conquering flight,
  Angel, onward speed!
Morning bursts upon our sight,
  Lo! the time decreed:
Now the Lord his kingdom takes,
  Thrones and empires fall;
Now the joyous song awakes,
  "God is All in All!"

AMERICA. (*Concluded from p. 314.*)

3 Let music swell the breeze,
And ring from all the trees
  Sweet freedom's song;
Let mortal tongues awake,
Let all that breathes partake,
Let rocks their silence break,
  The sound prolong.

4 Our father's God! to thee,
Author of liberty!
  To thee we sing;
Long may our land be bright
With freedom's holy light;
Protect us by thy might,
  Great God, our King.

MISSIONARY HYMN. 7s & 6s.

Dr. L. MASON.

1. From Greenland's icy mountains, From India's coral strand, Where Afric's sunny fountains Roll down their golden sand. From many an an-cient riv-er, From many a palmy plain, They call us to de-liv-er Their land from error's chain.

825 *Missionary hymn.* (1285)

2 What though the spicy breezes
   Blow soft o'er Ceylon's isle—
Though every prospect pleases,
   And only man is vile!
In vain with lavish kindness
   The gifts of God are strewn;
The heathen, in their blindness,
   Bow down to wood and stone.

3 Shall we, whose souls are lighted
   By wisdom from on high—
Shall we, to man benighted,
   The lamp of life deny?
Salvation! oh salvation!
   The joyful sound proclaim,
Till earth's remotest nation
   Has learned Messiah's name.

4 Waft—waft, you winds, his story,
   And you, yon waters, roll,
Till, like a sea of glory,
   It spreads from pole to pole;
Till, o'er our ransomed nature,
   The Lamb for sinners slain,
Redeemer, King, Creator,
   In bliss returns to reign.

826 *The fields are white already, etc.* (476)

1 Ho, reapers of life's harvest,
   Why stand with rusted blade,
Until the night draws round thee,
   And day begins to fade?
Why stand ye idle, waiting
   For reapers more to come?
The golden morn is passing,
   Why sit ye idle, dumb?

2 Thrust in your sharpened sickle,
   And gather in the grain;
The night is fast approaching,
   And soon will come again.
Thy Master calls for reapers;
   And shall he call in vain?
Shall sheaves lie there ungathered,
   And waste upon the plain?

3 Come down from hill and mountain,
   In morning's ruddy glow,
Nor wait until the dial
   Points to the noon below;
And come with the strong sinew,
   Nor faint in heat or cold;
And pause not till the evening
   Draws round its wealth of gold.

THE CHORUS OF ANGELS, No. 2. (New.) A. SQUIRE.

1. Hark! what joyful notes are swell-ing On the qui-et mid-night air!
'Tis the voice of an-gels tell-ing,
2. See all darkness dis-ap-pear-ing, As the Star be-gins to rise!
Sin and death stand trembling, fearing,

Jesus comes our sins to bear! Now the music, in its gladness, Breaks and swells and glides a-
As the light falls on their eyes; Now, again the earth rejoices, Satan's powerful kingdom

long! Now, earth, waking from her sadness, Joins the cho-rus of the song!
shakes, As from all the heavenly voic-es, Loud-er still the cho-rus breaks!

Chorus.
Glo-ry in the high-est heav-en! Peace on earth, good will to man!

CHORUS TO LAST VERSE.
Glo-ry in the high-est heav-en! Sound a-loud the joy-ful strain!

Let all praise to God be given, For re-demp-tion's glo-rious plan.

Glo-ry to the Lamb be giv'n, Who for sin-ners once was slain.

827   *Chorus of the angels.*   (134)

3 Rise and shine, Star of Salvation!
  Spread thy beams o'er all the earth,
Till each distant land and nation
  Owns and speaks thy matchless worth
Till all tongues, thy praises singing,
  Shall thy mighty wonders tell!
Till all heaven with joy is ringing,
  As our hearts the chorus swell!

4 When our days on earth are ended,
  And we rise to worlds above,
Then our songs shall all be blended
  In one song of pardoning love!
Then we'll tell the wondrous story,
  And our blessed Lord adore,
In our home of bliss and glory
  We shall sing for evermore!

MISCELLANEOUS. 323

GREENVILLE. 8s & 7s, Double. (316)

Fine.

840
1. Hear, O sin-ner! mer-cy hails you, Now with sweetest voice she calls;
Bids you haste to seek the Sav-ior, Ere the hand of jus-tice falls.
D. C. Trust in Je-sus, trust in Je-sus, 'Tis the voice of mer-cy calls.
2. Haste, O sin-ner! to the Sav-ior, Seek his mer-cy, while you may;
Soon the day of grace is o-ver, Soon your life will pass a-way.
D. C. Haste to Je-sus, haste to Je-sus, You must per-ish if you stay.

D. C.

Trust in Je-sus, trust in Je-sus, 'Tis the voice of mer-cy calls;
Haste to Je-sus, haste to Je-sus, You must per-ish if you stay;

I LOVE JESUS. (660) Arranged by T. E. PERKINS.

841 Oh thou Fount of ev'-ry bless-ing, Tune my heart to sing thy grace;
Streams of mer-cy, nev-er ceas-ing, Call for songs of loudest praise.

I love Je-sus, Hal-le-lu-jah! I love Je-sus, yes I do;

I do love Je-sus, he's my Sav-ior, Je-sus smiles and loves me too.

CHORUS. (To be sung after any suitable hymn, in Key A, A♭, or G.)

842 Oh how I love Jesus, Oh how I love Jesus, Oh how I love Jesus, Because he first loved me.

MISCELLANEOUS.

LEANDER. C. M., Double.

Go on, you pilgrims, while below, In the sure path of peace, Determined nothing else to know But Jesus and his grace. Observe your leader, follow him; He through this world has been Often reviled; but, like a lamb, Did ne'er revile again.

843   *Go on, you pilgrims.*   (486)

2 Oh, take the pattern he has given,
   And love your enemies;
And learn the only way to heaven
   Through self-denial lies.
Remember, you must watch and pray
   While journeying on the road,
Lest you should fall out by the way,
   And wound the cause of God.

3 Go on, rejoicing night and day;
   Your crown is yet before,
Defy the trials of the way,
   The storm will soon be o'er.
Soon we shall reach the promised land,
   With all the ransomed race,
And join with all the glorious band,
   To sing redeeming grace.

PILGRIM, WATCH AND PRAY.   T. E. PERKINS.

1. Softly on the breath of evening, Comes the tender sigh of day;
Lonely heart, by sorrow laden, ... 'Tis the time to pray.

Chorus.
Weary pilgrim, cease thy mourning, Weary pilgrim, cease thy mourning, Rest beyond forever.

844   *Watch and pray.*

2 'T is the hour when hallowed feelings
   Chase our doubts and fears away;
'T is the hour for calm devotion,
   Pilgrim watch and pray.

3 Tho' temptations dark oppress thee,
   Jesus guides thee on the way;
He will hear the lightest whisper,
   Pilgrim, watch and pray.

THE
CHRISTIAN HYMNAL.

SUPPLEMENT.

THERE IS A FOUNTAIN.

1
2 The dying thief rejoiced to see
That fountain in his day;
And there have I, as vile as he,
Washed all my sins away.

3 O Lamb of God! thy precious blood
Shall never lose its power,

Till all the ransomed Church of God
Be saved, to sin no more.

4 And when this lisping, stamm'ring
Lies silent in the grave, [tongue
Then in a nobler, sweeter song,
I'll sing thy power to save.

3 Tell me the story softly
   With earnest tones, and grave;
   Remember! I'm the sinner
   Whom Jesus came to save.
   Tell me that story always,
   If you would really be
   In any time of trouble,
   A comforter to me.
      Tell me, etc.

4 Tell me the same old story,
   When you have cause to fear
   That this world's empty glory
   Is costing me too dear.
   Yes, and when that world's glory
   Is dawning on my soul,
   Tell me the old, old story,
   "Christ Jesus makes thee whole."
      Tell me, etc.

3 I love to tell the story;
  'Tis pleasant to repeat
What seems, each time I tell it,
  More wonderfully sweet.
I love to tell the story;
  For some have never heard
The message of salvation
  From God's own holy word.
    I love to tell, etc.

4 I love to tell the story;
  For those who know it best
Seem hungering and thirsting
  To hear it like the rest.
And when, in scenes of glory,
  I sing the new, new song,
'Twill be—the old, old story
  That I have loved so long.
    I love to tell, etc.

HOME OF THE SOUL.

PHILIP PHILLIPS. By per.

1. I will sing you a song of the beau-ti-ful land, The far-a-way home of the soul, Where no storms ev-er beat on the glit-ter-ing strand, While the years of e-ter-ni-ty roll, While the years of e-ter-ni-ty roll; Where no storms ev-er beat on the glit-ter-ing strand, While the years of e-ter-ni-ty roll.

2. Oh, the home of the soul, in my vis-ions and dreams, Its bright jas-per walls I can see, Till I fan-cy but thin-ly the veil in-ter-venes Be-tween the fair cit-y and me, Be-tween the fair cit-y and me; Till I fan-cy but thin-ly the veil in-ter-venes Be-tween the fair cit-y and me.

3 There the great tree of life in its beauty doth grow,
    And the river of life floweth by;
For no death ever enters that city, you know,
    And nothing that maketh a lie.

4 That unchangeable home is for you and for me,
    Where Jesus of Nazareth stands;
The King of all kingdoms forever is he,
    And he holdeth our crowns in his hands.

5 Oh, how sweet it will be in that beautiful land,
    So free from all sorrow and pain!
**With songs on our lips and with harps in our hands,
    To meet one another again.**

SUPPLEMENT. 329

THE NINETY AND NINE.
IRA D. SANKEY, by per.

1. There were ninety and nine that safe-ly lay In the shel-ter of the fold, But one was out on the hills a-way, Far off from the gates of gold— A-way on the mount-ains wild and bare, A-way from the tender Shepherd's care, Away from the tender Shepherd's care.

2. "Lord, thou hast here thy ninety and nine; Are they not e-nough for thee?" But the Shepherd made an-swer: "This of mine Has wan-dered a-way from me; And although the road be rough and steep, I go to the desert to find my sheep, I go to the desert to find my sheep.

3 But none of the ransomed ever knew
How deep were the waters crossed;
Nor how dark was the night that the Lord passed through,
Ere he found his sheep that was lost;
Out in the desert he heard its cry—
'Twas helpless and sick, and ready to die.

4 And all through the mountains, thunder-riven,
And up from the rocky steep,
There rose a cry to the gate of heaven,
"Rejoice! I have found my sheep!"
And the angels echoed around the throne,
"Rejoice, for the Lord brings back his own."

DOVER. S. M.
English.

1. Great is the Lord our God,
   And let his praise be great;
He makes the churches his abode,
   His most delightful seat.

The Lord is great in Zion. (452)

2 These temples of his grace,
   How beautiful they stand!
The honors of our native place,
   And bulwarks of our land.

3 In Zion God is known,
   A refuge in distress;
How bright has his salvation shone,
   Through all her palaces!

SUPPLEMENT. 331

SWEET BY AND BY. Concluded.

meet on that beau-ti-ful shore, by and by! In the sweet by and by,
sing on that beau-ti-ful shore, by and by! In the sweet by and by,
praise on that beau-ti-ful shore, by and by! In the sweet by and by,

by and by,
In the sweet by and by, We shall meet on that beau-ti-ful shore.
In the sweet by and by, We shall sing on that beau-ti-ful shore.
In the sweet by and by, We shall praise on that beau-ti-ful shore.

ALMOST PERSUADED.*

P. P. BLISS.

1. "Al-most per-sua-ded" now to be-lieve; "Al-most per-sua-ded"
Christ to re-ceive. Seems now some soul to say, "Go, spir-it,
go thy way, Some more con-ven-ient day On thee I'll call."

2 "Almost persuaded," come, come to-day;
"Almost persuaded," turn not away.
Jesus invites you here,
Angels are ling'ring near,
Prayers rise from hearts so dear;
O wand'rer, come!

3 "Almost persuaded," harvest is past;
"Almost persuaded," doom comes at last!
"Almost" can not avail;
"Almost" is but to fail!
Sad, sad that bitter wail—
"Almost, *but lost!*"

* By permission of JOHN CHURCH & Co.

SUPPLEMENT.

WE SHALL KNOW. Concluded.

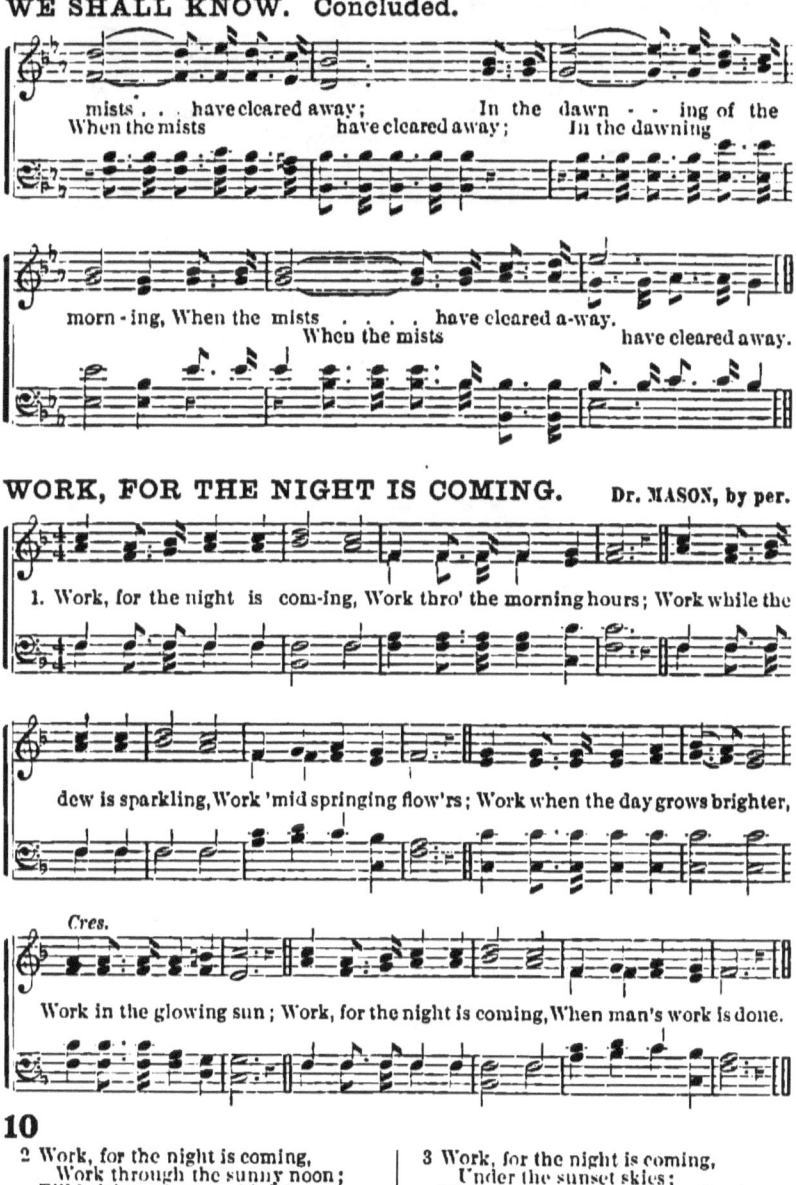

mists... have cleared away; In the dawn - - ing of the
When the mists have cleared away; In the dawning

morn - ing, When the mists .... have cleared a-way.
When the mists have cleared away.

WORK, FOR THE NIGHT IS COMING. Dr. MASON, by per.

1. Work, for the night is com-ing, Work thro' the morning hours; Work while the dew is sparkling, Work 'mid springing flow'rs; Work when the day grows brighter,

Cres.

Work in the glowing sun; Work, for the night is coming, When man's work is done.

10

2 Work, for the night is coming,
Work through the sunny noon;
Fill brightest hours with labor,
Rest comes sure and soon.
Give every flying minute
Something to keep in store;
Work, for the night is coming,
When man works no more.

3 Work, for the night is coming,
Under the sunset skies;
While their bright tints are glowing,
Work, for daylight flies.
Work till the last beam fadeth,
Fadeth to shine no more;
Work, while the night is dark'ning,
When man's work is o'er.

11

2 Your lofty themes, ye mortals bring,
In songs of praise divinely sing;
Salvation free, aloud proclaim,
And shout for joy the Savior's name.
    From all that dwell, etc.

3 In every land begin the song,
To every land the strains belong;
In cheerful sounds all voices raise,
And fill the world with loudest praise.
    From all that dwell, etc.

CREATION. L. M.
HAYDN.

1. Servants of God! in joyful lays, Sing ye the Lord Jehovah's praise; His glorious Name let all adore, From age to age, for evermore: His glorious Name let all adore, From age to age, for evermore.

12 *The glories of Jehovah.*

2 Who is like God? so great, so high,
He bows himself to view the sky;
And yet, with condescending grace,
Looks down upon the human race.

3 He hears the uncomplaining moan
Of those who sit and weep alone;
He lifts the mourner from the dust;
In him the poor may safely trust.

4 Oh then, aloud, in joyful lays,
Sing to the Lord Jehovah's praise;
His saving Name let all adore,
From age to age, for evermore.

SHAWMUT. S. M.

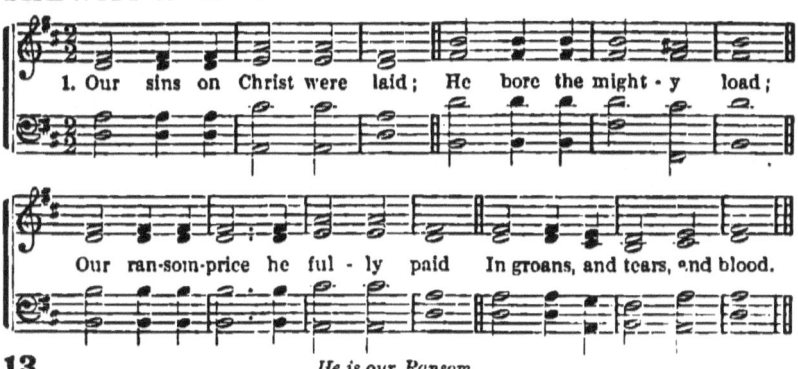

1. Our sins on Christ were laid; He bore the mighty load; Our ransom-price he fully paid In groans, and tears, and blood.

13 *He is our Ransom.*

2 To save a world he dies;
Sinners, behold the Lamb!
To him lift up your longing eyes;
Seek mercy in his name.

3 Jesus, we look to thee;—
Where else can sinners go?
Thy boundless love hath set us free
From wretchedness and woe.

SUPPLEMENT.

WAITING.

1. "A lit-tle while," our Lord shall come, And we shall wan-der here no more;
2. "A lit-tle while," he'll come again! Let us the precious hours re-deem;

He'll take us to our Fa-ther's home, Where he for us hath gone be-fore,
Our on - ly grief to give him pain, Our joy to serve and fol-low him;

To dwell with him, to see his face, And sing the glo - ries of his grace.
Watching and read-y may we be, As those who long their Lord to see.

14

3 "A little while," 'twill soon be past,
 Why should we shun the shame and
 Oh, let us in his footsteps haste, [cross?
 Counting for him all else but loss!
 Oh, how will recompense his smile,
 The sufferings of this "little while."

4 "A little while"—come, Savior, come!
 For thee thy Bride has tarried long;
 Take thy poor wearied pilgrims home,
 To sing the new eternal song,
 To sing thy glory, and to be
 In every thing conformed to thee.

LISBON. S. M.   DANIEL READ.
Glowing.

1. Welcome, sweet day of rest, That saw the Lord arise; Welcome to this reviving breast,

And these rejoicing eyes; Welcome to this reviving breast, And these rejoicing eyes.

15   *Welcome, sweet day of rest.*   (626)

2 The King himself comes near,
 And feasts his saints to-day;
 Here we may sit, and see him here,
 And love, and praise, and pray.

3 My willing soul would stay
 In such a frame as this,
 And sit and sing herself away
 To everlasting bliss.

SUPPLEMENT. 337

JESUS OF NAZARETH PASSETH BY.

1. What means this eager, anxious throng, Which moves with busy haste along—
These wondrous gath'rings day by day? What means this strange com - motion, say?

In ac-cents hushed the throng reply: "Je - sus of Naz - a - reth pass - eth by;"

In ac-cents hushed the throng re-ply: "Je - sus of Naz - a - reth pass - eth by."

16   *"He heard that it was Jesus of Nazareth."*

2 Ho! all ye heavy-laden, come!
Here's pardon, life, and pow'r, and home.
Ye wanderers from a Father's face,
Return, accept his proffered grace.
Ye tempted ones, there's refuge nigh;
"Jesus of Nazareth passeth by."

3 But if you still this call refuse,
And all his wondrous love abuse,
Soon will he sadly from you turn,
Your bitter prayer for pardon spurn.
"Too late! too late!" will be the cry—
"Jesus of Nazareth *has passed by.*"

WARWICK. C. M.   S. STANLEY.

1. Thou art our Shepherd, glo-rious God! Thy lit - tle flock be - hold,

And guide us by thy staff and rod, The chil-dren of thy fold.

17   *Thou leadest thy people like a flock.*   (729)

2 We praise thy name that we were brought
To this delightful place,
Where we are watched, and warned, and taught,
The children of thy grace.

3 May all our friends, thy servants here,
Meet with us all above,
And we and they in heaven appear,
The children of thy love.

RINDGE. C. M.

English Arr.

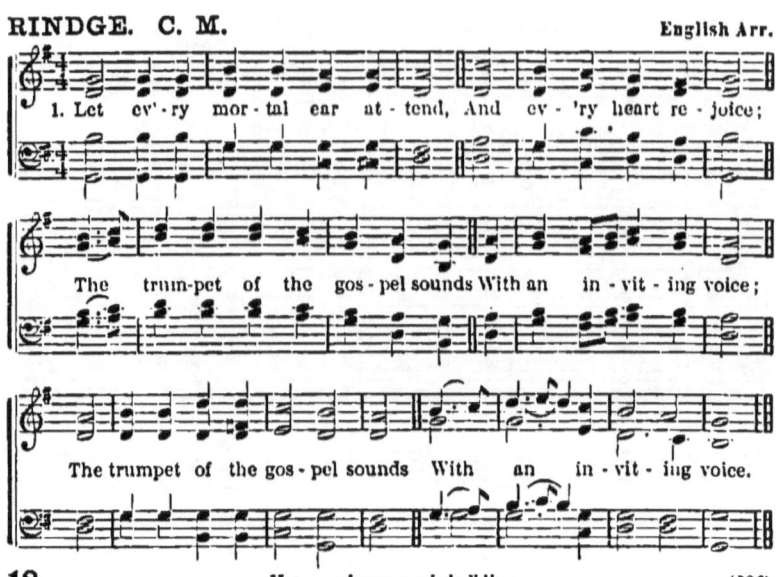

1. Let ev'-ry mor-tal ear at-tend, And ev-'ry heart re-joice;
The trum-pet of the gos-pel sounds With an in-vit-ing voice;
The trumpet of the gos-pel sounds With an in-vit-ing voice.

18 *Hear, and your soul shall live* (286)

2 Ho! all you hungry, starving souls,
Who feed upon the wind,
And vainly strive with earthly toys
To fill an empty mind;

3 Eternal wisdom has prepared
A soul-reviving feast,

And bids your longing appetites
The rich provision taste.

4 Ho! you that pant for living streams,
And pine away and die,
Here may you quench your raging thirst
With springs that never dry.

GIVE. C. M.

J. GRIGGS, Jr.

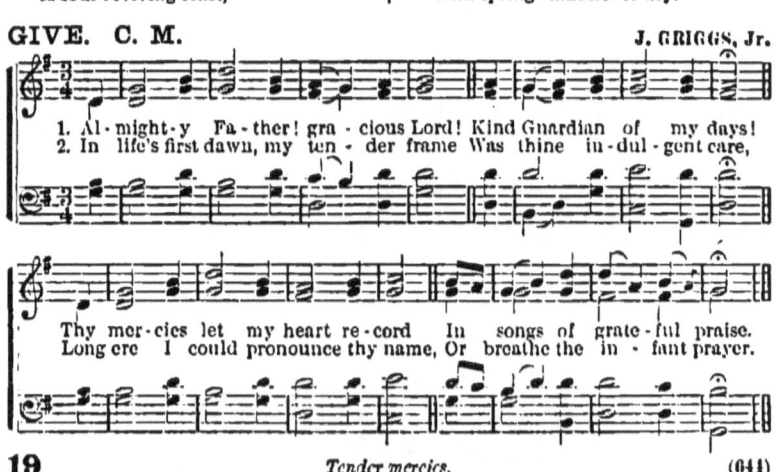

1. Al-might-y Fa-ther! gra-cious Lord! Kind Guardian of my days!
2. In life's first dawn, my ten-der frame Was thine in-dul-gent care,
Thy mer-cies let my heart re-cord In songs of grate-ful praise.
Long ere I could pronounce thy name, Or breathe the in-fant prayer.

19 *Tender mercies.* (644)

3 Each rolling year new favors brought
From thine exhaustless store;
But, ah! in vain my laboring thought
Would count thy mercies o'er.

4 Still I adore thee, gracious Lord!
For favors more divine –
That I have known thy sacred word,
Where all thy glories shine.

SUPPLEMENT.

ALIDA. C. M. Double.
D. B. THOMPSON.

1. How hap-py ev'-ry child of grace, Who knows his sins for-given!
This earth, he cries, is not my place; I seek my home in heaven:
D.S. The land of rest, the saints' de-light,—The heaven prepared for me.

A coun-try far from mor-tal sight, Yet oh, by faith, I see

20 Newness of life. (404)

2 Oh, what a blessed hope is ours,
While here on earth we stay;
We more than taste the heavenly powers,
And antedate that day:

We feel the resurrection near,—
Our life in Christ concealed,—
And with his glorious presence here,
Our earthen vessels filled.

GUIDE. 7s.
M. M. WELLS.

1. Bless-ed Sav-ior, faith-ful Guide, Ev-er near the Christian's side;
Gen-tly lead us by the hand, Pil-grims in a des-ert land.
D. S. Whisp'ring soft-ly, wand'rer, come! Fol-low me, I'll guide thee home.

Wea-ry souls, for-e'er re-joice, While they hear that sweetest voice;

21 Peace in believing.

2 Ever present, truest friend,
Ever near, thine aid to lend,
Leave us not to doubt and fear,
Groping on in darkness drear.
When the storms are raging sore,
Hearts grow faint and hopes give o'er;
Whisper softly, wanderer, come!
Follow me, I'll guide thee home.

3 When our days of toil shall cease,
Waiting still for sweet release,
Nothing left but heaven and prayer,
Wondering if our names are there;
Wading deep the dismal flood,
Pleading naught but Jesus' blood;
Whisper softly, wanderer, come!
Follow me, I'll guide thee home.

SUPPLEMENT.

STATE STREET. S. M. — WOODMAN.

1. Lord, in this sa-cred hour, With-in thy courts we bend,
And bless thy love, and own thy power, Our Fa-ther and our Friend.

22 *In his courts.*

1 Lord, in this sacred hour
  Within thy courts we bend,
And bless thy love, and own thy power,
  Our Father and our Friend.

2 But thou art not alone
  In courts by mortals trod;
Nor only is the day thine own
  When man draws near to God.

3 Thy temple is the arch
  Of yon unmeasured sky;
Thy Sabbath the stupendous march
  Of grand eternity.

4 Lord, may that holier day
  Dawn on thy servant's sight;
And purer worship may we pay
  In heaven's unclouded light.

SEASONS. L. M. — PLEYEL.

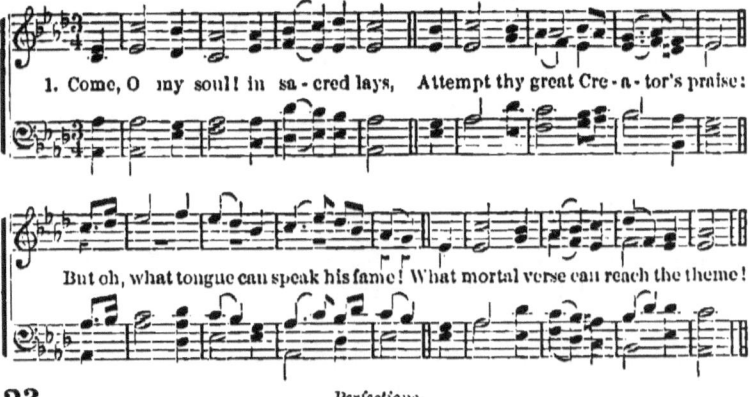

1. Come, O my soul! in sa-cred lays, Attempt thy great Cre-a-tor's praise:
But oh, what tongue can speak his fame! What mortal verse can reach the theme!

23 *Perfections.*

1 Come, O my soul! in sacred lays,
  Attempt thy great Creator's praise;
But oh, what tongue can speak his fame!
  What mortal verse can reach the theme!

2 Enthroned amid the radiant spheres,
  He glory, like a garment, wears;
To form a robe of light divine,
  Ten thousand suns around him shine.

3 In all our Maker's grand designs,
  Almighty power, with wisdom, shines;
His works, thro' all this wondrous frame,
  Declare the glory of his name.

4 Raised on devotion's lofty wing,
  Do thou, my soul, his glories sing;
And let his praise employ thy tongue,
  Till listening worlds shall join the song!

ST. ANN'S. C. M.
DR. CROFT.

1. The Lord our God is full of might, The winds obey his will;
He speaks, and in his heavenly height The rolling sun stands still.

24 *Power.*

2 Rebel, ye waves, and o'er the land
With threatening aspect roar;
The Lord uplifts his awful hand,
And chains you to the shore.

3 Howl, winds of night, your force combine;
Without his high behest
Ye shall not, in the mountain-pine,
Disturb the sparrow's nest.

4 His voice sublime is heard afar,
In distant peals it dies;
He yokes the whirlwind to his car,
And sweeps the howling skies.

5 Ye nations, bend—in reverence bend;
Ye monarchs, wait his nod,
And bid the choral song ascend
To celebrate our God.

WINCHESTER. L. M.
DR. CROFT.

1. Our Helper, God! we bless thy name, Whose love forever is the same;
The tokens of thy gracious care Open, and crown, and close the year.

25 *God our Helper.*

1 Our Helper, God! we bless thy name,
Whose love forever is the same;
The tokens of thy gracious care
Open, and crown, and close the year.

2 Amid ten thousand snares we stand,
Supported by thy guardian hand;
And see, when we review our ways,
Ten thousand monuments of praise.

3 Thus far thine arm has led us on;
Thus far we make thy mercy known;
And, while we tread this desert land,
New mercies shall new songs demand.

4 Our grateful souls, on Jordan's shore,
Shall raise one sacred pillar more;
Then bear, in thy bright courts above,
Inscriptions of immortal love.

EVENING HYMN. L. M.

TH. TALLIS.

1. Glo-ry to thee, my God, this night, For all the bless-ings of the light:
Keep me, oh, keep me, King of kings! Beneath the shad-ow of thy wings.

26   *Hide me under the shadow, etc.*   (1189)

2 Forgive me, Lord, for thy dear Son,
The ill which I this day have done;
That with the world, myself, and thee,
I, ere I sleep, at peace may be.

3 Teach me to live, that I may dread
The grave as little as my bed;
Teach me to die, that so I may
Rise glorious at thy Judgment-day.

4 Be thou my Guardian while I sleep,
Thy watchful station near me keep;
My heart with love celestial fill,
And guard me from th' approach of ill.

5 Lord, let my soul forever share
The bliss of thy paternal care;
'Tis heaven on earth, 'tis heaven above,
To see thy face, and sing thy love!

WILLINGTON. L. M.

GREATOREX COLL.

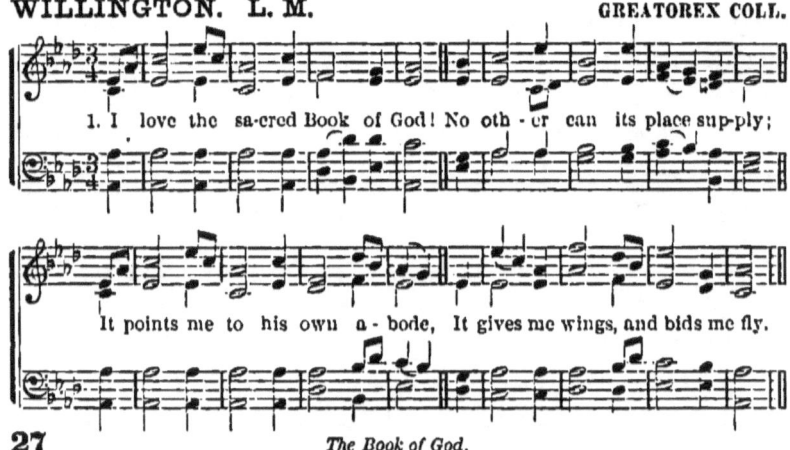

1. I love the sa-cred Book of God! No oth-er can its place sup-ply;
It points me to his own a-bode, It gives me wings, and bids me fly.

27   *The Book of God.*

2 Sweet Book! in thee my eyes discern
The very image of my Lord;
From thine instructive page I learn
The joys his presence will afford.

3 In thee I read my title clear
To mansions that will ne'er decay;—
Dear Lord, oh, when wilt thou appear,
And bear thy prisoner away!

4 While I am here, these leaves supply
His place, and tell me of his love;
I read with faith's discerning eye,
And gain a glimpse of joys above.

5 I know in them the Spirit breathes
To animate his people here;
Oh, may these truths prove life to all,
Till in his presence we appear!

BRADFORD. C. M.
HANDEL.

28   *A merciful and faithful High Priest.*   (233)

2 On earth he washed our guilt away
  By his atoning blood;
  Now he appears before the throne,
  And pleads our cause with God.

3 Clothed with our nature still, he knows
  The weakness of our frame,
  And how to shield us from the foes
  Which he himself o'ercame.

4 Nor time, nor distance e'er shall quench
  The fervor of his love;
  For us he died in kindness here,
  For us he lives above.

5 Oh, may we ne'er forget his grace,
  Nor blush to wear his name!
  Still may our hearts hold fast his faith,
  Our lips his praise proclaim!

PILESGROVE. L. M.
MITCHELL.

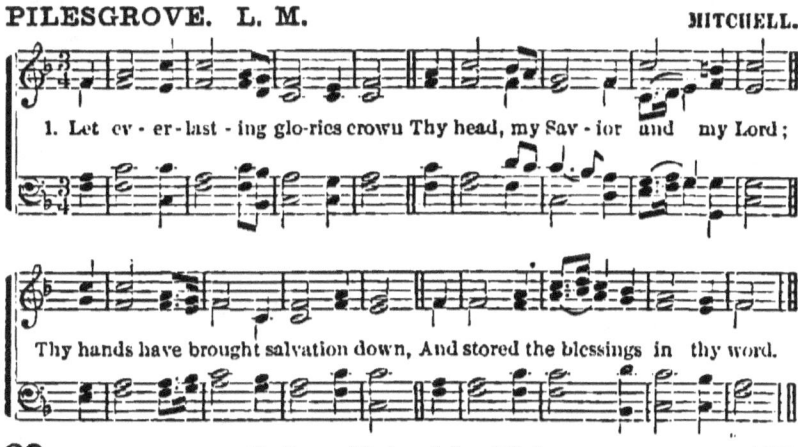

29   *Excellency of the knowledge of Christ.*   (221)

1 Let everlasting glories crown
  Thy head, my Savior and my Lord;
  Thy hands have brought salvation down,
  And stored the blessings in thy word.

2 In vain the trembling conscience seeks
  Some solid ground to rest upon;
  With long despair the spirit breaks,
  Till we apply to Christ alone.

3 How well thy blessed truths agree!
  How wise and holy thy commands!
  Thy promises, how firm they be!
  How firm our hope and comfort stands.

4 Should all the forms that men devise
  Assault my faith with treacherous art,
  I'd call them vanity and lies,
  And bind the gospel to my heart.

CROSS AND CROWN. C. M.

1. Must Jesus bear the cross alone, And all the world go free? No, there's a cross for ev'ry one, And there's a cross for me.

30

2 The consecrated cross I'll bear,
　Till death shall set me free,
And then go home my crown to wear,
　For there's a crown for me.

3 Upon the crystal pavement, down
　At Jesus' pierced feet,
Joyful, I'll cast my golden crown,
　And his dear name repeat.

4 And palms shall wave, and harps shall ring,
　Beneath heaven's arches high;
The Lord that lives, the ransomed sing,
　That lives no more to die.

5 Oh, precious cross! oh, glorious crown!
　Oh, resurrection day!
Ye angels, from the stars come down,
　And bear my soul away.

WOODSTOCK. C. M.
D. DUTTON.

1. Dear Father, to thy mercy-seat My soul for shelter flies; 'Tis here I find a safe retreat When storms and tempests rise.

31　　　　*Psalm* 145: 18.　　　(1309)

1 Dear Father, to thy mercy-seat
　My soul for shelter flies;
'Tis here I find a safe retreat
　When storms and tempests rise.

2 My cheerful hope can never die,
　If thou, my God, art near;
Thy grace can raise my comforts high,
　And banish every fear.

3 My great Protector, and my Lord!
　Thy constant aid impart;
Oh! let thy kind, thy gracious word
　Sustain my trembling heart.

4 Oh, never let my soul remove
　From this divine retreat;
Still let me trust thy power and love,
　And dwell beneath thy feet.

INDEX OF FIRST LINES.

No. of Hymn in Christian Hymn Book.	No. in this Work.	No. of Hymn in Christian Hymn Book.	No. in this Work.
1227 Abide with me	807	597 Behold the mountain of the Lord	462
347 A broken heart, my God	281	175 Behold the Savior of mankind	123
876 A charge to keep I have	615	444 Behold the sure foundation-stone	327
789 Acquaint thee, O mortal	518	118 Behold the woman's promised seed	68
828 A few more years shall roll	598	149 Behold where in a mortal form	101
933 After the toil	673	549 Benignant God of love	570
696 Again our earthly cares we leave	501	898 Be still, my heart	559
694 Again the Lord of light	500	675 Be thou exalted, O my God	522
1118 Ah, guilty sinner, ruined	747	840 Beyond the smiling	618
364 Ah, what avails my strife	267, 832	259 Beyond the starry skies	196
240 Alas! and did my Savior bleed	165	164 Beyond where Kedron's	109
872 Alas! what hourly dangers	642	307 Bleeding hearts, defiled by sin	229
203 All hail the power of Jesus' name	152	411 Blessed are the humble souls that	300
743 All ye nations, praise the Lord	785	741 Blest are the pure in heart	335
321 All you that are weary	245	488 Bless'd be the dear uniting love	361
496 All you that have confessed	647	495 Blest be the tie that binds	365
87 Almighty Father of mankind	48	679 Bless'd hour when mortal man retires	301
733 Almighty God, thy word	643	712 Blest is the hour when cares depart	476
1045 Almighty Maker of my frame	704	183 Bless'd morning, whose young	130
403 Amazing grace! how sweet the sound	286	406 Bless'd Savior, Friend divine	289
883 Am I a soldier of the cross	638	273 Blow ye the trumpet	198
166 Among the mountain trees	113	21 Book of grace and book of glory	256
365 And can I yet delay	266	895 Breast the wave	612
173 And did the holy and the just	122	954 Bright source of everlasting love	684
143 And is the gospel peace and love	99, 835	229 Bright was the guiding star	164
1133 And is there, Lord	711	283 Broad is the road	209
739 And let our bodies part	543	318 Burdened with guilt	241
1196 Another day is past	830	382 Buried beneath the yielding wave	284
189 Angels, roll the rock away	135	202 Burst, ye emerald gates	151
530 A parting hymn we sing	371	1211 By cool Siloam's shady rill	801
150 A pilgrim through this lonely world	100	855 By faith in Christ	636
564 Approach, my soul, the mercy-seat	420		
199 Arise, ye people, and adore	76	123 Calm on the listening ear of night	131
877 Arise, ye saints, arise	646	498 Children of the heavenly King	374
1288 Arm of the Lord, awake	455	322 Child of sin and sorrow	246
1032 As down in the sunless	404	602 Christian! see thou orient morning	471
1088 As flows the rapid river	610	934 Christian, the morn breaks	675
381 Ashamed of Christ! our souls disdain	280	1003 Christ leads me through	382
1028 Asleep in Jesus	700	190 Christ, the Lord, is risen to-day	134
176 As on the cross the Savior hung	121	372 Cling to the crucified	303
823 As the hart, with eager looks	305	265 Cling to the Mighty One	319
1040 As the sweet flower	702	927 Come, all ye saints of God	406
1195 A sweetly solemn thought	789	720 Come, Christian brethren, ere we	458
648 Awake and sing the song	503	324 Come, come, come to the Savior	811
434 Awake, my soul, to joyful	495	501 Come, dear friends; we are all	653
866 Awake, my soul, stretch every	640	670 Come, every pious heart	133
105 Awake, my tongue, thy tribute bring	60	1267 Come from the east with gifts	456
856 Awake, our souls	630	291 Come, humble sinner, in whose breast	217
630 Awake, ye saints	494	478 Come in, thou blessed of our God	354
518 Away from earth my spirit turns	310	1212 Come, let us anew	817
950 A weak and weary dove	674	206 Come, let us join our cheerful songs	153
		494 Come, let us join our friends	359
1157 Beautiful Zion, built above	768	618 Come, let us join with one	463
674 Before Jehovah's awful throne	521	824 Come, my Christian brethren	588
53 Begin, my soul, the lofty strain	27	598 Come, O thou mighty Savior	731
145 Behold! the blind their sight receive	259	666 Come, saints, let us join	517
194 Behold! the bright morning appears	142	1135 Come, sing to me of	743
236 Behold the glories of the Lamb	174	285 Come, sinners, to the gospel	210

345

INDEX OF FIRST LINES.

HYMN BOOK.	HYMNAL.
702 Come, sound his praise abroad	195
1319 Come to Calvary's holy mountain	15
292 Come to the ark	175
570 Come to the house of prayer	426
1228 Come unto me, when	440
281 Come, weary souls with sin distressed	211
701 Come, we that love the Lord	537
1236 Come, ye thankful people	812
586 Come, ye disconsolate	447
312 Come, you sinners, poor and needy	231
481 Come, you that love the Lord	355
230 Come, you that love the Savior's name	502
205 Crown his head with endless blessing	400
888 Dark and thorny is the desert	652
160 Dark was the night and	102
605 Daughter of Zion, awake	467
1117 Day of judgment, day of	742
1056 Dear as thou wast and	698
1054 Death can not make our souls	686
330 Delay not, delay not, O sinner	250
363 Desponding soul, oh cease thy	745
161 Did Christ o'er sinners weep	264
355 Didst thou, Lord Jesus, suffer shame	282
721 Dismiss us with thy blessing	461
973 Down the dark future	444
154 Draw near, ye weary	115
1075 Dropping down the troubled	714
698 Early, my God, without delay	531
396 Earth has a joy unknown in heaven	297
61 Earth with her ten thousand flowers	226
25 Ere mountains reared their forms	19
592 Eternal Lord, from land	453
1283 Eternal Lord, whose power	805
730 Eternal source of life and light	810
976 Every day bath toil	685
1210 Fading, still fading	800
1205 Faintly flow, thou	790
326 Fair shines the morning star	199
1073 Fallen on Zion's battle-field	712
459 Far down the ages now	331
1098 Far, far o'er hill and dale	724
709 Far from mortal cares retreating	341
977 Far from my thoughts	560
429 Far from these narrow scenes	315
749 Father, glory be to thee	140
908 Father, I know thy ways are just	425
584 Father, in thy mysterious presence	441
925 Father, oh hear me now	663
467 Father of mercies, bow thine ear	326
81 Father of mercies, God of love	45
10 Father of mercies, in thy word	7
671 Father of spirits, humbly bent	535
27 Father of spirits, nature's God	18
1209 Father Supreme, thou high	799
558 Father, whate'er of earthly bliss	416
869 Father, whene'er our	715
1316 Flee as a bird to your	803
267 Fling out the banner	192
873 Forever with the Lord	600
395 Forgiveness! 'tis a joyful sound	295
764 Fountain of light and living breath	184
1090 Friend after friend departs	114
718 From all that dwell below the skies	527
547 From every stormy wind	408
1255 From Greenland's icy	825
303 From the cross uplifted high	224
548 From the recesses of	450
139 From the regions of love, lo! an	94
1024 Full of trembling expectation	545
1175 Gently, Lord, oh gently lead us	449
817 Give me the wings of faith to rise	533
209 Give to the Lord thine heart	222
880 Give to the winds thy fears	619
747 Glorious in thy saints appear	83
460 Glorious things of thee are spoken	340

HYMN BOOK.	HYMNAL.
664 Glory, glory everlasting	623
698 Glory to God on high	520
734 Glory to God, who deigns	481
339 God calling yet; shall I	242
802 God doth not leave his own	576
60 God Eternal, Lord of all	689
268 God in the gospel of his Son	6
711 God is in his holy temple	549
991 God is in the loneliest spot	690
116 God is love; his mercy brightens	55
96 God is the fountain whence	59
442 God is the refuge of his saints	324
79 God moves in a mysterious way	47
412 God of my life, thy boundless grace	309
1174 God of my life, to thee	83
995 God of my life, to thee I call	718
897 God of our salvation	606
756 God of our salvation, hear us	625
1272 God of the prophet's power	562
7 God's law demands one living faith	5
486 Go on, you pilgrims, while below	843
162 Go to dark Gethsemane	225
1082 Go to the grave, in all thy glorious	719
1069 Go to thy rest, fair child	709
1094 Go to thy rest in peace	726
1221 Go watch and pray; thou canst not	816
579 Go when the morning shineth	496
405 Grace! 'tis a charming sound	293
394 Gracious Savior, we adore thee	551
1229 Gracious Source of every blessing	793
680 Great God, attend while Zion sings	526
40 Great God! thy penetrating eye	22
213 Great God! whose universal sway	159
1255 Great Maker of unnumbered worlds	733
269 Great was the day; the joy was great	193
115 Guide me, O thou great Jehovah	64
745 Guide us, Lord, while band in hand	814
257 Had I ten thousand gifts beside	104
1217 Hail, gracious, heavenly Prince	548
614 Hail, morning known among the	394
328 Hail, ransomed world! awake to	824
430 Hail, sweetest, dearest tie that binds	313
138 Hail the blest morn, when the great	92
628 Hail the day that saw him rise	188
136 Hail, thou long expected Jesus	140
608 Hail to the brightness of Zion's glad	469
218 Hail to the Prince of life and peace	69
924 Hallelujah! best and sweetest	624
1077 Happy soul, thy days are ended	546
441 Happy the church, thou sacred place	323
140 Hark! from the world on high	321
132 Hark, hark! the notes of joy	84
272 Hark how the gospel trumpet sounds	200
334 Hark, sinner, while God from on	252
663 Hark! ten thousand harps and voices	14
124 Hark the glad sound! the Savior	74
126 Hark! the herald angels sing	82
600 Hark, the song of jubilee	465
178 Hark, the voice of love and mercy	66
134 Hark! what joyful notes are	87, 827
135 Hark! what mean those holy voices	89
599 Hasten, Lord, the glorious time	137
306 Haste, O sinner! to be wise	228
276 Haste, traveler, haste! the night	204
1162 Have you heard, have you heard of	780
742 Head of the church triumphant	555
587 Hear, Father, hear our prayer	445
316 Hear, O sinner! mercy hails you	810
271 Hear the royal proclamation	201
172 He dies! the Friend of sinners dies	113
165 He knelt! the Savior knelt	111
768 He leadeth me! oh blessed thought	36
891 Here behold me as I cast me	626
859 Here I sink before thee lowly	403
544 Here, O my Lord, I see thee face to	313
829 Here, we are but staying pilgrims	602
68 He sendeth sun, he sendeth shower	37
969 He that goeth forth with weeping	792

INDEX OF FIRST LINES. 347

HYMN BOOK.	HYMNAL.
1138 High in yonder realms of light	763
20 Holy Bible! book divine	12
476 Ho! reapers of life's harvest	826
234 Hosanna! raise the pealing hymn	80
213 Hosanna to our conquering King	166
185 Hosanna to the Prince of light	129
270 How beauteous are their feet	197
141 How beauteous were the marks	97
1042 How blest are they whose transient	707
1039 How blest the righteous when he dies	701
479 How blest the sacred tie that binds	357
186 How calm and beautiful the morn	110
454 How charming is the place	332
792 How firm a foundation, ye saints of	438
287 How free and boundless is the grace	213
92 How gentle God's commands	116
1018 How gracious and how wise	367
408 How happy are they who their Savior	302
401 How happy every child of grace	287
402 How happy is the Christian's state	285
1051 How happy is the pilgrim's lot	746
588 How honored, how dear is that sacred	439
457 How honored is the place	336
831 How long, O Lord, our Savior	609, 833
23 How painfully pleasing the fond	16
627 How pleased and blest was I	31
515 How pleasing to behold and see	392
686 How pleasant, how divinely fair	528
9 How precious is the book divine	9
659 How shall I my Savior set forth	510
15 How shall the young secure their	11
1052 How short and hasty is our life	584
493 How sweet, how heavenly is the...358	837
111 How sweetly flowed the gospel sound	96
247 How sweet the name of Jesus sounds	172
638 How sweet the praise, how high	460
560 How sweet to be allowed to pray	417
548 How sweet to leave the world awhile	378
1015 How tender is thy hand	366
426 How vain is all beneath the skies	308
652 How various, and how new	294
393 Humble souls, who seek salvation	401
703 Hungry, and faint, and poor	540
965 Hush the loud cannon's roar	651
1154 I am a stranger here	765
837 I am weary of straying; oh fain	616
86 I can not always trace the way	432
1317 I come to thee to-night	819
926 I did thee wrong, my God	668
520 If human kindness meets return	360
439 If life's pleasures charm you	547
571 If 't is sweet to mingle where	270
1158 I hear thee speak of the better land	782
803 I know not it or dark or bright	565
219 I know that my Redeemer lives	160
72 I 'll praise my maker while I 've	41
8 I love the volume of thy word	42
453 I love thy kingdom, Lord	330
562 I love to steal awhile away	418
1134 I love to think of heaven	787
1146 I 'm but a stranger here	760
865 I 'm not ashamed to own my Lord.639	836
380 In all my Lord's appointed ways	281
1173 In all my ways, O God	607
1010 In every trouble sharp and strong	534
1109 In expectation sweet	736
119 In hymns of praise, Eternal God	70
524 In memory of the Savior's love	364
261 In seasons of grief, to my God I 'll	189
950 In silence of the voiceless night	717
1152 In that world of ancient story	603
1149 In the Christian's home in glory	771
713 In thy name, O Lord, assembling	550
543 I saw the cross of Jesus	126
1153 Is it a long way off	775
751 Israel's Shepherd, guide me, feed us	402
778 Israel the desert trod	563
120 It came upon the midnight clear	73

HYMN BOOK.	HYMNAL.
1220 I think, when I read that sweet story	814
533 It is finished, man of sorrows	208
798 I will not let thee go, thou help	571
836 I would not live always; I ask	614, 828
44 Jehovah reigns; he dwells in light	26
28 Jehovah reigns; his throne is high	735
821 Jerusalem, my glorious home	586
820 Jerusalem, my happy home	585, 834
373 Jesus, and shall it ever be	276
805 Jesus, guide, our way	317
541 Jesus has died for me	322
251 Jesus, I love thy charming name	173
923 Jesus, I my cross have taken	654, 839
242 Jesus, in thee our eyes behold	170
238 Jesus, in thy transporting name	167
529 Jesus invites his saints	370
390 Jesus, Lamb of God, for me	304
499 Jesus, Lord, we look to thee	274
262 Jesus, lover of my soul	187
375 Jesus, my all, to heaven is gone	838
209 Jesus shall reign where'er the sun	156
1188 Jesus, Sun of righteousness	788
1207 Jesus, tender Shepherd, hear me	796
220 Jesus, the Spring of joys divine	161
227 Jesus! the very thought is sweet	162
241 Jesus, thou art the sinner's friend	216
513 Jesus, thou joy of loving hearts	351
482 Jesus, thou Shepherd of the sheep	350
225 Jesus, thou Source of calm repose	182
156 Jesus wept! those tears are over	105
551 Jesus, where'er thy people meet	379
793 Joyfully, joyfully, onward I move	567
125 Joy to the world! the Lord is come	75
343 Just as I am, without one plea	240
755 Keep us, Lord! oh keep us ever	554
477 Kindred in Christ, for his dear sake	347
208 King Jesus, reign for evermore	155
1136 Know ye that better land	761
537 Lamb of God, whose bleeding love	238
16 Lamp of our feet, whereby we trace	10
842 Lead us, heavenly Father, lead us	622
205 Let earth, with every isle and sea	181
1248 Let every heart rejoice and sing	806
286 Let every mortal ear attend	212
651 Let every heart and tongue	601
823 Let me go: my soul is weary	593
497 Let party names no more	368
667 Let us awake our joys	519
1323 Let us sing the King Messiah	627
1055 Life is a span, a fleeting hour	697
284 Life is the time to serve the Lord	203
196 Lift up your heads, ye gates	144
197 Lift up your stately heads, ye doors	147
436 Like Noah's weary dove	334
315 Listen to the gospel telling	233
1104 Lo! he comes with clouds descending	743
1103 Lo! he cometh! countless trumpets	629
615 Long as I live, I 'll praise thy name	498
207 Look, ye saints, the sight is glorious	128
1218 Lord, a little band and lowly	797
35 Lord, all I am is known to thee	21
725 Lord, at this closing hour	373
523 Lord, at this table we behold	395
723 Lord, cause thy face on us to shine	530
754 Lord, dismiss us with thy blessing	552
397 Lord, I am thine, entirely thine	489
955 Lord, lead thou the way the Savior went	681
32 Lord, thou hast searched and seen me	25
708 Lord, we come before thee now	507
822 Lord, we expect a day	538
109 Lord, what is man? extremes how	61
732 Lord, when together here we meet	552
1121 Lo! round the throne a glorious	752
1112 Lo! the seal of death is breaking	741

348 INDEX OF FIRST LINES.

HYMN BOOK.	HYMNAL.
710 Love divine, all love excelling	514
367 Love for all I and can it be	272
1274 Love of God, all love excelling	235
1087 Lowly and solemn be	723
250 Majestic sweetness sits enthroned	171
95 Make channels for the streams of	683
192 Mary to the Savior's tomb	138
752 May the grace of Christ our Savior	515
361 Mercy alone can meet my case	288
516 'Mid scenes of confusion and	390
191 Morning breaks upon the tomb	136
121 Mortals awake, with angels join	77
889 Must Simon bear the cross alone	660
485 My Christian friends in bonds of love	356
1251 My country, 't is of thee	822
800 My days are gliding swiftly by	781
146 My dear Redeemer and my Lord	98
512 My faith looks up to thee	405
843 My feet are worn and weary with the	720
64 My God in whom are all the springs	34
581 My God, is any hour so sweet	431
900 My God, my father, while I	433
979 My God, my heart with love inflame	146
635 My God, my King, thy various praise	459
657 My gracious Redeemer, I love	509
1124 My heavenly home is bright and fair	754
921 My Jesus, as thou wilt	667
226 My prophet thou, my heavenly guide	183
838 My rest is in heaven, my home is not	361
249 My Savior, my almighty friend	163
781 My Shepherd's mighty aid	561
834 My spirit longs for thee	575
779 My spirit, on thy care	427
875 My soul, be on thy guard	644
691 My soul, how lovely is the place	499
95 My soul, repeat his praise	52
1006 My times of sorrow and of joy	383
928 Nearer, my God, to thee	669
536 Near the cross our station taking	397
163 Night with ebon pinion	112
65 No change of time shall ever	631
1092 No, no, it is not dying	725
1144 No seas again shall sever	613
1148 No shadows yonder	769
1160 No sickness there	779
531 Not all the blood of beasts	372
799 Now as long as here I roam	579
211 Now be my heart inspired to sing	158
683 Now begin the heavenly theme	506
440 Now I have found a friend	320
297 Now is the accepted time	220
298 Now is the day of grace	831
527 Now let each happy guest	369
235 Now let our cheerful eyes survey	169
806 Now let our souls on wings sublime	633
715 Now may the Lord, our Shepherd	529
1186 Now the shades of night are gone	691
1278 Now to heaven our prayer ascending	821
340 Now to the Lord who makes	491
93 Oh bless the Lord, my soul, let all	149
650 Oh bless the Lord, my soul, his	505
1302 Oh how thine ear, Eternal One	808
325 Oh come in life's gay morning	611
152 Oh could I speak the matchless worth	103
1134 Oh could our thoughts and wishes fly	587
280 Oh do not let the word depart	205
1289 O'er the gloomy hills of darkness	553
790 Oh eyes that are weary, and hearts	615
620 O Father, though the anxious fear	479
687 O Father, with protecting care	380
913 Oh for a closer walk with God	424
353 Oh for a faith that will not shrink	665
811 Oh for a heart to praise my God	421
1063 Oh for an overcoming faith	666

HYMN BOOK.	HYMNAL.
930 Oh for the peace that floweth as a	412
883 Oft in sorrow, oft in woe	580
38 O God, my heart is fully bent	604
73 O God of Bethel, by whose hand	28
521 O God, unseen yet ever near	580
508 Oh happy children, who follow Jesus	388
398 Oh happy day that fixed my choice	483
922 Oh how kindly hast thou led me	594
902 Oh let my trembling soul be still	263
665 O Jesus, the giver of all we enjoy	516
610 Oh let the joyful tidings fill the wide	477
169 O Lord, when faith with fixed eyes	120
108 O love, beyond conception great	62
505 O love divine, how sweet thou art	384
66 O love divine, that stooped to	25
110 O love of God, how strong and true	63
846 O my soul, what means this sadness	655
263 One there is above all others	234
431 On Jordan's stormy banks I stand	314
1226 Only waiting till the shadows	595
604 On the mountain's top appearing	344
885 Onward, Christian, though the region	657
1275 Onward, onward, men of heaven	91
1246 Onward speed thy conquering	823
1120 On Zion's glorious summit stood	751
760 O peace of God, sweet peace of God	558
966 Oh praise our God to-day	539
637 Oh render thanks to God above	208
177 O sacred head, now wounded	125
893 O Savior, whose mercy severe in its	253
30 O source divine, and life of all	524
399 Oh sweetly breathe the lyres above	299
641 Oh tell me no more of this world's	59
826 Oh that I had wings like a dove	591
640 Oh thou fount of every blessing...512, 841
1030 O thou, in whose presence my soul	695
554 O thou pure light of souls that love	637
1005 O thou, who driest the mourner's	692
729 Oh turn you, oh turn you, for why	249
580 Our Father in heaven	436
1067 Our Fathers, where are they	710
75 Our God, our help in age, past	29
195 Our Lord is risen from the dead	145
376 Our Savior bowed beneath the wave	277
907 Our souls are in the Savior's hand	664
280 Oh what amazing words of grace	176
830 Oh when shall I see Jesus.........608, 829
451 Oh where are kings and empires now	154
102 Oh worship the king all glorious	56
750 Peace be to this congregation	513
506 Peacefully, tenderly, here as we part	386
974 Peace, peace on earth; the heart	573
380 Peace, troubled soul, whose plaintive	262
1247 Peace, the welcome sound proclaim	813
947 Pity, Lord, this child of clay	209
487 Planted in Christ, the living vine	362
252 Plunged in a gulf of dark despair	180
1235 Praise, and thanks, and cheerful love	487
728 Praise God, ye heavenly hosts above	20
101 Praise, my soul, the king of heaven	65
58 Praise the Lord, his glories show	687
1252 Praise the Lord, ye heavens adore	818
673 Praise the Lord, ye saints adore him	257
1249 Praise to God, immortal praise	375
24 Praise ye the Lord, 'tis good to raise	17
565 Prayer is the soul's sincere desire	419
22 Precious Bible what a treasure	13
835 Purer yet and purer	605
920 Quiet, Lord, my froward heart	307
649 Raise your triumphant songs	501
401 Redeemed from guilt, redeemed from	490
640 Rejoice, O earth, the Lord is king	556
336 Repent the voice celestial cries	283
1110 Rest for the toiling hand	737
461 Restore, O Father, to our times	312

INDEX OF FIRST LINES. 349

HYMN BOOK.	HYMNAL.
796 Rest, weary heart... 569	1111 The chariot, the chariot, its wheels.... 740
982 Return, my roving heart, return... 413	794 The child leans on its parent breast... 759
288 Return, O wanderer, now return... 215	266 The Christian banner dread no loss... 190
296 Return, O wanderer, to thy home.... 214	1100 The church has waited long... 599
201 Rise, glorious conqueror, rise... 203	1208 The day is ended; ere I sink to sleep. 686
832 Rise, my soul, and stretch thy... 237	1044 The glories of our birth and state... 705
860 Rise, O my soul, pursue the path... 641	1234 The God of harvest praise... 407
261 Rock of ages, cleft for me... 185	378 The Great Redeemer we adore... 279
	1 The heavens declare thy glory, Lord.. 1
629 Safely through another week... 486	294 The King of heaven, his table... 209
254 Salvation, oh the joyful sound... 79	1113 The last lovely morning... 749
1202 Savior, breathe an evening blessing... 791	90 The Lord descended from above... 46
1102 Savior haste, our souls are waiting... 626	41 The Lord is great! ye hosts of heaven 186
216 Savior, I lift my trembling eyes... 578	214 The Lord is King; lift up thy voice... 577
784 Savior, teach me day by day... 568	103 The Lord is my Shepherd; no want../ 617
656 Savior, thy gentle voice... 670	187 The Lord is risen indeed... 484
387 Savior, thy law we love... 290	57 The Lord Jehovah reigns, and royal.. 30
578 Savior, when in dust to thee... 429	56 The Lord Jehovah reigns: let all... 32
500 Say, whence does this union arise... 511	70 The Lord my pasture shall prepare... 33
957 Scorn not the slightest word or deed... 682	94 The Lord my Shepherd is... 51
462 See I from Zion's sacred mountain... 346	1106 The Lord will come; the earth shall.. 732
1184 See how the rising sun... 738	1200 The mellow eve is gliding... 680
669 See the shining dew-drops... 536	1185 The morning light returns... 739
1070 Servant of God, well done... 542	606 The Prince of salvation in triumph... 473
1164 Shall we sing in heaven forever... 770	1086 There is a calm for those who weep... 716
500 Shed kindly light amid th' uncircling. 451	1132 There is a fold where none can stray.. 759
525 Shepherd of souls, refresh and bless.. 363	253 There is a fountain filled with blood.. 179
575 Shepherd of thy little flock... 275	1129 There is a land, a happy land... 758
133 Shepherds, hail the wondrous... 88	1145 There is a land immortal... 757
1276 Shout the tidings of salvation... 809	1119 There is a land mine eye hath seen.... 753
346 Show pity, Lord, O Lord, forgive... 233	428 There is a land of pure delight... 312
1201 Silently the shades of evening... 794	416 There is a name I love to hear... 328
131 Silent night, hallowed night... 93	1130 There is an hour of peaceful rest... 756
434 Since I can read my title clear... 316	1159 There is a place where my hopes... 776
55 Since o'er thy footstool here below... 71	4 There is a stream whose gentle flow... 3
260 Sing of Jesus, sing forever... 435	1143 There is no night in heaven... 766
508 Sinner, art thou still secure... 430	1147 There's a region above... 248
319 Sinner, come 'mid thy gloom... 244	1167 There's a land far away 'mid the... 783
327 Sinner, go, will you go... 247	1125 There is a region lovelier far... 767
335 Sinners, come, no longer wander... 255	52 There's not a tint that paints the... 23
311 Sinners, seek the priceless treasure... 541	239 The Savior! oh what endless charms. 168
304 Sinners, turn, why will you die... 227	179 The Son of Man they did betray... 127
314 Sinners, will you scorn the message... 233	43 The spacious firmament on high... 24
1076 Sister, thou wast mild and lovely... 715	892 The Sun above is gleaming... 661
884 Sleep not, soldier of the cross... 466	851 The tempter to my soul hath said... 635
1199 Softly now the light of day... 784	332 The voice of free grace cries... 95
514 Soft be the gently breathing notes... 377	1074 They are going, only going... 596
879 Soldiers of Christ, arise... 648	1142 This is not my place of resting... 54
654 Songs of praise awoke the morn... 508	621 This is the day the first ripe sheaf... 480
465 Son of God, our glorious head... 376	619 This is the day the Lord hath made... 478
844 Soon and forever the breaking of day. 620	624 This is the glorious day... 483
1269 Soon may the last glad song arise... 296	658 This Lord is the Lord we adore... 143
275 Sound, sound the truth abroad... 202	49 Thou art, O God! the life and light... 621
919 Sovereign ruler of the skies... 589	223 Thou art the Way, and he who sighs. 191
967 Sow in the morn thy seed... 650	248 Thou art the Way; to thee alone... 177
427 Stand up, my soul, shake off thy... 632	231 Thou dear Redeemer, dying Lamb... 581
797 Star of morn and even... 572	336 Though all the world my choice... 260
1294 Star of peace to wanderers weary... 254	583 Though faint, yet pursuing, we go on 437
577 Stealing from the world away... 688	1017 Though I walk through the gloomy... 703
484 Still one in life, and one in death... 352	100 Though troubles assail and dangers... 54
801 Still will we trust, though earth... 565	1093 Thou God of love, beneath thy... 727
317 Stop, poor sinner, stop, and think... 239	555 Thou Savior, from thy throne on... 410
978 Sun of my soul, thou Savior dear... 672	167 Thou sweet gliding Kedron... 117
550 Sweet hour of prayer, sweet hour of.. 414	1187 Thou that dost my life prolong... 748
615 Sweet is the fading light of eve... 409	200 Thou who didst stoop below... 150
366 Sweet is the friendly voice... 265	1206 Through the day thy love has spared. 106
611 Sweet is the work, my God, my king. 393	787 Through the love of God, our Savior.. 561
812 Sweet land of rest, for thee I sigh... 582	1190 Thus far the Lord hath led me on... 319
538 Sweet the moments, rich in blessing.. 399	951 Thy footsteps, Lord, with joy we... 457
941 Sweet was the time, when first I felt. 422	83 Thy goodness, Lord, our souls confess 49
	455 Thy kingdom, gracious Lord... 333
949 Take me, O my father, take me... 658	740 Thy name, almighty Lord... 485
1219 Take my heart, O father, mold it... 659	419 Thy Spirit shall unite... 292
1203 Tarry with me, O my Savior... 795	159 'Tis midnight, and on Olive's brow... 108
1165 That clime is not like this dull clime. 773	782 'T is religion that can give... 230
1107 That day of wrath! that dreadful day 734	737 To bless thy chosen race... 349
62 The Almighty reigns, exalted high... 33	279 To-day, if you will hear his voice... 207
193 The angels, that watched round the... 141	323 To-day the Savior calls... 40
857 The billows swell, the winds are high 634	727 To God, the great, the ever blest... 194

INDEX OF FIRST LINES.

HYMN BOOK.	HYMNAL.
736 To God, the only wise	541
937 To heaven I lift mine eye	387
646 To him that loved the sons of men	497
672 To him who did salvation bring	385
827 To Jesus, the crown of my hope	592
302 To-morrow, Lord, is thine	223
643 To our Redeemer's glorious name	464
631 To spend one sacred day	493
2 To thee, my heart, Eternal King	4
95 To thee, O God! to thee	798
705 To thy temple we repair	571
122 To us a child of hope is born	78
198 Triumphant Christ ascends on high	148
591 Triumphant Zion, lift thy head	452
517 'T was on that night, when doomed	119
1050 Unveil thy bosom, faithful tomb	705
1168 Upon the frontier of this	776
1284 Wake thee, O Zion! thy morning is	470
128 Watchman, tell us of the night	81
1141 We are on our journey home	764
801 We are too far from thee, our Savior	671
313 We are on the ocean sailing	236
392 Weary souls, that wander wide	306
423 We ask for peace, O Lord	679
310 Weeping sinners, dry your tears	273
946 Weeping soul, no longer mourn	368
1153 We have no home but heaven	612
632 Welcome, delightful morn	492
626 Welcome, sweet day of rest	482
516 Welcome, ye hopeful heirs of heaven	348
374 We love thy name, we love thy laws	278
331 We're bound for the land of the pure	251
1161 We're going home; we've had	786
320 We're traveling home to heaven	243
503 We shall meet no more to part	381
174 We sing the Savior's wondrous death	124
1150 We speak of the realms of the blest	772
1105 We wait for thee, All-glorious One	730
1031 We will not weep, for God	443
305 What could your Redeemer do	139
935 Whate'er my God ordains is right	677
11 What glory guides the sacred page	8
1079 What is life? 't is but a vapor	107
1081 What's this that steals upon my	721
968 What though earthly friends may	676
556 What various hindrances we meet	411
78 When all thy mercies, O my God	44
1058 When blooming youth is snatched	699
437 When for eternal worlds we steer	318
999 When gathering clouds around I	39
777 When I can trust my all with God	72

HYMN BOOK.	HYMNAL.
5 When Israel through the desert	2
512 When I survey the wondrous cross	353
117 When Jordan hushed his waters	67
1008 When languor and disease invade	694
938 When our purest delights are nip'd in	446
1016 When overwhelmed with grief	675
501 When shall we meet again	415
1238 When spring unlocks the flowers	820
1101 When the King of kings comes	728
1091 When the spark of life is waning	722
1114 When thou, my righteous Judge	744
1151 When we hear the music ringing	774
1156 When we reach a quiet dwelling	597
180 When we the sacred grave survey	157
952 While others pray for grace to die	412
561 While thee I seek, Protecting Power	423
1243 While with ceaseless course the sun	815
886 Whither goest thou, pilgrim stranger	777
767 Whither, oh whither should I fly	311
1137 Who are these in bright array	762
1057 Why do we mourn departing friends	693
1043 Why should we start and fear to die	703
690 Within thy house, O Lord	532
71 With Israel's God, who can compare	43
228 With joy we meditate the grace	163
469 With joy we own thy servant	329
971 With my substance I will honor	628
29 With one consent, let all the earth	523
1231 With songs and honors sounding	802
278 With tearful eyes I look around	619, 206
389 With willing hearts we tread	291
465 Ye Christian heralds	325
681 Ye nations round the earth, rejoice	525
545 Ye saints, your music bring	86
472 Ye servants of the Lord	337
99 Yes, for me, for me he careth	53
104 Yes! our Shepherd leads with gentle	389
188 Yes! the Redeemer rose	132
603 Yes, we trust, the day is breaking	472
301 Ye trembling captives, hear	221
309 Ye who in his courts are found	271
293 Ye wretched, hungry, starving	218
813 You glittering toys of earth, adieu	583
463 You may sing of the beauty of	434
470 You messengers of Christ	338
917 Your harps, ye trembling saints	428
474 You servants of God	57
593 Zion, awake! thy strength renew	454
464 Zion stands, with hills surrounded	345
607 Zion! the marvelous story be telling	475

The following, in the HYMNAL, are not found in the Christian Hymn Book:

Come, come to Jesus	474	Oh how I love Jesus	542
Come to Jesus just now	448	Our Father, who art in heaven	468
Is this the way, my Father	729	Softly on the breath of evening	844

INDEX OF FIRST LINES

OF HYMNS IN THE CHRISTIAN HYMN BOOK, NOT FOUND IN THIS WORK.

N.B.—The figures on the left indicate the Number of the Hymn in the Christian Hymn Book. The figures on the right indicate the page in this work, where a suitable tune may be found.

Number in Hymn Book.	Page in Hymnal.
1004 Affliction is a stormy deep..................	12
341 Ah, wretched vile, ungrateful heart..	80
1089 Alas, how poor, and little worth........	139
931 A little longer still.............................	163
970 All around us, fair with flowers..........	23
904 All as God wills, who wisely heeds.....	21
644 Almighty Father, gracious Lord.........	40
1245 Almighty Sovereign of the skies.........	62
446 A mother may forgetful be.................	50
705 And are we yet alive..........................	102
1011 And can my heart aspire so high.......	152
360 And must I part with all I have........	242
1191 And now another day is gone.............	302
1240 And now, my soul, another year.......	322
300 And will the judge descend...............	102
137 Angels from the realms of glory.........	89
616 Another six days work is done............	137
349 Around Bethesda's healing wave........	69
148 As much have I of worldly good........	44
871 As o'er the past my memory strays...	64
997 As oft with worn and weary feet.......	101
1221 At evening time, when day is done....	101
342 Awake from sin's delusive sleep........	100
847 Awake, my soul, lift up.....................	230
1181 Awake, my soul, and with the sun.....	128
815 Awake, you saints, and raise your.....	192
1095 Away from his home..........................	159
941 Before thy throne, with tearful eyes.	121
1115 Behold the day is come......................	85
19 Behold the lofty sky...........................	234
171 Behold the man, how glorious he......	39
271 Behold the morning sun.....................	234
956 Beneath the shadow of the cross.......	7
684 Be still, be still, for all around.........	80
84 Beyond, beyond that boundless sea...	61
420 Bless'd are the sons of God................	173
182 Bless'd be the everlasting God...........	176
916 Bless'd be thy love, dear Lord...........	134
699 Bless'd day of God, most calm, most.	132
532 Bless'd feast of love divine................	154
953 Bless'd is the man, whose..................	64
772 Bless'd is the man, who shuns the....	64
1192 Bless'd Sov'reign, let my evening song	133
534 Bread of heaven, on thee we feed......	8
975 Breathe thoughts of pity o'er a.........	262
127 Bright and joyful was the morn........	185
661 Brightness of the Father's glory.......	324
662 Bright the vision that delighted........	323
948 Brother, hast thou wandered far.......	104
421 Call Jehovah, thy salvation................	196
574 Child, amid the flowers at play..........	101
1097 Christian, the vision before...............	171
861 Christians, keep your armor bright...	201
386 Come and behold the place................	195

Number in Hymn Book.	Page in Hymnal.
377 Come, happy souls, adore the Lamb...	80
522 Come in thou blessed of the Lord......	144
233 Come, let us join in songs of praise....	132
1213 Come, let us join the hosts above......	64
569 Come, let us pray; 'tis sweet to feel..	44
357 Come, let us to the Lord, our God.....	168
697 Come, Lord, and warm each.............	192
509 Come on, my partners in distress......	273
693 Come, O thou king of all thy saints...	21
113 Come, ye that know and fear the......	182
1309 Dear Father, to thy mercy seat.........	151
1037 Dear is the spot where Christians......	137
1212 Dear Jesus ever at my side................	21
1072 Deathless spirit, now arise................	71
994 Deem not that they are blest along...	92
369 Does the gospel word proclaim.........	71
766 Do not I trust in thee, O Lord..........	18
717 Ere to the world.................................	6
1288 Eternal Father, strong to save...........	18
1230 Eternal source of every joy...............	306
112 Eternal wisdom, thee we praise.........	7
210 Exalted Prince of life, we own...........	62
352 Faith adds new charms to earthly....	14
458 Far as thy name is known..................	22
507 Farewell, my friends, time rolls........	130
1068 Far from my heavenly home..............	320
985 Far from the world, O Lord, I flee....	64
986 Father divine, thy piercing eye.........	278
707 Father, hear our humble claim.........	104
111 Father, how wide thy glory shines...	20
775 Father, I know that all my life........	61
415 Father, I wait before thy throne.......	151
773 Father of love, our guide and friend..	115
1299 Father of the human race..................	252
589 Father, to us thy children.................	262
748 For a season called to part................	87
678 Forth from the dark and stormy sky.	18
1178 Forth in thy name, O Lord, I go.......	128
1244 For thy mercy and thy grace.............	104
595 For Zion's sake I will not rest...........	152
1232 Fountain of life and God of love........	168
168 From Calvary a cry was heard..........	43
535 From the table now retiring..............	23
1022 Gently, gently lay thy sod.................	87
1034 Gently, my Savior, let me down.......	6
609 Gird on thy conquering sword..........	180
107 Give to our God immortal praise......	16
1320 Glory, glory to our King....................	113
1189 Glory to thee, my God, this night	62
1289 Glory to thee whose powerful word...	51
1270 Go and the Savior's grace proclaim...	302
1250 God, bless our native land.................	314

351

INDEX OF FIRST LINES.

HYMN	BOOK.	HYMNAL.
114	God, my supporter and my hope........	21
1253	God of mercy, do thou never.............	23
882	God of mercy, God of love.................	87
1223	God of my childhood and my youth...	64
1179	God of the morning, at whose voice...	128
1201	God that madest earth and heaven....	204
130	God with us! O glorious name...........	185
466	Go, messenger of peace and love........	110
833	Go up, go up, my heart.....................	112
471	Go with thy servant, Lord.................	123
46	Greatest of beings, Source of life	5
39	Great God! how infinite art thou	168
677	Great God! the followers of thy	39
1239	Great God, we sing that mighty.........	25
452	Great is the Lord our God	234
82	Great Ruler of all nature's frame.......	21
1001	Great Source of boundless power.......	121
413	Great Source of life and light	259
480	Had I the tongues of Greeks and Jews	202
13	Hail, sacred truth, whose piercing	12
1193	Hail, tranquil hour of closing days....	62
1007	Happy are they who learn in thee......	30
1312	Happy the child whose tender years...	322
1171	Happy the home when God is there ...	152
719	Happy the saints whose lot is cast.....	129
491	Happy the souls to Jesus joined.........	144
1131	Hark, hark the voice of censeless	137
878	Hark, how the watchmen cry	531
116	Hark, ye mortals, hear the trumpet...	272
170	Have we no tears to shed for him	49
344	Hear, gracious God, a sinner's cry.....	92
1321	Hear my prayer, O heavenly..............	299
601	Hear what God the Lord hath............	323
572	Heavenly Father, to whose eye..........	252
795	He bids us come, his voice we know...	273
155	He came not with his heavenly	30
129	He has come, the Christ of God..........	185
212	He lives, the great Redeemer lives	62
964	Help us, O Lord, thy yoke to wear.....	302
318	Here is my heart, I give it thee..........	17
388	Here, Savior, we would come.............	22
246	He who on earth as man was known...	66
1251	High as the heavens above the............	8
887	Holy Father, thou hast taught me.....	236
576	Holy Lord, our hearts prepare............	103
413	Honor and happiness unite................	131
1099	Hope of our hearts, O Lord, appear ...	30
1292	How are thy servants blest, O Lord...	322
909	How bright these glorious spirits......	279
415	How did my heart rejoice to hear	106
868	How oft, alas! this wretched heart....	68
1279	How sweet the gospel trumpet	115
1027	How vast is the tribute I owe.............	186
816	I am thy workmanship, O Lord.........	322
385	I come, the great Redeemer cries.......	66
819	I have no resting-place......................	30
1139	I journey forth.................................	222
912	I look to thee in every need................	44
237	Infinite excellence is thine................	106
785	In heavenly love abiding....................	222
142	In Jordan's tide the Baptist...............	69
1301	In sweet exalted strains.....................	180
845	In thee, O Lord, I put my trust..........	6
1026	In the floods of tribulation................	23
788	In time of fear, when trouble's near.	302
910	In trouble and in grief, O God...........	10
1180	I praise thy name, O God of light......	6
50	I sing the almighty power of God......	302
761	Is there a lone and dreary hour.........	137
1056	It is not death to die..........................	102
568	It is the hour of prayer......................	205
906	It is the Lord enthroned in light........	168
1060	I will extol thee, Lord, on high...........	125
780	Jesus, cast a look on me.....................	8
1322	Jesus hail enthroned in glory.............	279

HYMN	BOOK.	HYMNAL.
811	Jesus has died that I might live........	243
245	Jesus, immortal king, arise................	302
807	Jesus, my love, my chief delight........	120
557	Jesus, my strength, my hope.............	134
204	Jesus, our Lord, ascend thy throne....	152
920	Jesus, Savior, all divine.....................	71
915	Jesus, take me for thine own..............	8
526	Jesus the friend of man.....................	127
776	Jesus, these eyes have never seen.....	176
295	Jesus, thy blessings are not few.........	192
391	Jesus, to thy wounds I fly..................	101
1259	Judges who rule the world by laws....	19
864	Kind Father, look with pity now.......	322
647	Let earthly minds the world pursue..	152
224	Let everlasting glories crown............	28
810	Let me be with thee when..................	114
989	Let my life be hid in thee...................	101
1060	Let not your hearts with....................	255
425	Let others boast their ancient line....	29
1281	Let the land mourn through all.........	302
89	Let the whole race of creatures lie.....	151
338	Let thoughtless thousands choose.....	231
97	Let us with a joyful mind..................	71
594	Let Zion and her sons rejoice.............	208
1271	Light of the lonely pilgrim's heart...	182
1282	Light of them that sit in darkness.....	199
409	Like morning, when her early breeze	137
258	Like sheep we went astray.................	248
791	Long did I toil, and knew no earthly.	126
688	Look from on high, great God...........	129
483	Lord bless thy saints assembled here.	19
722	Lord, how delightful 'tis to see..........	6
853	Lord, I have foes without, within......	261
414	Lord, in whose might the Savior trod	182
1307	Lord, let thy goodness lead our land.	190
417	Lord, let thy Spirit penetrate............	308
1232	Lord, Lord, defend the desolate.........	8
519	Lord, may the Spirit of this feast......	121
26	Lord, my weak thought in vain.........	26
724	Lord, now we part..............................	16
639	Lord of all being, throned afar...........	28
1177	Lord of all eternal truth and might...	6
1394	Lord of hosts, to thee we raise............	185
1182	Lord of my life, O may thy praise.....	308
1473	Lord of the harvest, hear...................	122
1237	Lord of the harvest, these we hail......	18
714	Lord of the worlds above...................	34
1237	Lord, thou hast bid thy people pray..	19
33	Lord, thou hast formed mine every...	105
345	Lord, when my thoughts delighted...	305
1285	Lord, while for all mankind we pray.	153
1295	Lord, whom winds and seas obey......	136
354	Mistaken souls that dream of heaven	182
1241	My few revolving years......................	85
1306	My God, how endless is thy love.......	80
106	My God, how excellent thy grace......	39
80	My God, how wonderful thou art......	12
915	My God, my strength, my hope.........	203
704	My God, permit my tongue................	154
769	My God, the spring of all my joys.....	182
42	My God, thy boundless love I praise..	41
1069	My God, thy service well demands....	192
557	My only Savior when I feel................	148
612	My opening eyes with rapture see.....	6
553	My precious Lord, for thy dear name.	129
996	My spirit looks to God alone..............	202
881	My soul, it is thy God........................	195
436	My soul triumphant in the Lord........	7
911	My times are in thy hand..................	134
45	Nature, with all her powers, shall.....	58
867	Nay, tell us not of dangers dire.........	182
1176	New every morning is the love..........	125
1049	No bitter tears for thee he shed..........	63
1169	No night shall be in heaven...............	202

INDEX OF FIRST LINES. 353

HYMN BOOK.	HYMNAL.	HYMN BOOK.	HYMNAL.
1059 Not for the pious dead we weep	121	77 Oh why despond in life's dark vale	7
1298 Not for the summer hour alone	21	1028 Oh why this disconsolate frame	57
839 Not here, not here! not where the	160	1324 O you immortal throng	54
147 Not to condemn the sons of men	11		
449 Not to the terrors of the Lord	133	1140 Psalms of glory, raiment bright	281
181 Now for a song of lofty praise	230	368 People of the living God	71
1198 Now from labor and from care	103	655 Praise on, thee in Zion's gates	8
440 Now I have found the ground	18	51 Praise ye the Lord, immortal choir	61
746 Now may he, who from the dead	8	1021 Prince of peace! control my will	104
1014 Now to thy heavenly Father's praise	65		
		770 Rejoice, believers in the Lord	176
959 O be not faithless with the more	29	333 Restless thy spirit, poor wandering	171
685 O blest the souls, forever blest	110	1122 Return, my soul, and sweetly rest	114
215 O Christ, our King, Creator, Lord	5	1273 Rise, gracious God, and shine	184
682 O come, loud anthems let us sing	13	642 Rise, tune thy voice to sacred song	278
987 O could I find from day to day	243	1291 Rocked in the cradle of the deep	49
633 O day of rest and gladness	222	1287 Roll on, thou mighty ocean	317
763 O Father, gladly we repose	80		
759 Of thy love, some gracious token	9	998 Savior, through my rebellious	62
731 O God, by whom the seed is given	230	596 Say, who is he that looks abroad	14
1238 O God of love! O King of peace!	262	1263 See! gracious God, before thy throne	255
1016 O God! thy grace and blessing give	165	379 See how the willing converts trace	105
36 O God! we praise thee and confess	53	896 Shall we grow weary in our watch	156
962 O gracious Lord, whose mercies rise	153	960 She loved her Savior; and to him	144
1216 O happy is the man who hears	255	1062 She was the music of our home	151
492 O happy they who know the Lord	308	848 Silent, like men in solemn haste	231
972 O he whom Jesus loved has truly	262	85 Since all the varying scenes of life	64
371 O holy Savior, friend unseen	92	407 Since first thy word awaked my	293
358 O how divine, how sweet the joy	106	88 Since God is mine, then present	182
14 O how I love thy holy law	12	1297 Since Jesus freely did appear	308
850 O Israel, to thy tents repair	58	47 Sing to the Lord with cheerful voice	11
244 O Jesus, King, most wonderful	168	1041 So fades the lonely, blooming flower	137
559 O Jesus, Savior of the lost	153	37 Songs of immortal praise belong	53
639 O let your mingling voices rise	41	738 Soon we shall meet again	177
410 O Lord, and shall thy Spirit rest	100	59 Source of being, source of light	71
383 O Lord, and will thy pardoning love	255	919 Sovereign Ruler of the skies	8
1313 O Lord, another day is flown	151	700 Stand up and bless the Lord	270
67 O Lord, how full of sweet	110	221 Still nigh me, O my Savior, stand	101
582 O Lord, how happy should we be	139	988 Still with thee, O my God	319
566 O Lord, I would delight in thee	151	76 Sweet is the morning of thy grace	20
765 O Lord, thy heavenly grace impart	28	981 Sweet is the prayer whose holy	121
18 O Lord, thy perfect word	123	625 Sweet is the task, O Lord	177
17 O Lord, thy precepts I survey	121		
899 O Lord, thy counsels	120	1308 Teach us, in time of deep distress	152
1256 O may the power which melts the	6	1246 Thanks be to him, who built the	26
1048 O mourner, who with tender love	261	744 Thanks for mercies past received	8
546 Once the angel started back	86	894 The captive's ear may pause upon	262
511 One baptism and one faith	46	846 The Christian warrior! see him	28
256 O North, with all thy vales of	273	1197 The day is past and gone	102
771 O not to fill the mouth of fame	12	818 The dove, let loose in eastern skies	250
725 O present still, though still unseen	62	217 Thee we adore, O gracious Lord	16
613 O sacred day of peace and joy	306	1290 The floods, O Lord, lift up their	19
945 O Savior, lend a listening ear	192	1036 The God of mercy will indulge	92
1313 O shadow in a sultry land	61	1233 The harvest dawn is near	85
786 O strong to save and bless	264	54 The heavenly spheres, to thee, O God	115
157 O suffering friend of human kind	49	1051 The hour of my departure's come	256
981 O that I could forever dwell	28	936 Their hearts shall not be moved	54
433 O there 's a better world on high	152	447 The Lord of glory is my light	176
1085 O think that while you 're weeping	200	158 The morning dawns upon the place	6
762 O this is blessing, this is rest	321	1035 The morning flowers display their	28
862 O thou from whom all goodness flows	20	695 The offerings to thy throne which	106
74 O thou my light, my life, my joy	182	1300 The perfect world by Adam trod	105
424 O thou that hearest prayer	78	448 There is a little, lonely fold	151
939 O thou that hearest when sinners cry	100	1126 There an hour of hallowed peace	278
676 O thou to whom in ancient times	16	48 There seems a voice in every gale	26
809 O thou to whose all searching sight	49	1127 There 's music in the upper heaven	30
1012 O thou to whom the olive shade	64	63 There 's nothing bright above, below	276
1303 O thou whose own vast temple	105	870 The Savior bids us watch and pray	192
942 O thou whose tender mercy hears	68	870 The Savior calls; let every ear	152
422 Our blest Redeemer, ere he breathed	131	622 The Savior, risen to-day, we praise	53
450 Our Christ hath reached his	53	1035 The spring-tide hour	12
1260 Our earth we now lament to see	69	3 The starry firmament on high	11
983 Our Father, God, not face to face	150	151 The winds were howling o'er the	133
523 Our heavenly Father calls	154	438 The world may change from	76
1222 Our pathway oft is wet with tears	259	573 They who seek the throne of grace	8
1017 Out of the depths of woe	134	617 Thine earthly Sabbaths, Lord, we	129
1166 O where can the soul find relief	142	490 Think gently of the erring one	121
858 O where is now that glowing love	114	1172 This book is all that 's left me now	321
1055 O where shall rest be found	297	874 This world is poor from shore to	273

30

INDEX OF FIRST LINES.

HYMN BOOK.	HYMNAL.	HYMN BOOK.	HYMNAL.
1026 Thou art gone to the grave, but we....	38	1043 Weep not for the saint that ascends...	286
543 Thou art my hiding-place, O Lord.....	14	359 Welcome, O Savior, to my heart.........	322
771 Thou art my portion, O my God.........	308	1314 We left our hearts to thee	193
729 Thou art our Shepherd, glorious God.	106	1019 We love this outward world	85
1071 Though I walk the downward shade.	309	1305 We've no abiding city here.............	111
1311 Thou grace divine, encircling all......	53	905 We wait in faith, in prayer we wait..	2?0
839 Thou hidden love of God, whose......	69	901 What grace, O Lord, and beauty	21
1310 Thou, Lord of life, whose tender care	8	692 What shall I render to my God.........	243
222 Thou only Sovereign of my heart.....	39	808 What sinners value, I resign	114
1170 Thou Sovereign Lord of earth and....	129	1064 What though the arm of conquering.	253
1020 Thou very present aid....................	297	963 When adverse winds and waves........	101
911 Through all the changing scenes......	11	854 When darkness long has veiled my....	80
716 Through all this life's eventful road..	183	1108 When downward to the darksome.....	151
932 Through cross to crown	126	992 When far from the hearts where our..	38
1266 Thus Abrah'm, full of sacred awe....	21	337 When human hopes and joys depart..	128
1123 Thy Father's house, thine own.........	128	852 When in the hour of lonely woe........	6
443 Thy kingdom, Lord, forever stands...	255	1318 Whene'er I think of thee.................	147
1225 Thy mercy heard my infant.............	139	362 When I sink down in gloom or fear..	302
1293 Thy way is in the deep, O Lord ,.....	154	849 When Israel, of the Lord beloved......	105
91 Thy way is in the sea.....................	123	351 When marshaled on the nightly.......	28
913 Thy way, not mine, O Lord	108	432 When musing sorrow weeps the past.	20
993 Thy will be done; I will not fear.....	261	435 When reft of all, and hopeless care...	106
1081 Time is winging us away.................	91	502 When shall we all meet again..........	86
1023 'T is my happiness below...............	136	1060 When the vale of death appears	27
1029 'T is not a lonely night-watch...........	249	623 When the worn spirit wants repose...	40
1079 Tossed no more on life's rough billow	238	1296 When through the torn sail the wild.	38
757 To thee be praise forever...............	319	370 When we can not see our way.........	252
1183 To thee let my first offerings rise.....	182	963 Where shall the child of sorrow find.	302
1002 To thee, my God, whose presence.....	308	552 Where two or three with sweet........	143
641 To thee, my Shepherd, and my	183	540 While in sweet communion feeding..	23
758 To thee our wants are known..........	54	1214 While in the slippery pathway of....	152
153 To the hall of that past came the....	225	277 While life prolongs its precious light.	128
901 To weary hearts, to mourning hearts	17	683 While now thy throne of grace we....	129
		1254 While o'er our guilty land, O God	190
31 Unchangeable, All-perfect Lord	321	929 While thou, O my God, art my help...	38
6 Upon the gospel's sacred page	16	1025 Why should I, in vain repining.........	299
726 Up to the hills I lift mine eyes.........	5	282 Why will ye waste on trifling cares...	80
		1013 With earnest longings of the mind....	53
783 Vainly through night's weary hours.	104	689 With sacred joy we lift our eyes.......	14
468 Vouchsafe, O Lord, thy presence	153	753 Worship, honor, glory, blessing........	299
69 Wait, O my soul, thy Maker's will....	202	1053 Ye golden lamps of heaven..............	7
1277 We are living, we are dwelling.........	239	184 Ye humble souls that seek the Lord..	243
940 Weary of wandering from my God....	69	1215 Ye joyous ones, upon whose brow....	30
232 We bless the prophet of the Lord	152	489 Ye men and angels, witness now......	265

INDEX TO SUPPLEMENT.

Tunes in italic, First lines of Hymns in Roman.

	PAGE		PAGE
Alida...	339	*Lisbon*...	336
Almost Persuaded...........................	331	Must Jesus bear the cross alone........	341
Almighty Father gracious.................	338	Our Helper, God I we bless thy name.....	341
"A little while," our Lord shall come.....	336	Our sins on Christ were laid.............	335
Bradford..	343	*Pilesgrove*.....................................	343
Blessed Savior, faithful Guide...........	339	*Rindge*..	338
Come, let us join our songs of Praise.....	343	*Seasons*...	340
Come, O my soul in sacred lays.........	340	Servants of God! in joyful lays..........	335
Cross and Crown.............................	344	*Shawmut*.......................................	335
Creation..	335	*State Street*...................................	340
Dear Father, to thy mercy seat.........	344	*St. Anns*..	441
Dover..	329	*Sweet By and By*.............................	330
Eternal are thy mercies, Lord...........	331	The Lord our God is full of might.......	341
Evening Hymn................................	342	*The Ninety and Nine*.......................	329
From all that dwell.........................	331	*There is a Fountain*........................	325
Give...	338	There's a land that is fairer than day.....	330
Glory to thee, my God.	342	Thou art our shepherd.....................	337
Great is the Lord..............................	329	Tell me the old, old Story.................	326
Guide..	339	*Waiting*..	336
Home of the soul............................	328	*Warwick*.......................................	337
How happy every child of grace........	339	Welcome, sweet day of rest..............	336
I love the sacred book of God............	342	*We shall know*................................	336
I love to tell the story......................	327	What means this eager anxious throng...	337
I will sing you a song of the beautiful land	328	When the mists have rolled in splendor..	332
Jesus of Nazareth passeth by............	337	*Willington*.....................................	342
Let everlasting glories crown............	343	*Winchester*....................................	341
Let every mortal ear attend..............	338	*Woodstock*....................................	344
Lord, in this sacred hour..................	340	Work for the night is coming............	333

ALPHABETICAL INDEX OF TUNES.

	PAGE.		PAGE.		PAGE.
Abide with me	306	Brest	272	Duane Street	73
Adoration	188	Brown	132	Duke Street	26
After the toil	246	Browne	203	Dundee	21
Ain	194	Burlington	173	Dunlap's Creek	255
Alberte	124				
Aletta	103	Caddo	14	Edmeston	40
A little while	226	Calm	44	Effingham	276
Allen	59	Camden	125	Eltham	309
All's well	263	Cambridge	302	Eupar	264
All will be well	204	Canaan	322	Evergreen mount'ins	295
Amboy. I	55	Chelmsford	121	Excelsior	221
Amboy. II	321	Chestnut Street	200	Expostulation	96
America	314	Child of sin & sorrow	94		
Amoy	18	Christmas	233	Fading	265
Amsterdam	91	Chimes	64	Faith	237
Antioch	31	China	253	Fanning	209
Anvern	166	Clarington	57	Farewell Hymn	304
Ardon	254	Cling to the mighty	118	Federal Street	120
Ariel	41	Clure	248	Fellowship	144
Arlington	53	Come	93	Fenelon	144
Aspiration	117	Come to Jesus just	163	Ferguson	177
Atwater	321	Come, thou mighty	268	Flee as a bird	303
Autumn	208	Come to me	226	Florida	198
Avon	12	Come to thy rest	289	Folsom	140
Aylesbury	248	Come, ye disconsolate	163	Forever with the Lord	219
Azmon	106	Comfort	25	Forest	80
		Cookham	87	Fountain	68
Bealoth	122	Coronal	52	Fountain of life	94
Balerma	152	Coronation	61	Fraternity	130
Bankoke	258	Coventry	250	Frederick	224
Beacon Light	247	Cranbrook	109	From the depths	165
Bearing the Cross	240			Frontier	291
Beautiful world	296	Dalston	15		
Beautiful Zion	284	Daughters of Zion	170	Geneva	20
Beethoven	11	Dayton	141	Gerar	22
Behold the Lamb	52	Dedham	133	Gethsemane	43
Benevento	310	De Fleury	186	Glad homage	193
Bennett	139	Dennis	134	God doth not leave his	210
Bethany	244	Desire	114	God speed the right	314
Be with us thro' the	60	Devizes	168	Going home	213
Billow	99	Devotion	100	Golden Hill	319
Bonar	218	Dew-drops	193	Go to the grave	202
Boonton	29	Dickinson	111	Go to thy rest in peace	266
Boylston	195	Doom	274	Gratitude	39
Bradbury	50	Dorrnance	23	Greenville	323
Brattle Street	259	Dort	78	Haddam	34

355

ALPHABETICAL INDEX OF TUNES.

	PAGE.		PAGE.		PAGE.
Hail, ransomed world	316	Lead thou me on	165	Olivet	147
Hail to the brightness	171	Leander	324	Olmutz	154
Halle	113	Lenox	76	Oriel	261
Hallen	207	Let every heart rejoice	305	Ortonville	66
Hamburg	129	Let me go	216	Our Father	170
Happy clime	292	Lexington	205	Ozrem	297
Happy day	179	Lischer	180	Park Street	28
Happy Zion	228	Longing for rest	212	Parting hymn	131
Hark, the song of	169	Loving kindness	181	Parting in hope	201
Harmony Grove	322	Lucas	311	Patience	251
Harwell	9	Luther	184	Paul	241
Haste, traveler, haste	79	Luton	58	Paxan	308
Hastings	236	Lynch	241	Peace troubled soul	101
Heavenly Fatherland	290	Lyons	24	Pendleton	141
Heber	7	Manor	36	Perez	312
Hebron	128	Marlow	8	Perfect day	284
He leadeth me	17	Marton	172	Peron	27
Hendon	185	Martyn	56	Peterboro	176
Henly	160	McChesney	117	Petition	181
Henry	183	Mear	242	Pilgrim	290
Here and yonder	220	Memory	319	Pilgrim, watch and	324
Home	142	Mendon	13	Pinkerton	320
Homeward	260	Mercy seat	149	Pleading Savior	196
Hope	238	Merdin	60	Pleyel	252
Horton	104	Meribah	273	Pomeroy	265
Houston	116	Messiah	214	Portuguese hymn	158
Hour of prayer	156	Migdol	110	Prayer	153
How firm a foundat'n	159	Missionary Hymn	317	Refuge	300
How long, O Lord	320	Molucca	89	Resolution	84
I come to thee	312	Montague	51	Rest	256
Idumea	102	Moore	143	Rest for the weary	286
I love Jesus	323	Mount Blanc	282	Retreat	148
Importunity	62	Mount Pisgah	232	Return	83
Invitation	88	Mount Vernon	260	Rockingham	16
Iowa	286	Mozart	322	Rock of Ages	70
Ives	281	Naomi	151	Rock of salvation	197
Jesus bread of life	146	Nashville	19	Rockvale	315
Jesus is mine	119	Nature and life	275	Rosefield	86
Jesus waits for thee	173	Nettleton	187	Rothwell	230
Jesus wept	42	New Haven	189	Rowley	112
Joyful Day	267	New Richmond	321	Sabbath	178
Joyfully	206	Night with ebon	45	Sacred tears	47
Judgment hymn	269	Nillen	112	Salem	49
Kendrick	287	No night in heaven	283	Scotland	38
Kentucky	85	Nuremberg	136	Sessions	62
Kimmel	225	Oak	280	Shall we know each	288
		Oakland	297	Shall we sing in	285
Laban	234	Oh, how I love Jesus	323	Shepard	268
Land of promise	95	Old Hundred	190	Shining shore	293
Lanesboro	192	Oh, let the joyful	175	Shirland	123
Lanman	243	Olive's brow	43	Shout the tidings	307

ALPHABETICAL INDEX OF TUNES. 357

	PAGE.		PAGE.		PAGE.
Siberia	199	The day is ended	251	Vesper	320
Sicily	239	The Eden above	97	Victory	251
Sidmouth	247	The family Bible	10		
Silent devotion	146	The future rest	138	Ward	6
Silent night	37	The golden shore	90	Ware	74
Siloam	302	The gospel feast	81	Warning	98
Silver Street	75	The guiding hand	267	Watchman	33
Sing of Jesus	157	The heavenly mans'n	277	Watchword	310
Sing to me of heaven	277	The home in heaven	292	Wayne	30
Somerset	215	The house of the Lord	157	We are too far from	245
Soon and forever	227	The land of Beulah	279	Webb	222
Sorrows	45	The land of promise	95	Weep not for me	262
Star in the East	37	The last beam	301	Wells	19
Stearns	145	The last lovely morn	275	Welton	202
Still will we trust	201	The Lord is great	70	Western	319
St. Martins	182	The peace of God	249	We wait for thee	268
Stockwell	299	There is a land	278	Wilbor	155
Stonefield	105	The Rock	72	Will you go	93
St. Petersburg	18	The royal proclama'n	77	Wilmot	8
St. Thomas	108	Thy will be done	131	Wilson	71
Sunset	249	To thee we bow	300	Winchester	306
Supplication	162	To whom shall we go	162	Windham	231
Sweet hour of prayer	150	Triumph	200	Woodland	278
Sweet Kedron	48	Trumpet	174	Woodworth	92
Sweet story	301	Trust	164	Wyatt	211
				Wyman	126
Thanksgiving	313	Unity	150		
Thatcher	270	Urmund	77	Yoakley	69
The betrayal	46	Uxbridge	5		
The better land	294			Zanesville	308
The burial	266			Zebulon	54
The chariot	271	Vain world adieu	118	Zephyr	137
The cho. of angels	35, 318	Van Pelt	140	Zerah	32
		Varina	115	Zion	127

METRICAL INDEX.

L. M.

	PAGE
Anvern	166
Beethoven	11
Desire	114
Devotion	100
Dickinson	111
Duke Street	26
Effingham	276
Federal Street	120
Forest	80
Fraternity	130
Gratitude	39
Hamburg	129
Happy day	179
Haste, traveler, haste	79
Hebron	128
Judgment hymn	269
Loving kindness	181
Luton	58
Mendon	13
Mercy seat	149
Migdol	110
Moore	143
Old Hundred	190
Olive's brow	43
Oriel	261
Park Street	28
Rest	256
Retreat	148
Rockingham	16
Rothwell	230
Salem	49
Sessions	62
Stonefield	105
The gospel feast	81
Uxbridge	5
Ward	6
Ware	74
Wells	19
Welton	202
Winchester	306
Windham	231
Woodworth	92
Zephyr	137

L. M. D.

	PAGE
Amboy. II	321
Duane Street	73
Parting hymn	131
Sweet hour of prayer	150

L. M., 6 lines.

He leadeth me	17
Peace troubled soul	101
St. Petersburg	18
Yoakley	69

L. P. M.

Canaan	322
Nashville	19
The heavenly mans'n	277

C. M.

Allen	59
Antioch	31
Arlington	53
Aspiration	117
Atwater	321
Avon	12
Azmon	106
Balerma	152
Bradbury	50
Brown	132
Caddo	14
Cambridge	302
Chelmsford	121
Chimes	64
China	253
Christmas	233
Coronation	61
Coventry	250
Dedham	133
Devizes	168
Dundee	21
Dunlap's Creek	255
Edmeston	40
Fellowship	144
Fountain	68
Geneva	20
Going home	213
Harmony Grove	322
Heber	7

	PAGE
Henry	183
Houston	116
Importunity	82
Lanesboro	192
Leander	324
Longing for rest	212
Marlow	8
Mear	242
Mount Pisgah	232
Naomi	151
Ortonville	66
Parting in hope	201
Peterboro	176
Prayer	153
Resolution	84
Return	83
Siloam	302
St. Martins	182
The land of Beulah	279
Woodland	278
Zanesville	308
Zerah	32

C. M. D.

Brattle Street	259
New Richmond	321
Varina	115
Wayne	30

C. H. M.

Boonton	29
Calm	44
Watchword	310

C. P. M.

Ariel	41
Bennett	139
Meribah	273

S. M.

Alberte	124
Aylesbury	248
Bankoke	258
Boylston	195
Cranbrook	109
Dennis	134
Ferguson	177
Gerar	22

358

Golden Hill ... 319	Sidmouth ... 247	How long, O Lord ... 320
Idumea ... 102	Watchman ... 33	Merdin ... 60
Kentucky ... 85	Wilbor ... 155	Missionary Hymn ... 317
Laban ... 234	Wilson ... 71	Montague ... 51
Luther ... 181	**8s & 7s.**	Petition ... 181
No night in heaven ... 282	Dorrnance ... 23	Sunset ... 249
Ohnutz ... 154	Homeward ... 260	There is a land ... 278
Ozrem ... 297	Mount Vernon ... 260	Webb ... 222
Pinkerton ... 320	Perez ... 312	Western ... 319
Shirland ... 123	Sicily ... 239	**11s.**
Silver Street ... 75	Stearns ... 145	Adoration ... 188
Sing to me of heaven 277	Stockwell ... 299	Daughter of Zion ... 170
St. Thomas ... 108	The golden shore ... 90	Expostulation ... 96
Thatcher ... 270	**8s & 7s, Double.**	Frederick ... 224
Vesper ... 320	Autumn ... 298	How firm a foundat'n 159
S. M. D.	Camden ... 125	Home ... 142
Ain ... 194	Faith ... 237	Kimmel ... 225
Bealoth ... 122	Greenville ... 323	Memory ... 319
Bonar ... 218	Hastings ... 236	Portuguese hymn ... 158
Browne ... 203	Here and yonder ... 220	Sweet Kedron ... 48
Forever with the Lord 219	I love Jesus ... 323	**10s.**
	Let me go ... 216	Abide with me ... 306
S. H. M.	Manor ... 36	Go to the grave ... 262
The betrayal ... 46	Mozart ... 322	Joyfully ... 206
	Nettleton ... 187	Wyman ... 126
S. P. M.	Pleading Savior ... 196	
Dalston ... 15	Rest for the weary ... 286	**6s & 4s.**
	Shall we know each .. 283	America ... 314
7s.	Shining shore ... 293	Amoy ... 18
Cookham ... 87	Shout the tidings ... 307	Bethany ... 244
Hendon ... 185	Trust ... 164	Child of sin & sorrow. 94
Horton ... 104		Cling to the mighty ... 118
Nuremberg ... 136	**8s, 7s & 4s.**	Dort ... 78
Pleyel ... 252	Brest ... 272	Eupar ... 204
Wilmot ... 8	Coronal ... 52	Jesus is mine ... 119
	Florida ... 198	Lynch ... 241
7s, 6 lines.	Happy Zion ... 228	New Haven ... 189
Aletta ... 103	Hope ... 238	Oak ... 280
Halle ... 113	Invitation ... 88	Olivet ... 147
Oakland ... 297	Marton ... 172	**6s & 5s.**
Rock of Ages ... 70	Molucca ... 89	Dew-drops ... 193
Rosefield ... 86	Peron ... 27	Excelsior ... 221
Sabbath ... 178	Siberia ... 199	Jesus waits for thee ... 173
	Zion ... 127	Shepard ... 208
7s, Double.		The last lovely morn. 275
Amboy. I. ... 55	**8s.**	Unity ... 150
Benevento ... 310	Clarington ... 57	
Eltham ... 309	De Fleury ... 186	**H. M.**
Hark, the song of ... 169	Iowa ... 286	Haddam ... 34
Ives ... 281	Somerset ... 215	Lenox ... 76
Martyn ... 56	**7s & 6s.**	Lischer ... 180
Messiah ... 214	Amsterdam ... 91	Zebulon ... 54

METRICAL INDEX.

8s & 3s.
	PAGE.
All's well	263
Will you go	93

8s & 4s.
All will be well	204
Hour of prayer	156
Lexington	205
Nature and life	275
Urmund	77
Vain world adieu	118
Weep not for me	262

8s & 5s.
| Patience | 251 |
| Sing of Jesus | 157 |

10s & 11s.
Comfort	25
Folsom	140
Lyons	24
Sacred tears	47
Soon and forever	227

11s & 10s.
Come, ye disconsolate	163
Hail to the brightness	171
Henly	160
Star in the East	37

12s.
| Scotland | 38 |
| The house of the Lord | 157 |

12 & 11s.
| The family Bible | 10 |
| Warning | 98 |

11s & 12.
Fading	265
The chariot	271
The Rock	72

11s & 8s.
Ardon	254
Sweet story	304
The Lord is great	70

10s, 11s & 12s.
| Paul | 241 |
| Trumpet | 174 |

6s.
Come	93
Lanman	243
Nillen	112

P. M.
After the toil	246
A little while	226
Beacon Light	247
Bearing the Cross	240
Beautiful world	296
Beautiful Zion	284
Behold the Lamb	52
Be with us thro' the	60
Billow	99
Burlington	173
Chestnut Street	200
Clure	248
Come, thou mighty	268
Come to Jesus just	163
Come to thy rest	289
Dayton	141
Doom	274
Evergreen mount'ins	295
Fanning	209
Farewell Hymn	304
Fenelon	144
Flee as a bird	303
Fountain of life	94
From the depths	165
Frontier	291
Gethsemane	43
Glad homage	193
God doth not leave his	210
God speed the right	314
Go to thy rest in peace	266
Hail, ransomed world	316
Hallen	207
Happy clime	292
Harwell	9
Heavenly Fatherland	290
I come to thee	312
Jesus bread of life	146
Jesus wept	42
Joyful Day	267
Kendrick	287
Lead thou me on	165
Let every heart rejoice	305
Lucas	311
McChesney	117
Mount Blanc	282
Night with ebon	45
Oh, how I love Jesus	323
Oh, let the joyful	175
Paxan	308
Pendleton	141
Perfect day	284
Pilgrim	290
Pilgrim, watch and	324
Pomeroy	265
Refuge	300
Rock of salvation	197
Rockvale	315
Rowley	112
Shall we sing in	285
Silent devotion	146
Silent night	37
Sorrows	45
Still will we trust	204
Supplication	162
Thanksgiving	313
The better land	294
The burial	266
The cho. of angels..35,	318
The day is ended	251
The Eden above	97
The future rest	138
The home in heaven	292
The land of promise	95
The last beam	301
The peace of God	249
The royal proclama'n	77
To thee we bow	300
To whom shall we go	162
Triumph	200
Van Pelt	140
Victory	271
We are too far from	245
We wait for thee	268
Wyatt	211

CHANTS.
Come to me	226
Our Father	170
The guiding hand	267
Thy will be done	131

www.ingramcontent.com/pod-product-compliance
Lightning Source LLC
Chambersburg PA
CBHW031425230426
43668CB00007B/441